Contem
Rhetorical
Citizenship

RHETORIC IN SOCIETY

Contemporary Rhetorical Citizenship

EDITED BY CHRISTIAN KOCK AND
LISA VILLADSEN

LEIDEN UNIVERSITY PRESS

Cover design en lay-out: Mulder van Meurs, Amsterdam

ISBN 9789087282165
e-ISBN 9789400601918 (e-pdf)
e-ISBN 9789400601925 (e-pub)
NUR 610

This book is distributed in North America by the University of Chicago Press (www.press.uchicago.edu).

Contents

Introduction

Rhetorical Citizenship as a Conceptual Frame: What We Talk About When We Talk About Rhetorical Citizenship

CHRISTIAN KOCK AND LISA VILLADSEN

Under the heading "Rhetoric in Society" scholars have met four times: in Aalborg, Denmark; Leiden, The Netherlands; Antwerp, Belgium; and Copenhagen, Denmark. These events arguably make up the first series of rhetoric conferences on European soil. This volume is a manifest indication of the increasing interest this topic attracts in Europe and beyond. We welcome this growing attention to the role of rhetoric in public life, but for the purposes of constructive scholarly exchange we also felt the need to delimit the notion of "rhetoric in society" in selecting a theme for RiS4, the conference on which this book is based. Hence, we took rhetorician Gerard Hauser's words to heart: "A public's essential characteristic is its shared activity of exchanging opinion. Put differently, *publics do not exist as entities, but as processes; their collective reasoning is not defined by abstract reflection but by practical judgment; their awareness of issues is not philosophical but eventful*" (1999, p. 64; emphasis in original). This creative, collective, and processual understanding of rhetoric's place in society struck us as highly resonant with the concept of rhetorical citizenship, which we had worked with earlier. By choosing "Contemporary Rhetorical Citizenship: Purposes, Practices, and Perspectives" as the theme of the RiS4 conference, we hoped to learn more about how colleagues near and far would challenge, develop, or make use of this notion to conceptualize the discursive, symbolic, and otherwise participatory aspects of civic life.

Since public discourse should not be studied merely as a theoretical or idealized notion the conference theme also called for scholarly endeavors in accounting for and critiquing actual practices. Focusing on how citizens actually engage each other across various forms of public fora allows us to consider both macro and micro practices – always with an eye to the significance for the individuals involved. For example, what forms of participation does a particular discursive phenomenon encourage – and by whom? How are speaking positions allotted and organized? What discursive norms inform a particular forum? What possibilities – and obstacles – are there for "ordinary" citizens to engage in public discourse? How do individuals come to see themselves as legitimate "voices" in public debate – and is there any sign of resonance? How does one assess arguments presented on public issues?

While we think that rhetoric has something valuable to contribute to the study of such questions, it cannot possibly do the work alone. Exploring rhetorical citizenship and fleshing out the concept should, we believe, be a much wider, cross-disciplinary scholarly project including political scientists, media scholars, philosophers, and discourse analysts – to mention just a few.

The array of papers in this book reflects the breadth of what the notion of rhetorical citizenship can cover and subsume as well as its limits. In this introduction, we open with some comments on the scope and relevance of the concept, and then lay out the structure of the book and the various ways in which its chapters relate to the theme of rhetorical citizenship and each other.

Rhetorical citizenship as a conceptual frame

Rhetorical citizenship was from the beginning meant as an umbrella term for studying what rhetoricians Robert Asen and Dan Brouwer call "modalities" of public engagement (2010). While we maintain an interest in more traditional public and political debate, we want to heed Asen's call to attend to the "fluid, multimodal, and quotidian enactments of citizenship in a multiple public sphere" (p. 191) where democracy is seen more as a "guiding spirit that informs human interaction" than a "set of institutions or specific acts" (p. 196). In our conceptualization, rhetorical citizenship may be theoretically accessed via the notion of rhetorical agency, i.e., citizens' possibilities for gaining access to and influencing civic life through symbolic action; or it may be embraced from a focus on how people may be involved with, and evaluate, public rhetoric – not as participants, but as recipients. We think it important to maintain this dual focus on what one might call, respectively, the participatory and the receptive aspects of civic interaction.

It bears underscoring that rhetorical citizenship is not a new idea (and not even a new term). The notion that rhetoric is what makes civilized society possible goes back to the ancients, and many great thinkers and scholars have prepared the way for thinking of citizenship as something that is, at least in part, discursively or symbolically constituted. Also, plenty of theorists have written about how citizenship is not just a formal or rights-based category but also a more qualitative, participatory process. Thus, we see rhetorical citizenship as a conceptual frame accentuating the fact that legal rights, privileges and material conditions are not the only constituents of citizenship; discourse that takes place between citizens is arguably more basic to what it means to be a citizen.

With this conceptual assumption it becomes natural to wish for a research platform that allows different strands of rhetorical scholarship to come into contact, including studies in public argumentation and deliberation on the one hand and studies in rhetorical agency on the other. At best, such efforts can enrich each other. Whereas argument and deliberation theories tend to rely on normative standards that are often pure and clinical, rhetorical agency theory for its part could sometimes do with more conceptual precision. In any case either might benefit from being brought into contact with the other. For example, argumentation studies and deliberative democracy theory might look more at real and less-than-ideal practices, and rhetorical agency theory might be more systematically applied and exemplified in case studies with an eye to evaluation. If not synthesis, there might be synergy. Complementary strengths and perspectives might coalesce in a common pursuit.

To take rhetorical citizenship as one's conceptual frame in scholarship has a descriptive and a normative side, and its purpose is ultimately critical, as in any other kind of rhetorical criticism. But the focus is less on what a particular utterance is like, or how effective it is, but more on how suited it is to contribute to constructive civic interaction. The late rhetorician Thomas Farrell defined the constructive potential of rhetoric, which again is the basis for a normative approach, by saying that rhetoric builds not on "an *a priori* validity claim in advance of speech" - rather, "*rhetorical practice enacts the norms of propriety collaboratively with interested others*" (1991, p. 200; emphasis in the original). More specifically, he argued, "important civic qualities – such as civic friendship, a sense of social justice – are actively cultivated through excellence in rhetorical practice" (p. 187). This line of thought echoes that of founding rhetorical thinkers like Isocrates and Cicero who believed that human societies could not have been built and sustained without rhetoric; and recently, Robert Danisch (2012) has maintained that the sophists, from Protagoras on, saw rhetoric as a "prudential pragmatism" and taught it to equip citizens to participate in their polity. If this is so, then citizenship inherently has a rhetorical side. And rhetoric is not merely persuasion in a narrow sense, but in fact a form of society building.

The place of rhetoric and rhetorical criticism, constructive or otherwise, in society and civic life is addressed below by Chaput, Mifsud, and Zarefsky in their respective chapters. At a theoretical level, Chaput interrogates the implications of the metaphors we use to conceptualize democracy: commodity and the common. Mifsud focuses on Aristotle's notion of the audience as "simple judges" and argues that it represents an archaic concept of citizenship, based on mutual sympathy, deeper than the Rhetoric's more technical notion of persuasion. The potential societal consequences of rhetorical criticism of public discourse are the topic of Zarefsky's chapter. He asks if rhetorical criticism may have a degenerative effect by virtue of the risk it entails for cultivating cynicism and systematic suspicion. The study of individual rhetors' utterances has different levels. Most fundamentally, there is a descriptive element in simply mapping how rhetors, whether elite or "common," actually present arguments or positions in the public realm. In this volume, we have included case studies of various types of discursive practices, from the large public hearings in three states in the US on same-sex marriage, studied by Karen Tracy, to Gene Navera's cross-presidential study of the evolving uses made of the concept of "people power" in Philippine national politics, to Carolyne Lee and Judy Burnside-Lawry's study of small group conversations as breeding grounds for rhetorical citizenship. Kuroiwa-Lewis' and van Belle's chapters both focus on individual rhetors' conceptions of civic cohesion and division. While Kuroiwa-Lewis' reading of Franklin D. Roosevelt's rhetoric on taxes as a collective social responsibility shows how FDR attempts to create moral consensus around a contested political topic, van Belle's study focuses on the Dutch immigrant poet Bouzza's embrace of polarization as a means of igniting public debate.

Provocation to reflect on social membership and civic norms of communication is also the theme of Olmos' critical analysis of the Rico affair in Spain, named after a a well-known intellectual, accused of deceiving the public regarding his status as a smoker in a debate on smoking bans.

Olmos' study ventures the step from analytic criticism toward a normative assessment of how well a rhetor has performed in a debate, and how that debate might more profitably have continued. Such analyses, which necessarily imply norms of rhetorical merit, may lead to questions about how rhetors' various practices reflect ruling discursive norms. By examining these norms, whether they are recognized or not, one has a better basis for critique – one that takes into account the ruling *doxai* and social and other constraints, which can sometimes be at odds with more abstract idealizations of civic discourse. Such grounded criticism is, we believe, a meaningful supplement to existing cross-disciplinary scholarship on citizenship, which often is either primarily theoretical or focused on greater trends and quantifiable generalizations. Case studies are useful in at least two respects: first, they are useful for pedagogical purposes because they are concrete and thus easy to remember. Second, detailed analysis can further nuanced understanding, regardless of whether the analyzed artefact is representative of many or somehow odd or marginal. Whether under the aegis of rhetorical agency or not, rhetorical critics of, e.g., minority and women's rhetoric have thus expanded our appreciation of the multiple ways in which rhetorical citizenship is manifested. Hannken-Illjes' study of the celebration of trees as concrete material entities in a controversy over the new train station in Stuttgart is one such example of how social protest argumentation displays an expanded understanding of the stakeholders in the controversy and their means of symbolic expression. Similarly, Goggin's study of "yarn bombing" as a protest form with global appeal illustrates how citizens, whether anonymously or not, contribute to the array of symbolic expressions inviting critical reflection on civic issues.

So, thinking of rhetorical citizenship becomes an impetus for forging more explicit links between particular utterances and their role in the maintenance and development of civic life. This may give renewed emphasis to the *critical and social potential* of rhetoric by teaching students to appreciate that the way we "do" citizenship discursively and the way we talk about society are both constitutive of and influential on what civic society is and how it develops.

Rhetorical citizenship: participatory and receptive

Rhetorical Citizenship as a conceptual frame emphasizes the fact that laws, rights, and material conditions are not the only constituents of citizenship; discourse broadly conceived among citizens (in other words: rhetoric in society) is arguably just as important. The concept unites under one heading citizens' own discursive exchanges, in public or in private conversation, i.e., the active or *participatory* aspect of rhetorical citizenship, and the public discourse of which citizens are *recipients*. On a more fundamental level Thomas Farrell described this as "a dual sense of constraint and opportunity" (1991,

p. 199). With this bi-focal sensibility, Farrell wanted to capture the creative tension of customary practice on the one hand and on the other the inevitable uncertainty with regard to the constraints of the particular situation. Together, these competing forces explain how rhetoric can be at once adaptive and inventional. He calls it "reflective participation" and suggests that it also implies that propriety has both an ethical and an aesthetic dimension. When we talk about the receptive aspects of rhetorical citizenship, we may link that with the "constraint" aspect posited by Farrell. Rhetorical encounters are circumscribed by situation, genre, and discursive norms; but that is precisely part of what makes it possible for us to identify better or worse instantiations of public argument. Farrell's "opportunity" aspect is closer to ideas about how rhetorical agency can emerge, even where it is unexpected, when individuals do not let convention or habit constrain them, but begin to see themselves as citizens and even citizens with a point to make – be it in traditional oratorical form or some other kind of symbolic behavior.

A more concrete way of expressing these ideas is to see rhetorical citizenship as integrating two complementary aspects of both these categories: on the one hand, there are the *rights* that we, as citizens, are accorded, and the expectations that citizens may rightfully have in regard to discourse among citizens; on the other hand there is all that which other citizens are entitled to expect from *us*, precisely because we are citizens; we may also refer to this aspect as comprising discursive *responsibilities or duties* as citizens.

The two dimensions, active/passive and rights/responsibilities, define, much like the cardinal directions of a compass rose, four broad areas of interest. The "North-South" axis may represent the active or participatory aspect versus the passive or receptive aspect; the "West-East" axis may then represent citizens' rights versus their responsibilities or duties (see Figure 1).

FIGURE 1

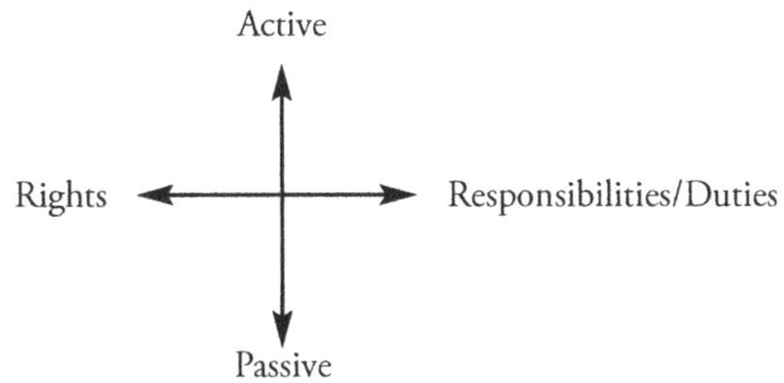

This figure illustrates how various rhetorical concerns are connected, but also how much recent thinking in other disciplines addresses rhetorical concerns; thus interdisciplinary contact becomes an obvious agenda. For example, the idea that citizenship involves not only citizens' rights but also what might be expected or demanded of them is stated clearly as an emerging insight in an overview on citizenship research by the philosophers Will Kymlicka and Wayne Norman: "most theorists now accept that the functioning of society depends not only on the justice of its institutions or constitutions, but also on the virtues, identities, and practices of its citizens, including their ability to co-operate, deliberate, and feel solidarity with those who belong to different ethnic and religious groups" (2000, p. 11).

As for the distinction between the active and the receptive aspects of rhetorical citizenship, it parallels what political theorists Amy Gutmann and Dennis Thompson call the "principles of accommodation." These principles, they say, "make two kinds of general demands on citizens; one concerns how citizens present their own political positions, and the other how they regard the political positions of others" (1996, p. 80).

As for citizens' rights or rightful expectations with regard to rhetoric in society, citizens not only have the right to speak, they also need the capacity and position to speak so that they may be heard. Studies of rhetorical agency and how it is achieved by some and denied to others belong here. How is rhetorical agency manifested or contested? What does it take to gain a hearing? What counts as participation in public debate? How do we determine what points of view are to be considered legitimate and appropriate forms of expression on issues of common concern? How can we account for changes in these categories?

Are there certain responsibilities or duties incumbent on those who speak – such as standards of responsible discourse or even of deliberation? Many scholars in disciplines other than rhetoric have reflected on what those standards might be. Recently, political theorist John Dryzek has recognized rhetoric as a necessity in democracy, while not per se a constructive factor. He argues for a "systemic" criterion to distinguish between "desirable and undesirable uses of rhetoric," and after analyzing how rhetoric may be either "bridging" or "bonding," and how both kinds may play positive roles, he concludes that we should be "asking whether or not the rhetoric in question contributes to the construction of an effective deliberative system joining competent and reflective actors on the issue at hand" (2010, p. 335).

Simone Chambers is another political theorist who has addressed the standards issue. She believes that deliberation is needed in a democracy, but also that "the mass public can never be deliberative." Democratic deliberation in small groups of citizens is fine, but not enough. However, she believes that the public rhetoric we hear, mainly through the media, has the potential for providing deliberation. Regrettably, very often it provides none: failing to engage citizens' "capacity for practical judgment," it becomes what she calls "plebiscitary," based on pandering and manipulation. So we must critically assess public rhetoric and the media that bring it to us, because we do have the task and at least some means of "making the mass public more rather than less deliberative." "If rhetoric in general is the study of how speech affects an audience then deliberative rhetoric must be about the way speech induces deliberation in the sense of inducing considered reflection about a future action" (2009, p. 335).

Public rhetors' responsibilities may also be expressed in terms of individual citizens' rights. We citizens have a right to expect that public rhetoric helps us identify, understand and reflect on issues of common concern – by providing information and reasons that call on us to engage public issues and assist us in developing informed views on them.

The political theorist Robert Goodin has emphasized the importance of what he calls "deliberation within," pointing out that "very much of the work of deliberation, even in external-collective settings, must inevitably be done within each individual's head." In modern nation states there is no way everyone can speak up and be heard by everyone else on any issue. But we may "ease the burdens of deliberative democracy in mass society by altering our focus from the 'external-collective' to the 'internal-reflective' mode, shifting much of the work of democratic deliberation back inside the head of each individual." Goodin adds that "internal-reflective deliberations might hope to secure better representation of the communicatively inept or the communicatively inert than external-collective deliberations ever could" (2000, p. 83).

In this volume, Jørgensen's chapter on politicians' and especially the media's abuse of the concept of election "promises" calls on us to be critical when presented with hasty or disingenuous characterizations of political statements as speech acts of various kinds. Similarly, Navera's and Olmos's chapters focus on evolving and ambiguous rhetoric presented by elite rhetors to the public.

Just as we have a right to expect deliberative public rhetoric, the polity may also expect from us that we will indeed weigh in our minds the information and reasons we hear. Indeed, a major emphasis on rhetoric as a capacity to listen, deliberate and assess, justifying its centrality in civic education, is evident in one of the most influential rhetoricians in history, the Renaissance theologian and educator Philipp Melanchthon, whose work informed the organization of general education in all of Protestant Europe. In the opening of his *Elementa rhetorices* (1531) he declares that the precepts of rhetoric were developed not just for aspiring rhetors, but for every young person, and not primarily so that they can become orators, but because it helps them in the reading of excellent writers and in judging upon complex issues ("in longis controversiis judicandis"). Even citizens who do not actively participate in debate and other discursive exchanges have a responsibility to listen to reasons, including those supporting views other than their own, and to information that is new and perhaps unwelcome. One important reference here might be to the rhetorician Wayne Booth's concept of "listening-rhetoric" (2009). McKerrow's contribution to the present volume addresses the criteria of the enactment of citizenship and points to issues of voice and silence and the respective motives that may lie behind the choice of speaking or remaining silent.

Rhetorical citizenship has potential as an interdisciplinary conceptual frame in which to interpret and assess rhetoric, in its practical as well as its theoretical and/or critical manifestations. Dahlgren's chapter below on the interfaces between discourse studies and rhetorical studies provides a helpful overview of mutual points of interest and of areas where they either overlap or have yet to do so. Deneire, Eelbode, and Lauwers' application of game theory to the study of political debate offers a completely new perspective on how to understand campaign rhetoric, and how to reform it.

One thing rhetorical citizenship might certainly be is a pedagogical project. With an increasingly heterogeneous population, public education has a growing responsibility to teach students not only about democracy and civic rights, but also about their own roles and obligations in civic life; and that should include training them in the practical skills necessary to participate in, and to receive, public discourse, including intercultural communication.

In 1998, a committee in Britain, led by the political theorist Bernard Crick, published a report, *Education for Citizenship and the Teaching of Democracy in Schools* (Crick 1998). The report pointed to a number of "skills and aptitudes" that schools should teach, most of which might clearly be seen as mainstays of a rhetorical education. Among them were: "to make a reasoned argument both verbally and in writing," "to consider and appreciate the experience and perspective of others," "to tolerate other view points," and "to recognise forms of manipulation and persuasion" (p. 44). So, without ever mentioning rhetoric, the report confirmed that citizenship is in large part a rhetorical concept, and that citizenship education should in large part be rhetorical, too. In her present study of a pedagogical project in a Greek school, Egglezou describes an educational program aimed at preparing students to consider for themselves and discuss with each other complex topics of civic importance, exemplified by the case of GMO food products. While Kuehl's starting point for talking about citizenship in the classroom is also local, her argument in this book is that rhetorical citizenship should be introduced to students as not just an invitation to participate in local concerns, but as a global awareness. Ulrich, in her chapter on the TV series The West Wing, shows how this series refutes the common notion that the portrayal of politics in popular film and TV fiction rests on a basic attitude of cynicism. Rather, she finds the series to be at once entertaining and educational in its celebration of rhetoric in the political culture as an important civic and aesthetic craft.

The Structure of the Book

As we said above, we hoped, when these papers were first invited, to learn how colleagues near and far would challenge, develop, or make use of the concept of rhetorical citizenship. They did all these things, and they did so in numerous divergent ways. Despite the diversity in theoretical starting points, methodology, and studied discourse, we found that the submissions nevertheless converged in broad groups. We have therefore organized the book in three sections, each headed by one of the three invited keynote lectures by internationally celebrated scholars.

In the first section, "Rhetorical Criticism from the Viewpoint of Rhetorical Citizenship," David Zarefsky asks, "Is Rhetorical Criticism Subversive of Democracy?" He reminds us that rhetoric builds communities and makes citizenship active, but also cautions that rhetorical criticism may be subversive by fostering cynicism and thus apathy with regard to rhetorical invention and practice. This is so if, with systematic negativity, it suggests that individuals can have no agency, or that discourse is always a mere mask for power, or a tool for ideological false consciousness. Deliberative rhetoric is the core of democracy, but criticism that claims always to see sinister underlying motives, or sees rhetoric as manipulation that obfuscates people's self-interest, paralyze democracy by suspending deliberation. Rather than that, we need constructive rhetorical criticism that may help us work through our predicaments.

Paula Olmos, in "On Rhetorical Ethos and Personal Needs: A Spanish 2011 Public Controversy," focuses on the Aristotelian notion of *ethos* and then discusses, by means of a borderline case, the classic question of what constitutes the basis of a speaker's ethos: the discourse alone or a more comprehensive impression including the speaker's biography. The aforementioned Rico affair illustrates the conundrum of ethos: a well-known author made an ethotical statement known by the public to be untrue, thus stirring up intense speculation about his intentions and widespread disapproval of his letter and person.

Charlotte Jørgensen, in "The Hunt for Promises in Danish Political Debate," criticizes the obsessive media focus on politicians' promises and alleged breaches thereof, arguing that this orientation undermines the deliberative ideal of informed public debate. Along with so-called "contract politics" it renders argumentation superfluous, demotivating citizens from engaging themselves in the issues that arise in the contingent realm of politics.

In her paper "Keep[ing] profits at a reasonably low rate: Invoking American civil religion in FDR's rhetoric of tax equity and citizenship," Nathalie Kuroiwa-Lewis highlights aspects of Roosevelt's presidential rhetoric that appear striking today: he presented taxation, even progressive taxation, as a civic good and a matter of social justice – a means for citizens to enact their citizenship and a part of a "civil religion." Both Jørgensen's and Kuroiwa-Lewis' chapters may be said to represent the kind of appreciative and constructive criticism of rhetoric in the public sphere that Zarefsky suggests as a necessary counterbalance to systematically negative criticism.

Maureen Daly Goggin, in "Yarn Bombing: Claiming Rhetorical Citizenship in Public Spaces," investigates how knitted patches, sewn together and displayed prominently at sites of civic controversy, become a global form of agency and an instantiation of contemporary feminist protest tactics on issues such as war and environmental sustainability. Yarn bombing, graphically exemplified, is conceptualized as a materialist epistemology in the form of DIY activism.

Establishing a linkage of two concepts: materiality and argumentation, Kati Hannken-Illjes, in "On Trees: Protest Between the Symbolic and the Material," investigates a related aspect of the rhetoric of protest: how non-discursive entities – things – influence discourse, frame argumentation and thereby function rhetorically. Hundreds of old trees, destined to be cut down in a grand remodeling of Stuttgart's main station, became a strong and central theme of dispute, and this can teach us something about the status of "things" and their materiality in public discourse.

Anne Ulrich, in her chapter "'Cicero Would Love This Show': The Celebration of Rhetoric and Citizenship in *The West Wing*," shows us how fictional narratives in the successful TV series *The West Wing* teach us "an entertaining civics lesson" and constitute a "celebration of rhetoric." She considers Aaron Sorkin, the creator of the series, a political orator actively engaging in public discourse and openly performing his vision of citizenship. Analyzing crucial scenes in the activities of the White House oratorical team, Ulrich discusses how Sorkin conceives rhetoric and in what way one can understand the series itself as, literally speaking, epideictic rhetoric, i.e., a demonstration of rhetoric apt to enhance political participation and identification, that is, citizenship.

The second section of the book, "Studies in the Practice and Cultivation of Rhetorical Citizenship," raises the perspective from the rhetorical criticism of intriguing cases to a more general level, namely what we might call rhetorical culture (or cultures).

Karen Tracy, in "Rhetorical Citizenship in Public Meetings: The Character of Religious Expression in American Discourse," analyzes citizen testimony at public hearings on same-sex marriage bills, pointing to linkages for Americans among citizenship, public hearings participation, and religious talk. She identifies patterns of invoking religion as relevant to civic issues and calls for increased attention to rhetorical citizenship as a culturally inflected practice. Talk at such public hearings, she maintains, serves important functions, even if at odds with stringent norms of deliberation. Thus, rhetorical citizenship becomes a more useful concept if it can maintain a productive balance between deliberation and advocacy.

Carolyne Lee and Judy Burnside-Lawry consider, in "The Communicative Construction of Rhetorical Citizenship in Small Groups," how people in small groups practice a continuous feedback loop of articulating one's position, listening to the positions of others, and finally responding appropriately to them. A triad of concepts helps explain this: voice – understood as the opportunity for people to speak and be heard on what matters in their lives; narrative; and listening. Narrative is an essential means for individuals to drive the feedback loop, and small group talk may thus be seen as a micro-model of what rhetorical citizenship could be like.

"Argumentative Literacy and Rhetorical Citizenship" is Fotini Egglezou's detailed account of an 'Isocratean' program of rhetorical education implemented in a modern Greek primary school. A wide range of argumentative and reflective verbal activities concerning the same controversial issue led a group of twelve-year-olds to a measurable increase in "the Isocratean qualities of sophia or phronesis." Egglezou thus makes an empirically supported case that the internalization of rhetorical argumentation, with the implied dimensions of criticism, evaluation and choice, lays a foundation for the cultivation of civic virtue; citizenship, as Isocrates believed, is grounded rhetorically.

Gene Segarra Navera, under the title "'People Power' in Philippine Presidential Rhetoric: (Re)framing Democratic Participation in Post-authoritarian Regimes," traces the term "people power" in five Philippine presidents' rhetoric as a malleable resource for talking about and performing democracy. Using concepts from cognitive linguistics, particularly "frames" stemming from seminal "conceptual metaphors," he highlights the fluidity in the conceptualization of a hallowed phrase in its various metamorphoses from a form of resistance to an element of nation building.

In "On Being a Simple Judge," Mari Lee Mifsud explores the notion of the *haplous kritēs* in Aristotle's *Rhetoric*. This "simple judge" who judges public rhetorical argument is a citizen who understands the fundamental of *eudaimonia*: the "happiness" that the polis should seek to provide for all citizens. Aristotle here refers to Homeric examples. At the core of civic happiness are solidarity and mutual benefaction, central to archaic norms for gift-giving, which honors those who give and reciprocate gifts. Rhetoric and rhetorical citizenship built on this basis is "simpler," i.e., deeper and more essential than, rhetorical technē based on persuasion.

Raymie McKerrow's chapter is also an essay into thinking deeper on the nature of rhetoric and the social motives that carry it. "The Rhetorical Citizen: Enacting Agency" considers the nature and enactment of agency in the guise of the rhetorical citizen as a person whose actions within the public sphere encompass considerations of race, class, sex, and gender lines. Premised on a Burkean sense of motive, McKerrow explores two major criteria undergirding the enactment of citizenship: the constraints provided with respect to access and the role of motive in highlighting why one acts in giving voice to one's role as a citizen. The role of voice includes that of silence, and the author suggests that the refusal to act is as much a rhetorical statement, provided the motive is clear, and is an overt action.

In the third and last section of the book, "Crossing Borders, Disciplinary, Political and Otherwise," we have brought together five chapters that each in their different ways explore borders between theoretical, disciplinary, and cultural assumptions about what communication in society is and should be like.

In "Rhetorical Analysis and Discourse Analysis: Probing the Interface," Peter Dahlgren highlights key similarities and differences between rhetorical analysis and two prominent schools of discourse analysis to render them mutually accessible. All three do qualitative analysis of discourse in society and may learn from each other. He focuses on two strands of discourse analysis: Critical Discourse Analysis (Fairclough et al.) in a sense updates ideology critique, taking a constructionist view of language. Discourse Theory (Laclau & Mouffe et al.) adds theoretical weight to discourse analysis, with the aim of enabling us to "think and do otherwise." Dahlgren finds that rhetorical analysis typically extrapolates readers' and listeners' responses to communication, but the subject and subjectivity remain less theorized.

Hilde van Belle's chapter, "A Stowaway of Emigration: Polarization in Hafid Bouazza's Work" deals with the Dutch writer Hafid Bouazza's practice of challenging widely held assumptions that polarization in debate is undesirable and detrimental to constructive rhetorical citizenship. Bouazza is a full-blooded exponent of diversity and complexity, in fiction and drama as well as in his polemical writings, which castigate Islamic fundamentalism and tendencies in Holland, and the West generally, to seek appeasement and deny polarization. His driving force is passion for all colors of the spectrum, in language, literature, and society.

Under the title "Extending Civic Rhetoric: Valuing Rhetorical Dimensions of Global Citizenship in Civic Education," Rebecca A. Kuehl argues that civic rhetoric would benefit from a rhetorical view of global citizenship in extending the practices of rhetorical education. She defines civic rhetoric as a specific component of civic education, focusing on teaching skills such as critical thinking, speaking, and writing. Global citizenship, defined as a specific type of rhetorical citizenship, including issues that span nation-states, is claimed to be useful in extending the civic rhetoric tradition via arousing people's emotions about political issues. In this way, Kuehl connects concepts of interconnectedness and social belonging as central to the notion of civic republicanism and civic liberalism.

Catherine Chaput argues that rhetoric, concomitant with democracy, has long helped capitalism appear inevitable in a "triple helix of freedom." But this "triumphant knot" is unraveling. In "Rhetorical Citizenship beyond the Frontiers of Capitalism," she posits that the core metaphor of capitalism is the commodity, emphasizing individual ownership and profit as central to citizenship. An alternative metaphor is the common. Both conceptions of citizenship are rhetorically constituted, but the "common" metaphor nudges us toward a sense of citizenship based on shared resources (such as history, knowledge, the environment). Jason Barker's documentary *Marx Reloaded*, as Chaput sees it, revitalizes Marx's thinking and imaginatively visualizes the commodity and the common as structuring myths of citizenship.

Finally, Tom Deneire, David Eelbode and Jeroen Lauwers in "A Game with Words: Rhetorical Citizenship and Game Theory" represent a fresh look at how political argumentation might be construed. Conceptualizing rhetorical behavior, and in particular: political discourse, with the metaphor of the "game," the authors explore the hermeneutic questions whether the critical potential of mathematically formalized game theory for rhetorical criticism. The authors argue that rhetorical discourse can be interpreted as a game, speakers as players, and the rhetorical situation as providing the constraints on the actions the players can take. These lead to consequences with a certain pay-off, or rhetorically speaking to discourse capable of altering reality. The partisan nature of rhetoric is used as a starting point for discussing the speaker from the point of view of a rational decision-maker, thus linking to game-theoretical analysis. The authors compare rhetorical action to the so-called "prisoner's dilemma," and a location game model suggests that it is rational for politicians to stay close to the middle and at times concentrate on particular swing votes while ignoring many other voters. Finding this result unattractive, the authors conclude by suggesting the basic premise of an alternative voting system that they envision as fostering more responsible political debate.

Closing remarks

We believe rhetoric has a place in the study of civic life in virtue of the discipline's dual nature as an everyday practice and a field of academic inquiry. Lots of rhetoric takes place every day. Sometimes it inspires us, sometimes it irks us, sometimes we are part of it, sometimes we don't even notice it. Rhetoric makes society hang together. By paying close attention to what people say and do in various civic settings, we stand to learn about how people understand their society and their own role in it. The way they speak and what they say are keys to this understanding, which rhetorical analysis and criticism might promote. Studying the kind of argumentative "work" that certain viewpoints or topoi are being used to accomplish, or how they travel from vernacular settings to government discourse (or not), may be a way of understanding the workings of society better. Expectations may be confirmed, but at other times new arguments or new angles may emerge.

As rhetorician Robert Hariman noted, "understanding, appreciating, and improving democratic participation is impeded by both the rationality standards of deliberative democracy theorists and classical rhetoric's ideal of eloquence" (2007, p. 222). We take this as a call for scholarly approaches that better account for, and can offer suggestions for, actual vernacular discourse. We as academics can assist in showing how praxis is both inventional and reflects civic norms and cultural values. As a practice, rhetoric holds a built-in impetus of improvement. This is where the normative aspect rests, both on the practical and the theoretical level. With its keen eye for contingency and indeterminacy, rhetoric is equipped to deal with the imperfect nature of civic discourse, at once serving as a resource for improvement and a sober acknowledgement of the constraints of the situation. Rhetoric, in the words of Thomas Farrell, is "practical reasoning in the presence of collaborative others" (1991, p. 189). It is, he believed, "more than the practice; it is the entire process of forming, expressing, and judging public thought in real life. ... this enhanced understanding needs to include the condition of being a rhetorical audience. This is a condition in which we are called to exert our own critical capacities to a maximum extent. We have to decide – quite literally – what sort of public persons we wish to be" (p. 208).

References

Asen, R. and D. C. Brouwer (2010). Introduction: Public Modalities, Or the Metaphors We Theorize By. In: D. C. Brouwer and R. Asen (Eds.), *Public Modalities: Rhetoric, Culture, Media, and the Shape of Public Life* (pp. 1-32). Tuscaloosa: University of Alabama Press.

Asen, R. (2004). A Discourse Theory of Citizenship. *Quarterly Journal of Speech* 90, 189-211.

Booth, W.C. (2004). *The Rhetoric of Rhetoric: The Quest for Effective Communication.* Malden, MA: Blackwell.

Chambers, S. (2009). Rhetoric and the Public Sphere: Has Deliberative Democracy Abandoned Mass Democracy? *Political Theory* 37, 323-350.

Crick, B. (1998). *Education for Citizenship and the Teaching of Democracy in Schools.* London: Qualifications and Curriculum Authority.

Danish, R. (2012). Stanley Fish Is Not a Sophist: The Difference Between Skeptical and Prudential Versions of Rhetorical Pragmatism. *Rhetoric Society Quarterly* 42, 405-423.

Dryzek, J.S. (2010). Rhetoric in Democracy: A Systemic Appreciation. *Political Theory* 38, 319-339.

Farrell, T. (1991). Practicing the Arts of Rhetoric: Tradition and Invention. *Philosophy and Rhetoric* 24, 183-212.

Goodnight, T. (1993). A "New Rhetoric" for a "New Dialectic": Prolegomena to a Responsible Public Argument. *Argumentation* 7, 329-342.

Goodin, R.E. (2000). Democratic Deliberation Within. *Philosophy & Public Affairs* 29, 81-109.

Gutmann, A., and D. Thompson. (1996). *Democracy and Disagreement.* Cambridge, MA: Harvard University Press.

Hauser, G.A. (1999). *Vernacular Voices: The Rhetoric of Publics and Public Spheres.* Columbia, SC: University of South Carolina Press.

Ivie, R.L. (2002). Rhetorical Deliberation and Democratic Politics in the Here and Now. *Rhetoric and Public Affairs* 5, 277-285.

Kock, C. and L. Villadsen (2012). Introduction: Citizenship as a Rhetorical Practice. In: C. Kock and L. Villadsen (Eds.), *Rhetorical Citizenship and Public Deliberation* (pp. 1-10). University Park: Pennsylvania State University Press.

Kymlicka, W. and W. Norman. (2000). *Citizenship in Diverse Societies.* Oxford: Oxford University Press.

Melanchthon, P. (2001). *Elementa rhetorices. Grundbegriffe der Rhetorik. Mit den Briefen Senecas, Plinius' d. J. und den "Gegensätzlichen Briefen" Giovanni Picos della*

Mirandola und Franz Burchards, hrsg., übers. und kommentiert von Volkhard Wels. Berlin: Weidler.

Tracy, K., J. P. McDaniel and B. E. Gronbeck. (2007). *The Prettier Doll: Rhetoric, Discourse and Ordinary Democracy.* Tuscaloosa: University of Alabama Press, 2007.

PART I

Rhetorical Criticism from the Viewpoint of Rhetorical Citizenship

Is Rhetorical Criticism Subversive of Democracy?

DAVID ZAREFSKY

Statement of the problem

For nearly 45 years I have studied and taught rhetorical criticism, the analysis and interpretation of public discourse in order to explain, evaluate, and change social practices. I saw myself as contributing in a small way to democratic life. I still do – rest assured that I am not entering into some late midlife crisis. But as I have thought about public discourse, and about governance in democracy, and about our complicated current predicaments, I'm not sure that rhetorical criticism is always a positive force. There may be a dark side to both popular and academic rhetorical criticism which we would do well to identify and try to ameliorate.

Rhetoric builds community through appeals to common bonds and transcendent values. There is an element of mystery in such appeals, and by demystifying rhetoric, explaining everything, criticism may prevent rhetoric from doing its work. This risk is especially serious for democracies since rhetorical appeals are their only means for mobilizing public judgment and decision. Can we have strong rhetorical practice and strong criticism too, or are the two inherently at odds?

I have raised a provocative question, perhaps even an outlandish one: Is rhetorical criticism subversive of democracy? To forecast my answer, it is "not necessarily." Yet the danger is real. The argument I'll advance is somewhat indirect. Most of my examples will come from the United States, because I know it best, but I believe that the questions and concerns I raise speak to the human condition at this moment, without geographical limitation. I will proceed in four steps: (1) clarifying what I mean by "citizenship," "rhetoric," and "democracy," (2) explaining how "rhetorical citizenship" is achieved through "democratic deliberation" which is itself a rhetorical enterprise, (3) describing how democratic deliberation builds identification as a counter to the natural divisions among people, and (4) identifying and discussing potential threats to democratic deliberation posed by rhetorical criticism, and also their possible remedies.

Citizenship, rhetoric, and democracy

My argument pivots around the relationships among three key terms: citizenship, rhetoric, and democracy. All three terms are used in multiple ways, so I need to make clear where I am going with each of them.

Citizenship is the enactment of the individual's relationship to the polity, whether it is local, state or regional, national, or global. Most of us, in fact, enact this attachment at multiple levels. "Thin" expressions of citizenship include voting, paying taxes, performing military service, and holding a passport. In these cases the attachment to the polity may be weak or indirect. Other forms, such as attending to the news, campaigning for public office, and undertaking legal action to protect one's rights, require more active engagement.

Kock and Villadsen propose that citizenship be understood as rhetorical, "in the sense that important civic functions take place in deliberation among citizens, and that discourse is not prefatory to real action but is in many ways constitutive of civic engagement" (2012, p. 1). I share their view: what makes citizenship active rather than passive is its rhetorical character.

Once freed of its widespread negative stereotypes in everyday usage, *rhetoric* is understood as both an academic discipline and a social practice. Ordinary people engage in it and academics study it. Our studies seek both to strengthen and perpetuate the discipline through the deepening of theoretical insight, and also to analyze and interpret the practice of rhetoric in society. We understand rhetoric broadly as about the relationships between messages and people.

We tend to distinguish between rhetorical practice and rhetorical criticism – between performance, on the one hand, and analysis, interpretation, and judgment on the other. But this is in some sense a false dichotomy. Analysis and criticism of rhetoric in society should also help to improve rhetorical practice, whether of the rhetors we study, or others, or our own. Likewise, efforts to develop or improve skills should make us more sensitive to how, and how well, those skills are deployed in society. In practice, however, we have reified the distinction, teaching and studying the arts of rhetoric separately from the analysis and criticism of rhetoric. The former forms the substance of courses in public speaking and the goal of consultants and coaches of politicians and business executives. The latter becomes the province of academics. The former emphasizes rhetoric's potential; the latter, its limitations. The former is typically local and private in its orientation; the latter concerns discourse in the public sphere. Rhetoricians may train people to be good speakers or writers, but critics may argue that these people deploy their newly acquired skills in futile pursuits if they aim to make a difference in the public sphere, because rhetoric may be only a cover for the impersonal forces that really control public life. If it conveys the message that individuals have no agency, rhetorical criticism is indeed subversive of democracy. It "teaches" that individuals might as well opt out of public life and it implies that the inevitable stalemates in the public sphere ultimately will be overcome not through discursive engagement but through anarchy; surrender to authoritarianism; whim, fashion, or caprice; a crisis so dire that it upends presumptions about what is possible; or even violence. Even democracies fall victim occasionally to these forces, but to depend on them is to deny the prospect of democracy itself.

Fortunately, the converse is also true. If rhetorical criticism and rhetorical practice can be rejoined, if academic and scholarly critics adopt Kenneth Burke's comic rather than tragic frame[1] so that rhetoric is seen as the comic corrective to impersonal social forces, then rhetorical criticism can strengthen rather than subvert democracy. Rhetoric can become a means for working through seemingly intractable conflicts, exploring alternative frames of reference, identifying what is at issue and distinguishing between the trivial and the crucial, determining when consensus is possible and when it is not, and building legitimacy for a majority's decision while respecting the minority's rights.

But I am getting ahead of myself here. I have talked about what I mean by "citizenship" and "rhetoric," but not yet about "democracy." And "democracy" is a charismatic term[2] – positive in its connotations (at least it is now, unlike in the 18th century when it was equated with mob rule) but

[1] See Burke (1959) [1937], esp. pp. 92-105, for a discussion of the comic and tragic frames.

[2] The concept of "charismatic terms," terms of great potency but unclear referents, is explained in Weaver (1953), pp. 227-232.

attached to widely differing referents. Abraham Lincoln perhaps defined it best when he called it "government of the people, by the same people."[3] Sovereignty resides ultimately and collectively with those who also are subjects of the regime. Rulers and ruled are the same. If government violates the people's rights or liberties, the people have the prerogative of altering it. If the people desire an outcome that is within the scope of government, they have the power through majority vote to bring it about. But since a majority vote could be used to enshrine tyranny and to undercut democracy itself (as happened in Germany in 1934), fundamental rights of the minority are protected. Anti-majoritarian provisions assure that a regime based on majority rule can prevail since the minority of one day becomes the majority of the next.

The core elements of democracy, then, are the identity between rulers and ruled, majority rule, and minority rights. Certainly democracy is not a necessary condition for rhetoric. One need only recall the public address of Hitler and Stalin to recognize that totalitarian rulers can evoke raw emotion, constitute individuals as a mob, and convert the will to act into violent action. These in large measure are rhetorical outcomes, despise them though we may. They remind us of Aristotle's dictum that rhetoric is a neutral instrument that can be used for good or for ill.

On the other hand, rhetoric may well be a necessary condition for democracy, or at least for a healthy and functioning one. It fits comfortably with the recognition that people must come to collective decisions and act in the face of matters that are uncertain and contingent, about which we do not have all the information we would like. It recognizes that people are fallible, that decisions and commitments can be reviewed, that majorities and minorities may trade places, that controversies often are managed rather than ultimately resolved, and that great issues can remain contested over time.[4]

Democracy is sometimes confused with two other notions that share its trappings but not necessarily its substance. One is elections. They are a valuable and efficient means to determine the will of the majority, but they are not democracy itself. What if only a single candidate is allowed to

[3] "Message to Congress in Special Session, July 4, 1861." In: *Collected Works of Abraham Lincoln* (1953), 4:426. The phrasing anticipates that of the Gettysburg Address.

[4] On the importance of democracy's acknowledging human fallibility, see especially Thorson (1962).

run? What if there is an "inside" candidate and opposition supporters are intimidated so that they do not vote? What if the turnout is very low or the voters are unrepresentative of the total population? What if the counting of the ballots is suspect? Each of these things has happened in my lifetime, and each undercuts the legitimacy of an election. The citizen-voters are not in fact the rulers; the will of the majority is not being carried out; the rights of the minority are not protected. These are not democratic elections.

Second, democracy is sometimes confused with an extreme form of populism, in which an inherent division is assumed between "elites" and "the people." Rulers and ruled are not drawn from the same category. Elites never can represent the wishes of the people, even if chosen by them, because their interests as elites are at odds with the interests of the people. The goal of the elites is to preserve and build upon their own power. One way to do that is to oppress the people, but that might precipitate revolution. A better way is to appear to share the people's values and interests while actually co-opting them. Thus, for example, an officeholder may claim to support "family values" while opposing specific legislative measures to benefit families, such as family medical leave or child care allowances, even if a majority of the people support them. The officeholder is not necessarily being dishonest (although he or she may be), but according to this view of democracy, the officeholder is undemocratic. There is no doubt that this scenario in which elites co-opt the people sometimes develops. But it is a mistake to think that it is *inherent*, that there is a perpetual class struggle. To believe that is to advocate not democracy but anarchy, for there is no way by which the will of the people can be made effective. And the critic of public discourse who presumes that the practice of the culture is in such a state will have a ready-made and all-purpose interpretation at the ready: discourse is a mask for power, pure and simple. The critic may argue that individuals lack agency because their discourse is smothered by the intractable power struggle. Nuance does not matter; audience adaptation does not matter. These are only clever tricks to instill a kind of false consciousness among the people. Such an account, to say the least, is overdetermined.

There is another understanding of "democracy" that makes good sense at first glance. If the goal is for decisions to reflect the will of the people, why not ask each person (or a representative sample) his or her opinion, tabulate the responses, and present the answer? But the view of democracy as polling has two basic flaws. First, it neglects a sense of the commons and makes the public nothing more than an aggregate of individuals. "What is best for the country (or society)" reduces to "What do I like?" when these in fact are not identical. Second, this is at best a "thin" form of democracy. Poll numbers generally do not reflect either intensity of belief or the degree of information on which it is based. They yield inconsistent results, partly because people may be inconsistent (approving of social programs but not wanting to fund them, for instance) but also because answers to the pollster may be superficial or because answers are highly sensitive to the specific wording of a question. A richer, or "thicker" conception of democracy would promote the expression of reasoned, considered opinions as the basis for public judgment. For this reason, political scientist James Fishkin and his colleagues have experimented with what they call "deliberative opinion polling," obtaining people's opinions after they have been involved in structured discussion on the topic.

Deliberative opinion polling has been criticized on grounds of practicality, but it reflects the insight that rhetorical scholars often find congenial: that deliberation is the essence of democracy, or (as it is sometimes said) that democracy exists in communication. Realizing this insight, some have theorized about what they have called "deliberative democracy." The term, coined in 1980 by Joseph M. Bessette, refers to a system in which conflict is resolved and disagreement addressed through "open and uncoerced discussion."[5] The assumption is that "political agreement can be reached on the basis of principles that can be justified to others."[6] What determines the value of an idea or proposal is its ability on its own merits to influence others. Deliberation is characterized by giving and seeking reasons. What emerges is collective rationality – what the decision-making group as a whole considers to be reasonable. This is not necessarily the same as a simple aggregation of individual preferences, because presumably individuals will transform their preferences to take others' views into account. This approach to decision making is fundamentally rhetorical, because the justifications people provide for their views are justifications *to an audience*. They are not deduced like syllogisms but are premised on the beliefs and values of a deliberating community in a specific situation.

[5] I discuss strengths and flaws of the deliberative-democracy research in Zarefsky (2008), pp. 131-153.

[6] Guttman and Thompson (2003), p. 33.

Nevertheless, the deliberative democracy literature is largely theoretical and abstract. There are but a few empirical applications, and they involve contrived situations. The literature is based on the normative but counterfactual situation of "open and uncoerced discussion," which seldom if ever obtains. Deliberative democracy also envisions relatively small discussion groups as the model, not an entire society or its representatives pursuing collective decisions about war or peace, taxation, the role of government in the economy, the tension between national and local interests, the general welfare, or any of the other topics usually placed under "public policy." But deliberative democracy does make clear that rhetoric has a central role to play. Rhetorical sensitivity can rehabilitate the concept of deliberative democracy and can invigorate its practice – if rhetorical criticism will allow it to.

Democratic deliberation and rhetorical citizenship

Armed with that premise, scholars such as Kock and Villadsen are fleshing out a concept of rhetorical citizenship based upon a more empirical understanding of deliberation, and scholars such as Tracy are conducting empirical studies, particularly of representative governing bodies at the local level.[7] These studies reflect the fact that discussion is not usually "open and uncoerced." People bring with them the baggage of their own circumstances, ranging from class and economic self-interest to personal identity and political ideology, and they evaluate others' ideas within the context of these commitments. Discussion moves that might violate conventional norms of decorum or politeness are not condemned out of hand; they are examined for an understanding of their function in widening or narrowing the viewpoints under consideration, and for facilitating decisions or slowing the rush to consensus.

What is not so generally realized is that the same processes of rhetorical deliberation evolve as a larger society works toward public decisions. Citizens read and listen about issues from a wide variety of information sources, incorporating what they learn into a pre-existing set of knowledge and beliefs, adjusting the set when necessary to incorporate new or discordant elements. Leaders write and talk about these issues, trying to make connections between their ideals and proposals, on the one hand, and the audience's beliefs and values, on the other. Interested parties try to arouse others' interest

[7] See, for example, Tracy (2010).

and support through a wide variety of media and presentational choices. On the surface, the process hardly resembles a conversation, much less a meeting of a decision-making body. But in a larger sense, that is exactly what it is – a wide-ranging conversation across space and time in which a loosely defined but vast body of individuals comes to a collective sense of its identity, its values, and its priorities – or, in the case of a stalemate, fails to do so.

A rhetor anticipating or confronting such a broad audience does not begin in a vacuum. Every society, as Bourdieu asserts, has unquestioned assumptions that are widely believed as if they were facts – whether because, as he claims, those in power want to present contestable claims as if they were settled, or simply as a result of socialization into a culture.[8] For example, many Europeans find it hard to understand why in the United States gun control is such a troublesome issue even in the face of clear evidence that guns easily get into the wrong hands and lead to unnecessary violence, sometimes on a massive scale. It *is* hard to understand, at least until one recognizes this issue as the latest instantiation of ideas that trace back to the American founding: distrust of and hostility toward government, which is seen as the people's enemy rather than as their agent; a strong emphasis on individualism and self-reliance rather than communal action as the best guarantor of safety and security; the historical experience of colonists in Boston in the 1770s who were forced to quarter British soldiers in their private homes and who sought means of self-defense; and the belief that local militias offered better defense against enemies than did national standing armies which easily could be turned against the people instead. Taking stock of these cultural facts does not decisively tip the scales against gun control, of course, for there are multiple considerations on the other side. But it does help to explain why the question is controversial and divisive, even in the face of tragedies such as the recent mass shooting at Sandy Hook Elementary School in Newtown, Connecticut. And it does make clear the burden on the advocates of gun control: either to demonstrate to the public's satisfaction that proposed measures will not jeopardize this set of prevailing beliefs or to provide a convincing explanation for why the set should be altered or overthrown.

Participants in a controversy such as this one on gun control may not consciously recognize that this is their task, caught up as they are in their own advocacy. But that is where the rhetorical critic comes in, either con-

[8] Bourdieu (1979), cited in von der Lippe (2012), p. 165.

structively by advising advocates on the structure of audience beliefs and the burden the advocates face, or analytically by accounting for the presence and significance of these predispositions. Too often, references to context treat it just as historical background, useful for knowing what is happening at the time, without recognizing its constitutive nature with regard to the controversy at hand. Understanding public discourse as extended democratic deliberation might make us more sensitive to this problem.

Democratic deliberation and identification

How are we to understand what happens in a deliberating group or society? What is the rhetorical process involved, how is it democratic, and in what ways might it be threatened by rhetorical criticism?

People are by nature divided, Kenneth Burke has written.[9] They are separated from one another by differences in experience, thought, feeling, motivation, and interest, among other things. Each of us is a solitary being, yet persistent solitude is unpleasant and uncomfortable, so we are also by nature social. Burke's maxim is that "identification is compensatory to division."[10] We identify with others when they fit our ideas into their values and vice-versa. When that happens, we can understand how they think and what they value. We see their viewpoint as fitting within our own. More than that, Burke employs religious imagery in maintaining that we become "consubstantial" with them – metaphorically, we become one. We come to see ourselves as parts of the same whole, with which we both affiliate.

But how does this happen? Participants in deliberation try out their stories on one another, exchanging them and comparing others' stories with their own. In referring to stories, I mean the accounts that people offer to explain their world-views or frames of reference. The stories may be narratives with characters and plot, but they also may take the form of arguments, descriptions, or explanations. The participants' goal is to have stories that match, so that you can see yours in mine and vice-versa. When that happens, the deliberation has produced a common story. Sometimes all or nearly all will need to accept the story for the deliberation to be successful; sometimes a supermajority will be required; sometimes a simple majority. Sometimes the deliberation will not succeed in its primary goal but nevertheless will have

[9] Burke (1969) [1950], esp. p. 22.

[10] Burke, (1969) [1950], p. 22.

identified the precise matters about which there is disagreement and will succeed in clarifying the different positions and developing an understanding of how they will be tested.

This abstract model of deliberation, of course, is enacted in real time, with real actors operating with real baggage. They will try to do one or more of three things. First, advocates may seek *transcendent* appeals – ones that will subsume whatever are the matters on which the advocates disagree. In the recent fiscal-policy debates in my country, for example, the conviction that we must not go over the "fiscal cliff" induced the deliberators to reach at least a semblance of agreement. The need to build "a common European home" during the 1990s likewise subsumed competing nationalistic desires even though those forces remained active. If deliberators can see their interests subsumed within a common vision, to that degree they will see themselves as united, members of the same community pursuing the same goal.

A second possibility is for advocates to develop *multivocal* appeals, messages that attract people's support for different reasons and that may even mean different things to different people. Division is overcome through a unified message that people can understand each in his or her own way yet all can support. A contemporary example is "income tax reform," which can be understood as meaning anything from eliminating loopholes and deductions to making tax rates sharply more (or less) progressive. A wide swath of the U.S. public views "tax reform" favorably as an essential component of a solution to the problem of the U.S. national debt, but they do not all mean the same thing by the phrase. A famous 19th century example was the term "popular sovereignty," which for a decade papered over differences within the Democratic Party about whether territories did or did not have the right to prevent the introduction of slavery before they became states. Multivocal appeals depend on a certain degree of ambiguity; their power to build consensus is lost if they are rendered too precise. They function in a way similar to what political scientist Murray Edelman, borrowing from anthropologist Edward Sapir, called "condensation symbols"; they condense into one symbol a wide range of ideas and referents that might otherwise diverge.[11]

A third option is for advocates to formulate *displacement* appeals, those that lead advocates to abandon one commitment and to replace it with another, having been convinced that the new commitment is more compatible

[11] Edelman (1964), p. 6; Sapir (1934).

with the person's belief system than was the old. This is the most overt case of people changing their minds. This happens occasionally, especially if the original commitment is not very strong. What is more likely is to establish that a person's original commitment leads him or her to results that he or she finds unacceptable, rejecting it for that reason, and adopting the proposed alternative in order to avoid a vacuum. This is a particular illustration of the circumstantial *ad hominem* argument.[12] For example, a person believing that there should be absolutely no government involvement in the economy might be confronted with the knowledge that this position is at odds with a call for government to provide funds to rebuild one's town after it has been hit by a major national disaster – a view which our hypothetical citizen also supports, having been a victim of a hurricane in the past. The pull of personal interest might prove stronger than that of abstract principle, and being aware of the tension between the two might induce our hypothetical citizen to abandon the unyielding opposition to any and all government involvement in the economy.

Transcendence, multivocality, and displacement are three examples of strategic appeals that a deliberating group or a larger society can use to move from division toward identification. But exactly how they work involves something of a "black box." Forty years ago, Ernest Bormann (1972) proposed that people tell stories exchanging what he called "fantasy themes" and that these "chain out" in a group as they resonate with others. People pick up on a particular theme because it "speaks to them." They elaborate on its meaning, develop additional implications, carry a metaphor further, or find an additional application, and thereby join with others in commitment to the theme. Bormann used "fantasy theme" as a somewhat technical term, but the process of "chaining out" may have more general application.

An obvious example would be the acceptance of "war" as a metaphor to describe what took place on September 11, 2001. The dominant story might have been that there was a monstrous crime, or that it was the act of insane and deluded people on a massive scale, or that this was the assertion by a non-state actor of the prerogatives of a state, or something else. But these options gained little traction because the metaphor of "war" so quickly chained out that it became the normalized way to describe these terrible

[12] On this use of the *ad hominem* argument, see Johnstone (1959), p. 73, p. 76; Walton (1998), pp. 2-6.

events. More recently, the September 11, 2012 attack on the U.S. mission in Benghazi, Libya, has come to be understood as a terrorist act rather than – as some in the U.S. intelligence community had maintained – only the spontaneous and unplanned consequence of a protest demonstration. As a different story chained out from the one the early commentators had used, they were perceived not just as mistaken but as dangerously naïve.

The trajectory by which a story chains out, however, is not predetermined and always could be otherwise. It is contingent and depends upon intervening variables ranging from contemporaneous events to the ideological predisposition of the decision makers. This fact underscores the rhetorical nature of deliberation. Rhetoric is situational; it is grounded in particulars rather than following law-like generalizations. It is an art, not a science. Its outcome depends upon the inventional resources and aptitude of individuals in a given moment. And since it cannot be fully or definitively explained, it contains an element of mystery. This element keeps rhetorical practice open and potential, not closed and definitive. It preserves the possibility of rebuttal, and therefore is foundational to democracy.

Rhetorical criticism and threats to democratic deliberation

This brings me at last to the concern I raised at the outset. If rhetoric in society depends on an element of mystery, then rhetorical criticism, in seeking to demystify what is going on, poses a potential threat. It may contribute to the paralysis of democratic deliberation that is so often noted today. Surely this paralysis has many other causes, such as sharply increased political polarization, the recognition of limits, and the emergence of seemingly intractable positions. But rhetorical criticism, if it presumes to explain too fully, may leave no room for rhetors to use the resources of invention to work creatively in the face of these challenges. And, of course, if democracy is paralyzed and grinds to a halt, necessary decisions will be made and actions taken by non-democratic means.

Both everyday and academic rhetorical criticism can reveal this dark side, in two different ways in each case. I begin with the everyday. First, political actors can too easily become rhetorical critics, not accepting others' words at face value nor even retaining a healthy skepticism, but scrutinizing their discourse to determine what it "really" means beneath the surface. Recent politics furnishes some examples. Unencumbered by evidence, a non-trivial number of people continue to believe that President Obama is a

Muslim socialist who was born in Kenya. Documents establishing the contrary are dismissed as forgeries or otherwise inauthentic, as clever devices to obscure the truth and prop up illegitimate holders of power. German chancellor Angela Merkel's call for a more integrated euro zone is disdained on the grounds that what she "really" is trying to do is to reassert German dominance of the European continent. U.S. Secretary of State Hillary Rodham Clinton's recent illness was said to be faked, statements of medical experts to the contrary notwithstanding, because she wanted to avoid having to testify before the Congressional committee investigating the Benghazi tragedy that was, it was said, highly critical of the State Department.

These examples are especially disconcerting because they call into question such fundamentals as the nature of fact and evidence. Even more, they divide people into radically different communities with different standards of knowledge and belief – each of which can perpetuate itself by insulating its members from exposure to alternative viewpoints – rather than a single community of people who hold diverse opinions. Without sharing such basic beliefs about the world, they cannot deliberate together and instead either withdraw into their separate enclaves or else engage in full-scale culture wars.

It is easy to disparage such blatant disregard for fact. But a second way by which advocates try to become rhetorical critics is harder to dismiss. Consider as an example a book that appeared almost a decade ago, Thomas Frank's *What's the Matter with Kansas?* (2004). While he writes specifically about the state of Kansas, Frank's argument applies far more broadly to significant elements of the U.S. population. Noting that a century ago Kansas was a hotbed of radical populism, Frank asks how it has happened that the state has come to be dominated by social conservatives who do not represent the economic self-interest of the people. His answer, in a nutshell, is that a generation of people has been led to vote against its own self-interests, rejecting government economic policies that actually would help them, because they have given priority to ideologically conservative beliefs about social topics such as abortion, religion, and marriage, which somehow trump their economic self-interest. I happen to share Frank's wish that Kansas would return to its more radical roots, but I find his analysis flawed. It reduces legitimate grounds for voting to personal economic self-interest alone, implying that the people of Kansas are misguided if they cast their votes on any other grounds. This both exalts the economic over other dimensions of a person's life and also suggests that people should select officials and policies not on the basis of what they think is good for society as a whole but only on the basis of what will benefit them personally. The people of Kansas surely are not the only ones who sometimes allow the common good to trump their personal self-interest. I myself have sometimes supported measures for which I would need to pay even though I would not benefit from them personally, in the belief that they were beneficial to society as a whole and that, in the given case, that was more important. This preference for the public over the private is what the 18th century understood as the meaning of virtue.

If Frank's recommendations to vote based on economic self-interest were widely adopted, there would be no need for deliberation, because there would be nothing to discuss with others. Each person could calculate his or her own self-interest and vote on that basis; the results could be tallied up; and the outcome would be that choice which the greatest number of individuals saw as being in their self-interest. This approach would stop deliberation in its tracks and would substitute a thin for a robust sense of democracy. If one agrees with Frank's underlying ideological position, then one should focus not on the fact that social values can trump self-interest but on the particular social values that the people of Kansas have been persuaded to accept.

The two approaches to amateur rhetorical criticism I've described here seem to be opposites. One is marked by disregard for "the facts" and the surface claims of discourse, in the belief that they are but a cover for deeper underlying motivations that the would-be critic would expose. The other is marked by reduction of discourse to *only* "the facts," and to a narrow conception of them at that – economic self-interest. But they actually share a most disturbing feature. They stymie continued deliberation. If "the truth" really is secret and known only to a privileged few, then deliberation is pointless. If "the truth" reduces to facts that are not disputable, then deliberation is unnecessary. And if, as I've claimed above, deliberation is constitutive of democracy, then discouraging deliberation is indeed subversive of democracy.

What is worse, these positions are not easily refuted. Can one prove conclusively that the President is not a Muslim or that he was not born in Kenya? The documents on which one would rely would be dismissed by the would-be critic as forgeries or corrupted by misinterpretation. The reaction is the same as that to conspiracy rhetoric:[13] if a suspect denies that he or she is in on the plot, isn't that exactly what you would expect a devious conspirator

[13] An excellent review of the literature on conspiracy arguments is Pfau (2005), chap. 1.

to do? The argument that seemingly would deny the charge is reinterpreted to support it instead. The preposterous claims become self-sealing.[14] If the allegations cannot be dislodged on their own terms, the remedy must be to shift the terms – objecting to the line of argument because it is destructive of individual freedom, or perhaps subjecting it to ridicule through a circumstantial *ad hominem* showing that the self-sealing argument can be used against its own perpetrator.

But it is not just the amateur critics about whom I worry. There are problematic tendencies in academic rhetorical criticism as well. Here I am understanding "critical" in "rhetorical criticism" as meaning "analytical" or "reflective," not "negative" or "hostile." The academic subfield of rhetorical criticism has made immense advances in the past sixty years, evolving from a formula-based approach that proved primarily that any discourse could be sorted out into pre-defined categories taken from Aristotle's *Rhetoric*. One of the more significant advances has been the productive complication of the concept of agency. Even sixty years ago, it seemed strange to judge a speech a failure in a situation in which the speaker had no realistic possibility of success to start with. Assuming complete agency on the speaker's part was undoubtedly naïve. Attributing a more limited sense of agency to the speaker, and granting agency to situational, social, economic, and ideological forces has made the critic's task more difficult but has produced criticism of greater sophistication and force.

One very strong move in this direction was the "critical rhetoric" project undertaken by Raymie McKerrow (1989). McKerrow urged a special focus on the relationship between rhetoric and power. Discourse can be used by the powerful as an instrument to maintain power, even if it professes neutrality or openness to critique. Meanwhile, it can be extremely difficult for insurgent challengers to employ discourse as a means to equalize or threaten power in the way enacted by social protest movements of the 1960s. These are important insights, and one of the clearest trends in rhetorical criticism over the past decade is the growing emphasis on power and ideology as explanations for the strength or weakness of discourse.

Here too, though, I think there is at least a potential problem. It is tempting to infer from the influence of power and ideology that they are

[14] The concept of "self-sealing arguments" comes from Robert J. Fogelin. See, for example, Fogelin and Sinnott-Armstrong (1997), pp. 353-357.

completely deterministic, explaining the outcome of rhetorical acts without remainder. If it is all power, all the way down, then as a practical matter there is no need to undertake the criticism, because we already know the answer before we ask the question. If everything can be explained by patriarchy, or exploitation of labor, or white privilege, or any other ideology to which one might subscribe, then rhetoric itself is rendered inert. And from the viewpoint of the rhetors we study, if our criticism were convincing and they came to understand that rhetoric was inert, then there would be no reason for them to engage in deliberation. Deliberation is a sham, on this view; the real game is amassing or overturning power, and – with apologies to Clausewitz – rhetoric becomes the continuation of warfare by other means.

Furthermore, ideological criticism, when "taken to the end of the line" in the manner I am imagining, is also self-sealing. A critic who disputes the force of ideology easily could be accused of displaying "false consciousness," having been seduced by the hegemony of that ideological force. Not realizing the determinism of ideology, he or she would posit the existence of rhetorical agency, thereby revealing only that he or she didn't "get it" and causing the challenging criticism to be dismissed rather than taken seriously. This result is even more likely to come about if the discourse being examined is itself ideologically driven, situated in a controversy in which the participants appear to have completely different world-views and the dispute among them is marked by "deep disagreement."[15]

The problem with this approach is that it is at odds with what we know about rhetoric itself: that it is grounded in specific situations and that it arises in moments that are uncertain and contingent. Robert Ivie put it this way in an e-mail exchange he and I had on this topic: "Our field seems inclined to locate rhetoric under the sign of ideology, which sacrifices rhetoric's potential for addressing pragmatically the problem of perceived incommensurability. Rhetoric doesn't require us to solve these divisions completely or universally. It is situational and adaptive."[16] I would add that we sell our own subject short when we pretend otherwise.

I suspect that I have constructed a caricature of ideological criticism; I hope so. There is no particular example I can cite of criticism that

[15] I discuss the problem of "deep disagreement" and some possible rhetorical moves to overcome it in Zarefsky (2012). The term "deep disagreement" comes from Fogelin (1985).
[16] Robert L. Ivie, e-mail message to the author, March 16, 2012.

takes ideology all the way "to the end of the line," certainly not the work of McKerrow. But I confess that I occasionally read essays in our journals that make me wonder if this is the direction in which we are heading, and that lead me to issue a pre-emptive warning against following that path. We need to find and produce criticism of rhetorical moments when ideology is present and yet not deterministic, in which creative invention blunts, sets aside, limits, or challenges its influence. Periods of ideological turbulence and change offer especially rich resources for such studies.

Another potential challenge to academic rhetorical criticism is that, despite what I said before that "critical" does not mean "hostile," there may be a tendency for critics to "go negative." It's my sense, and I could be wrong, that we write more often in condemnation of our subjects than in praise. In part, there is a natural asymmetry here. The sublime does not require detailed analysis. In fact, to explain its success is to detract from its artistry: great art conceals art. Rhetorical masterpieces are to be appreciated for what they are. It is perhaps not surprising, then, that there are relatively few critical works, for example, that examine the speeches ranked near the top of the rhetorical scholars' "top 100" list.[17] On the other hand, weaker performances may cry out for critical attention – to explain where they went wrong and to propose how they might have gone better, or at least what other, more promising alternatives might have been available.

Even beyond this basic asymmetry, however, I suspect that there may be a critical preference for the negative. It may reflect the tendency of many scholars to be skeptical generally. Or it may reflect a tendency not to write approvingly of rhetorical efforts if one disagrees with the conclusions they advance. The furor caused almost 40 years ago by Forbes Hill's sympathetic reading of Richard Nixon's "Vietnamization" speech is still with us.[18] I find it noteworthy that, while there are guarded readings of President George W. Bush's address to Congress after the tragedy of September 11,[19] there is hardly any sympathetic reading of any of his other speeches, including his

[17] In 1999, a panel of over 130 rhetorical scholars was asked to identify the top 100 speeches delivered in the United States during the twentieth century. The list and copies of the top 100 texts can be found in Lucas and Medhurst (2009).

[18] Hill (1972a). For alternative viewpoints, see Newman (1970); Campbell (1972); Hill (1972b).

[19] For example, Murphy (2003); Zarefsky (2004).

Second Inaugural Address, which – like it or not – is a masterful presentation of the theories of democracy promotion and American exceptionalism, on which his presidency was based. Likewise, there are few if any attempts to read sympathetically the discourse of the Tea Party in defense of limited government that has echoes of Thomas Jefferson, or the social-policy discourse of conservatives who oppose abortion consistently without exceptions. I do not agree with any of these positions, but the fact is that they are legitimate rhetorical stances, rich in *topoi* with deep historical resonance. For that matter, with the exception of one or two specific speeches he gave before becoming president, there have been few sympathetic readings of the speeches of Barack Obama.

Now, a preference for condemnation over appreciation might have no serious consequences if we did not imagine academic rhetorical criticism having any impact beyond illustrating the act of criticism itself. But we usually imagine that criticism can make a difference in shaping the course of public deliberation. Critical discourse that is long on blame and short on praise will offer little guidance about how to advance discussion of important public issues, other than a steady stream of admonitions to "avoid this." Moreover, it will induce cynicism about the critics, or about the act of criticism itself, that will harm the prospects for its use in deliberation. The cynicism will be justified, especially if critics hold the rhetorical performance up to the standards of an impossible ideal, as is done in some of the "deliberative democracy" literature. As Hauser points out, if everyday debates are measured by the standards of ideal speech, negative evaluation will be guaranteed.[20] This too is essentially a non-rhetorical evaluation because it does not reflect the grounding of rhetoric in specific situations.

Perhaps even more than sympathetic criticism, there is a need for constructive criticism, that is, rhetorical criticism that not only identifies our predicaments but also proposes ways to work through them. The needs for such "work around" proposals can be seen acutely in the United States, which now has experienced 20 years of persistent political gridlock and stalemated discourse, but it probably characterizes much of the world facing seemingly intractable problems without deep reservoirs of political sensitivity or good will. Ivie expressed this concern to me when he wrote, "There probably is more of this kind of constructive rhetorical scholarship going on

[20] This is one of the themes of Hauser (1999). It is referred to in Klujeff (2012), p. 101.

than I know about, but I suspect there is relatively little of it and certainly less of it than is needed to direct the field's considerable intellectual capital toward constructively addressing the challenges of the present era."[21]

Situations perceived as deadlocked, after all, are tailor-made for rhetorical intervention – for imagining things in a different way, for shifting the frame of reference, for introducing a new term or a new hierarchy of terms or a new definition of a term, for all the ways in which rhetors and audiences might take a new look at an old problem. To the degree that such conversations take place, they are usually proprietary, between political leaders and their advisers, and they are dismissed by others as nothing more than "spin." But democratic deliberation would be enhanced if the conversation were broadened, if rhetorical critics took up topics like these: How can we overcome the frustrating impasse about the size and role of government that is at the heart of the "fiscal crisis" in the United States and, I suspect, in the European Union as well? How can we reconcile the seeming deep disagreement between faith in the government and faith in the market? How do we decide what values are universal and exportable and which are culture-specific and not the business of 'outsiders,' and how do we regard a value such as "democracy" that belongs to some degree in both categories? In a time of increased religiosity around the world and the rise of fundamentalism in all religions, how can we respect religious differences while also respecting religious belief and practice? How can those who believe that prophecy has ceased engage in productive dialogue with those who claim to have received the word of God? How can we reconcile a commitment to equal opportunity with the realities of unequal achievement? And how can we reconcile a commitment to free and unfettered expression with the recognition that speech has consequences?

Hard questions, these. They pose seemingly sharp dichotomies. But if that is the final answer, they cannot be resolved by democratic deliberation. They will be subject to the whims of shifting majorities or through deference to authority or appeal to force. Democracy will wither as citizens withdraw from the public sphere in the belief that democratic deliberation is futile and that the outcome will not matter to them anyway. If, on the other hand, rhetorical critics can take up these questions and begin to offer constructive alternatives, the benefits are huge. We can revitalize the study of invention

[21] Ivie, e-mail message to the author, March 16, 2012.

by rhetoricizing the situational context and then deriving possibilities from our own creativity and our understanding of rhetorical traditions. We can give more credibility to our critical judgments by suggesting alternatives to those we criticize, rather than merely offering critiques. We can give potency to what Robert Asen has called "a discourse theory of citizenship" (2004) by explaining and showing how it works, how the process of public deliberation is the enactment of citizenship. And we thereby can make rhetorical criticism an instrument of democracy rather than a possible threat to it.

The four potential threats to democracy I've discussed – two from everyday rhetorical criticism and two from academic rhetorical criticism – have in common that they deny the richness of rhetoric itself, especially its grounding in specific situations and its inventional possibilities. Revitalization of democracy springs from a healthy respect for and use of these very features of rhetoric. This is only one of many ways in which we might orient our intellectual resources. We will need to respond to cynics who may accuse us of being overly optimistic or naïve, but the potential rewards of this effort are vast. Perhaps most of all, we will take the idea of "rhetorical citizenship" seriously and we will strengthen democratic deliberation as the way to achieve it. Surely that is a worthy task.

References

Asen, R. (2004). A Discourse Theory of Citizenship. *Quarterly Journal of Speech* 90, 189-211.

Bormann, E.G. (1972). Fantasy and Rhetorical Vision: The Rhetorical Criticism of Social Reality. *Quarterly Journal of Speech* 58, 396-407.

Bourdieu, P. (1979). *Outline of a Theory of Practice*. Cambridge: Cambridge University Press.

Burke, K. (1959) [1937]. *Attitudes toward History*, 2d. rev. ed. Boston: Beacon Press.

Burke, K. (1969) [1950]. *A Rhetoric of Motives*. Berkeley and Los Angeles: University of California Press.

Campbell, K.K. (1972). Conventional Wisdom – Traditional Form': A Rejoinder. *Quarterly Journal of Speech* 58, 451-454;

Edelman, M. (1964). *The Symbolic Uses of Politics*. Urbana: University of Illinois Press.

Fogelin, R.J. (1985). The Logic of Deep Disagreements. *Informal Logic* 7, 1-8.

Fogelin, R.J. and W. Sinnott-Armstrong (1997). *Understanding Arguments: An Introduction to Informal Logic*. 5th ed. New York: Harcourt Brace.

Frank, T. (2004). *What's the Matter with Kansas? How Conservatives Won the Heart of America*. New York: Henry Holt.

Guttman, A. and D. Thompson (2003). Deliberative Democracy Beyond Process. In: J.S. Fishkin and P. Laslett (Eds.), *Debating Deliberative Democracy* (pp. 31-52). Malden, Massachusetts: Blackwell.

Hauser, G.A. (1999). *Vernacular Voices: The Rhetoric of Publics and Public Spheres.* Columbia, SC: University of South Carolina Press.

Hill, F.I. (1972a). Conventional Wisdom – Traditional Form. The President's Message of November 3, 1969. *Quarterly Journal of Speech* 58, 373-386.

Hill, F.I. (1972b).Reply to Professor Campbell. *Quarterly Journal of Speech* 56, 454-460.

Johnstone, H.W., Jr. (1959). *Philosophy and argument.* University Park: Pennsylvania State University Press.

Klujeff, M.L. (2012). Provocative Style: The Gaarder Debate Example. In: C. Kock and L. Villadsen (Eds.), *Rhetorical citizenship and public deliberation* (pp. 101-114). University Park: Penn State University Press.

Kock, C. and L. Villadsen (2012). Introduction: Citizenship as a Rhetorical Practice. In: C. Kock And L. Villadsen (Eds.), *Rhetorical Citizenship and Public Deliberation* (pp. 1-10). University Park: Pennsylvania State University Press.

Lincoln, A. (1953). Message to Congress in Special Session, July 4, 1861. In: R.P. Basler (Ed.), *Collected works of Abraham Lincoln.* New Brunswick, N.J.: Rutgers University Press.

Lucas, S.L. and Martin Medhurst. (Eds.) (2009). *Words of a Century: The Top 100 American Speeches, 1900-1999.* New York: Oxford University Press.

McKerrow, R.E. (1989). Critical Rhetoric: Theory and Praxis. *Communication Monographs* 56, 91-111.

Murphy, J.M. (2003) 14-20. "Our Mission and Our Moment": George W. Bush and September 11th. *Rhetoric & Public Affairs* 6, 607-632;

Newman, R.P. (1970). Under the Veneer: Nixon's Vietnam Speech of November 3, 1969. *Quarterly Journal of Speech* 56, 168-178.

Pfau, M.W. (2005). *The Political Style of Conspiracy: Chase, Sumner, and Lincoln.* East Lansing: Michigan State University Press.

Sapir, E. (1934). Symbolism. In: E.R.A. Seligman (Ed.). *Encyclopedia of the Social Sciences.* New York: Macmillan

Thorson, T.L. (1962). *The Logic of Democracy.* New York: Holt, Rinehart, and Winston.

Tracy, K. (2010). *Challenges of Ordinary Democracy.* University Park: Pennsylvania State University Press.

von der Lippe, B. (2012). Rhetoric of War, Rhetoric of Gender. In: C. Kock and L. Villadsen (Eds.), *Rhetorical Citizenship and Public Deliberation* (pp. 153-168). University Park: Pennsylvania State University Press.

Walton, D. (1998). *Ad Hominem Arguments*. Tuscaloosa: University of Alabama Press.

Weaver, R.M. (1953). *The Ethics of Rhetoric*. Chicago: Henry Regnery.

Zarefsky, D. (2004). George W. Bush Discovers Rhetoric: September 20, 2001 and the U.S. Response to Terrorism. In: M.J. Hyde (Ed.), *The Ethos of Rhetoric* (pp. 136-155). Columbia: University of South Carolina Press.

Zarefsky, D. (2008). Two Faces of Democratic Rhetoric. In: T.F. McDorman and D.M. Timmerman (Eds.), *Rhetoric & Democracy: Pedagogical and Political Practices* (pp. 115-137). East Lansing: Michigan State University Press.

Zarefsky, D. (2012). The Appeal for Transcendence: A Possible Response to Cases of Deep Disagreement. In: F.H. van Eemeren and B. Garssen (Eds.), *Topical Themes in Argumentation Theory* (pp. 77-89). Dordrecht: Springer.

On Rhetorical Ethos and Personal Deeds: A 2011 Spanish Public Controversy[1]

PAULA OLMOS

The two sides of *ēthos* theory

Within the conceptual framework of Rhetorical Citizenship, the notion of the individual citizen's identity and its enactment through rhetorical participation becomes a crucial concern. Any rhetorical act both takes advantage of and helps to construe the orator's identity as a public image, for public purposes. In other words, her disclosed and received character or public ēthos is both a substantial ingredient and one of the most conspicuous outcomes of her involvement in civic interaction. That is why rhetorical attention to ēthos theory and ēthos-centered criticism of argumentative discourse are an inescapable feature in any study of rhetorical agency.

According to Aristotle's *Rhetoric* (1356a9-10), ēthos, the orator's character – a basic source of persuasion, together with *logos* and *pathos* – should be understood by means of the orator's own discourse (*dia tou logou*) and not through any previous information and opinions we may have about her acts and person (*alla mē dia to prodedoxasthai*, i.e., "but not through what was previously known/opined"). In this Aristotelian caution, we may see the origins of a long and complex rhetorical tradition, a conception of ēthos as "the self-image that a speaker, either willingly or unwillingly, construes through her own discourse" (Bokobza Kahan 2009, p. 2; cf. Amossy 1999, 2006 [2000], 2009), as something distinguishable from her biographical self. Contemporary rhetoricians and discourse analysts seek to study the relationships between such a *discursive* ēthos and: i) the speaker's discourse as such, ii) the speaker's biographical and social self

[1] Supported by Research Project FFI2011-23125, funded by the Spanish Ministry of Economy and Competitiveness.

and iii) the social and institutional context of her discursive practice; in what constitutes a "complex conception of ēthos."[2]

According to R. Amossy (1999), the analyst's aim is not at all to exclusively identify the speaker's ēthos with either of the two extremes: her biographical self or her pure discursive image, but rather to articulate an integrated approach to the concept of ēthos as a constellation of relationships including both textual and extra-textual elements. Amossy also alludes to the possible differences between what the speaker projects and what the audience receives, which is ultimately beyond her control. Literary studies have particularly focused on the exploration of various "ethotic games" which might be described and analyzed through the use of a collection of opposable notions, such as "author/author's image," "responsible/responding author," 'actor-author/*auctor*-author.'[3]

But going back to Aristotle's *Rhetoric* and regarding, then, the "orator's character" as an "available means of persuasion" (1355b25-26) and not just a literary proposal, Aristotle's caution that we should focus on the explicitly discursive ēthos (*ēthos dia tou logou*) does not seem to be entirely justified; least of all if we are thinking about a civic context and an audience that is to decide on political matters (the paradigmatic referent of ancient rhetoric). Why should we renounce the information we already have about the orator in our reception of her discourse? Is this at all operative or commendable in such contexts?

In spite of the contemporary rhetorical and literary resonance of Aristotle's caution for a modern informed reader, the philosopher was in fact responding in an innovative way to certain aspects of 4th c. BCE Greek rhetorical theory. The allegedly more conventional *Rhetoric to Alexander*, attributed to Anaximenes of Lampsacus, and what we know about Isocrates' rhetorical teachings reveal to us the crucial importance placed by these two authors and their schools on the opposition between an interlocutor's dis-

[2] A complex conception of ēthos would try to include and account for a whole array of notions, ranging from the speaker's own real traits and characteristics, her widely and publicly known traits, her visible traits, to their translation into her verbal and discursive traits (as "sujet de l'énonciation") and even explicit ethotic self-references (as "sujet de l'énoncé").

[3] Cf. Mainguenau (2009), who talks about a complex "ontology of authorship" which we could reconstruct as an "ontology of ēthos."

course and her previously known character. The contrast between these two aspects is a conspicuous part of the argumentative techniques studied and recommended by the *Rhetoric to Alexander* (*RA*). Several "types of proof" or means of persuasion defined and proposed in this text are based on the rhetorical exploitation of possible pragmatic inconsistencies between a person's discourse and her deeds or character. M. Kraus (2011) offers the following schema of the types of proof presented and studied in the *RA*.

Internal proofs	**External proofs (epithetoi)**
a. *eikos* (based on what is plausible)	a. *doxa tou legontos*
b. *paradeigma* (example)	b. witnesses
c. *tekmērion* (indication of a pragmatic inconsistency)	c. torture
d. *enthymema* (indication of a contradiction)	d. oaths
e. *gnomē* (maxim)	
f. *sēmeion* (sign)	
g. *elenchos* (direct effective refutation)	

The type of counter-argumentative proof known as *tekmērion* explicitly concentrates on well-, or in any case previously, known information about the interlocutor's character (Noël 2011). The *tekmērion* exploits, thus, the notion of an *ēthos dia tōn ēthōn* (a biographical ēthos) with a constant reference to the extra-discursive realm of the arguers' real biographical characteristics. Moreover, Pisani (2011) explores the contrast between the *RA*'s *enthymeme* and *tekmērion* in a way that points to a conception of the former which may also be rather *ethotic* in content.

Kraus (2011) also notes another ethotic element present in the *RA*, namely the kind of external proof rather ambiguously called *doxa tou legontos*: i.e., the opinion "of" or "about" the speaker, according to divergent interpretations. Kraus's own position is that it is more plausible to interpret this as the "speaker's reputation," rather than referring to his own opinions (2011, pp. 275-278). This would mean that there is something akin to Aristotle's ēthos in the *RA*, although precisely and explicitly pointing to a biographical ēthos that is somewhat opposed to Aristotle's explicit caution.[4]

[4] Kraus ultimately claims that there is still the possibility of accepting a reasonable amount of ambiguity in the expression, which would thus refer to the speaker's reputation *as based on* his known opinions. This possibility would make the *doxa tou legontos* a type of proof,

We could try to solve the theoretical conflict between Aristotle and Anaximenes in a rather trivial way, by claiming that with his caution Aristotle is simply giving instructions to a prospective orator. He would be talking about what the speaker can control, i.e. her *ēthos dia tou logou*, the only possible *technical ēthos*. Her previous life, character or actions known to the audience would be *atechnoi*, i.e. beyond rhetorical control. We could then say that the *RA*, for its part, shows a characteristic practical bent towards controversy (especially legal *adversarial* controversy). This would contrast with Aristotle's focus on a single orator's "persuasive discourse," and thus, it would be consistent for it to emphasize the role of dialectical moves (arguments and counter-arguments between proponent and opponent). In neither case would we be reading about technical recommendations or suggestions for "argument assessment" by either the audience or an "external analyst," an omnipresent figure today, but rather absent in Greek rhetorical theory.

I contend, nevertheless, that we can make more fruitful use of Aristotle's caution and its focus on discursive *ēthos* within the context of a contemporary approach heedful of the normative evaluation of arguments. We could ask ourselves how an argument analyst should proceed in the face of the ethotic aspects of discourse. Should she focus on the argumentative interchange or exploit the information she has from other sources? Is it reasonable and legitimate to bring in external information? Or is it reasonable, on the other hand, to neglect such information and ask for a "candid" reception of the discourse?

My position is not that we should always do either one or the other. These are not entirely incompatible approaches and a judicious combination of the two is surely the best option, depending on the context and the social practice involved. However, I believe that Aristotle's caution deserves additional attention. Although it should not be taken as a permanent rule (that would preclude exposure, in the appropriate context, of the speaker's imposture), it is nevertheless a useful initial imperative of ethical value, embodying a defeasible presumption about the speaker's pragmatic consistency which may help us better understand her discourse.

Aristotle's indication seems to dictate a somewhat difficult, almost unnatural, attitude on the part of the audience and the analyst (and this

a means of persuasion, rather akin to the modern and complex idea of a doubly conceived (intra- and extra-discursive) ēthos.

will be clearly revealed in the case we are going to present and analyze). Additionally, it recommends a stance that is intellectually problematic in epistemic terms, suggesting a temporary cancellation of information we may have about the people involved in a controversy. However, we could take it as a methodological suggestion, a tactical presumption that may help us examine certain possibilities which could be relevant from an argumentative and communicative point of view and which might pass unnoticed.

To maintain an initial presumption about the exclusive internal relevance of the discursive ēthos (vs. a biographical ēthos) may help us comply with the ethical imperative of offering the speaker a renewed opportunity (independent of her previous life) to put forth her arguments. It is also the basis of the exercise of advocacy, allowing an orator to represent other people's interests, which she may or may not share. Finally, an initial focus on discursive ēthos and a cautious subsequent broadening of perspective to take into account other available information may in certain cases help us examine issues related to the relevance and right to participate of some voices in a particular controversy. This is also something that the "Rico Scandal" we are about to examine will shed light on.

A 2011 Spanish Controversy: The Rico Scandal

During the early months of 2011, an article published in the opinion section of the Madrid newspaper *El País* by a rather well-known university professor and specialist in Spanish literature, Francisco Rico, gave rise to a prolonged scandal in which very different people took part quite passionately. A critical analysis and rhetorical assessment of this interesting case – involving a publicly conducted and extended exchange of opinions on an issue of public policy by people not directly engaged in politics – may help us see the workings, the perils and the role of discursive ēthos in the context of rhetorical interaction and conscious representation of both receptive and participatory citizenship.

The original article by Rico criticized the new smoking bans enacted by the government and offered a number of arguments against the prospective policy. However, it contained a very controversial claim that aroused the anger of many readers. Let us take a look at the overall chronology of the scandal in order to get a general picture of its length, scope and actors:

Jan. 11 Article published by Francisco Rico in *El País*: "Teoría y realidad de la ley contra el fumador" ("Theory and reality of the law against smokers").

Jan. 16 Long commentary by *El País* ombudswoman Milagros Pérez de Oliva: "La impostura del fumador" ("The smoker's deception"), including excerpts from some letters to the editor and from Rico's oral and written responses.

Jan. 19 Additional letter by Rico published in *El País*: "Sobre la prohibición del tabaco" ("On smoking bans").

Feb. 13 Written defense of F. Rico published in *El País* by writer and friend Javier Cercas "Rico, al paredón" ("Rico, facing the firing squad").

Feb. 15 Satirical rejoinder against Cercas, published by Arcadi Espada in rival paper *El Mundo*.

Feb. 20 Final "judgment" by the *El País* ombudswoman: "En defensa de Cercas y de la verdad" ("In defense of Cercas and truth").

Mar. 06 Syntactic note and clarification by writer and *El País* contributor Javier Marías: "Dos postdatas" ("Two postscripts").

The original article by Rico, in a literary style, offered a particularly well-written and rather structured argumentation – although, of course, defeasible and subject to contrary opinion – against prospective smoking bans that could have begun an argumentative dialogue on certain quite substantive issues. We can summarize his arguments and reasons for opposing the government's policy as follows:

R0 (mentioned but left unjustified by means of an explicit *praeteritio*, "let's leave aside…"): There is lack of scientific rigor in "arguments against tobacco."

R1: the law is a *low blow* against freedom, because the excessive expansion of bans represents a change in policy, from "space segregation" to "impediment."

R2: There is "stolidity" in the law's wording (he uses a difficult, bookish word and provides the definition: "*estolidez*" is "lack of reason and discourse"). Articles 7 and 8 provide a list of places where smoking is banned which could be compared in its unintelligibility with the well-known classification found in J.L. Borges' Chinese Encyclopedia.

R3: It also advocates a "vile" procedure, encouraging people to report violators (moreover, anonymous, online reporting). This kind of "vileness" ("*vileza*," another bookish word) is explicitly associated with the social blindness of the legislators: "sons of an abstract morality and deprived of any human understanding, they despise real people and real situations."

So far, so good. However, the article included a *postscriptum* which we will for these purposes call reason R4. It did not provide an additional direct argument against the law, but sought to grant credibility and authority to the entire argumentation by means of an ethotic assertion about the writer (as "sujet de l'énoncé"): "I haven't smoked a single cigarette in my whole life" ("En mi vida he fumado un solo cigarrillo"). This *postscriptum* was the source of the scandal.

Five days after publication of this piece, Milagros Pérez de Oliva, the paper's ombudswoman, issued a long commentary stating that she had received a number of complaints from the newspaper's readers, had passed them on to Francisco Rico and obtained from him an initial reaction. The title of this commentary was quite expressive: "The smoker's deception." In her report, Pérez de Oliva mentioned several remarks about R0, many of them made by doctors, who could not imagine how the alleged "lack of rigor" could be supported. There were also complaints about the article's aggressive and contemptuous tone, but mainly infuriated denunciations of Rico's own compulsive smoking habits. According to these readers, he had simply lied.

The ombudswoman would have to hear both parties, however, before issuing a verdict. As she claimed that she did not fully understand Rico's reaction on the phone, she chose to transcribe parts of a letter which he had subsequently sent to her:

> The *postscriptum* means some things literally, and others not so literally, but these are obvious: that "Je est un autre" (Rimbaud), that writing isn't autobiography, that "truth is true, whether it is Agamemnon or his pigman who tells it" (A. Machado). The *postscriptum* has given me the sad satisfaction of confirming my diagnosis: this law is a school of vileness. Most of those who are against my article are prying into my life and habits, spying on my friends and looking for criminal records. They scarcely touch my arguments.

He also insisted on a particularly sensitive point for him, mentioning "the vileness [again] of certain articles in the law: especially the smoking ban on hospitalized, particularly dying patients." But the ombudswoman was not very sympathetic to Rico's stance, nor touched by his concerns. Her evaluation was entirely negative: "lies" such as Rico's were not admissible in the opinion section:

> An article in the opinion section is not a piece of literary fiction, and less so in the case of a text with so many political implications. It isn't an error or witticism. It is a question of truth and falsity. In the end, the question is if it is acceptable to use a lie to defend a true position.

She simply assumed that Rico had only tried, unsuccessfully, to conceal his biographical reality in an attempt to claim a lack of personal concern and made it clear who could legitimately be considered to have no "conflict of interest" with regard to legislation on tobacco:

> [it] is usually assumed that the absence of a conflict of interest may reinforce an argumentative stance. In this case, those who have no links to tobacco companies or are non-smokers are free from a conflict of interest.

Rico probably felt he had not been at all understood by either the readers or Pérez de Oliva, but apparently did not find much else to say on R4, so he gave up pursuing that point further. But he was still interested in the discussion and in having his main arguments stand. So, just three days later, he sent an additional letter to the paper entitled "On smoking bans," in which he sought to justify his support for R0, the only one of "his substantive arguments" that had been duly opposed by the infuriated readers. He was not talking about the scientific rigor of medical studies identifying the physical damage suffered by individual active or passive smokers. He referred instead to the more controversial studies about the real social effects of such restrictive measures as those prescribed by Spain's forthcoming law. He cited academic studies (published in the *British Academic Review*, for example) in which it was claimed that smoking bans in leisure spaces had the effect of restricting smoking to private homes, which were less suitable places for such a habit, with further exposure for children, etc. Thus, he could insist on his cherished point about the necessity to understand real social situations instead of thinking about "abstract" laboratory conditions.

This might have been the end of it, because nobody tried publicly to continue discussing either this or any of his other arguments against smoking bans with Rico. The infamous *postscriptum* and the angry reactions to it had apparently succeeded in "poisoning the well." However, about a month later, Javier Cercas, a widely known writer and Rico's pupil and friend, attempted to defend him from his critics, focusing again, almost exclusively, on his ethotic assertion. Cercas' column – published in the same paper, *El País*, under the title "Rico, facing the firing squad" – was long and rather confusing. It advanced different lines of argument, not all of them adequately coordinated, in defense of Rico's *postscriptum*. It contained first a rather polemic *argumentum ad Hitleri* directed at his critics: "Beware of those who demand truth at all costs: Hitler did that," combined with a paradoxical kind of maxim: "emphasis on truth usually reveals a liar." It subsequently engaged in a defense of "literary license" in both fiction and history (supported by R. Carr's "imaginative conception of history"), only to assume in the end that the assertion was simply a joke, made after a piece of argumentation that nobody had really tried to respond to. It was a joke because: "Everybody knows that Rico is like a *chimney*." So, the intelligent thing would have been to disregard it with humor – the critics and the ombudswoman had proved to be "humorless people." The *postscriptum* had no real argumentative value and the critics had not taken on the true arguments. Cercas thus assumed, in the long run, the irrelevance of R4, and incidentally of all ethotic resources, because he insisted on claiming that arguments are "independent" of their source.

In my opinion, Cercas' defense was not very brilliant, nor was it really effective. Javier Cercas is also somewhat of a public figure in Spain, who often writes opinion and literary columns and has his friends as well as his enemies in the literary world. He had probably exposed himself too much with his complicated and confusing defense, had revealed too many weak spots, and someone was prepared to take advantage of this. Two days after the publication of Cercas' column, another well-known polemist and columnist, Arcadi Espada, tried to show in the pages of the rival paper, *El Mundo*, that he, at least, was not at all a humorless person. He played a rather mischievous joke on Cercas, making use of his own supposed literary precepts. In his column, Espada feigned sorrow at the (totally fictitious) arrest of J. Cercas at a brothel in Madrid's Southern district of Arganzuela. This "unfortunate situation" was preventing him from responding, in due form, to Cercas' article on Rico and about literary and rhetorical imposture:

> I feel terrified and ashamed that his name has been dragged through the mud of brothels which are not those of Arganzuela. The story reveals that we're just innocent soldiers, solely interested in the maneuvers of rhetoric, style and truth.

The tone was satirical enough and the irony was not much disguised, but Cercas was indignant and sued Espada for libel. His own paper, *El País*, considered this article "a defamation of Cercas."

This second scandal, in which Rico took no part, led Milagros Pérez de Oliva to return to the issue in a rather self-reassuring piece entitled "In defense of Cercas and truth." It contained a maternal rejoinder against Cercas along the lines of: "look what may happen if one follows Rico's practices that you so advocate..." and a complete reassertion of her initial stance: "Lies cannot be used in defending truth"; "Journalism has nothing to do with fiction." She also rejected Cercas' thesis that Rico's *postscriptum* was a joke, because the larger audience did not know him personally. Pérez de Oliva's final sentence again condemned Rico's choice, claiming that Arcadi Espada had clearly shown that, if we leave that possibility open, there is no limit to what can be expected.

Things calmed down somewhat after this sober and commonsensical commentary and it seemed as though there was nothing more to be said about either Rico's *postscriptum* or his other arguments, completely forgotten by now, against smoking bans. However, about two weeks later, another well-known writer and friend of Francisco Rico (and regular contributor to *El País*), Javier Marías, decided to try a different line of defense in a shorter column entitled "Two postscripts." His was just a grammatical note that attempted to clarify something pointed out by Rico in his first written answer to Pérez de Oliva: "The *postscriptum* means some things *literally*." Marías claimed again that it was a kind of joke, but not simply an ironic remark, because it had in fact played with the syntactic ambiguity of the sentence:

> It seems it was just me, but when I read the infamous *postscriptum*, knowing that Rico is an even more compulsive smoker than myself, I didn't take it as a lie, but as a syntactic witticism: "I haven't smoked a single cigarette in my whole life" means, for me, literally "Never a single one; never in my whole life; always more than one." Or: "It was always the same cigarette. Only one: i.e. it has been a *continuum*."

This was a nice and funny final remark that at least granted Rico some literary merit and linguistic ingenuity. Nevertheless, although such a witticism might have been present in Rico's mind during the process of selecting the wording of the *postscriptum* (or, at least, at the moment he wrote his first answer to the ombudswoman), I seriously doubt there was nothing more to it. We have to take into account that Marías' interpretation is not a natural one, nor even an absolutely correct one from the point of view of Spanish grammar. But, more importantly, the widespread "negative" interpretation of the *postscriptum* was not only due to the application of syntactic rules. It was of course also a question of pragmatic relevance, in this case, of specifically argumentative relevance.

An appraisal of R4 from a rhetorical point of view

So there were ultimately three different public evaluations of Francisco Rico's R4. For M. Pérez de Oliva, it was an inadmissible – false and dishonest – ethotic argument. Rico wanted to deceive the readers and had failed and been exposed. In the event he wanted to continue with the discussion, he should withdraw the claim and start again. But this time there was a presumption against the rest of his arguments, as the newly revealed ethotic information (that he was, indeed, a smoker) meant that he had a conflict of interest with regard to the issue under discussion.

For J. Cercas, it was simply a joke for the (many) people who know him. In any case, those who did not know him did not have to react, because it was not a substantive part of his argument and Cercas maintains that arguments should be understood and assessed independently of their author. In short, he was not trying to deceive, but only being ironic with an argumentatively irrelevant *postscriptum*. Finally, for J. Marías, it was just a syntactic witticism; a joke, again, but more sophisticated than simple irony, although also irrelevant to his argument. None of these interpretations took it seriously as a relevant move from a discursive or rhetorical point of view. Nor did they feel that it should be read in combination with the rest of his arguments as building a particular ēthos, selected for a concrete stance in relation to the issue at hand.

The first thing we have to take into account is that, in my opinion, Rico could never have thought that the falsehood would simply prevail (as Pérez de Oliva assumed time and again). Of course, not everybody knows him, but he is enough of a public figure and the people who know him best are in fact women and men of letters, writers and journalists: it was impossible that it could pass unnoticed or undisclosed. So my first claim, which I think is more than reasonable, is that he *wanted* to "continue the discussion," he *wanted* it to be pointed out to him that he is a smoker and he already had part of his response prepared. I cannot imagine he wanted the deception to stand permanently.

But with this starting point in mind, we may still allow for a rather cynical interpretation of his move, as a dialectical trap. According to this possibility, he would have foreseen his critics attacking his position as a "contaminated" arguer and not taking on his more substantive points. This would have granted him the opportunity to crush them with the "sad satisfaction" mentioned in his first letter, his recourse to the "vileness" spread by the spirit of the law (thus reinforcing one of his "substantive" reasons), etc. A certain superior tone in Rico's language and attitude may support this idea, which would make his *postscriptum* a kind of *red herring* argument that, in the end, would block further discussion by humiliating the opponent. I think, however, that this was only a possibility which emerged later, when Rico realized that the initial reactions to his proposal were so negative, and it made his first written response neither very satisfactory nor constructive. Nevertheless, the fact that he sent the second letter about what we have called R0 would seem to indicate that he was still interested in discussing his stance and that the point about "the scientific rigor of studies on smoking bans" was not a completely independent line of argument, but instead was rather coherent with his main position against "abstract or symbolic legislation."

To maintain, instead, that the *red herring* outcome was Rico's idea from the beginning presupposes his complete lack of confidence in his other arguments, yet he certainly took pains to present them carefully, in an orderly manner and with carefully chosen vocabulary and wording. A methodological "principle of charity" encourages us to seek a more sympathetic account of *at least* his initial intentions. We might thus assume the *postscriptum* can be viewed as a "sincere" ethotic argument – one that could even have been presented face to face with a cigarette in hand, in which case, I presume it might have been more successful – not precisely referring to Rico's biographical ēthos, but rather to a discursive ēthos assumed and construed on a specific occasion, for a particular discussion. In such a case, it would simply mean that the entire argumentation was presented *as* defended by, and thus *as* defensible by, a non-smoker (it would have been an undisguised, overt "Je est un autre").

Under this interpretation, instead of counting on avoiding exposure, Rico would have (probably too naively) counted on the stark evidence of the irony (as J. Cercas suggested), not, however, to make a joke, but to bring to our attention the allegedly "universal" character of his arguments. R1 to R3 in fact focus on issues like "a suitable balance of freedoms," "the legal requirement for comprehensible and univocal principles," "the problems of abstract morality and symbolic policy making" and seem to be carefully selected to address a "universal audience" (Perelman and Olbrechts-Tyteca, 1958). These are questions about which citizens in general should, in principle, be concerned and pose possible problems that create a presumption in favor of, at the very least, further examination of the case at hand. In my opinion, although they can of course be contested and are not conclusive in any sense, they at least succeed in passing the onus on to the respondent (Pinto 2001).

The problem is that with the large and varied audience represented by the readers of a national newspaper (with different degrees of personal knowledge about the author), this ethotic game was somewhat difficult to manage ... unless they had all been devoted followers of Aristotle's *Rhetoric* and its caution about discursive ēthos (not a very plausible presumption). Both the initial reactions on their part and Rico's own initial response did not succeed in reestablishing the grounds for mutual understanding. Rico's choice was ultimately not effective in rhetorical terms as it was unsuitable for such a large audience. He could have chosen a different way of signaling the alleged "objectivity" and "universality" of his stance; for example, by making its independence from his personal status as a smoker explicit or by openly stating as an assumption that he was arguing "*as* a non-smoker." He chose instead the rhetorical impact of an unexpected claim in an ambiguously positioned *postscriptum*, naively trusting in the unpredictable outcome of a process of revelation and possible objection – in addition to (according to J. Marías' interpretation) taking advantage of a certain syntactic ambiguity. But things got somewhat out of hand.

Now, leaving aside Rico's own mindset when designing his strategy, I also think there is another significant point to this story that is worth emphasizing and which is in fact related to the concept of Rhetorical Citizenship (Kock and Villadsen 2012). Rico's confidence that he could naturally adopt the role and ēthos of a non-smoker places him in direct opposition to Pérez de Oliva's explicit account of the agents to which we could attribute a "conflict of interest" in this particular matter. The *El País* ombudswoman claimed that both "tobacco companies" and "smokers" were in such a dubious position, as opposed to "non-smokers unrelated to the tobacco business." But Rico's stance against the smoking bans had, according to his own projected ēthos, nothing to do with defending interests like those of the tobacco companies. After his habit is revealed, Rico presents himself as only incidentally a smoker, but more precisely as a conscious citizen with other concerns in mind, seeking a solution that he allegedly believes is better for a mixed community of smokers and non-smokers. For him, the relevant distinction is not, therefore, the one between smokers and non-smokers, who are all individual citizens, very possibly changing sides over the course of their lives, and whose interests cannot be equated with those of the tobacco companies. In fact, with some political and economic imagination, the distribution of tobacco could conceivably be organized as a non-profit activity.

For Rico, the relevant dichotomy in this case, mentioned repeatedly in all his texts throughout the controversy (and never taken on by any other participant), would be the divide between "abstract thinkers and symbolic policy makers" on one side, and "people interested in the workings of social reality" on the other. Pushing this line of interpretation even further, Rico's ethotic claim could be understood as a way of protesting against hasty "presumptions of partiality" and a vindication of the speaking rights of both smokers and non-smokers in the debate, provided that they act as conscious citizens in a proper deliberation based on issues and principles of common interest (Vega and Olmos, 2007).

His assumed discursive ēthos, although not exactly coincident with some of his biographical traits, was in principle a coherent one for a "generic citizen" allegedly concerned with principles such as those tacitly used to warrant his "substantive reasons." His ethotic choice, although controversial and defeasible, should not, in my opinion, have been attacked by simply revealing the pragmatic inconsistency between his biographical and his discursive ēthos, but ultimately by rebutting the plausibility of a non-smoker presenting and defending R1 to R3, given that Rico himself was not, in the end, an example of confirmation of such a claim.[5] It was not a question of the truth or falsity of the ethotic *postscriptum*, but of the plausibility and coherence of the assumed discursive ēthos together with the rest of the arguments. However, unfortunately, nobody (to my knowledge) took up that challenge.

Of course, under this more qualified interpretation, Rico's rhetorical strategy and discursive decision cannot be equated with or compared to something like Arcadi Espada's practical joke on Cercas, which was in any

[5] i.e. The claim that "R1 to R3 are reasons which a non-smoker could plausibly present and defend."

case a satirical, although rather extreme and somewhat defamatory, response to the latter.

Absolutely True *Postscriptum*

I (Paula Olmos' biographical ēthos speaking) have never been a smoker. Additionally, I do not think that Francisco Rico's argumentation against smoking bans was especially conclusive, strong or truly difficult to oppose. Regardless of this, I do believe it was a more interesting and qualified argumentative piece than the subsequent controversy assumed. Rhetorical theory has helped us to suggest alternative interpretations that link Rico's move to a tradition of adopting a somewhat detached and civil ēthos in a deliberation about a public policy, a tradition that is an essential part of rhetorical agency and citizenship.

References

Amossy, R. (2006) [2000]. *L'argumentation dans le discours*. Paris: Armand Colin.

Amossy, R. (2009). La double nature de l'image d'auteur. *Argumentation et Analyse du Discours* 3, online, accessed 06/03/2012, http://aad.revues.org/662.

Amossy, R. (Ed.) (1999). *Images de soi dans le discours. La construction de l'ethos*. Geneva: Delachaux et Niestlé.

Bokobza Kahan, M. (2009). Introduction: Ethos discursif et image d'auteur. *Argumentation et Analyse du Discours* 3, online, accessed 07/03/2012, http://aad.revues.org/658.

Booth, W.C. (1961). *The Rhetoric of Fiction*. Chicago: University of Chicago Press.

Cercas, J. (2011). Rico, al paredón. *El País* (02.13.2011). http://elpais.com/diario/2011/02/13/opinion/1297551604_850215.html

Chiron, P. (2011). Relative Dating of the *Rhetoric to Alexander* and Aristotle's *Rhetoric*: A Methodology and Hypothesis. *Rhetorica* 29, 236-262.

Espada, A. (2011). Diarios de Arcadi Espada. *El Mundo* (02.15.2011).

Kock, C. and L. Villadsen (Eds.) (2012). *Rhetorical Citizenship and Public Deliberation*. University Park: Pennsylvania State University Press.

Kraus, M. (2011). How to Classify Means of Persuasion: The *Rhetoric to Alexander* and Aristotle on *pisteis*. *Rhetorica* 29, 263-279.

Mainguenau, D. (2009). Auteur et image d'auteur en analyse du discours. *Argumentation et Analyse du Discours* 3, online, accessed 06/03/2012, http://aad.revues.org/660.

Marías, J. (2011). Dos postdatas. *El País* (03.06.2011). http://elpais.com/diario/2011/03/06/eps/1299396425_850215.html

Meizoz, J. (2009). Ce que l'on fait dire au silence: posture, ethos, image d'auteur.

Argumentation et Analyse du Discours 3, online, accessed 07/03/2012, http://aad.revues.org/667.

Noël, M.-P. (2011). Isocrates and the *Rhetoric to Alexander*: Meaning and Uses of *tekmerion*. *Rhetorica* 29, 319-335.

Perelman, C. and L. Olbrechts-Tyteca (1958). *Traité de l'argumentation. La nouvelle rhétorique*. Paris: PUF.

Pérez de Oliva, M. (2011a). La impostura del fumador. *El País* (01.16.2011). http://elpais.com/diario/2011/01/16/opinion/1295132405_850215.html

Pérez de Oliva, M. (2011b). En defensa de Cercas y de la verdad. *El País* (02.20.2011). http://elpais.com/diario/2011/02/20/opinion/1298156405_850215.html

Pinto, R.C. (2001). *Argument, Inference and Dialectic*. Dordrecht: Kluwer.

Pisani, G. (2011) The *ekstastikon eidos* of the *Rh.Al.* and Parallels in Aeschines' *Against Timarchus* and Demosthenes' *On the False Embassy*. *Rhetorica* 29, 336-356.

Rico, F. (2011a). Teoría y realidad de la ley contra el fumador. *El País* (01.11.2011). http://elpais.com/diario/2011/01/11/opinion/1294700405_850215.html

Rico, F. (2011b). Sobre la prohibición del tabaco. *El País* (01.19.2011). http://elpais.com/diario/2011/01/19/opinion/1295391608_850215.html

Vega, L. and P. Olmos (2007). Deliberation: A Paradigm in the Arena of Public Argument. In: H.V. Hansen et al. (Eds.), *Dissensus and the Search for Common Grounds*, Proceedings of the 7th OSSA Conference, CD-ROM.

The Hunt for Promises in Danish Political Debate

CHARLOTTE JØRGENSEN

Introduction

In recent years promises have played an increasing role in Danish political debate, a development that has culminated in the so-called "breach of promises debate."[1] The corresponding Danish word "løftebrudsdebatten" was coined in the wake of the general election in September 2011 to characterize the political debate after the Thorning-Schmidt government took over. This theme has persisted as the dominant frame throughout this government's reign.

In my view the intensified focus on promises has deteriorated into a "hunt for promises" that has gotten out of hand. The purpose of this paper is neither to defend the government nor to discuss how many election promises the two "red" political parties – S (the Social Democrats) and SF (the Socialist People's Party) – have fulfilled or walked away from. My concern is with a general tendency that works against the deliberative ideal of informed public debate and does not promote rhetorical citizenship. In what follows I discuss why indiscriminate accusations about broken promises are a problem.

Since the breach of promises debate is a culmination of a general development, the background leading up to this debate is outlined in section 2. Section 3 evidences how it exploded. In section 4, I argue that the debate reveals confusion between policy statements and actual election promises in the proper sense of "promises" as described in speech act theory. Finally, the implications for rhetorical citizenship and political debate are discussed in section 5.

[1] This development is not peculiar to Danish affairs. The debate focus on promises and breaches appears to be an international trend. For instance, the political commentator Nielsen (2013) refers to similar debates as "political wars about breach of promises" in a number of European democracies.

The background

Election promises and accusations of breaking them play natural roles as *topoi* of political argumentation before and after an election. The issuing of promises that a political party commits itself to, if elected, obviously has a positive function for the electorate, helping citizens decide how to vote. Especially promises *not* to take certain actions if elected may provide relevant information in the election process. If a politician afterwards acts in a way that is contrary to the promise, the citizens who voted for him or her have reason to feel deceived. Such cases are relatively frequent. Some attract little public attention and are soon forgotten. Others create public outrage, fed by massive media coverage, and persist for a long time in public memory. A notorious example is Danish Prime Minister Jens Otto Krag. In 1966 he formed his Social Democratic government with SF as its supporting party, the so-called "Red Cabinet," although he had declared that he would never do so. His remark: "You hold a position until you take another"[2] has become a formula for the *topos* of broken election promises, often referred to by Danes in similar situations.[3]

The most significant event that prepared the ground for the breach of promises debate is what has become known as "the case of the early retirement allowance" ("efterlønssagen") from 1998. About eight months after the general election in that year, Prime Minister Poul Nyrup Rasmussen struck a political compromise with the opposition to implement cuts in the early retirement allowance. Since during the election campaign he had made it a top issue to preserve the program, this caused a media storm.

This case has hampered the Social Democrats severely in the long run, drawing heavily on the party's "ethos account" (McCroskey 1997, p. 95). It has attained status as a textbook example of broken election promises that political opponents and commentators return to time and again when, for instance, opinion polls look bad for the Social Democrats.

To prevent something similar from happening to himself, Nyrup Rasmussen's successor, Anders Fogh Rasmussen, introduced the so-called "contract politics" at the 2001 election. The expression was used to refer to a list of governmental policies that he promised to uphold unconditionally until the next election. The mantra went: what we say before the election is

[2] "Man har et standpunkt til man tager et nyt."

[3] The *topos* is used both negatively and positively. It is often quoted in order to expose the absurdity of the idea that politicians should not be allowed to get wiser and change their minds.

also what we do after the election! Thus, contract politics was launched as a strategy to meet the general distrust of politicians that Nyrup Rasmussen's broken promise had stirred up in the electorate.

On the face of it, contract politics seems a sound principle – pure common sense, a voter might think. Upon reflection, however, it poses various problems. As it later turned out, it restricted the government's room for maneuvering as the financial crisis developed, and Fogh Rasmussen's successor Lars Løkke Rasmussen eventually took steps to depart from it. With respect to the democratic ideal of deliberation, the foremost problem with contract politics is that it renders argumentation by politicians about the current issues more or less superfluous: if the course of action is settled, why should politicians deliberate the pros and cons of the issue? This means that contract politics undermines rhetorical citizenship because it demotivates citizens from engaging in the issues that arise in the contingent realm of politics. Instead, it invites citizens to sit on their hands between elections, reducing them to voters who reward or punish politicians for having implemented or walked away from what they once promised.

The attention to promises has been heightened by the fact that the opposition parties tended to adopt the idea of contract politics that had worked successfully for the Fogh Rasmussen government. Thus, although the era of contract politics is over, it seems probable that Danes after a decade of this kind of politics have become accustomed to it and, in turn, more prone to expect and demand promises from politicians. Either way, much attention was devoted to promises in the election campaign of 2011. On the one hand, politicians across the spectrum spent much energy on blaming each other on this account and, on the other, they were constantly confronted in the media by journalists repeatedly asking whether they could promise this or that.

The debate frame is launched

We now turn to the breach of promises debate itself. It exploded almost from day one after the S-R-SF government took office.[4] As R (the Danish

[4] SF left the government in the beginning of 2014 in consequence of the increasing turmoil in the party's political backing caused by the discrepancy between the policy that SF stands for according to its members and the policy that the party leadership shouldered as their share of the responsibility for in government – generally referred to as the party leaders' many breaches of promise.

Social Liberal Party) had come out strengthened from the election, and the two "red" parties weakened, essential parts of S and SF's collective election program *Fair løsning 2020* (A fair solution) were taken out, even negated, in the government program negotiated by the coalition parties after the election and then presented to the public.

According to a study by the weekly *Mandag Morgen*, the word "løftebrud," i.e., "breach of promise" or "broken promise," occurred in as many as 1,200 newspaper articles within the first eight months of the new government (Andersen 2012a). My own investigations indicate that the compound noun "løftebrudsdebat," i.e., "breach of promises debate," is a new word in the Danish vocabulary that was triggered by the opening debate in the Danish parliament on October 6, 2011, shortly after the election. Promises given and broken were the main theme in this 15-hour opening debate, turning it into an extremely hostile confrontation and a conspicuous display of futile and repetitive argumentation (transcript in *Folketingstidende*, October 6, 2011). According to my searches on *Google* and the database *Infomedia*, the word "løftebrudsdebat" ("breach of promises debate") yields only one result before that date. This *hapax legomenon* had occurred in an online editorial from February 2010 predicting that no parties would risk being caught up in "a breach of promises debate of the sort that hit" Poul Nyrup Rasmussen.[5] Used here as an indefinite noun I consider it a nonce word created momentarily by the author for the specific instance. The next result occurs in *Berlingske*'s online edition on October 6, 2011, this time used by the political commentator Thomas Larsen in reference to the opening debate while it was still taking place in the Danish Parliament. From that day on the word "løftebrudsdebat" abounded in the media for months to come.[6] The fact that it is often used in the definite form shows that the word has now become conventionalized with direct reference to the unremitting debate succeeding the election – primarily as a frame directed against the Thorning-Schmidt government.

[5] 180grader.dk, 24.02.2010: "... Efter valget vil ingen af partierne turde ende som centrum i en løftebrudsdebat af samme slags, som ramte tidligere statsminister Poul Nyrup Rasmussen, og derfor..."

[6] Thomas Larsen's active part in this development is evidenced by the information in *Mandag Morgen* that over the period of eight months he wrote 34 political analyses – "almost once a week" – about the case that he has called "the century's breach of promise" (Andersen 2012b).

Is an election promise a promise?

What strikes me as a major problem with the breach of promises debate is that politicians and commentators as well as members of the electorate seem to extend the meaning of an "election promise" beyond a "promise" in the proper sense as described in speech act theory (Austin 1975, Searle 1969). This problem raises the questions: Are election promises proper promises? Do they count as true promises? In other words: Do the same speech act rules for performing a promise apply to election promises? Or does the election context make them a special case of promising? In that case we must evaluate them by different rules than we do proper promises. These questions relate primarily to the *essential* felicity conditions, i.e., the obligation to undertake the responsibility for fulfilling the promise and perform the promised act. The questions are of special relevance for evaluating argumentation in the breach of promises debate. Moreover, I suggest that a major problem with the breach of promises debate stems from the contamination of election promises in the proper sense and the word used in a broader sense. The following examples serve to explicate my points.

The first example illustrates a clear-cut election promise counting as a proper promise in accordance with speech act theory. In her election campaign 2005 to become Lord Mayor of Copenhagen, the Social Democrat Ritt Bjerregaard issued a promise to provide housing that ordinary people could afford under the slogan: "Five thousand flats for five thousand crowns in five years." As I have argued elsewhere (Jørgensen 2011, 2012), she did indeed make a promise, explicitly saying that she had *promised* to build the "cheap flats," and that she had *committed* herself to doing so. Yet, two years later when it became more and more obvious that her plan would fail, she denied the promise in a newspaper interview (Weiss 2007). She now claimed that she had "merely stated what [she] intended to work towards" (Jørgensen 2011, p. 910).

The second example, a paraphrase of a passage from the opening debate in the Danish parliament mentioned above, illustrates the massive accusations in the breach of promises debate. The leader of the Conservatives, Lars Barfoed, describes what he sees as the enormous political turnaround of S and SF as "voter deception" (*vælgerbedrag*). While underscoring that he – a Conservative – of course appreciates these policy changes, he attacks the government on this account: it makes a politician untrustworthy to run away from a policy presented in the election campaign once the election is won. Claiming that there are lots of similar examples, he points to one of "the 12 SF promises." It allegedly promised less money to millionaires and more to those with low incomes, but now SF wants lower taxes for all, including millionaires! (*Folketingstidende* October 6, 2011, 84, 8.09 p.m.)

Also, this example illustrates the duplicity of an arguer who, on behalf of others, accuses an opponent of breaking a promise to do something he himself agrees with. The main point here, however, concerns the 12 SF promises Barfoed refers to. You cannot accuse someone of breaking a promise unless that person has made a promise. This self-evident condition was met in the former case of the cheap flats. Now, had SF actually issued a promise? The question in this second case is tricky.

The alleged promises were presented in SF's election pamphlet *Friske øjne på Danmark* (2011). The front page announces 12 concrete *goals* to achieve a stronger Denmark and to measure the party by. Next follows a list of these goals, arranged in threes under four headings. Goal no. 3 under the heading New Growth says: "Less to millionaires, more to pensioners and wage earners." However, on the last page these goals are suddenly called *election promises*. In other words, the pamphlet uses the word in a weak sense as interchangeable with *goals* or *policy statements* in election programs. An "election promise" now refers to a future act that the politician *promises to work for* – a significant shift from the obligation undertaken in a proper promise, where the speaker is committed to *do* the future act, not just work for it.

This notion of an election promise as something different from a regular promise is adapted and explicated in an editorial in the newspaper *Politiken* (August 11, 2011) after party leader Villy Søvndal's presentation of SF's election program. The 12 items are called *election promises* (*valgløfter*) one moment and the next moment *goals* or *policy aims* (*målsætninger*). The expression "promises that [SF] wishes to be measured by" is first criticized because it conjures up bad memories of the failed and now abandoned notion of contract politics. However, the editor adds, Søvndal has wisely distanced himself from this interpretation: he has made a crucial distinction, saying that they are "promises which he cannot *guarantee*, but shall work for."[7] In that case the obvious reply would be: Why then call it a promise? A promise that you cannot guarantee is not much of a promise.

Note that Ritt Bjerregaard defended herself with the very same dis-

[7] "Der er tale om løfter, som han ikke vil *garantere*, men som han vil arbejde for."

tinction when she denied her promise. Only, she did it in retrospect. As the journalist at that time remarked in the interview, one has to be in politics for a lifetime to apprehend this subtlety.

One is tempted to suspect that politicians parade goals as promises, reckoning that citizens will see them as binding commitments, while not doing so themselves. Using *election promise* in this weak sense may thus serve as a wild card to capture votes. Whether politicians do this manipulatively or unwittingly, they should consider the loss of credibility they risk when their more or less obtainable goals, masked as promises, are not – or cannot be – realized.

Back to Barfoed's accusation: Is it fair argumentation to say that SF has broken a promise on the criterion that the accusation presupposes that a promise has actually been made? My answer is: No. Barfoed's accusation cannot be sustained on this account. As long as he censures the disparity between, on the one hand, the policy that SF put forward in the election campaign and the policy they usually stand for and, on the other, the policy they are now willing to implement, so far so good. But when he frames it as a broken promise, his argumentation becomes a violation of the standard of fairness as defined by Onsberg and Jørgensen (2008, see Jørgensen 2007, pp. 170-173).

Admittedly, the leaders of SF have themselves been partly to blame since they did use the word "promise" in their election program; had they stuck to "goals" they could legitimately be censured for having held up unfeasible policy prospects in the election campaign, but they would not have laid themselves bare to the accusation of breaking a promise.

However, to maintain, as Barfoed does, that SF issued promises in the proper sense in the pamphlet is based on a skewed reading: it takes the word out of context and neglects the fact that SF obviously used it in the weak sense, as supported by the editorial. Speaking as if SF unequivocally issued promises and did not talk of goals, Barfoed clearly presents a false picture of SF's speech act in the pamphlet. Although SF may be accused of making a blunder, or even of manipulative language, in using the word promise, Barfoed is still to be criticized for contributing to the general slippage of terms referring to political speech acts in debate. I thus see the accusation as an example of *unfair argumentation*, more specifically as a case of distortion by *oversimplification* (Jørgensen 2007, p. 171). Furthermore, I consider it as rather seriously unfair on the following grounds. To accuse a person of breaking a promise is a strong attack on that person's *ethos*. This increases the burden of proof on the accuser. Performing this speech act legitimately requires that the accuser has solid grounds for making it and is able to produce convincing evidence that the politician did in fact issue a proper promise. The Ritt Bjerregaard case serves as an example of such an election promise.

By contrast, if we accept that an election promise is merely a goal that the politician will "work for," the implication is that the essential condition for the speech act of promising does not apply. In turn, we cannot talk of a broken promise. The accusation of breaking election promises now becomes just another of the hollow strategic maneuvers that politicians perform to attack each other. In the broader context of public debate, the indiscriminate outcry of "broken promise" becomes feed for the media, which seek conflict according to the notion that the good story is a bad story. As for the electorate, a "broken promise" becomes an outlet for frustrated citizens who feel let down by the politicians they voted for – politicians whose actions in power they find inconsistent with the policy their party represents.

I have taken the Barfoed example as representative of many of the accusations in the breach of promises debate; it illustrates some of the confusions that the hunt for promises, to my mind, has created. To be fair, I should add that Barfoed was one of the least eristic arguers among all those who made breaches of promise the main theme in the opening debate, making those accusations on loose grounds. He, after all, could provide some evidence that a promise had been made.

Some implications

In conclusion, let me sum up the views put forward in this paper. The implication is not that politicians should abstain from issuing promises, but that they should confine themselves to only those promises they intend to keep and are confident that they will be able to fulfill after the election. In all other cases, they should stick to "goals" and insist that this is what they are, resisting the temptation to dress them up as promises in order to get a short-term advantage, and not give in to the constant pressure from the media or to demands from the electorate. Journalists, for their part, should let up on their efforts to nail politicians to promises that they can afterwards blame them for having broken.

Nor do I mean to imply that politicians should not be held accountable for promises they have clearly made, or that they should not be exposed and censured severely when breaking them. Rather, it is the inflation in "promising" and, in particular, the escalation of the *topos* of broken election promises that I have argued against – the ever more widespread assumption that promises are what matters most in politics.

An idealistic, probably utopian, hope is that the breach of promises debate has exhausted itself so that the hunt for promises will not turn out to be an enduring condition in future political debate. Looking back at the era of contract politics and at the last couple of years of the breach of promises debate, a political journalist on national TV news predicted that the focus on promises will be absent in the next election campaign and that the ensuing debate will be "completely different" from the breach of promises debate that has "raged" since the 2011 election (Ringberg 2013).

The prospects for a positive development, however, seem bleak. Politicians may well have learned a lesson, be less inclined to make promises, take pains to specify that a party's goals are not promises, and guard themselves against later attacks for running away from them. But apart from that, one should preserve a right to skepticism. Although the intensity of the breach of promises debate has dropped somewhat over the years since the election, it remains the dominant *topos* in contemporary Danish political debate, constantly popping up across the field. A curious example to illustrate the wide range of the *topos* is a newspaper advertisement inserted by the new Neoliberalist party *Liberal Alliance*, attacking former Prime Minister Lars Løkke Rasmussen, leader of the right wing party *Venstre*, as a Social Democrat in disguise. The upper half of the ad is a close-up photo of his face with the headline above: *Løftebryder!*, i.e., *Promise breaker!* The main argument is that Løkke Rasmussen in the election campaign said that it "must not cost more to be a Dane,"[8] but now he has struck a compromise on energy with the Government that will cost Danes more and make it harder for businesses to compete (Liberal Alliance 2012). In view of the ubiquity and frequency of the *topos*, I suspect that the breach of promises debate will not die out in the near future. My guesses for the next election campaign is that politicians will continue to holler *løftebryder* (*promise breaker*) at each other, that the media will continue their hunt for promises, that interviewers will keep asking if the politicians can promise or guarantee this or that, and that after the

[8] "Det må ikke blive dyrere at være dansker."

election journalists as well as voters will condemn them indiscriminately for breaches of promise.

As for the alleged semantic slide from "goals" to "promises," one might object that the word "promise" has always in election contexts been used in the weak sense, sometimes referring to "goal," as for instance in the expression "manifesto promise." True enough, the expression *gyldne løfter* (*golden promises*) is well on in years in Danish usage. But it has been used figuratively – as a dead metaphor. In the breach of promises debate, however, "promise" is used in a more literal sense where "promise" is synonymous with "goal" (what the politician will work for), and, at the same time, it carries the same commitment as a regular "promise" (what the politician has undertaken an obligation to do).

My main objections to this muddle is that it empties the speech act of promising of its meaning – it erodes its illocutionary force, namely that promising is among those speech acts that place the heaviest load of commitment on the speaker,[9] and, in turn, that accusing someone of breaking a promise is a very serious charge against that person's ethos. Both promises and accusations of breaking them should therefore be uttered with utmost caution. If done indiscriminately, political debate will deteriorate into a populist rhetoric that distrusts electors' sound judgment, and into toxic eristic that departs from the notion of deliberative democracy where dissent is considered potentially valuable and politicians are supposed to respect their opponents' views (see for instance Jørgensen 1998, Kock 2007, 2009).

If politicians and the media continue on the path of the breach of promises debate, the implications are thus negative from a normative point of view. In relation to a notion of rhetorical citizenship, the general tendency to use "goals" and "promises" synonymously in the contexts of elections and parliamentary debate poses several problems. In the first place, voters need party goals, especially in a democracy like the Danish, characterized by a fairly large number of political parties and a tradition of coalition governments. The political debate obviously becomes absurd if parties cannot set up their individual goals, i.e., policy statements, without being accused

[9] Cf. Searle, who argues that the reason why we sometimes use the locution *I promise* emphatically, i.e., in utterances that do not count as promises, is that it is among "the strongest illocutionary force indicating devices for *commitment* provided by the English language" (1969, p. 58).

afterwards of being promise breakers every time they make a compromise. In this connection, the breach of promises debate is a pseudo-debate that sidesteps the real issue, namely how far a party in power can deviate from the goals and policies they stand for in the eyes of the voter, without losing its integrity.

Further, as indicated in section 2, the problem in relation to rhetorical citizenship pointed out in connection with contract politics is transferred to the breach of promises debate, namely that the focus on promises reduces the deliberating citizen to a *consumer*-like position (Kock and Villadsen 2012, p. 3). The citizen, on this view, is nothing but a voter whose democratic participation is limited to election day, and who, in voting every few years, either rewards or punishes the politicians in power for either delivering or failing to deliver the desired products. More specifically, the semantic slide from "goals" to "promises" appeals to a passive recipient role, in contrast to the active and responsible listener role suggested by Kock and Villadsen's discussion of rhetorical citizenship in their introduction above: see especially figure 1. The crucial distinction in the present context is that as long as we talk of "goals," the voters share the communicative responsibility with the party they vote for in the sense that they partly have themselves to blame if these goals are unrealistic or obviously unfeasible. Talk of "promises" involves citizens less in the sense that it makes the promise-maker solely accountable for the feasibility of the propositional content of the promise. The risk is that this invites voters to assume an uncritical position, allowing them to blame the politician alone, not themselves, when the promises afterwards are not kept, whether the reasons for this are good or bad. For instance, many citizens, including left-leaning voters, by all accounts found S and SF's election program *Fair løsning* too "rosy," i.e., full of idealistic political goals and loose proposals that seemed too far from reality. Afterwards seeing this as a case of broken promises is to trivialize a much more important and urgent issue, involving big questions such as demagogy, manipulative argumentation and the gulf between political elites and the electorate. This way, the focus on promises may promote a passive and irresponsible attitude, detrimental to the ambition of creating better conditions for rhetorical citizenship, and the breach of promises debate may be regarded as a symptom of the problems that contemporary Western democracies are facing.

References

Andersen, T. K. (2012a). "Løftebruds-regeringen" er en myte. *Mandag Morgen* 23, June 20, 44-51.

Andersen, T. K. (2012b). Otte måneder i modvind. *Mandag Morgen* 23, June 18, 52-58.

Austin, J. L. (1975) [1962]. *How to Do Things with Words*. Second Ed. Oxford: Oxford University Press.

Bjerregaard, R. (2005). København må ikke blive en velhaverghetto. *Information*, October 27.

Folketingstidende. 2011, October 6. http://www.ft.dk/Dokumenter/Tingdok/ErrorPages/No_tingdok_pdf_file_founded.aspx

Friske øjne på Danmark. 2011.http://www.sf.dk/uploads/media_items/sf-s-valgprogram-2011.original.pdf,

Jørgensen, C. (1998). Public Debate – an Act Of Hostility? *Argumentation* 12, 431-443.

Jørgensen, C. (2007). The Relevance of Intention in Argument Evaluation. *Argumentation* 21, 165-174.

Jørgensen, C. (2011). Fudging Speech Acts in Political Argumentation. In F. H. van Eemeren, B. Garssen, D. Godden and G. Mitchell (Eds.) *Proceedings of the 7th Conference of the International Society for the Study of Argumentation*, 906-913. Amsterdam: Rozenberg/Sic Sat (CD-ROM).

Jørgensen, C. (2012). Snyd med sproghandlinger: Et retorisk casestudie fra den danske politiske debat. *Sakprosa* 4, 2 1-13. https://www.journals.uio.no/index.php/sakprosa

Jørgensen, C. and M. Onsberg (2008). *Praktisk argumentation*, Third Ed. København: Nyt Teknisk Forlag.

Kock, C. (2007). Norms of Legitimate Dissensus. *Informal Logic* 27, 179-196.

Kock, C. (2009). Choice Is Not True Or False: The Domain of Rhetorical Argumentation. *Argumentation* 23, 61-80.

Kock, C. and L. S. Villadsen (2012). Introduction: Citizenship as a Rhetorical Practice. In C. Kock and L. S. Villadsen (Eds.) *Rhetorical Citizenship and Public Deliberation* (pp. 1-9). University Park, Pennsylvania: The Pennsylvania University Press.

Liberal Alliance (2012). Løftebryder! *Politiken*, March 25.

McCroskey, J. C. (1997). *An Introduction to Rhetorical Communication*, 7th Ed. Boston: Allyn and Bacon.

Nielsen, S. W. (2013). Helle og Lars' løfteskænderi kræver en richterskala. *Politiken*, June 9.

Politiken. (2011). Duelig. Valgløfter giver fingerpeg om SF's ansvarlighed. August 11.

Ringberg, J. (2013). ANALYSE: Næste valgkamp bliver uden løfter. Accessed May 2014. http://www.dr.dk/Nyheder/Politik/Politiske_analyser/Jens_Ringberg/2013/02/27/110154.htm

Searle, J. R. (1969). *Speech Acts: An Essay in the Philosophy of Language*. London: Cambridge University Press.

Weiss, J. (2007). Jeg har aldrig lovet 5.000 billige boliger på fem år. *Berlingske Tidende*, July 10.

"Keep[ing] Profits at a Reasonably Low Rate": Invoking American Civil Religion in FDR's Rhetoric of Tax Equity and Citizenship

NATHALIE KUROIWA-LEWIS

The tax wars

In the midst of the 2012 Republican debate in Florida and under pressure from both the Right and Left to release his tax returns, then presidential candidate and self-professed multi-millionaire Mitt Romney informed Americans, "You'll see my income, how much taxes I've paid, how much I've paid to charity." He then affirmed, "I pay all the taxes that are legally required and not a dollar more. I don't think you want someone as the candidate for President who pays more taxes than he owes."[1] Effectively, in this moment, Mr. Romney asked his audience to identify with his opposition to paying a higher tax rate. Implicit in this statement is the premise that it is socially acceptable for the very wealthy to pay only the bare minimum. Not surprisingly, Mr. Romney's tax returns revealed that he paid a 13.9 % tax rate in 2010, and would likely pay a 15.4 % tax rate in 2011, lower than what many middle class Americans pay (Peralta 2012).

Approximately one year later, following the re-election of President Obama to the White House, House Speaker John Boehner argued in an opinion piece for *The Wall Street Journal* that President Obama had altered bipartisan plans to reduce the budget by calling for new taxes. From a perspective commonly voiced by the Republican party, Mr. Boehner opposed paying for the national deficit through taxes. In order to offset a growing deficit, Mr. Boehner proposed instead increasing spending cuts in lieu of raising tax revenue, writing that "[t]he president has repeatedly called for even

[1] *Republican Debate Transcript.* Transcript. January 23, 2012. Council on Foreign Relations, accessed July 10, 2013, http://www.cfr.org/elections/republican-debate-transcript-tampa-florida-january-2012/p27180. 9.

more tax revenue, but the American people don't support trading spending cuts for higher taxes. They understand that the tax debate is now closed" (Boehner 2013). What Mr. Boehner failed to mention, however, was the economic feasibility of balancing the federal deficit via spending cuts only.

Now compare Mr. Romney's and Mr. Boehner's views on taxation to Franklin Delano Roosevelt's perspective on the role that taxes play in 1930s civil society. In his famed June 19, 1935, message to Congress, FDR calls for an estate and inheritance tax, along with a graduated tax for corporations. He justifies curbing inherited wealth and the profits of big business, arguing that great wealth is evidence of the elite's capacity to pay more to the public sphere. Similarly, he voices opposition to the idea of a wealthy elite owning the majority of society's wealth. It is thus he makes the case for a uniquely American tax imperative, providing a powerful philosophical rationale for progressive taxation. He points to the 1913 Income Tax Law as representative of the ideal "that taxes should be levied in proportion to ability to pay and in proportion to the benefits received." He affirms further that "taxation according to income is the most effective instrument yet devised to obtain just contribution from those best able to bear it and to avoid placing onerous burdens upon the mass of our people" (Roosevelt 1935). Consider here how FDR, using a rhetoric that may at first appear politically reckless (particularly from today's perspective), places the burden of tax responsibility on the wealthy, carefully constructing an ideal of tax equity as a civic good. By asking the audience to participate in a vision of economic equity, FDR appeals to the audience's sense of social justice, whereby wealthy private individuals come second to the needs of the collective. In the later years of his presidency, FDR would shape the civic sphere further by making a direct correlation between taxes and the funding of war, arguing in particular that the wealthy have unique fiscal obligations in contributing to society and nation building.

A premise underlying this article is that FDR employs the progressive tax system as a powerful means of inculcating the audience to rhetorical citizenship, and in so doing paves the way for a model of public moral argument articulating fiscal responsibility as a moral principle. To assert this premise, I refer to William Keith and Paula Cossart's definition of rhetorical citizenship that focuses on praxis as a means of creating spaces for citizens to participate in the public sphere (Keith and Cossart 2012). To demonstrate how FDR's rhetoric invokes taxes as a means of performing moral citizenship, I draw on Robert Bellah's theory of American civil religion. As outlined in his formative critique titled, "Civil Religion in America" Bellah contends that American civil religion is a "religious dimension" manifest "in a set of beliefs, symbols, and rituals" of the public sphere (1988, p. 42). Bellah further contends there is a religious element to American political society and that the US possesses a unique civil religion guiding its culture, history and sense of nationhood. In particular, Bellah argues that American civil religion propels nation-building and that American presidents play a unique role in acting as the chief officers of this religion (1988, pp. 110, 115). In this article, I propose that the construct of American civil religion informs how FDR frames tax equity as an ethical principle that is distinct to the American people. I assert that the power of FDR's tax rhetoric lies in his ability to use taxes to formulate a moral principle and therefore call on his audience to act as moral agents who will contribute to nation building. To assert this claim, I analyze FDR's 1936 "Address at Worcester Massachusetts" and his 1942 "Call for Sacrifice" speeches and contend that in these speeches FDR creates a rhetorical framework from which to discuss and perceive taxes through a public moral discourse.

Civil religion and the poor

In contrast to the mantra of a highly individualistic, right leaning popular discourse expressed in much of contemporary tax discourse today, it may appear almost unthinkable to even consider how FDR was able to speak so candidly about shared values such as equity and self-denial for the common good.[2] To understand FDR's rhetoric of taxation and its potential contribu-

[2] Thompson (2003). Understanding critical historical-political moments influencing today's current tax rhetoric can lend insight to the Republican Right's relative success in being able to shape the rhetoric of taxation and influence the mainstream public's perception of taxes as a social burden rather than an investment into civic society. In his article, Thompson outlines a brief history of tax reform following WWI and WWII through George W. Bush's administration's implementation of tax cuts in 2003. Thompson argues that following the World wars, many government officials agreed that they wanted progressive taxes and that they could be employed as a means of managing the economy. He describes how Keynesian economics in the 1950s and 1960s motivated fiscal spending for a larger government and that most Americans profited from a progressive tax structure and therefore sanctioned progressive taxes. Interestingly enough, during this period, there existed an anti-tax rhetoric that equated higher taxation with lack of productivity, however,

tions to contemporary American tax discourse, it is important to consider how FDR assumed the role of chief magistrate that characterizes civil religion and used his position as president to assert a religious conception of nationhood (Bellah 1988, p. 105). In this regard, a Christian social activist element permeated much of FDR's tax discourse and vision of nationhood (Smith 2006, pp. 191-220). For in many of FDR's public remarks on taxes, he professed a commitment to fiscal fairness that drew on a specific Christian orientation deeply concerned with the plight of the needy[3] as he placed particular attention on the responsibility of the wealthy towards improving the lot of the poor. Although FDR was by no means entirely successfully in promoting these values throughout the duration of his many administrations, and did prove himself to be fallible on a host of domestic and foreign policy issues, it is, nonetheless, not unusual for many scholars to point to FDR's acumen as a moral leader, particularly in his tax rhetoric.

For FDR expressed his moral leadership by making a strong case that tax equity was fundamental to the progressive tax system. Such a view drew on a shared, historical understanding of the progressive tax system. As Joseph Thorndike explains, the progressive tax system is the philosophical base for the American tax system. At its roots lies the fundamental belief in contributing to one's "fair share" in democracy. This understanding of the progressive tax system shaped much of FDR's rhetoric. So much so, in fact, that a case can be made that FDR employed the progressive tax system as a rhetorical device for illustrating the principle of tax equity where the responsibility for shouldering taxes would lie most with the upper classes. Ronald

according to Thompson, this discourse received no "political support from the citizenry of the United States and also any empirical support from the social science establishment." Thompson points to the 1970s as a turning point in American attitudes towards taxes because during this decade, many Americans began to benefit economically and climb larger tax brackets and therefore were required to pay more taxes than in the past. Due to this change, the redistributive advantages that Americans had previously enjoyed did not appear as palpable as in the past. Hence, a public pressure led to a conservative movement under the auspices of the Reagan administration in the 1980s. What is fascinating in Thompson's account is his contention that the logical result of a conservative rhetoric in favor of tax cuts "is a gradual destruction of the public sector and the expansion of the market to more domains of society."

[3] Gal. 2:10; Isa. 1:17; Luke 6: 20, 24; Ps. 9:18; Ps. 41:1; Ps 82: 3-4 (NRSV).

Isetti compares Leuchtenburg's critique of FDR to Hofstadter and shows how Leuchtenburg viewed FDR as a moral individual, distinct from his advisors, and one who through the office of the presidency, taught and preached to the public (Isetti 1996, p. 678). Thorndike describes FDR as revealing a nascent fidelity to the system of progressive taxation. Progressive taxation to FDR lay in his conviction that the wealthy were obligated to contribute more taxes than the needy, particularly in times of crisis (2013, p. 45).

The fact that FDR was able to empathize with others and communicate that empathy with the struggling poor and middle class (and by some historical accounts was both pragmatic and sincere) is testament to FDR's adept use of rhetorical skills to lead as a moral leader, particularly so, at least when it came to the topic of taxation.

Situating FDR's tax rhetoric in history

The Great Depression and WWII were historical events that made possible FDR's ability to use civil religion for nation building purposes. Like President Lyndon Johnson, who was influenced by the social foment of the era and drew on civil religion to rally support for voting rights (Bellah 1988, p. 110), FDR utilized civil religion to shape a tax policy that would respond to the needs of his times.

For this reason, it would be next to impossible to understand the power of FDR's rhetoric of taxation without first considering how the economic and social scene of his era shaped his tax rhetoric and policies. The state of the economy during the Depression, for example, was so severe that it had a far-reaching impact adversely touching not only the lower class, but large numbers of the middle class. Interestingly enough, McElvaine suggests that it was the middle class that pushed values for a morality-based reform of the economy, thereby shaping FDR's rhetoric, and not the other way around. He makes this case when he remarks that "[t]he Great Depression served to confirm the poor in their belief that moral considerations ought to have a role in economic practices" and that it was through experiencing the Great Depression that "the middle class [came to] identify their interests and values with those of the poor" (McElvaine 1984, p. xiv). McElvaine, in this light, paints the portrait of an era preoccupied with the values of economic fairness and equity (p. 206), where social attitudes leaned towards governmental actions favoring the equitable distribution of the nation's wealth.

With this point in mind, we can see that for FDR the summer of 1935 signaled a politically motivated though sincere shift to the left, as McElvaine contends. He describes FDR as moving "in the same direction that a majority of the people at the time was going – towards the left, toward humanitarian, cooperative values" (McElvaine 1984, p. 263). According to McElvaine, 1936 was the year where FDR "was casting his lot with the forgotten man (who seems most often to be remembered during and just prior to election years). It would be 'us' against 'them' in 1936, and FDR clearly wanted to be one of 'us'" (1984, p. 261). On June 19, 1935 (the day that Social Security had been passed through the Senate and the Wagner bill approved by the House), FDR told Congressmen that the excessive concentration of wealth was leading to a "perpetuation of great and undesirable concentration of control in a relatively few individuals over the employment and welfare of many, many others" and used the occasion to ask for a variety of tax solutions ranging from federal gift taxes to a graduated corporate income tax to increased income taxes for the very wealthy (McElvaine 1984, p. 260).

In addition to the much talked about influence that the summer of 1935 had on FDR, Thorndike contends that the years of 1933 and 1934 played a formative role in setting the themes of tax evasion and tax avoidance in national debate, which in turn influenced the rhetoric of FDR (Thorndike 2013, p. 75). In particular, the 1935 Revenue Act or Wealth Tax, which in reality did little to change the distribution of taxes, nonetheless signaled a profound cultural shift in FDR's ability to speak to the left (Thorndike 2013, p. 131). Influential academics such as Herman Oliphant, the general counsel to the treasury, for example, aided FDR on key tax issues and were inspired by the Supreme Court Justice, Louis Brandeis, who distrusted corporate concentration of wealth and advocated for tighter regulation of big business (Thorndike 2013, pp. 138, 139). Others like Robert Jackson, the Chief counsel of the Bureau of Internal Revenue, studied the tax evasion practices of wealthy families and helped inform FDR's tax message denouncing tax avoidance (Thorndike 2013, pp. 141, 152).

Linking taxes to the American Revolution

A significant aspect of FDR's tax rhetoric that deserves attention is how FDR frames his position on taxes within a historical context specific to the 1776 American Revolution, therefore appealing to a powerful symbol of American civil religion (Bellah 1988, p. 105). Consider how, for example, in FDR's October 21, 1936, "Address at Worcester Massachusetts," FDR associates taxes with the concept of the American revolution, creating a model of democratic citizenship. To enact this concept of citizenship, FDR interprets the cause of the revolution as that over "the doctrine of democracy in taxation," highlighting tax inequity and stressing the colonists' rejection of a British imposed tax. In this way, FDR frames the conflict between the British and the colonists over taxes as America's burgeoning attempt to become independent from the British.

Such a presentation of leadership draws on a narrative structure of American civil religion, where, as Bellah asserts, Washington becomes "the divinely appointed Moses who led his people out of the hands of tyranny" (Bellah 1988, p. 105). Through this narrative, FDR frames the British, like the wealthy who oppose paying higher taxes, as the undesirable Other, while aligning himself with the national leaders who guided the nation away from a foreign colonial power to a higher law.

FDR plays with this narrative further, equating the colonists' fight for American independence in 1776 with his defense of the New Deal during a presidential election year. By placing himself and his audience in the subject position of the colonists fighting the British in 1776, he frames the colonists' fight as not only for autonomy from England, but for US civilization. He creates this construction when he states: "In 1776, the fight was for democracy in taxation. In 1936 that is still the fight. Mr. Justice Oliver Wendell Holmes once said: 'Taxes are the price we pay for civilized society.'" In comparing 1776 to 1936, FDR links the goal for tax equity in 1936 to the quest for national autonomy during the revolution. This idea, in particular, suggests that tax inequity is undemocratic because it is threatening to nationhood.

Demonizing tax avoiders

Another noteworthy feature of FDR's tax discourse is how he uses taxes to create powerful lines of division and identification. Although FDR's tax discourse is not explicitly religious in nature, he invokes the concept of a "higher criterion" or notion of right and wrong with roots in the philosophy of American civil religion.[4] Framing tax equities as a civic good and tax in-

[4] Bellah (1988), p. 100. As outlined in Bellah's discussion of American civil religion, American governance is traditionally influenced by the concept of political sovereignty in God and presidential allegiance to a "higher criterion."

equities as a moral ill allows FDR to articulate a standard of right and wrong, swaying the audience to a moral ideal based on the concept of a higher law.

To do this, FDR frames the standard of right and wrong by creating lines of division between citizens willing to pay taxes and those unwilling to do so. Importantly, he defines citizens unwilling to pay taxes as those "who still do not recognize their advantages and want to avoid paying their dues," framing them as Undesirable Others. This construction frames those who oppose paying higher taxes as morally delinquent in their responsibilities to the collective, thus arousing feelings of indignation in the audience.

At the same time as FDR draws lines of division by stating a "they and we," he blurs them by positing a shared motive between "they and we." Observe how he identifies common ground between business persons and the middle class by asserting that "the overwhelming majority of business men are like the rest of us. Most of us whether we earn wages, run farms or run businesses are in one sense business men. All they seek and we seek is fair play based on the greater good of the greater number – fair play on the part of the Government in levying taxes on us and fair play on the part of Government in protecting us against abuses." Drawing on the precepts of American civil religion, FDR utilizes the concept of fair play as a moral standard or higher criterion to strive for. This appeals to the audience's collective allegiance to fairness and calls on the audience to act as moral agents participating in the civic good of tax equity. At the same time, FDR prioritizes government as guardian of the civic good, leading the audience to want to participate as agents of that good.

Influenced by the precepts of American civil religion, an additional element of FDR's tax rhetoric worthy of consideration is the focus on sacrifice, which was a pertinent theme in much of FDR's WWII rhetoric (Bellah 1988, p. 107). In FDR's later years, particularly throughout World War II, FDR's tax rhetoric would evolve into a discourse that increasingly came to link the concept of self-denial with the overall maintenance of the general economy. As the government, under the leadership of FDR, anticipated the potential threat of price inflation during World War II, it sought to employ taxes as a tool for curtailing consumption.[5] It was at this time, not surprisingly, that

[5] Thorndike (2013), pp. 207, 214, 216. According to Thorndike, World War II led to an increased understanding of how taxes could be used to control inflation, and even corporate profiteering. (Emphasis on profiteering, 216). The intellectual scene during

FDR's rhetoric became strongly influenced by the work of the Nye Committee, which targeted war profiteering and advocated for war profits taxation (Thorndike 2013, p. 221). According to Thorndike, World War II brought a significant change in the American tax structure. The federal government perceived a need to fund the war through taxes, and taxes came to be seen as a way of managing the economy. As a consequence, in spite of opposition from the business community, FDR demanded an increase in higher taxes for the wealthy, along with the creation of new taxes for those in the low and middle income brackets (Thorndike 2013, p. 275).

Paying taxes for war as a privilege

Nowhere is the need to rally a nation towards a unified goal made more manifest than in wartime. Here FDR's discourse, like that of many presidents before him, draws on a salient facet of American civil religion through its focus on the commendable goal (Bellah 1988, p. 111). In his 1942 speech titled "A Call for Sacrifice," FDR puts the focus on the laudable goal – asking Americans to pay more taxes to fund the war – at the center of his rhetoric. He shapes the civic discourse by framing fiscal responsibility as a method of fighting the war. To do this, he blurs the lines of identification and division, situating the citizen in the subject position of the soldier who has the "privilege" of fighting. The enthymeme that logically emerges from this construction is that fighting for one's country in war-time entails self-denial. This conclusion, in a sense, attempts to lower the audience's expectations about what the government can do to contribute to the war effort.

As FDR instills a sense of duty in the audience, arousing a collective desire to fiscally contribute to the war, he prepares the audience to anticipate paying higher taxes as a means of funding the war effort. FDR's use of the positive term "privilege" in the theme of "fighting as a privilege" simultaneously identifies and divides two groups of people – civilians not participating directly in the war with soldiers/workers physically active in military preparation for war. While calling fighting a "privilege," he states that "not all of us can have the privilege of fighting our enemies in distant parts of the world" and that "not all of us can have the privilege of working in a munitions factory." Here, FDR associates soldiers fighting in war with workers

World War II was inspired by heavy weights such as Randolph Paul who saw taxation as a vehicle for decreasing inflation, and imparted this belief to FDR (pp. 222, 223).

laboring for the war effort. By arguing that soldiers and workers are both uniquely "privilege[d]," FDR frames fighting as a civic good and the negative "not all of us" creates a line of division and assigns guilt to those not privy to this civic good.

Such a construction creates an ambiguous space that serves to both include and exclude civilians removed from the war effort, suggesting that all Americans may share the goal of fighting though not all are directly involved in military preparation for war. Consider how FDR extends the theme of privilege, creating a space for civic action in the domestic sphere, when he states: "But there is one front and one battle where everyone in the United States – every man, woman, and child – is in action," adding that "[t]hat front is right here at home, in our daily lives, in our daily tasks. Here at home everyone will have the privilege of making whatever self-denial is necessary, not only to supply our fighting men, but to keep the economic structure of our country fortified and secured during the war and after the war." Here FDR equates soldiering abroad with soldiering at the home front. By stressing words such as "daily," "self-denial" and "home," FDR creates a domestic space for the average American to express citizenship through fiscal self-restraint.

The legacy of FDR's tax rhetoric

A central preoccupation that recurs throughout FDR's tax rhetoric is the notion of social justice. The fact that FDR strove to actively induce his audience to participate in an ideal of tax equity and collective sacrifice for war illustrates a view of social justice influenced by Christian values that informed much of FDR's thinking, specifically in regard to the economy. In the role of socio-economic redeemer, crucial to the philosophy underpinning American civil religion, FDR articulates a social activist Christian message of fiscal fairness, prioritizing the needs and interests of the poor over the rich. His rhetoric was one that drew on arguments based on fiscal capacity to pay for taxes, which he employed to rationalize higher taxes on both the rich and the voluminous corporate sector (Thorndike 2013, pp. 139, 140).

The tendency for FDR to be critical of what he saw as an overzealous corporate American drive to make profits allowed him to blame an excessive free market model for the fiscal ills of the nation and create a powerful argument that took sides with the financial underdog – the nation's poor and unemployed.

In sum, the strength in FDR's discourse on taxes lies in his use of

American civil religion to construct and lead the nation towards ethical precepts of equity and self-denial. FDR was not altogether able to push tax policies representing this ideal through Congress. However, his progressive tax argument and public chastising of tax avoidance, along with the emphasis on taxes as a social contract necessary for promoting a civil society, created a rhetorical framework that makes a viable, public moral argument possible in the civic sphere. The subtle power in FDR's tax rhetoric lies in the endeavor, at least, to frame tax equity as a moral principle. In this, FDR appeals to his audience's belief in fairness and calls on his audience to consider participating as moral agents in a tax structure conducive to a larger civic good – namely, tax distribution as a form of social justice.

References

Bellah, R. (1988). Civil Religion in America. *Daedalus* 117. 3, 40-55.

Boehner, J. (2013). John Boehner: The President is Raging Against a Budget Crisis He Created. *Wall Street Journal*, February 20.

Isetti, R. (1996). The Moneychangers of the Temple: FDR, American Civil Religion, and the New Deal. *Presidential Studies Quarterly* 26, 678-693.

Keith, W. and P. Cossart. (2012). The Search for 'Real' Democracy: Rhetorical Citizenship and Public Deliberation in France and the United States, 1870-1940. In C. Kock and L.S. Villadsen (Eds.), *Rhetorical Citizenship and Public Deliberation* (pp. 46-60). University Park: Pennsylvania State University Press.

McElvaine, R. (1984). *The Great Depression: America 1929-1941*. New York: Times Books.

Peralta, E. (2012). Mitt Romney's Tax Returns Show $43 Million Income in Past Two Years. *Npr,* January 24, 2012. http://www.npr.org/blogs/thetwo-way/2012/01/24145690405/mitt-romneys-tax-returns-show-43-million-income-in-past-two-years.

Roosevelt, F. D. (1935). Message to Congress on Tax Revision. *The American Presidency Project*. Accessed July 21, 2014. http://www.presidency.ucsb.edu/ws/?pid=15088.

Roosevelt, F. D. (1936). Address at Worchester, Massachusetts. *The American Presidency Project*. Accessed October 1, 2012. http://www.presidency.ucsb.edu/ws/?pid=15201.

Roosevelt, F. D. (1942). A Call for Sacrifice. *Modern History Sourcebook*. Accessed October 1, 2012. http://www.fordham.edu/halsall/mod/1942roosevelt-sacrifice.html.

Smith, G. S. (2006). *Faith and the Presidency: From George Washington to George W. Bush*. New York: Oxford University Press.

Thompson, M. (2003). Taxing Democracy: Politics and the Bush Tax Cut. *Logos: a journal of modern society and culture* 2.3, n.p. Accessed June 2nd, 2014.

Thorndike, J. (2013). *Their Fair Share: Taxing the Rich in the Age of FDR*. Washington D.C.: The Urban Institute Press.

Yarn Bombing: Claiming Rhetorical Citizenship in Public Spaces

MAUREEN DALY GOGGIN

> *Put simply, rhetorical citizenship is the search for, and practice of, methods of communication capable of guiding public decision and judgment*
> (Danisch 2011, p. 38)

Robert Danisch captures the theoretical thrust of this edited collection when he calls attention to the "importance of communication practices in grounding habits of citizenship." He fittingly observes that:

> Contemporary conceptions of citizenship have been qualified in a number of different ways: social citizenship, multicultural citizenship, citizen-soldiers, or citizen-workers are just a few examples. Although these are useful elaborations of the concept of citizenship, they fail to recognize the importance of communication practices in grounding habits of citizenship. The earliest Ancient Greek model of citizen was so closely tied to speech acts that the word 'rhetor' could be used as a place holder for citizen. (2011, pp. 37-38).

Indeed, as Christian Kock and Lisa Villadsen point out in the introduction to this collection, rhetoric has been central to the concept of Western citizenship since the sophists in Ancient Greece. For example, J. H. Freese observes that "The object which Isocrates professedly had in view was to train young men in the art of speaking and writing on political subjects, in order to fit them to fulfil the active duties of life in a manner worthy of the citizens of the Hellenic world" (1973, p. xiv). This important co-constructive connection between rhetoric and citizenship remains with us today, a significant connection Kock and Villadsen have termed "rhetorical citizenship" for the 2008 "Rhetorical Citizenship" conference in Copenhagen from which selected papers were published in *Rhetorical Citizenship and Public Deliberation*. There they define "rhetorical citizenship" as "a way of conceptualizing the discursive, processual, participatory aspects of civic life" (2012 "Introduction," p. 5).

Protesting is but one way to lay claim to rhetorical citizenship in public spaces. This deliberative rhetoric calls for co-active participation from both those creating/circulating protest agendas and those consuming/debating such agendas. Such a view calls on us to examine everyday practice to see how active agents participate in public protests both as contributors and as listeners. In short, rhetorical citizenship recognizes publics as practices not as abstractions, as fluid not as stable, as active in practical judgment not as passive recipients, and as operating in the here and now not in some imagined future (cf. Kock and Villadsen "Rhetorical Citizenship"). While rhetorical citizenship has a long history, how it plays out in the world, the actions it engages, shifts over time and space.

In the twenty-first century, Western feminist activism has taken a radical turn, moving beyond traditional rhetorical strategies of public protest and confrontation among throngs of gatherers. As Stacey Sowards and Valerie Renegar point out, today feminist activism also includes tactics such as "creating grassroots' models of leadership, using strategic humor, building feminist identity, sharing stories, and resisting stereotypes and labels" (2006, p. 58). I call this political turn "soft power." This oxymoronic phrase for contemporary feminist activism challenges the connotation of "soft" as flimsy, weak, stereotypical feminine and the connotation of "power" as brute force, strong, stereotypical masculine. Both words are turned inside out in many current activist movements: Soft is strong and power is nonaggressive. Soft is physical and power is cerebral. Soft is durable and power is creative. In this essay, I examine the practice of yarn bombing as one instantiation of contemporary feminist protest tactics. Specifically, I examine protest yarn bombing as an act of rhetorical citizenship across different countries on issues concerning: war, political decisions, economic problems, and environmental sustainability.

Yarn bombing[1] is a relatively new form of outsider street art[2] that is popping up all over the world in unexpected places, for unexpected reasons,

[1] The term "yarn bombing" was coined by Leanne Prain (a graphic artist, writer, knitter, and crafter) for her 2009 co-authored book titled *Yarn bombing: The art of crochet and knit graffiti* (Moore and Prain 2009). The term "bombing" comes from graffiti slang meaning

and toward unexpected ends (Greer 2008; Knitshade 2011; Tapper 2011; Werle 2011). Globally, women and men are taking up their knitting needles and crochet hooks to make political, social, cultural, aesthetic, and artistic statements.[3] Thus, in describing yarn bombing as a feminist activity, Beth Ann Pentney usefully conceives of feminist knitting practices horizontally along a continuum that recognizes "while they may differ in tactics, scope, and purpose they nevertheless contribute to a feminist ethos" (2008). This continuum moves from "women's community building and celebration of knitting as a domestic art (located at one end of the continuum), ... into a consideration of outreach and fundraising activities ... (located towards the middle of the continuum) [and ends with] knitting used in public forms of political protest, including rallies, marches, and public displays (located at the other end of the continuum)." More recently the practice has become

to paint a surface. The practice is also known by other names such as yarn storming, yarn graffiti, urban crochet and knitting, and guerilla crochet and knitting. Prior to Prain and Moore's book, knitting and crocheting had been used for various feminist activist projects but these terms of the art were yet in play. See, for example, Sabrina Shirobayashi (2007); and David Revere McFadden and Jennifer Scanlan (2007). These works include several yarn bombing pieces described as performative, subversive, and activist art.

[2] On outsider art, see John Maizels (2009); Lucienne Peiry (2001); Lyle Rexer (2005); Colin Rhodes (2000); and Susan Goldman Rubin (2004).

[3] The origins of yarn bombing are fuzzy at best. Books, magazine articles, newspaper accounts, and blogs typically report that the first recorded yarn bombing took place in Den Helder in the Netherlands in 2004 and that in the US it was founded in 2005 in Houston, Texas by Magda Sayeg. A yarn store owner who rounded up friends to form a group called "Knitta Please," Sayeg and the group used leftover yarns and unfinished projects to yarn bomb decorative pieces in unusual places around the city. Their activities were a response to the dehumanizing qualities of the urban environment. However, as early as 1992, contemporary Canadian artist Janet Morton was covering up public spaces with crocheted and knitted pieces. Her first installation was a huge knitted sock that she laid on a memorial in Queen's Park, Toronto. The following year she covered a bicycle, calling the installation "Sweater Bike." In 1994 she exhibited a huge mitten she named "Big, Big Mitt" by hanging it off an urban building. Since then she has completed many yarn installations. See the CCCA Canadian Art Database for images of Janet Morton's knitted work at http://ccca.concordia.ca/artists/work_detail.html?languagePref=en&mkey=55160&title=Big+Big+Mitt&artist=Janet+Morton&link_id=5793).

mainstreamed: commodified and commercialized with some yarn bombers being called upon by Fortune 500 companies to create yarn installations for large sums of money. Ironically, this latter form of yarn bombing has become the very thing that outsider and contemporary artists in general and yarn bombers in particular are calling into question. In this piece, I do not take up this practice but focus instead on yarn installations as public protest that fall toward one end of Pentney's continuum and as concrete manifestations of everyday rhetorical citizenship.

Perspective by incongruity

Yarn bombing takes place in unexpected spaces. A car, tree, street lamp, parking meter, sidewalk, park bench, for example, are adorned to a lesser or greater extent with yarn pieces. (See figure 1 where trees are yarn bombed in a central square in Spain.)

These installations thus disrupt the *genius locus* of the space. In classical Roman times, *genius locus* referred to the resident spirit of a place and was represented in religious iconography by figures dedicated to specific protective or guardian spirits. Today *genius locus* refers to the distinctive character of a location. As Danielle Endres and Samantha Senda-Cook note in "Location matters: The Rhetoric of Place in Protest," "locations, bodies, words, visual symbols, experiences, memories, and dominant meanings all interact to make and remake place" (p. 277). Typically these makings and remakings are part of a schema and as such are expected. Yarn bombing disrupts the schema of the *making* and *remaking* of place to call attention to itself. In a word, the installations are ironic.

Yarn bombing installations offer what Kenneth Burke termed "perspective by incongruity" (1964; 1970) in that they disrupt patterns of expectations and experiences regarding both yarn and the *genius locus* of public space. Clothing outdoor 'things' in yarn disrupts the domestic use of yarn and the public use of space. As Burke explains, "perspective by incongruity" serves as an invention device – a "method of gauging situations by verbal 'atom cracking.' That is, a word belongs by custom to a certain category – and by rational planning you wrench it loose and metaphorically apply it to a different category" (1984 *Attitudes*, p. 308). In *Philosophy of Literary Form* he defines perspective by incongruity as "a rational prodding or coaching of language so as to see around the corner of everyday usage" (1973, p. 400). As Abram Anders points out, perspective by incongruity thus serves as "a tool

FIGURE I

Yarn bombing at Plaça d'Hondures, Valencia, Spain. Wikimedia Commons photograph by JoanBanjo. 27 October 2013. Creative Commons Attribution – Share Alike 2.0 Generic license.

for challenging and reshaping the orientations through which we experience the world" (2011). Perspective by incongruity is not a tool restricted to verbal language. Functioning through both words and images, "perspective by incongruity," in Ross Wolin's words, "pushes to the limit our ability to generate meaning and make sense of the world through rational, pragmatic means. Perspective by incongruity is a violation of piety for the sake of more firmly asserting the pious" (2001, p. 76; also see Biesecker 1997). This violation calls attention to itself to assert firmly the issue at stake in the yarn bombing – an issue that might be as crass and mundane as the marketing of a product to as sensitive and extraordinary as raising charitable funds to fight breast cancer.

As Kock and Villadsen explain about rhetorical citizenship as a conceptual frame in their introduction to this collection, the "focus is less on what a particular utterance is like, or how effective it is, but more on how suited it is to contribute to constructive civic interaction." Perspective by incongruity evokes and induces an interaction.

Yarn graffiti as a materialist epistemology

Grounding my exploration in "thing theory," I argue that yarn bombing can be understood to constitute a materialist epistemology, what Davis Baird has termed "thing knowledge," "where the things we *make* bear knowledge of the world, on par with the words we speak" (2002, p. 13, emphasis added; also see Baird 2004 and Latour 2005). Indeed, the term yarn *graffiti* underscores this discursive construct as the word "graffiti" comes from the Greek term γράφειν – *graphein* – meaning "to write." What is written? When the graffiti artist who is credited with beginning the contemporary graffiti movement in Tehran, Iran, was asked about the meaning of graffiti, the artist self-named A1one (a.k.a. Taṇhā[4]) said: "A drawing on the street is similar to a letter: It proves that there is a writer. Whether people want to receive this letter or not is a different question" Graffiti confirms the presence and reality of the "maker" in a public space that is typically controlled by and reserved for those in power. Graffiti – whether in yarn or paint – bears knowledge of the world; it expresses dynamically "thing knowledge." The question of what

[4] Taṇhā is one of the Four Noble Truths of Buddha meaning "thirst" literally but defined as the craving to hold onto pleasurable and neutral experiences and to be separated from unpleasant ones.

audiences think about the graffiti message is open because audiences will vary deeply in their responses.

Without official permission or a permit, yarn bombing like graffiti is illegal which is why many yarn bombers use pseudonyms to conceal their identities. Where yarn bombing differs from graffiti is that yarn bombing doesn't damage property; it is easily removed and leaves no mark. In some spaces it is more tolerated than others; nevertheless, it is seen in 'public spaces' as 'defacing property.' Of course, yoking the phrases 'public spaces' and 'defacing property' blurs public and private worlds. This blurring is a hegemonic reading of graffiti, delimited it to the narrow notion of violation rather than expression.

Yarn bombing may be understood as a form of "girlie feminism," a term coined by Jennifer Baumgardner and Amy Richards in their *Manifesta: Young Women, Feminism, and the Future* to describe the pro-femininity line of young feminists (2000, p. 136). Girlie feminism is a strand of third-wave feminism that seeks to validate traditional female activities by "valuing knitting, cooking and dressing up" while challenging their stereotypical and hegemonic charac terizations (2010, 216). As Beth Ann Pentney notes, "If second-wave feminists have been historicized as women who put down their knitting, third-wave feminists may be characterized as those who have picked it back up again" (2008). Jack Z. Bratich and Heidi M. Brush refer to this resurgence of interest especially among young women as "fabriculture," "a whole range of practices usually defined as the 'domestic arts': knitting, crocheting, scrapbooking, quilting, embroidery, sewing, doll-making" (2011, p. 234).

Of course, third-wave feminism, like first and second waves, is comprised of many contradictory strands of feminism; however, what most strands share is a vibrant critique of earlier waves of feminism as impotent and a political stance that is much gentler than the "kick the door" down strands of some first- and second-wave feminists. This softer tactic is evident in what some guerilla yarn bombers say about the act. For instance, Deadly Knitshade (a pseudonym for a guerrilla yarn bomber in London) says:

> Change and making the world a better place can be done with a grin instead of a grimace, a whisper instead of a bellow. What we do *can* alter the way people look at their world. How it [yarn storming] alters it is up to them. That's really our point. (2011, p. 124)

Deadly Knitshade coined the term "yarn storming" to deflect the association of the term "bombing" with war and violent tactics. Her point calls attention to the dialogic nature of protest with both rhetor and interlocutors who will vary in their responses to the rhetor's yarn installation. Further, as Dennis Stevens notes in discussing the Do-it-Yourself (DIY) movement in which many yarn bombers participate:

> Rather than bringing revolution to the front door and kicking it open, as their parents may have hoped to do, these independent [DIY] makers are using the disarming and unassuming aesthetic of DIY craft's remixed domestic creativity to make subversive statements about the world in which they live. (2009)

So how are women and men attempting to alter political and social practices and perspectives? We turn now to protest yarn bombing as acts of civil disobedience – a global practice for making subversive statements about political issues and engaging polypublics. The following sections address activism in yarn against war, political decisions, economic problems, and environmental sustainability.

Protests against war

In April 2006, Danish artist Marianne Jørgensen created a yarn bombing war protest against the US, British, and Danish involvement in the Iraqi war, covering in yarn a World War II tank that she borrowed after much negotiating with Danish government (Sandra 2011). Titled *Pink M.24 Chaffee Tank*, the installation was made up of more than 4,000 15 X 15 cm pink crocheted and knitted squares donated by more than one thousand contributors from the United States and European countries, then assembled together by a group of volunteers and fit over the borrowed WWII combat tank.

These squares of various crochet and knitted patterns, according to Jørgensen, "represent a common acknowledgement of a resistance to the war in Iraq" (n.d.). Catherine Mazza notes that "When pieced together from numerous individual contributions, as many knitted protest projects are, the works become a sort of handcrafted petition" (qtd. in Gohil 2007). As a known artist, Jørgensen did not hide her identity but the thousand or so square makers remain anonymous. The piece was displayed between April 7th and 11th in 2006 in front of the Nikolaj Contemporary Art Center in Copenhagen. As Ele Carpenter points out about this protest,

FIGURE 2

Pink M.24 Chaffee Tank *by Marianne Jørgensen. April 2006. Photograph courtesy of Marianne Jørgensen.*

> This symbolic transformation of military hardware into an object of comic irony seeks to disarm the offensive stance of a machine justified by its defensive capability. Whilst the sinister Trojan undertones of disguising a real weapon as soft and fluffy lead us to review the deaths from 'friendly' fire, as well as the women and children who suffer the largest percentage of deaths in most conflicts. Activist craft has many forms of symbolism and disguise. … [M]ost importantly the *Pink M.24 Chaffee* enables, or should enable, an alternative critical discourse about global militarism. (2010, p. 4)

Carpenter's point echoes Deadly Knitshade. Public spaces and the authority that typically regulates them are subverted and transformed when filled with color, difference, and domestic work in ways that demand some kind of response (cf. Shepphard 2012). Finally feminist Beth Ann Pentney rightly points out that:

> Combining what Jørgensen refers to as the symbolic 'home, care, closeness' [and, I would add, 'the traditionally feminine'] with the violence and trauma caused by war machines forces the viewer to reconsider the perceived ordinariness or inevitability of war. The ideological affiliation of knitting with the feminine is exploited rather than rejected by Jørgensen in this demonstration, to such a degree that the cultural meanings imbued in the colour pink – femininity, a lack of authority, and nostalgic ties to the domestic – are used to destabilize the tank's symbolic power. (2008)

The inverted sense of "soft power" is clear here. Power is, as Pentney notes, "destabilize[ed]" and soft takes on a new sense of strong. Here the alternative critical discourse about global militarism as Carpenter notes challenges the role of military warfare for peaceful ends by likening the cover to warmth and domesticity that brings to mind the many friendly fire accidents and civilian deaths, especially of women and children, that are the unforgivable fall out of hostile and aggressive fighting.

The incongruity of the yarn pieces against the military machinery function as "perspective by incongruity" that is, as heuristic that wrenches viewers out of their customary habits of perception by disrupting familiar habits of mind so as to move them towards another perspective.

Protest against political decisions

Yarn bombers challenge various political decisions. In April 2011, thousands of German citizens held an anti-nuclear protest, demanding the end of nuclear power. In Essen, Germany (near where the next yarn bombing took place), about 3,000 people participated in the nationwide anti-nuclear demonstration. As part of that protest, two young German university students who call themselves by the pseudonyms Strick and Liesel (named after "Strickliesel" or "Knitting Nancy," a toy that teaches children how to knit) conducted yarn bombings (C. G. 2011). (See figure 3.) In part, these protests were a response to the German parliament passing a law in fall 2010 to extend the operation time of the country's 17 nuclear power plants.

Figure 3 shows one of Strick and Liesel's yarn bombing installation. The piece echoes the yellow and black nuclear power signs scattered near reactors or nuclear facilities with a twist. The center circle is marked by "Xs" for eyes and a stitched mouth both referencing death. At the top right hand corner are two colorful flowers that juxtapose nature to the manmade, life

FIGURE 3

Strick and Liesil Yarn Bomb Protest against Nuclear Power. 4 September 2011. Wikimedia Commons photograph by Fluffy on Tour. Creative Commons Attribution – Share Alike 2.0 Generic license.

against death, powerful beauty against ugliness. The yarn patch stands out against the bleak walls drenched in graffiti. In another installation, Strick and Liesel again draw on the familiar nuclear activity logo at the top in the branded yellow and black and repeated at the bottom in white and black. The middle yellow and black section sports the words "Nein Danke" or "No thanks," a phrase that is part of the logo of the large international Anti-Nuclear Movement. The two young women hung banners of this design on trees, street lamps, bridge banisters, and the pillars in front of the state parliament building around Dusseldorf, Duisburg, and Essen. This low-key anonymous activism relying on a private domestic practice attached to public spaces offers a powerful example of perspective by incongruity. Although the streets in several cities throughout Germany were filled with protesters, this protest offers no shouting, no crowds, and no force. In doing so, it

FIGURE 4

Tramway to Hell Yarn Bombing, Edinburgh, Scotland. September 2012. Photograph by Mary Gordon.

makes a robust statement quietly but no less powerfully. The piece makes a passerby stop to ponder the "nuclear symbol" and the words "no thanks" together. The ironic twist makes the message serve as an invention device to get some people thinking and perhaps caring about the dangers of nuclear power and maybe even considering future actions.

Northwest of Germany in Scotland in September 2012, an unknown crochet artist yarn bombed a political protest against the underground expansion of the city of Edinburgh's tram line. The installation was put up on Princes Street in the city. Against a warm, soft, colorful blanket of crocheted squares is the message "Tramway to Hell." (See figure 4.)

The letters are on plain crocheted squares; the pattern of the other squares is worth noting as it is called Granny square. Embroidering the letters on plain colored crocheted squares surrounded by Granny squares calls attention to the incongruity of this piece and all it symbolizes – both in terms of granny and language. In reaction to this anonymous installation, Yarnivore Rose (also a yarn bomber and former yarn store owner) is reported to have said, "Actual political speech in yarnbomb form rather than 'mere' decoration! BRING IT ON!" ("Mystery" 2012).[5] Here "decoration" serves as a pun – yarn work as decoration and political speech as decoration. Of course, the contrast of decoration and political protest, softness of material and hardness of message, expectations for a respectable granny and the pseudo-swear "hell" makes this piece a sophisticated pun, meant to draw attention to the incongruity of its presence and message. In short, it is meant to spark a response and a reflection on the issue of the tram extension.

Protests against economic problems

We turn now to yarn bombing protests regarding economic problems. In June 2012, outside the Bank of America on 1715 North Vermont Ave, in Los Feliz, California (an affluent neighborhood in Los Angeles, California, USA), the KnitRiot Collective (a group of US guerrilla knitters and crafters) hung 99 hand-knitted houses among the ficus trees to protest the foreclosure crises ("Los Feliz" 2012). Ironically titled HOMEsweetHOME, this yarn storming was intended to demonstrate solidarity among Americans who have lost or are losing their homes to foreclosures. (See figures 5, 6, and 7.)

Hanging domesticated yarn houses along a clothes line structure with clothes pins – symbols of home – calls attention to the devastation of the home foreclosure problem during the economic collapse of 2009 onward. The clothes pins hold the houses on the line as if they were drying/driving home the point that homes like clothing are necessary shelters and coverings – something the flurry of home foreclosures, short sales, and home abandonments precluded. These problems, largely caused by inappropriate and shady mortgage practices, are all more distressing as they could have been avoided except for power and greed.

On the back of the knitted houses, KnitRiot attached a tag urging

[5] Rose's response resonates with the riot grrrl's perspective of an anti-corporate stance through self-sufficiency and self-reliance. See Sara Marcus's *Girls to the Front: the True Story of the Riot Grrrl Revolution*. Also see the video of Rose White (Yarnivore Rose's) talk on "The History of (Guerilla) Knitting," 24th Chaos Communication Congress, *Yovisto: Academic Video Search* (December 29, 2007). http://www.yovisto.com/video/9916.

FIGURE 5

HomeSWEETHome Yarn Bombing Protest of Home Foreclosures. Los Angeles, US. June 2012. Courtesy of and photograph by KnitRiot Collective.

FIGURE 6

Close-up of HomeSWEETHome Yarn Bombing Protest of Home Foreclosures. Los Angeles, US. June 2012. Courtesy of and photograph by KnitRiot Collective.

FIGURE 7

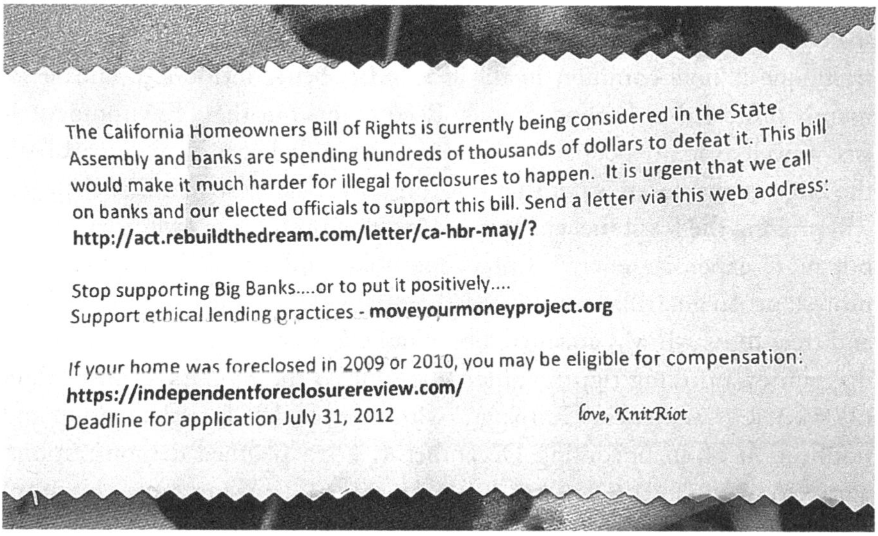

Tag on backside of knitted home. Yarn Bombing Protest of Home Foreclosures. Los Angeles, US. June 2012. Courtesy of and photograph by KnitRiot Collective.

viewers to call on banks and elected representatives in the State Assembly to vote in favor of the California Homeowners Bill of Rights, a bill to curtail illegal foreclosures. (See figure 6.) Calling on viewers to "stop supporting Big Banks" in favor of "ethical lending practices," the tag offered information on how to apply for compensation after a foreclosure. Each point was highlighted with a viable web address. The California Homeowners Bill of Rights passed and became law in January 2013.[6] The leftwing political position of this knitting group is clear in both the visual rhetoric and the written rhetoric on their installation.

Sustainability protests

The last kind of protest I examine concerns environmental sustainability protests specifically against two damaging practices: fracking and logging. On November 28, 2012, a yarn bombing protest against hydraulic fracturing or fracking took place at St. Annes Square in Blackpool, England

[6] For more information on this bill, see "California Homeowner Bill of Rights," State of California Department of Justice, Office of the Attorney General at http://oag.ca.gov/hbor.

("Yarnbombing" 2012). Fracking is a process of drilling and injecting fluid of various chemicals into the ground at a high enough pressure to fracture shale rocks to release the natural gas contained inside. The shale gas drilling technique is now common in the US and is being introduced and vehemently protested in Europe. Stanley Reed points out that "Environmentalists, as well as many people living near possible shale gas sites, worry about the huge quantities of water that fracking uses. They also fear that shale gas will prolong the fossil fuel era by reducing the incentive to switch to cleaner but more expensive energy sources like solar and wind" (2012). For this protest, urban guerrilla knitters tied blue triangular crocheted tags to railings and trees to which was attached a blue note. On one side of the note was a diagram of a drilling rig; the other side sported the phrase "Against Water F.O.W.L.E.R.S. Awareness Campaign" with contact details for the group and notification of an upcoming December 1, 2012 planned demonstration.[7] The acronym F.O.W.L.E.R.S. stands for "Fracking Our Water Leaves Environmental Residential Stress." The effects of fracking are still being discovered, but so far the chemicals used have been linked to kidney and liver damage. The practice has also "been linked to earthquakes in the US, witnessed in states such as California, Ohio, and Arkansas" ("Environmental" 2012). The blue triangles dangling from railings and trees drew attention to the protest. The color blue is an ironic pun, connoting both clean skies and sadness, signaling both purity and contamination.

On February 16, 2012, a stretch of Highway 774 near Pincher Creek in Alberta, Canada was yarn bombed by a group protesting the practice of logging that was taking place just 4 kilometers south of the highway. (See figure 8.)

Yarn bombers targeted trees so that those who passed by would "pause to reflect on the 'knitting together' of people, their communities, and the beauty in the space that surrounds them" (Castle 2012). With its perspective by incongruity – human made afghans in nature on trees – passersby would surely notice the installation and pause. A spokesperson for the group described the installation as "creating a voice for wild spaces" (Castle 2012). The knitted afghan on each tree works as a metaphor supplying warmth, nurturing, and protection against the devastation of logging while at the

[7] Over 300 protestors held a demonstration in London on December 2, 2012 ("Environmental" 2012).

FIGURE 8

Protest Against Logging, Pincher Creek, Alberta, Canada. February 16, 2012. Courtesy of and photograph by Barbara Amos, Art Works for Wild Spaces.

same time shouting a message of "do not touch me." The notion that knitting 'knits' folks together has a long history and this pun is certainly evoked by the colorful 'protected' trees in the 'wild.'

Ephemeral strength

Feminists Betsey Greer and Debbie Stoller[8] argue that the resurgence of interest in knitting and crocheting, especially among third-wave feminists, comes from an epistemic perspective that values *making over made* – that values production over consumerism, and process over product (Greer 2008; Stoller 2004). Yarn bombing fits this paradigm because it is an ephemeral, transient art. For example, self-described yarn bombers on Flickr were asked "How long do your yarn bombs last?" Over a dozen answered. All agreed that length of depends on the location and on the design. One reported, "I had one last less than 24 hours;" another said "we've got some that stay up until the weather kills them; others disappear much sooner for reasons unknown." Still another wrote: "Really depends on so many things. The shortest I've had was less than half an hour and another I've had up for over a year" ("How Long," 2009). Yarn installations are often taken down by the public who see them as a nuisance, the police who see them as vandalism, or even those who see the whimsy of them and appreciate the art and message often take them precisely because of those very reasons. Not everyone, in other words, is accepting of or enthusiastic and uncritical about the practice of yarn bombing. But we should not expect unified responses. What is important is that there are responses to the act. Given that it is unclear how long a piece will remain, yarn bombers are clearly more invested in the *process of creating* the installation than in the finished product itself. That is, it is the *performance* of yarn bombing that creates the meaning rather than thing itself and that engenders a response – whether good or bad.

Valuing the doing over the done and the self-made over the mass made is to claim slow process practices as a reaction against the staggering rate of technological change today, what Colin Bain calls "hyperculture" (2002). Paradoxically, however, it is this speedy race of communication technology that has facilitated yarn bombing to spread across the globe so quickly. In-

[8] Debbie Stoller is founder of *BUST* magazine and the writer of the *Stitch and Bitch* series of knitting and crochet books.

deed, the internet has been absolutely vital to circulating and sharing yarn bombing strategies through viral videos, blogs, and social networks. On the first International Yarn Bombing Day, June 11, 2011, founded by Joann Matvichuk of Lethbridge, Alberta, Canada, Matvichuk wrote on her blog:

> I had no idea when I came up with the idea for International Yarnbombing Day that it would have gotten this big. I figured a few hundred Canadians and Americans would be participating but I had no idea that I would have people from all over the World including countries like Iceland, Norway, Egypt, Israel, Germany and Australia. (2011)

Virtually every continent has participated. It has been an annual event across the world ever since 2011. This widespread and ongoing activity confirms that yarn bombing is a global community movement. In the words of one reporter, "This global reach is one reason why some yarn-bombers believe their work has the potential to make political statements" ("Yarn-Bombing" 2010). Crossing physical, ideological, and political borders via the internet, yarn bombers can find those who share similar political views even when the politics of their individual countries are very different. As Kock and Villadsen point out, "Globalization and digital media are two major factors creating increased attention to national and global citizenship, and to the opportunities and the need to communicate across space and other barriers" (2012, p. 4). Yarn bombing clearly fits this contemporary paradigm.

Conclusion

Throughout the globe, yarn graffiti activists juxtapose the softness of yarn against the hardness of the issues they protest and the sterility of the spaces on which they install them. Often, they juxtapose the beauty of the colors and design against the ugliness of the issues at hand. As one guerilla knitter puts it, "this style of folk craft renovation is ... integral to altering and beautifying ugly aspects of urban architecture" (van de Velde 2010). Not everyone shares their passion or vision; indeed, some are downright hostile to yarn graffiti. In some ways, it matters little what the exact response is as it is more important that there is a response, for as Simone Chambers, whom Kock and Villadsen also cite in "Rhetorical Citizenship as a Conceptual Frame in Academe," says: "If rhetoric in general is the study of how speech affects an audience then deliberative rhetoric must be about the way speech induces deliberation in the sense of inducing *considered* reflection about a future action" (2009, p. 335).

Yarn Bombing (re)presents the convergence of several contemporary political and cultural strands: third-wave feminists, craft activists, Do-It-Yourselfers, and contemporary artists. By engaging in practices that have been gendered in the past, feminist yarn bombers (men and women) seek to reclaim these "traditionally feminized" activities. Greer has termed this political strategy craftivism[9] (craft + activism for activists who use art as a medium). In terms of the Do-it-yourself movement (DIY), Dennis Stevens points out: "If there is anything cohesive about the DIY movement, it's that its practitioners choose to *reinvent tradition as a remix*, engaging with it through parody, satire and nostalgic irony. ... [T]his work makes its cultural [and I'd add political] statements indirectly and quietly" (2009, emphasis added).

Drawing these strands together, we can understand yarn bombing as a contemporary response to the separation of labor and domestic skills and the split of public and private. Yarn bombing is fully based on creativity rather than destruction, resists the legal restrictions on making and mending anything, and subverts impediments on displaying anything in public. This practice creates a perspective of incongruity; that is, it serves as an invention device, one that attracts attention to the strangely familiar markers of home, nurturing, protecting, and sheltering in an unfamiliar place of the outdoors.

Political activist theorist Randy Shaw offers the following advice to current activists: "Today's activists must … recognize that their participation in public life will make a critical difference in their world. By acting proactively and with tactical and strategic wisdom, social change activists can bring a degree of social and economic justice ... that has for too long been deferred"

9 Betsy Greer coined the term "craftivism" in 2003 to explain a third-wave feminist embrace of stitching, crochet, and knitting. *American Craft Magazine* put the term "craftivist" on one of the great moments in crafts to mark their 70th anniversary. See "Interactive Timeline [1940s-2000]," *American Craft Magazine* http://craftcouncil.org/timeline/2000s.html and "70 Years of Making: The Timeline," *American Craft Magazine* (August/September 2011). http://craftcouncil.org/magazine/article/70-years-making-timeline. On craftivism, Greer argues that "In promoting the idea that people can use their own creativity to improve the world, craftivism allows those who wish to voice their opinions and support their causes the chance to do just that...but without chanting or banner waving and at their own pace" (2007). Also see her blog at http://Craftism.com.

(2001, p. 279). What Shaw neglects in his advice are those who co-participate as interlocutors to take up the work on issues long deferred. As Kock and Villadsen remind us, "Public discourse is concrete, manifest, omnipresent, visible, and accessible for all; anyone can relate to it, and it is the conduit of numerous societal functions and dynamisms" (2012, p. 4). The global reach of the everyday rhetorical citizenship practice of yarn bombing offers the possibility of extending social and economic justice across the world. Bring it on.

References

Anders, A. (2011). "Pragmatisms by Incongruity: 'Equipment for Living' from Kenneth Burke to Gilles Deleuze". *KB Journal* 7.2. Accessed May 14, 2014. http://kbjournal.org/anders.

Bain, C. M., Dennis Des Rivieres, and Sean Dolan (2002). *Transitions in Society: The Challenge of Change*. Toronto: Oxford University Press.

Baird, D. (2002). Thing Knowledge - Function And Truth. *Techné* 6.2: 13-27.

Baird, D. (2004). *Thing Knowledge: A Philosophy of Scientific Instruments*. Berkeley: University of California Press.

Baumgardner, J. and A. Richards. (2000). *Manifesta: Young Women, Feminism, and the Future*. New York: Farrar Straus & Giroux.

Baumgardner, J. and A. Richards. (2010). *Manifesta [10th anniversary edition]: Young Women, Feminism, and the Future*, rev. ed. New York: Farrar, Straus and Giroux.

Biesecker, B.A. (1997). *Addressing Postmodernity: Kenneth Burke, Rhetoric, and a Theory of Social Change*. Tuscaloosa: University of Alabama Press.

Bowker, J. (2003). *The Concise Oxford Dictionary of World Religions*. Oxford, UK: Oxford University Press. Accessed May 14, 2014. http://www.oxfordreference.com/view/10.1093/acref/9780192800947.001.0001/acref-9780192800947-e-7197.

Bratich, J.Z. and H.M. Brush. (2011). Fabricating Activism: Craft-Work, Popular Culture, Gender. *Utopian Studies* 22.2, 233-60

Burke, K. (1984) [1959] *Attitudes Toward History*, 3rd ed. Berkeley: University of California Press. Originally published Los Altos, CA: Hermes Publications.

Burke, K. (1973) [1964]. *Philosophy of Literary Form: Studies in Symbolic Action*, 3rd ed. Berkeley: University of California Press. Originally published Baton Rouge: Louisiana State University Press.

Burke, K. (1970) [1961]. *The Rhetoric of Religion: Studies in Logology*. Berkeley: University of California Press. Originally published Boston: Beacon Press.

Burke, K. (1964). *Perspectives by Incongruity*, edited by S.E. Hyman. Indianapolis: University of Indiana Press.

Carpenter, E. (2010). Activist Tendencies in Craft. In G. Cox, N. Haq and T. Trevor (Eds.), *Concept Store 33: Art, Activism and Recuperation*. Bristol, UK: Arnolfini. Accessed May 14, 2014. http://eprints.gold.ac.uk/id/eprint/3109.

Castle 'Yarn Bombing.' (2012). *Stop castle logging* blog. February 17. Accessed May 14, 2014. http://stopcastlelogging.wordpress.com/2012/02/17/castle-yarn-bombing/.

Chambers, S. (2009). Rhetoric and the Public Sphere: Has Deliberative Democracy Abandoned Mass Democracy? *Political Theory* 37, 323-350.

Danisch, R. (2011). Jane Addams, Pragmatism, and Rhetorical Citizenship in Multicultural Democracies. In R. Danisch (Ed.), *Citizens of the World: Pluralism, Migration and Practices of Citizenship* (pp. 37-59). Amsterdam: Rodopi.

"Environmental Risk: UK Protests over Fears of Fracking Ban Lift." (2012). *RT Question More*. December 2. Accessed May 12, 2014. http://rt.com/news/uk-fracking-protest-environment-073/.

Freese, J. H., trans. (1973) [1894]. Introduction. In *Orations of Isocrates* vol. 1, ix-xxvii. London: Chiswick Press. Originally published London: George Bell & Sons.

G., C. (2011). Yarn Bombing: Knitting Against Nuclear Power. *The Economist*. Prospero blog. April 15. http://www.economist.com/blogs/prospero/2011/04/yarn_bombing.

Gohil, N.S. (2007). Activists Use Knitting Needles to Make Their Point. *Columbia News Service*. March 13. http://jscms.jrn.columbia.edu/cns/2007-03-13/gohil-knittinginprotest.html.

Greer, B. (2007). Craftivism. In G.L. Anderson and K. G. Herr (ed.), *Encyclopedia of Activism and Social Justice* (p. 402). Thousand Oaks, CA: Sage.

Greer, B. (2008). *Knitting for Good: A Guide to Creating Personal, Social, and Political Change, Stitch By Stitch*. Boston: Trumpeter.

How Long Has Your Graffiti Lasted? (2009). *Yarn Bombing DIY/Discuss*. Flickr. Accessed May 14, 2014. http://www.flickr.com/groups/yarnbombingukdiy/discuss/72157614269938076/.

Jørgensen, M. (n.d.). Pink M.24 Chaffee: A Tank Wrapped in Pink. Marianne Art. Accessed May 14, 2014. http://www.matianneart.dk.

KnitRiot (blog). http://www.knitriot.blogspot.com/.

Knitshade, D. (2011). *Knit the City: A Whodunnkit Set in London*. Chichester: Summersdale.

Kock, C. and L. S. Villadsen. (2012). Introduction: Citizenship as a Rhetorical Practice. In C. Kock and L.S. Villadsen (Eds.), *Rhetorical Citizenship and Public Deliberation* (pp. 1-10). University Park: Pennsylvania State University Press.

Kock, C. and L. S. Villadsen. (Forthcoming). Rhetorical Citizenship as a Conceptual Frame: What We Talk About When We Talk About Rhetorical Citizenship. In

C. Kock and L.S. Villadsen (Eds.), *Contemporary Rhetorical Citizenship*. Leiden, Netherlands: Leiden University Press.

Latour, B. (2005). *Reassembling the Social: An Introduction to Actor Network Theory*. New York: Oxford University Press.

Los Feliz Bank Gets 'Yarn-Bombed' in Foreclosure Protest. (2012). *The Eastsider LA*. June 9. Accessed May 14, 2014. http://www.theeastsiderla.com/2012/06/los-feliz-bank-gets-yarn-bombed-in-foreclosure-protest/.

Maizels, J. (Ed.) (2009). *Outsider Art Sourcebook: International Guide to Outsider Art and Folk Art*. Watford: Raw Vision.

Marcus, S. (2010). *Girls to the Front: The True Story of the Riot Grrrl Revolution*. New York: Harper Collins.

Matvichuk, J. (2011). The Birth of an Idea. *International Yarn Bombing Day* (IYBD) blog. June 11. Accessed May 14, 2014. http://iybd.blogspot.com/.

McFadden, D.R. and J. Scanlan. (2007). *Radical Lace and Subversive Knitting*. New York: Museum of Arts & Design.

Moore, M. and L. Prain. (2009). *Yarn Bombing: The Art of Crochet and Knit Graffiti*. Vancouver: Arsenal Pump Press.

Mystery Knitter Vents Edinburgh Trams Fury in 'Yarn-Bombing' Blanket Protest. (2012). *news.Scotsman.com*. September 27. Accessed May 14, 2014. http://www.scotsman.com/news/mystery-knitter-vents-edinburgh-trams-fury-in-yarn-bombing-blanket-protest-1-2549375.

Peiry, L. (2001). *Art Brut: The Origins of Outsider Art*. Paris: Flammarion.

Pentney, B.A. (2008). Feminism, Activism, and Knitting: Are the Fiber Arts a Viable Mode for Feminist Political Action? *thirdspace: a journal of feminist theory & culture*, 8.1. Accessed May 14, 2014. http://journals.sfu.ca/thirdspace/index.php/journal/article/viewArticle/pentney/210.

Reed, S. (2012). Fracking Still Controversial in Europe. *The New York Times*. November 2012. Accessed May 14, 2012. http://www.nytimes.com/2012/11/14/business/energy-environment/fracking-still-controversial-in-europe.html.

Rexer, L. (2005). *How to Look at Outsider Art*. New York: Abrams.

Rhodes, C. (2000). *Outsider Art: Spontaneous Alternatives*. London: Thames and Hudson.

Rubin, S.G. (2004). *Art Against the Odds: From Slave Quilts to Prison Paintings*. New York: Crown Books.

Sandra, C. (2011). Craft Process in Contemporary Art. The *Studio Stitch Art* blog. December 9. Accessed May 14, 2014. http://studiostitchart.blogspot.com/2011/12/craft-process-in-contemporary-art.html.

Shaw, R. 2001 [1996]. *The Activist's Handbook*, rev. 2nd ed. Berkeley and Los Angeles: University of California Press.

Shepphard, E. (2012). "'It's Not A Hobby, It's a Post-Apocalyptic Skill': Space, Feminism, Queer, and Sticks and String." *Bad Subjects*, 83. Accessed May 14, 2014. http://bad.eserver.org/issues/2012/notahobby.

Shirobayashi, S. (2007). *KnitKnit: Profiles and Projects from Knitting's New Wave*. New York: Harry N. Abrams.

Sowards, S.K. and V.R. Renegar. (2006). Reconceptualizing Rhetorical Activism in Contemporary Feminist Contexts. *The Howard Journal of Communications* 17, 57-74.

Stevens, D. 2009. "DIY: Revolution 3.0 – Beta." *American Craft Magazine*. October/November. http://craftcouncil.org/magazine/article/diy-revolution-30-beta.

Stoller, D. (2004). *Stitch 'n Bitch: The Knitter's Handbook*. New York: Workman Publishing.

Tapper, J. (2011). *Craft Activism: People, Ideas, and Projects from the New Community of Handmade and How You Can Join In*. New York: Potter Craft.

van de Velde, D. (2010). I Knit Brisbane. *The Fox is Black* blog. July 23. Accessed May 14, 2014. http://www.thefoxisblack.com/2010/07/23/i-knit-brisbane/.

Werle, S. (2011). *Urban Knits*. Munich: Prestel.

White, R. (2007). The History of (Guerilla) Knitting. 24th Chaos Communication Congress. *Yovisto: Academic Video Search*. December 29. Accessed May 14, 2014. http://www.yovisto.com/video/9916.

Wolin, R. (2001). *The Rhetorical Imagination of Kenneth Burke*. Columbia: University of South Carolina Press.

Yarn-bombing - a Sort of Graffiti with Wool - Has Glasgow Residents in Stitches. (2010). *Scotland on Sunday*. December 18. Accessed May 14, 2014. http://www.scotsman.com/lifestyle/fashion/yarn-bombing-a-sort-of-grafitti-with-wool-has-glasgow-residents-in-stitches-1-479869.

Yarnbombing St. Annes! (2012). *Residents Action on Fylde Fracking* blog. November 29. Accessed May 14, 2014. http://stopfyldefracking.org.uk/latest-news/yarnbombing-st-annes/.

On Trees: Protest between the Symbolic and the Material

KATI HANNKEN-ILLJES

Once there was a tree, and she loved a little boy.
And every day the boy would come and he would gather her leaves.
And make them into crowns and play king of the forest.
He would climb up her trunk and swing from her branches. And eat apples.
And they would play hide and go seek.
And when he was tired, he would sleep in her shade. And the boy loved the tree – very much.
And the tree was happy.
(Shel Silverstein, *The Giving Tree*)

Introduction

This paper is about trees. About the trees in the "Schlossgarten" – the castle garden – in the city of Stuttgart, Germany, and how they have shaped the protest against the remodeling of Stuttgart's main station. Thereby this paper also aims to establish a linkage of two terms and concepts: materiality and argumentation. It starts from the assumption that the role of "things" in argumentation and their relation to symbolic action are worth exploring. The interest in the materiality *of* communication and the materiality *in* communication has been growing in the last twenty to thirty years. One of the cornerstones of this interest is marked by a book edited by Gumbrecht and Pfeiffer (1988) with exactly this title: *Materiality of Communication.* The chapters of that volume circle around the material aspects of media that enable communication. Many of them stress the surface – aspects of communication, which do not necessarily refer to some deeper meaning, but rather function through (bodily) perception and experience. Gumbrecht, for instance, in his chapter (1988) already hints at his later theory of presence by formulating a tension between the rhythm (open to bodily experience) and the meaning of texts. The underlying assumption when discussing the materiality of communication is that it determines not only how something can be communicated but what can be communicated. A public park allows for other means today, with a combination of mobile, internet–based means of communication and 'traditional' paper-based forms like leaflets and posters, than it did twenty years ago. At the same time, a park still allows for entirely different forms of symbolic action than a parliament.

What I am interested in moves one step further and relates to work in the rhetoric of protest: how non-discursive entities – things – influence discourse, frame argumentation and thereby function rhetorically. This is somewhat in line with the actor-network theory as put forward by Latour (2005). He suggests describing practices while refraining from prior strong conceptions of human action. Rather, the researcher should stay open and describe the center of agency, and this center can be human as well as non-human. Latour applies the term "actor" also to non-human agents. However, when he applies the term "actor," the concept of "acting" is quite different from that in a strong human-action paradigm. As Latour puts it, "an 'actor' in the hyphenated expression actor-network is not the source of an action but the moving target of a vast array of entities swarming toward it" and "to use the word 'actor' means that it's never clear who and what is acting when we act since an actor on stage is never alone in acting" (2005, p. 46). It is in this sense that I am interested in the entanglement of different things and humans acting rhetorically. It might prove fruitful to conceive of the things – in this case the trees – not only as something that is being acted upon, but as things which themselves have agency. So the questions addressed in this essay are: How is the materiality of the specific trees incorporated in the protest? What kind of protest practices are the trees subjected to? How are the trees acted upon by the protesters? How could the trees in the Schlossgarten become such a strong and central argument theme? And also: what can a case study of the Stuttgart protests show about the status of "things" and their materiality for public discourse?

This focus is grounded in my interest in public discourse as a process between different participants/citizens and in my interest in the significance of rhetoric for a democratic society. As Kock and Villadsen put it: "Rhetoric is at the core of being a citizen" (2012, p. 5). The focus on processes rather than products of rhetorical action allows for *how* questions rather than *why* questions: how do participants take part in public discourse, how do they enact rhetorical citizenship? This then includes taking into account not only traditional rhetorical means (speeches and debates) but all forms employed by citizens performing citizenship. Asen stresses this notion of multimodality when he writes: "In drawing attention to the citizenship as a process, a discourse theory recognizes the fluid, multimodal, and quotidian enactments in a multiple public sphere" (2004, p. 191).

Before moving to the method section and my analysis, let me first set the scene by briefly describing the history of the protest movement against the remodeling of the train station. In 1995 the German federal railways, the federal government, the *Land* of Baden-Württemberg and the city of Stuttgart agreed on the project to remodel Stuttgart's main station and turn it from an over-ground dead-end into an underground through-station. This project has become known as Stuttgart 21 or just S21. From the beginning several environmentalist groups questioned the project for a variety of different reasons: among them cost, threat to the ground water (Stuttgart has mineral water springs), logistics, and the threat to the "Schlossgarten." This protest stayed within smaller circles. It existed, but was neither heard nor seen much publicly. Then in 2007 more than 60,000 citizens of Stuttgart moved for a public referendum about Stuttgart 21. The motion was dismissed by the majority of the city council.

In 2010 the beginning of the visible construction work drew closer, including the demolition of one part – the North wing – of the station building. Under the heading of the slogan "stay up" (*oben bleiben*) a form of public protest arose that Stuttgart had never encountered before. Since then Stuttgart has seen "Monday rallies" every week – ranging from a couple of hundreds of participants to 100,000. The label "Monday protests" was not chosen by chance: since the revolution in the former GDR, instigated by the "Monday protests" in Leipzig, among others, this label has been used by rallies that mean to place themselves in line with an oppressed people against an, at best, disengaged government. Then in July 2010, a steady picket was established in the Schlossgarten by the protesters, trees were occupied and some tree houses built.

On September 30, 2010 thousands of citizens, mainly high school students, rallied against the felling of 250 trees in the Schlossgarten. The police answered with pepper spray and water cannons. These means were widely perceived as too harsh and inappropriate. In a legendary TV-news interview anchor Marietta Slomka interrupted the Minister of the Interior, as he described and justified the police action, with the question: "Are you now actually talking about the Swabian citizenry? It sounds like you are talking about a war zone" ("Reden Sie denn jetzt über das schwäbische Bürgertum? Das hört sich an, als würden Sie über den Krieg berichten"). This quote puts in a nutshell the controversy that accompanied the S21 protests: what does it mean to be a good citizen? How should citizenship be enacted? On October 1 between 50,000 and 100,000 protesters rallied against Stuttgart 21. September 30 gave rise to an even stronger protest movement. The Schlossgarten at that time was an assemblage of tents, occupied trees, information booths, the picket, percussion groups, and overall a very lively, colorful crowd. The protests had altered the face of the city, and a specific mode of involvement, a specific mode of "being a citizen" (see Asen 2004, 195) had been introduced. And this way of being a citizen was not orderly, but loud and colorful, representing in some ways the "rowdiness" that Ivie (2002) identifies as central to rhetorical deliberation (see p. 279), although rowdiness might be too strong a term. At the same time the government of Baden-Württemberg initiated an arbitration procedure, which led to few results and only minor changes in the project. In 2012, already under the newly elected Green/Social Democrat administration, the majority of citizens in Baden-Württemberg (and in Stuttgart) voted for the continuation of the project. Shortly after that, 250 more trees were felled in the "Schlossgarten."

What struck me when looking more closely at the argumentative strategies of proponents, and especially opponents, was the motif of the tree. This motif in itself is not unusual in this kind of protest. The tree is an emblem often featured in environmentalists' discourse and protest, and it is a topos often taken up in arguments about "green" themes. What struck me in the protest against S21 was that it did not only take up the prominent topos of a tree discursively, but that the protestors' argumentation was inextricably bound to the concrete, particular trees. One could probably argue that the trees themselves protested, had agency in the protest. In this paper I want to offer an analysis of the S21 controversy by following a theme and a materiality through the discourse. I shall first lay out my method and then analyze how "the tree" as an argument and a materiality functioned during the controversy. Finally, I will tie this analysis to the discussion on materiality and discourse. I will argue that one cannot grasp the impact of the argumentation when taking it into account only as discursive entities, but that discourse and materiality are interwoven.

Method

This analysis performs a form of argumentation analysis that is informed by my interest in the development or career of argument themes: how do arguments develop over time in a specific discourse, how are they employed, how do they fail? So my interest is not in the argument as a product but rather as a becoming, as something that is in flux while it is employed in the discourse and itself influences the discourse it enables. In an earlier project on the career of statements in criminal cases this included following the career of arguments through different materialities: files, informal chats, lawyer-client conferences and trials.[1] For the current project on trees, I mainly relied on websites, info brochures, interviews, field notes and the trees themselves.

This interest is informed by ethnographic work – although in itself it does not represent "real" ethnographic work. As Endres and Senda-Cook (2011) argue, the rhetorical impact of "place" as a materiality can best be grasped when experiencing it, when "being there" is part of the research, as it allows one to access participant categories. This hints at an ethnographic approach where participant observation, or rather participating observation, is key. At the same time it needs to be accompanied by the alienation of that which is being seen, heard, experienced. As Ammann and Hirschauer stress, "ethnography is in some ways about, after having understood something, being even more astonished by it. Familiarity is not a goal, but a point that always needs to be overcome anew" (1997, p. 29).[2]

Focusing on the intertwinement of the material and the symbolic also invites what Marcus (1995) called "multisited ethnography." This approach answers the conditions of modern life, being held in a tension between the local and the global, as well as the attention to the ethnography of one's own culture, by suggesting that one not focus on a single, specially circumscribed field, but rather follow something (the people, the thing, the metaphor, the story, the conflict, the life) through discourse, practice, culture (Marcus 1995, p. 106) in order to be able to produce and appropriate analysis and thick description of cultural phenomena. In my analysis I am following two entities: the theme of the tree in the S21 controversy seen through the discourse, and the actual trees in Stuttgart. Two entities that, although distinguishable from each other, are intertwined at the same time. The underlying

[1] See for example Scheffer, Hannken-Illjes and Kozin (2010).

[2] Translation my own.

assumption here is that following the trees will also show how arguments and their premises are being produced. My interest is not so much in a single snapshot of an argument as product, but rather in the becoming of arguments. As Latour put it, "we are going from final products to production, from 'cold' stable objects to 'warmer' and unstable ones" (2005, p. 21). Thus this work is a hint at an ethnography of argumentation, as has been advocated by Prior (2005). Prior has asked argumentation studies "to give the diagrams a bit of a rest and consider seriously the implications of seeing argumentation as sociohistoric practice, to ask how pedagogies can help attune students to the work of appropriating situated knowledge practices, to open up the ethnography of argumentation as a branch of the larger ethnography of communication" (Prior 2005, p. 133). This includes focussing not so much on the premises and the inferential relationships between them but rather on the way these premises are constructed and become available. But note again: my approach and analysis in this research are not ethnographic, they rather borrow insights and concepts from ethnography to conduct a rhetorical analysis (and in certain ways an argumentation analysis). By doing so I mean to suggest that taking up ethnography in argumentation analysis would be extremely fruitful.[3]

As my starting point I utilized different forms of data: the website and the activities by a group called "die Parkschützer" (the park guardians) and "die Baumpaten" (the Godparents of trees), interviews with protestors and my notes. With all this, I followed the trees.

Trees

The tree is a central metaphor and material topos. It stands for knowledge, for life, for duration, for shelter. A vast number of literary works centering around childhood speak of trees – trees that protect, that become witnesses, become friends. It is not by accident that trees in *The Lord of the Rings* are the oldest creatures and among the most powerful. I would need an extra

[3] My reluctance to position this work more clearly in the ethnographic strand is twofold: most importantly, I started to work on this project after the trees were gone, so although I have experienced the protest in the Schlossgarten, I have not done so as a researcher. Also, this project stands currently at the beginning. I am still continuing to gather data, mainly from interviews with different activists. So what this paper presents are first outcomes to be supplemented in the future.

essay, if not an extra book, to lay out in what different senses "the tree" bears in different disciplines. Not only the tree in itself, but also the planting of trees can have a strong rhetorical impact. In 1985 Joseph Beuys, a German artist well known for his concept of "the social sculpture" and for the statement that every person is an artist, started his art project "7,000 oaks" at the documenta in Kassel. He framed this project as an act of creation: "... here, there is nothing to hope, or to believe, or to doubt, but here something is being created, that in itself is a creation" (Beuys, Blume and Rappmann 2006, p. 25).

In the Stuttgart protests, the planting of trees was one of the rhetorical practices: well-known protestors planted a "Stuttgart-21-resistance-tree". This tree became an object of controversy, being attacked by the proponents of S21 and planted anew, resulting in at least three "resistance trees" being planted.

Especially in environmentalists' discourse and protests the tree is a central theme. The beginning of the environmentalist concern in Germany in the 1970s, for example, was marked by the concern about the "German Forests," which were threatened by pollution and acid rain. This importance of the motif of the tree is also reflected by the label sometimes used for environmentalists: tree-huggers. This nickname – often pejoratively used – points to another important aspects of the tree as an argument theme:[4] it oscillates between the botanical and the human. Trees, it seems, are often granted personhood, anthropomorphized. Some statements of the "godparents of trees" in Stuttgart point to this: "A tree is a creature like you and me" (*Ein Baum ist ein Lebewesen wie du und ich*). "The animal, the human, the tree, they all share the same breath" (Das Tier, der Mensch, der Baum, sie alle teilen denselben Atem). "Who cuts – kills – a tree is a sinner" (*Wer einen Baum fällt – tötet – ist ein Frevler*).

Looked at from an argumentation point of view, one could argue with Cox (1982) that the tree is here taken as "unique." Cox introduces uniqueness as one aspect of the topos of the irreparable. This topos he takes from Perelman and Olbrechts-Tyteca "as one of several 'lines of argument relating to the preferable'" (1982, p. 228). The trees here are depicted as irretrievable once cut down and are thereby anthropomorphized. It also offers an explanation why the argument often brought forward by the proponents – that,

[4] On the difference of topos and argument theme see Hannken-Illjes (2008).

although 250 trees will have to go, 5,000 will be planted once the construction work is done – fails to persuade the protesters.[5] They reply that these trees will need a very long time to grow into trees of comparable strength. And something else seems to be at work here: that you cannot just replace a tree with another one, as you cannot just substitute a person for another one.

But I shall stop this line of analysis before it has really started. Conventional arguments employing the theme "tree" can easily be identified in the broader environmentalist discourse as well as in the specific protest against Stuttgart 21 (which is not solely a protest out of environmentalist considerations). Those would include the tree as a habitat: you cannot fell this tree because it gives shelter to insects and mammals. In the case of Stuttgart 21 this argument has been put forward with respect to the hermit beetle, which lived in the trees and is threatened with extinction. Also the trees would be depicted as useful, as they clean the air and provide a resting place. This argument for Stuttgart 21 would take into account the geography of the city, which sits like a cauldron within steep hills, with the park and its trees as a central area to provide the inner city with fresh air. It is not overly surprising that these common arguments can be found in the Stuttgart 21 discourse. Analyzing them could be an interesting and worthwhile undertaking. At the same time, these arguments seem to be interchangeable among various protest sites, had they not been accompanied by references to the concrete trees in the Schlossgarten and the practices that surrounded them. Here the conventional argument themes with their history are coupled with the materiality that can be experienced: a coupling of a general discursive unit with a specific thing that is open to experience.

This coupling and the notion of specificity are represented by many personal narratives, especially by older protesters. It is the theme of these trees as survivors. These trees were protected by the citizens during World War II, when the inner city of Stuttgart was bombed. This is a narrative with a clearly argumentative function that appears in very different forms and functions as one of the leading arguments.[6] And these trees were left standing during the cold winters ("hunger winters") just after the Second World

[5] See open letter by the Parkschützer to the mayor of Stuttgart who wrote in a public letter addressed to two children that although some trees would need to be felled, many more would afterwards be planted. http://www.parkschuetzer.de/wissenswertes/habensiekinder

[6] This was also apparent in one of the interviews with participants of the protest.

War, when the citizens of Stuttgart used pretty much everything they could find as firewood. As one user on the platform of the "Parkschützer" (the park guardians) writes:

> Stuttgart's green lung must not be excavated, otherwise we will all have shortage of breath. Also, the park was given to us by King Wilhelm, who was close to the citizens. Nobody can just take it away from us. In the hard winters of the 40ies in the last century, the freezing people saved this park and did not cut it down. Because it has given them and still gives us a place for recreation and health. Hence: "No excavators in the park!" ("Stuttgarts grüne Lunge darf nicht angebaggert werden, sonst bekommen wir alle Atemnot. Außerdem wurde uns der Park vom bürgernahen König Wilhelm geschenkt. Den Park darf uns niemand einfach wegnehmen. In den harten Wintern der 40er Jahre des vergangenen Jahrhunderts schonten frierende Bürger diesen Park und holzten ihn nicht ab, grade weil er ihnen und uns bis heute zur Erholung und Gesundheit dient. Also Bagger weg vom Park!!!!!" (roberta penz)).[7]

From a formal point of view, what is employed here is a classical "more or less" topos. At the same time it becomes obvious that this is about specific trees. So I want to shift the focus to those specific trees and how they were acted upon in order to make them meaningful and a part in the protest.

Guarding the guardian

In 2010 and 2011 the "Schlossgarten" was – next to the building of the main station itself – the central place for protest. Here 250 trees were supposed to be felled for preliminary construction work. Starting in the middle of 2010, protesters occupied the "Schlossgarten" and along with it some of the trees. Trees were being decorated, tents were built underneath the trees, the picket had its place among the trees, political and cultural events took place, there was music, there was food. The park was also a place for spiritual practices like prayers and meditations. The "Schlossgarten" and especially its trees became a place for protest and exemplified what Endres and Senda-Cook stated for places of protest in general: "Place is a performer along with activists in making and unmaking the possibilities of protest" (2001, p. 258). The trees were decorated and utilized in quite different ways. One tree had

[7] http://www.parkschuetzer.de/php/public.php?page=discussions, accessed 28.12.2012

so many teddy bears – large and small ones – strung around it that its trunk was barely visible. Others were decorated with teddy bears and political leaflets. One trunk held a large poster, reading "My friend, the tree. This tree must not die and must not fall. Then my heart would go with him." In the treetops many houses were built and constantly occupied. This image of the occupied tree is one I want to take a closer look at. Here two arguments, two topoi merge that at first sight might appear to be contradictory: the tree as shelter and the tree as in need of protection.

On the one hand there is the tree as a shelter: The occupation makes the notion of the tree as shelter open to experience. Unlike the argument of the habitat, the shelter for the hermit beetle, this shelter can be seen and felt. Anybody could climb into the tree house and experience what it means to be protected by a tree. And many people will probably remember what it meant to climb into a tree as a child and being protected and shielded from view by it. These trees were not *like* shelters, they *were* shelters. These same practices – exhibiting the tree as a shelter – feed into another topos. By making the strength of the trees visible, their vulnerability is stressed at the same time. The trees are at the same time depicted as in need of protection, most clearly in the notion by one group of protesters of the tree as a godchild. This group of protesters called itself "Baumpaten" (tree sponsors or tree godparents). I chose the latter translation because – as also evidenced by the teddy bears – at least some of the protesters related to the trees as to persons, vulnerable persons. Hence being a tree-godparent implied taking responsibility for someone vulnerable and possibly in need of protection. What is striking, again, is that these people were not "like godparents," they *were* godparents. This is underscored in their vow: "This tree has a godparent. I allow everybody to come to my godtree, to rest in his shade, to meet others there, to celebrate, sing, laugh, sleep, just do what you like. I would enjoy more godparents. I ask everybody to protect my godtree, It is prohibited to cause harm to my godtree."[8] ("Dieser Baum hat einen Paten. Ich erlaube jedem, meinen Patenbaum aufzusuchen, sich in seinem Schatten auszuruhen, sich mit anderen dort zu treffen, dort zu feiern, singen, lachen, schlafen, einfach zu tun was gefällt. Ich freue mich über weitere Paten. Ich bitte jeden, meinen Patenbaum nach besten Kräften zu schützen. Es ist verboten meinem Patenbaum Schaden zuzufügen"). This vow establishes a close relation of the individual protester to the individual tree.

[8] www.baumpaten-schlossgarten.de/?seite=zertifikat, as of 14.01.2013

By means of the specific, material tree, open to experience, two seemingly opposed arguments are integrated: the tree as shelter and the tree as godchild. Something (or someone) who protects is, while protecting, in need of protection. One could argue at this point that the tree functions simply as a non-technical proof in the Aristotelian sense and thereby in itself does not belong to the realm of rhetoric. As Aristotle puts it, those proofs are "not supplied by the speaker but are at the outset" (1980, p. 12). He also says of them that they are used rather than invented. However, the trees are not just employed by rhetors, but rhetors, by granting them personhood and turning them into shelters, act upon them in a way to turn them into actors that cannot be dismissed. It is an essential part of making the trees part of the protest to transform them into actors themselves. This position of the trees in the protest might also explain how the felling of the trees was treated.

In February 2012, 250 trees were cut down in the Schlossgarten. The trees are gone. You can look at what is left: a void – an empty space, a construction site. Thereby a place for protest, the central place of the movement, is gone and the tree as an argument has become unavailable, or rather, publicly invisible. At the same time the trees are still available for the protest, but in a very different form. Many of the trees – that is, their large trunks – have been taken to a forest, close to the city center. Here, in the Feuerbacher forest, I encountered what could be called a public viewing of the deceased and a death watch. I first saw this mourning ritual on a Youtube video,[9] documenting the whereabouts of the trees and talking about them. When I saw the video, my first impression was that now the protest had become somewhat obscure. Sanctuary lamps could be seen in the trees, the faces of the people on the videos were those of mourners. But when I went to the forest to look at this myself, my impression changed somewhat: there was a sign above the trees, stating that these were cut down in the Schlossgarten. I first went there around Christmas, and although there were no candles, the trees were decorated with stars made of straw. One could even argue that they still demanded attention, that they could not "just be dismissed" by the protesters. What they demanded was a form of burial and mourning. This was certainly no form of protest that

[9] http://www.youtube.com/watch?v=syciS9-ItJ4 (last access 05.07.2013), also http://www.youtube.com/watch?v=yAcFoOtELTs (last access 05.07.2013)

was directed towards other people, but it seemed to function for the protest movement as a form of internal identification work – a view also voiced by several protesters themselves.

Conclusion

In this analysis I have tried to show how the materiality of the trees in the Schlossgarten fed into the protest against Stuttgart 21, and how the material is related to the symbolic. Not only is the tree material and a "thing" acted upon, it even in a way becomes an actor of the protest itself. This is due to strategies of anthropomorphization – especially in evidence in the discursive and topical power of the tree and in the way the trees become a central locus of protest practices, discursive as well as material. The trees were taken up in their specificity in different ways: through personal narratives of the Schlossgarten and its history, by decorating them with political as well with personal items, and, not least, by inhabiting them and making them the very place of protest. All these ways of acting upon the trees used the experienceable materiality of the tree: the wood, which holds posters and tree houses, gives shelter, can be touched, smelled, leaned against. At the same time these ways of integrating the trees into the protest relate to the strength the tree has as a topos in very different discourses. Here the material and the symbolic are bound together and refer to one another. This interaction of a strong topos with the material trees that allowed for a wide range of practices could also explain its potency: the trees were common and specific enough to integrate very different forms of protest and political beliefs. Thereby "the trees" opened the protest up to a wider public and offered a form of common ground with personal experience attached to it. Thus they also offered a space for those protesters who usually would not take part in a public protest.

In this way the case of the S21 protests illustrates what the concept of rhetorical citizenship refers to: the focus on the enactment of citizenship and its rhetorical processes and forms. The S21 protests show that – and how – citizenship is not only a status but at the same time needs to be performed, to be enacted. The S21 protests achieved a broad mobilization of citizens by relying on practices and topoi that centered around the park and the trees that allowed a very diverse movement to unify. Interestingly enough, the notion of what it means to be a citizen in the city of Stuttgart, to take the park as a gift to the citizens of Stuttgart, addressed the concept of citizenship explicitly. After the felling, "the trees" allowed for rituals that might have helped some protesters to reform and regroup through symbolic action whose aim was more internal than external. The mourning here represents a strategy to use when something has been irreparably destroyed, aimed at the reintegration of a group rather than affecting an opponent in a controversy. At the same time the trees seemed to demand this kind of ritual treatment. In conclusion, the materiality of place and thing affected participants in such a way that the theme "tree" was taken up not only intellectually, but also by experience.

> "Well," said the tree, straightening herself up as she could, "well an old stump is good for sitting and resting. Come Boy, come sit down. Sit down and rest." And the boy did. And the tree was happy… The end. (Shel Silverstein, *The Giving Tree*)

References

Ammann, K. and S. Hirschauer. (1997). Die Befremdung der eigenen Kultur. Ein Programm. In K. Ammann and S. Hirschauer (Eds.), *Die Befremdung der eigenen Kultur*. Frankfurt am Main: Suhrkamp.

Aristoteles (1980). *Rhetorik*. München: Fink.

Asen, R. (2004). A Discourse Theory of Citizenship. *Quarterly Journal of Speech* 90, 189-211.

Beuys, J. B. Blume and R. Rappmann. (2006). *Gespräche über Bäume*. Wangen/Allgäu: FIU-Verlag.

Cox, R. (1982). The Die Is Cast: Topical and Ontological Dimensions of the Locus of the Irreparable. *Quarterly Journal of Speech* 68, 227-239.

Endres, D. and S. Senda-Cook. (2011). Location Matters: The Rhetoric of Place in Protest. *Quarterly Journal of Speech* 97, 257-282.

Gumbrecht, H.U. and K. L. Pfeiffer (Ed.). (1988). *Materialität der Kommunikation*. Frankfurt am Main: Suhrkamp.

Gumbrecht, H.U. Rhythmus und Sinn. (1988). In H.U. Gumbrecht and K.L. Pfeiffer (Eds.), *Materialität der Kommunikation* (pp. 714-729). Frankfurt am Main: Suhrkamp.

Hannken-Illjes, Kati, "On Building a Winning Team," in *Proceedings of the OSSA-Conference on Argumentation*, edited by Hans Hansen and Christopher Tindale Windsor 2008. CD-ROM.

Ivie, R.L. (2002). Rhetorical Deliberation and Democratic Politics in the Here and Now. *Rhetoric and Public Affairs* 5, 277-285.

Kock, C. and L. Villadsen. (2012). Introduction: Citizenship as a Rhetorical Practice. In

C. Kock and L. Villadsen (Eds.), *Rhetorical Citizenship and Public Deliberation* (pp. 4-15). Pennsylvania State University: Pennsylvania State University Press.

Latour, B. (2005). *Reassembling the Social.* Oxford: Oxford UP.

Marcus, G.E. (1995). Ethnography in/of the World System: The Emergence of Multi-Sited Ethnography. *Annual Reviews Anthropology* 24, 95-117.

Prior, P. (2005). Toward The Ethnography of Argumentation: A Response to Richard Andrews' 'Models of Argumentation in Educational Discourse.' *Text* 25, 129-144.

Scheffer, T. K. Hannken-Illjes and A. Kozin. (2010). *Criminal Defence and Procedure: Comparative Ethnographies in the United Kingdom, United States and Germany.* Basingstoke: Palgrave.

"Cicero Would Love This Show": The Celebration of Rhetoric and Citizenship in *The West Wing*

ANNE ULRICH

Television shows, citizenship, and the display of rhetoric

"The more diverse a society becomes, the more pressing is the need for public reflection on what is best for the society as such and not just for its segments – in other words, the need for deliberation, for rhetoric." According to Christian Kock and Lisa Villadsen (2012, p. 4), rhetoric plays a central role in defining citizenship and in connecting individuals and groups with abstract political entities like the "nation" or the "state." In a face-to-face democracy like the ancient *polis*, the communitarian aspect was very concrete because citizens knew each other and participated together in the *ekklesia* and *dikasteria* and therefore had a clear sense of membership and affiliation. But in contemporary societies, as Dominique Leydet (2011) rightly remarks, "[c]itizens do not meet under an oak tree to formulate the laws; they are basically strangers and citizens' involvement in the politics of representative democracies is episodic and diluted. Politics in this context cannot be expected to play a central role in most individuals' lives; something else must generate the trust and loyalty necessary to the functioning of a political community." But what are trust-generating factors in a fragmented and diverse society? In this paper, I argue that television can be an alternative forum for public deliberation and the formation of citizenship. Kock and Villadsen would claim that television involves citizens "at the receiving end of public deliberation" who engage themselves "in 'inner' deliberation." (2012, p. 5) The authors are certainly thinking of factual television, such as electoral debates, news broadcasting, talk shows or other forms of political journalism. But I want to show that fictional television, especially the political television series, can also be interpreted as both active and passive forms of public engagement and that their depiction of the art of rhetoric is worth investigating in the context of rhetorical citizenship. In fact, it is crucial to explore fictional forms of public engagement as a reaction to and extension of factual forms of citizenship.

There has been a renaissance of political issues in television series during the past years, for instance in series like *Borgen* (DR1, Denmark, 2010–), *The Thick of It* (BBC, UK, 2005-2012), *Veep* (HBO, USA, 2012–), or *Scandal* (ABC, USA, 2012–), to name only some of the most prominent. Their tradition goes back to UK series like *Yes, Minister* and *Yes, Prime Minister* (BBC Two, UK, 1980–1988; repr. Gold, UK, 2013–) or *House of Cards* which was recently re-adapted for the US (BBC, UK, 1990; repr. Netflix, USA, 2013–). Each of these series chooses politicians and their staff as the main characters and the political stage as central scenery, showing everyday political procedures like negotiations, photo-ops, press interviews, etc., as well as extraordinary situations like general elections, evolving national crises or private scandals.

Most of these series paint a rather cynical picture of politics. They use the political more as a backdrop against which a further drama or another sitcom unfolds. Thus, the plot has political connotations, but is not politically motivated – the only political purpose of such series is, at best, to question the uprightness of politics. *The West Wing*, in contrast, is more serious about politics – despite its orientation to entertainment. While other series mercilessly exaggerate the depiction of politicians and their staffers, *The West Wing* remains more realistic and therefore develops a fictional but quite plausible alternative to "real" politics. Aaron Sorkin, the creator of the series, imagined a fictional US administration that differed quite clearly from the Clinton Administration at the time. By making viewers identify with the fictional president and his staff, the series sought to activate their desire for political change; in this way, the series has a relatively strong political agenda.

Much has been already written about *The West Wing* as a political television series. But only a few studies have drawn attention to the political rhetoric of the show. I want to concentrate on the show's diverse depictions of political rhetoric in order to crystallize the show's own conception of deliberative rhetoric as a specific modality of public engagement. First, I will draw a sketch of the series' general plot and cast and introduce show runner Aaron Sorkin as a political orator. Then I will focus on three different rhetorical aspects to characterize the show's specific enhancement of rhetorical citizenship.

An entertaining civics lesson

The West Wing aired on NBC in the United States from September 1999 to May 2006 and was created by Aaron Sorkin, an award-winning US-American screenwriter and television producer. The show sought to entertain its viewers in a specific way, by addressing them *as* citizens and by showing them the process of making political rhetoric, and not just as an ordinary TV audience interested in primetime entertainment – even if the viewers were not US citizens. Its appeal to citizenship goes beyond national borders and involves the representation of politics and political rhetoric in a plausible and skillful way – almost based on the following aphorism quoted by *The West Wing* character Sam Seaborn, "Aristotle says, a probable impossibility is preferable to an improbable possibility" (Season 4, Episode 8: *Process Stories*). In seven seasons and 155 episodes in total, the series accompanied the fictional US-American President Josiah 'Jed' Bartlet and his well-educated and quick-witted White House staff during his two terms of office. *The West Wing* is not only a show about politics, it is a political show. According to the taxonomy of Terry Christensen and Peter J. Haas, *The West Wing* is a show with both political content and political intent and is therefore "explicitly political", i.e. it depicts various aspects of the political system as well as delivering a political message (2005, p. 8). That's why I consider Sorkin to be a political orator who was actively engaging in public discourse and openly performing his vision of citizenship through the show. Although a great number of people were involved in the production of the series (John Wells and Thomas Schlamme, for instance, were both important players), Sorkin had a crucial role in the creative production process and can therefore be considered to be the main author and producer of the show. From a rhetorical perspective, his name stands for the collective authorship of the show.

Who are the characters in the show, and what is their relation to rhetoric? Martin Sheen plays US President Jed Bartlet, a president that is often described as an idealized version of left-leaning presidents like Jimmy Carter or Bill Clinton (Rothöhler 2012, p. 19). The character is catholic, a Democrat, a Nobel-prize winning economist, a quick-witted, elitist wiseguy with an immense instinct for power, and a dedicated and responsible, but also very hard-to-assess, "leader of the free world". As a bit of a political pun, the fictional President is a direct descendant of a certain Josiah Bartlet, a real-world signatory of the Declaration of Independence (Clark 2005, p. 224). Jed Bartlet is conceived as a charismatic character for a well-educated public: he received a comprehensive education in the humanities, is well-versed in the Bible, and likes to "entertain" his staff with erudite anecdotes, preferably in Latin (Cicero would love that, too). Although he is thought to be a "good guy," the character becomes more ambiguous over the course of the series, which increases the "reality effect" of the show. But above all, Jed Bartlet is a rhetorical talent. The Bartlet "entourage," which consists of seven main characters, is conceived in a similar way: they are both admirable and sometimes reprehensible because of their flaws and weaknesses, in life as well as in politics – and they are depicted as masters of rhetoric in many different ways. Chief of Staff Leo McGarry (John Spencer), Bartlet's oldest and most like-minded political companion, is something like the White House "consigliere," laying out the strategic guidelines according to which the President's staff should act. The continuous dialogs between Deputy Chief of Staff Josh Lyman (Bradley Whitford) and his assistant Donna Moss (Janel Moloney) reveal quite a few absurdities of the Washington "political machine," and their mutual attraction (and denial of that attraction) is responsible for a certain soap opera feeling (see also van Zoonen 2005, pp. 19–35). Communications Director Toby Ziegler (Richard Schiff) and his Deputy Sam Seaborn (Rob Lowe) are both speech writers and spin doctors, and therefore represent hard-working "rhetorical craftsmen." Press Secretary C.J. Gregg (Alison Janney), another "rhetorical craftswoman," deals with the Washington journalists and the 24/7 news cycle. Finally, the President's personal aide Charlie Young (Dulé Hill) plays the part of an "ordinary young man" and functions as a rhetorical sidekick for the Bartlet character.

It has often been pointed out that Jed Bartlet is not the only character modeled on real world people. Several reviews of the series claim that many of these characters are based on real members of the Clinton administrations: Communications Director Toby Ziegler is supposed to depict Gene Sperling, Deputy Communications Director Sam Seaborn parallels George Stephanopoulos, Deputy Chief of Staff Josh Lyman is a mirror of Paul Begala, and Press Secretary C.J. Gregg is a stand-in for Dee Dee Myers (see Waxman 2003, p. 204, and Podhoretz 2003, p. 222). Former Clinton Press Secretary Dee Dee Myers also served as a consultant for the show and even as a screenwriter for several episodes – as did other former White House employees. Thus, with regard to the main characters, the setting, and the fact that the story is set in the present, there are a lot of direct references to actual political reality. This is very important in order to understand the political nature of the show and the Aristotelian "probable impossibilities" that Sorkin wants to propose to his audience. From a rhetorical perspective, his intention was to "realize" his White House and his portrayal of the presidency in order to open up new spaces for conceivable political possibilities. His inspiration was taken from the real White House and real American politics, but his goal was to depict another, "better" White House and a "better" American politics in order to work towards it in the real world.

The West Wing also focuses on citizenship by confronting the audience with political topics and political problems, and it becomes entertainment by presenting them in a very witty and amusing way. The show's ratings averaged between 8 and 17 million viewers per season. Its audience was interested in politics, stemmed from both the Democratic and the Republican electorate, and averaged an income over $100,000 (Finn 2003, p. 118f.; an analysis of this target demographic would be interesting, but is outside the scope of this paper). According to Jeannie Rutenburg, viewers claimed to enjoy "better looking staffers who are funnier and talk faster than real ones," (2003, p. 12) but they also enjoyed the regular "civil education" that came along with every episode. Critics such as Simon Rothöhler praised the "historically profound study of political institutions," as well as the ability to illustrate "sophisticated aspects of U.S.-American constitutional reality." (2012, p. 52) Over the course of seven seasons, the series went through almost every conceivable political scenario in both an informative and entertaining way: we witness a filibuster (Season 2, Episode 17: *The Stackhouse Filibuster*), a shutdown due to budget negotiations (Season 5, Episode 8: *Shutdown*), the nomination of judges for the Supreme Court (Season 5, Episode 17: *The Supremes*), the unfolding of a presidential electoral campaign (Seasons 6 and 7) and even a typo in the constitution (Season 7, Episode 21 *Institutional Memory*).

The show uses rhetorical *evidentia* and shows us democracy in the making. Other Sorkin TV shows like *Sports Night*, *Studio 60 on the Sunset Strip*, and, currently, *The Newsroom* are also backstage shows that cast an eye behind the scenes of television shows. The aesthetic concept of the backstage as the "frontstage" (Goffman 1959) on *The West Wing* may, at first glance, imply that politics is nothing but another television show, and may therefore recall academic discourse on the dramatization and mediatization of politics (Meyer 2002) or the so-called television malaise thesis, which holds that television only provides entertainment and transforms serious information or debate into entertainment. Yet, Sorkin's *The West Wing* turns the tables by overcoming the skepticism of TV through TV itself. It addresses its audience as a citizenry and *not* as an uninformed, misguided or manipulated "mass." I agree with Liesbet van Zoonen that series like *The West Wing* "enable people to think about the dilemmas that politicians and politics face" (2005, p. 137) and confront them with new knowledge about specific aspects of politics that allow them to adjust their image of politics again and again. Simon Rothöhler has said that an important effect of the show is that "almost every episode contains a detail you want to google," or provokes a question you want to answer (Rothöhler 2012, p. 52). By gradually getting to know both the various aspects of politics and the characters of the show, the audience is invited to engage in the process of 'making' politics.

The show relies on the principle of para-social interaction, a concept of television theory elaborated by Donald Horton and R. Richard Wohl (1956) that explains how viewers establish a virtual but vivid relationship to their favorite characters. By identifying with one or more characters, viewers take sides and therefore not only observe but also participate in their actions. This is underlined by the general "backstage" strategy. While the real President and his real staffers can only be seen by the public performing their professional roles on the "frontstage," the fictional characters of *The West Wing* are also shown "backstage," where viewers can see them as they "really" are. This strategy of creating authenticity was one of the main drivers of the show's success, not least because of the way it created a professional and entertaining manner for the subject matter of presidential politics to become pop culture. In the real world, we are either denied a look behind the scenes of the President and his staff, or the images that we do receive are completely staged – we thus never have the chance to get close to these figures. With *The West Wing*, on the other hand, we are able to develop an almost intimate relationship with the protagonists, and we identify with and pick up on their problems, which could, indeed, be our own political problems because of the way that Sorkin blends fiction and reality in the writing of the show. Over the course of the series, the aversions or affections that we have for the protagonists develop into political attitudes that increase our readiness for civic engagement.

Rhetoric behind the scenes

If we consider *The West Wing* to essentially be a show about rhetoric, the aesthetic concept of the backstage becoming the frontstage indicates an important deviation from the common display of rhetoric in film and television.

When political rhetoric is featured in film or television it is usually depicted by an actor delivering a speech accompanied by the "shot–reverse shot" technique, which shows the reaction of the audience. In such cases, the character rises to speak during some substantial crisis and becomes an "orator" through some kind of fundamental rhetorical speech act that resonates well in the represented audience. We can think of Marlon Brando as Mark Antony in the 1953 film adaption of Shakespeare's *Julius Caesar*, for example, or of Denzel Washington as Malcolm X in the Spike Lee movie (for further examples see the section "Movie Speeches" on www.americanrhetoric.com). These depictions of political orators are best described as the perfect combination of the Aristotelian *zōon politikon* and *zōon logon echōn*: a person that gains his (or, more rarely, her) status only through the power of speech that nature has given him or her. The speech is performed at its best and it is successful and effective beyond any doubt. In these depictions, only the frontstage is shown, and the orator doesn't show up on stage until he's already perfect.

The West Wing, on the other hand, isn't afraid of disenchanting us of this artificial image of rhetoric. In fact, it shows the manufacturing of speeches and other rhetorical forms by shifting the emphasis from the frontstage to the backstage and from the product to the production process (according to ancient rhetoric, the five canons of rhetoric). This reversal and its aesthetic appeal are implicitly referred to by *West Wing* character Leo McGarry in one of the first episodes when he remarks, "there are two things in the world you never want to let people see how you make 'em: laws and sausages." (Season 1, Episode 4: *Five Votes Down*) "And speeches," the rhetorician would add, for if the audience "sees how you make 'em," they would instantly lose their persuasiveness. This phenomenon was described by the ancient rhetorical notion of *dissimulatio artis*, the dissimulation of the rhetorical technique in order to inspire the confidence of the audience. Aaron Sorkin deliberately ignored this suggestion by showing and explicitly celebrating "how you make 'em." By analyzing crucial scenes in the activities of the White House orators, I want to show how Sorkin conceives of "rhetoric" and how we can understand the series itself as, literally speaking, *epideictic rhetoric*, i.e., a demonstration of rhetoric.

The collective fabrication of speeches

In *The West Wing*, speeches are perfectly delivered, but they are also shown as hard-earned achievements. The most important speech that the series centers on is the annual State of the Union, but there are also speeches at fundraising events, in front of lobbyist organizations or during electoral campaigns. The third of the five canons of rhetoric, the *elocutio*, is reflected upon in several episodes, for instance in Season 2, Episode 13 (*Bartlet's Third State of the Union*). In this episode, Communications Director Toby Ziegler discusses the concrete wording of the speech with another speechwriter and the president:

> TOBY: Delete "vigorously" from the first sentence.
>
> [...]
>
> SPEECHWRITER 2: We're not going to vigorously pursue campaign finance reform?
>
> TOBY: No, we're just gonna pursue it regularly.
>
> SPEECHWRITER 2: Not vigorously.
>
> TOBY: Not tonight. [to Leo] McGowan says we're fine. He feels the word "vigorously"'s inflammatory.
>
> [...]
>
> BARTLET: Bob Novak just said this was the speech of my political life. You know how many times I've heard that?
>
> TOBY: Sir, Senator McGowan say's we're fine if we cut "vigorously." (All quotes from *The West Wing* episodes are taken from http://www.westwingtranscripts.com)

In this scene, the quite vigorous claim that this is the "speech of my political life" is contrasted with the petty reservations of a powerful senator in regard to the adverb "vigorously." Besides being a nice joke, the scene shows how arduous the fabrication of a presidential speech is – especially in light of the annotations and reservations of countless powerful senators and other important government functionaries that have to be considered and incorporated up to five minutes before the speech is to be delivered. But this example also shows the love and the feeling for language that Sorkin puts in the mouths of the speechwriters. In Season 4, Episode 14 (*Inauguration*), speechwriter Will Bailey (played by Joshua Malina), says to the President, "there's a ... partnership, sir, that can develop between someone and his speechwriter. It happens over time. You get to know just where he likes his commas and why he says self-government instead of government. Why he doesn't like the word 'implement' but does like the word 'obfuscate'. Like jazz musicians ..." Additionally, Season 1, Episode 2 (*Post hoc, ergo propter hoc*) features speechwriter Sam Seaborn formally proclaiming:

"I'm a lawyer and a speechwriter. I argue for a living, and I'm sought after because I'm good at it."

But elocution and argumentation are not the only rhetorically relevant issues in the fabrication of speeches in *The West Wing*. In the previously mentioned episode *Five Votes Down*, President Bartlet gives a dinner speech promoting a bill on gun control that is supposed to pass Congress a few days later. We see him performing the final paragraphs of the speech, interrupted by several cuts to the President's staff backstage. At the same time, Toby Ziegler is watching the speech on a monitor and orchestrating the President like a conductor with a baton, "take a beat. [pause] There you go," – and the President is obviously "following" these instructions. But towards the end of the speech, Bartlet begins to extemporize for just a few moments. Toby – who has a penchant for skepticism and pessimism – complains to his deputy Sam about how the President high-handedly, "blew the D section," – while Sam clearly finds the speech "outstanding". Further on, Toby tells Press Secretary C.J. Gregg that, "Sam wrote two and a half paragraphs and I wrote thirty-seven pages." This makes it clear that the speech had at least three authors, and that there is a possible conflict between those who wrote it and the person who actually delivers it. This conflict results in an ironic exchange between the President and his Communications Director:

> BARTLET: What'd you think?
>
> TOBY: I thought my work was outstanding, Mr. President. [...] Couldn't help but notice you got a little extemporaneous there in the D section.
>
> BARTLET: Oh, you noticed that, did you? [...] Yes. I did a little polish right up there on my feet.
>
> TOBY: Yes indeed.
>
> BARTLET: Right in front of everybody. I looked to the side at one point, you know. I half expected to see you coming at me with a salad fork.

There is no doubt that Toby is none too happy with the President improvising and changing the speech deliberately before his eyes. We thus have to deal with a fragmented and collective oratorship, which is made even more difficult by the despicable "political machine" in Washington, as is shown, for example, in Season 1, Episode 12 (*He Shall, From Time to Time*).

In this episode, the speechwriting process is widely obstructed by characters other than the speechwriting team or the President – and their reservations are not merely concerned with elocutionary aspects. As the title indicates, the episode focuses once again on the annual State of the Union. *The West Wing* shows us how many people are involved in the shaping of both content and form of the speech. Drafts circulate weeks before the date (see also Schlesinger 2008), and Toby has to sit down with interest groups, party members, members of Congress and Cabinet Members that have their own agenda to write or change certain paragraphs. Thus, the speech is shown more as an object of diplomatic political negotiations than as a result of the best oratorical craft. In another episode, *The Portland Trip* (Season 2, Episode 7), the staff is working on a speech on education at the last minute while on a flight to Portland. Toby complains about how great oratory is being sacrificed to tactical decisions and political compromise.

> SAM: Toby, you're the one for the last six months who's been saying we need a radical approach...
>
> TOBY: [raising his voice] Yes, yes I have, and I got shouted down in every meeting! I'd love to write a speech about a radical new approach to education, but we don't have one! So unless we can come up with an idea and implement it before land in Portland, I'd prefer not to paint a picture in the interest of great oratory.

In this way, *The West Wing* explicitly reflects not only on the collective authorship inside the White House, but also on the mutual relationships between the President, his staff and the political machine that has "shouted [them] down in every meeting." What a president can say when he rises to speak obviously depends on his respective range of power. I wouldn't go so far as to say that the other political actors are also "authors" of the President's speech, but their agendas are a constraint that cannot be denied or ignored, and thus constitute what the sociologist Anthony Giddens (1984, p. 31) would call a structure of domination. Without going too far into detail, the staff's struggle for the right wording in every speech can be understood as a constant struggle for agency in a pre-structured communication environment – even if the actor is the "leader of the free world." This is also a struggle for public engagement and citizenship that the audience can take inspiration from. When it is successful in *The West Wing*, oratory isn't "magic," but rather a hard-won battle in a complex and challenging environment.

Another topic in *The West Wing's* depiction of "oratory" is the kind of self-referential presentation of a speech on television and the measurement of its effects on the audience. In *100,000 Airplanes* (Season 3, Episode 12), there is another State of the Union to prepare. Once more, we participate in the production process, but this time Sorkin starts at the end, as the delivery of the speech is shown on monitors in the rooms of the "National Strategic Group." As Sam Seaborn explains to a visiting journalist, the speech is being exposed to real-time polling. The polls are visualized as blue (Democrat), red (Republican) and green (independent) lines going up and down across a graph as the speech is being delivered. Sam predicts a peak of all three lines for the following paragraph in Bartlet's speech:

> BARTLET [on T.V.] Now in a new century, when we meet and master new forms of aggression and hatred, ignorance and evil, our vigilance in the face of oppression and global terror will be unequaled by any moment of human history.
>
> LISA [the journalist]: Now you're cooking.
>
> BARTLET [on T.V.]: And to the enemies of freedom, the enemies of democracy, the enemies of America, the enemies of humanity itself, we say here tonight with one voice. There is no corner of this earth so remote, no cave so dark, that you will not be found and brought to light and ended.

Here, we recognize a different tone in the speech of the fictional President following the real-world 9/11 event, but this change of tone is not the focus of this essay. Instead, it is the way that Sorkin stresses the importance of public opinion and visualizes the way it shapes and affects the speech. Once again, the delivery of the speech is only a vehicle in order to show what's normally behind the screen – in this case the submission of political rhetoric to polling and public opinion. This arrangement can be just as limiting as lobbyism and opposition, and it is one that is present throughout the whole series as the audience learns that political rhetoric is about seeking attention and goodwill, about compromise and, sometimes, about compromising on your ideals. But it is also about regaining the sovereignty of interpretation of political or social reality. Thus, *The West Wing* is absolutely ambivalent: it both praises and criticizes political rhetoric, while other TV series prefer to provide a purely cynical look at politics.

The "walk and talk" and "real" debates

The series' most significant aesthetic feature is not the monolog, but rather dialog. In the words of film scholar Thomas Morsch (2010, p. 228), "in terms of the series' portrayal of politics, the 'walk and talk' is assigned the role of visually dramatizing what, in itself, fails to provide interesting images, but is essential to the series' idea of politics: the verbal exchange of political arguments." There are several very long shots in almost every episode that illustrate the series' extensive depiction of dialog and debate. The characters walk through the labyrinthine corridors of the White House, talking at high speed and outperforming each other in quick-wittedness. The walks are orchestrated by Sorkin and his director Thomas Schlamme in a very sophisticated manner – the wit is not limited to one character but is the result of all characters performing the "art of argument." Not only does this prove to be the right tactic for making agreements internally, but it is also presented as a way to conduct political negotiations between the staff and lobbyists, members of Congress, opposition politicians and others. While in the real world such debates are held behind closed doors, *The West Wing* presents them openly – and as a very dynamic form of communication. As Morsch puts it, "to speak constitutes the chief form of action." (p. 230)

The last season focuses on the presidential race as Bartlet's second term in office comes to an end. The seventh episode, *The Debate*, features a quite remarkable rhetorical form: the two presidential candidates, Alan Alda as Arnie Vinick (Republican) and Jimmy Smits as a Latino candidate Matt Santos (Democrat), staged a live, improvised debate on television. This kind of live "improv debate" was an exceptional challenge for both actors because they were forced to debate *as if* they were real candidates. To increase the illusion of reality, the debate took place on the same set that had been used in the actual presidential debate between President George W. Bush and Senator John Kerry on NBC in 2004. And as in real life, the debate was surveyed by a pollster, with the following result, according to the *Washington Post* (de Moraes 2005), "before the episode, viewers between 18 and 29 preferred Santos over Vinick, 54 percent to 37 percent. But after the debate, in which veteran Alda gutted pretty-boy Smits without him even knowing it, Vinick now leads among viewers under age 30, 56 percent to 42 percent." Unique episode formats like this underline the show's perspective on political reality (Skewes 2009). But even in this "realistic" debate setting, the TV show leaves enough space for political fantasy by staging a "real debate," as the fictional Republican candidate Arnie Vinick puts it:

> VINICK: You know, I've watched every televised Presidential debate that this country has ever had. And every time I heard them recite the rules, I always thought that meant they're not going to have a real debate. When the greatest hero of my party, Abraham Lincoln, debated, he didn't need any rules. He wasn't afraid of a real debate. Now I could do a 2-minute version of my Sensible Solution stump speech and I'm sure Congressman Santos has a memorized opening statement ready to go. And then we could go on with this ritual and let the rules decide how much you're going to learn about the next President of the United States, or we could have a debate Lincoln would have been proud of. We could junk the rules. We could let our able and judicious moderator ask us questions. And we could forget about whether each of us has the exact same number of seconds to speak. We could have a real debate if that's all right with you, Matt.

So, NBC has a fictional "real debate" that exceeds every "real" debate because of its spontaneity and sincerity. The actors stage an idealized, somehow adjusted debate that contains only "good" rhetoric. It reproduces, as Jeannie Rutenburg put it, "values of this civic humanism – peace, reason, freedom, and the rule of law," and explains why "Cicero would love this show" (Rutenburg 2003, p. 14).

Conclusion

By creating a both realistic and idealistic White House, Sorkin proposes a concrete political and rhetorical message: what if the president and his staff were wittier, what if they made better decisions, what if participating in the political process was entertaining, what if constitutional history was fun, what if debates weren't tainted by spin doctors and polls, what if a nuclear accident changed a whole election – and, last but not least: what if a Latino like Matt Santos was elected president? Sorkin suggests that this would be better than the actual White House. It is no secret that Sorkin's team got in touch with Barack Obama's advisor David Axelrod as early as 2004. In this way, the election of Barack Obama in 2008 somehow "imitated" the election of Matt Santos in the final season of the show in 2006, and this certainly is the strongest "political fantasy" to be found in the *The West Wing* script.

There is also no doubt that as political orators, the executive producers of the show, Sorkin and later John Wells, were very pleased that the Obama team lived out their scripts (Freedland 2008). But all political fantasies are closely linked to political reality, either by being accurate or dramatically convincing. I want to call this strategy "visionary plausibility," and it is a sophisticated and intriguing interplay of reality and fictionality. Never one-dimensional and always ambivalent, Sorkin creates, in his own words, a, "kind of a valentine to public service" (quoted from Clark 2005, p. 226). I think the term "valentine," as Thomas Morsch has also said, refers to the series being performative in a way that the audience cannot ignore. It demands a reaction, and at the very least a virtual sense of involvement that enhances political participation and identification – even beyond U.S. borders. Most of the problems depicted in the show resonate in other modern Western democracies as well. Even if political systems may differ slightly and non-American viewers may miss some subtle allusions, the general problems of political rhetoric in Western democracies are clearly the same. Thus, as Trevor and Shawn Parry-Giles (2002, p. 211) put it, "fictionalized representations of politics are powerful and accessible rhetorical forms, increasingly influential as they improve in technological sophistication and mimetic capacity. Such discourses play a central role in the definition and expression of political culture and political leaders" – and, if I may add – in the definition of rhetoric and citizenship.

References

Christensen, T. and P.J. Haas. (2005). *Projecting Politics: Political Messages in American Films*. New York: M.E. Sharpe.

Clark, E. (2005). The Bartlet Administration and Contemporary Populism in NBC's *The West Wing*. In M. Hammond and L. Mazdon (eds.), *The Contemporary Television Series* (pp. 224-243). Edinburgh: Edinburgh University Press.

Finn, P. (2003). *The West Wing*'s Textual President: American Constitutional Stability and the New Public Intellectual in the Age of Information. In P.C. Rollins and J.E. Connor (Eds.), *The West Wing: The American Presidency As Television Drama* (pp. 101-124). Syracuse: Syracuse University Press.

Freedland, J. (2008). From West Wing to the Real Thing: Scriptwriters Modelled TV's Ethnic Minority Candidate on Young Barack Obama. *The Guardian*, 21 February. http://www.guardian.co.uk/world/2008/feb/21/barackobama.uselections2008, accessed January 13, 2013.

Giddens, A. (1984). *The Constitution of Society.* Cambridge: Polity.

Goffman, E. (1959). *The Presentation of Self in Everyday Life.* New York et al.: Doubleday.

Horton, D. and R.R. Wohl. (1956). Mass Communication and Para-Social Interaction. Observation on Intimacy at a Distance. *Psychiatry* 19, 215–229.

Kock, C. and L.S. Villadsen. (2012). Introduction: Citizenship as a Rhetorical Practice. In C. Kock and L.S. Villadsen (Eds.), *Rhetorical Citizenship and Public Deliberation* (pp. 1–10). University Park, Pennsylvania: The Pennsylvania State University Press.

Leydet, D. (2011). Citizenship. The Stanford Encyclopedia of Philosophy. http://plato.stanford.edu/entries/citizenship/, accessed August 2, 2013.

Meyer, T. (2002). *Media Democracy: How the Media Colonize Politics.* Cambridge: Polity Press.

Moraes, L. de. (2005). Vinick Sways Voters, er, Viewers on "West Wing." *The Washington Post,* November 8, 2005, http://www.washingtonpost.com/wp-dyn/content/article/2005/11/07/AR2005110701712.html, accessed January 13, 2013.

Morsch, T. (2010). Representation, Allegory, Ecstasy – Fantasies of The Political In Contemporary Television Series. In C. Dreher (Ed.), *Auteur Series: The Re-Invention of Television* (pp. 200–248). Stuttgart: Merz & solitude.

Parry-Giles, T. and S.J. Parry-Giles. (2002). The West Wing's Prime-Time Presidentiality: Mimesis and Catharsis in a Postmodern Romance. *Quarterly Journal of Speech* 88, 209–227.

Podhoretz, J. (2003). The Liberal Imagination. In P.C. Rollins And J.E. Connor (Eds.), *The West Wing: The American Presidency as Television Drama* (pp. 222–231). Syracuse: Syracuse University Press.

Rothöhler, S. (2012). *The West Wing.* Zurich: diaphanes.

Rutenburg, J. (2003). Television Fantasy, Political Reality, And Pop Culture in Aaron Sorkin's *The West Wing. Film International* 6, 10–15.

Schlesinger, R. (2008). *White House Ghosts: Presidents and Their Speechwriters.* New York et al.: Simon & Schuster Paperbacks.

Skewes, E.A. (2009). Presidential Candidates and the Press on *The West Wing* and in the Real World. *Quarterly Review of Film and Video* 26, 131–142.

van Zoonen, L. (2005). *Entertaining the Citizen: When Politics and Popular Culture Converge.* Lanham: Rowman & Littlefield Publishers.

Waxman, S. (2003). Inside *The West Wing's* New World. In P.C. Rollins And J.E. Connor (Eds.), *The West Wing: The American Presidency as Television Drama* (pp. 203-212). Syracuse: Syracuse University Press.

The West Wing Transcripts, http://www.westwingtranscripts.com, accessed June 2, 2014.

List of mentioned episodes (in chronological order):

Season 1, Episode 2: *Post hoc, ergo propter hoc*, original air date September 29, 1999.
Season 1, Episode 4: *Five Votes Down,* original air date October 13, 1999.
Season 1, Episode 12: *He Shall, From Time to Time*, original air date January 12, 2000.
Season 2, Episode 7 *The Portland Trip*, original air date November 15, 2000.
Season 2, Episode 13: *Bartlet's State of the Union*, original air date February 7, 2001.
Season 2, Episode 17: *The Stackhouse Filibuster*, original air date March 14, 2001.
Season 3, Episode 12: *100.000 Airplanes*, original air date January 16, 2002.
Season 4, Episode 8: *Process Stories*, original air date November 13, 2002.
Season 4, Episode 14: *Inauguration*, original air date February 5, 2003.
Season 5, Episode 8: *Shutdown*, original air date November 19, 2003.
Season 5, Episode 17: *The Supremes,* original air date March 24, 2004.
Season 7, Episode 7: *The Debate*, original air date November 6, 2005.
Season 7, Episode 21: *Institutional Memory*, original air date May 7, 2006.

PART II

Studies in the Practice and Cultivation of Rhetorical Citizenship

Rhetorical Citizenship in Public Meetings: The Character of Religious Expression in American Discourse

KAREN TRACY

> Speaking out is the patriotic duty of democratic citizenship.
> – Robert Ivie (2002), p. 281

> If we are concerned about the shape of our democracy, we would do well to start by exploring exactly those practices, by investigating the norms we already live by.
> – Gary Shiffman (2004), p. 112

Christian Kock and Lisa Villadsen (2012) begin their discussion of rhetorical citizenship by asserting that talk is not a precursor to real action but itself is "constitutive of citizen engagement" (p. 1). I strongly agree; this chapter evidences the essence of their claim even as a twist and a challenge are made. The twist I add is that rhetorical citizenship needs to recognize the degree to which it is a culturally-inflected practice. Citizenship for Americans involves distinctly different discourse activities than are typical for Europeans. In particular, American citizenship valorizes ordinary people speaking out at public meetings, and it legitimates the relevance of talk about God and religion in state policy-making debates. The challenge I make is of an assumed close relationship between deliberative democracy and rhetorical citizenship. I develop these claims by analyzing citizen testimony at three U.S. state legislative hearings considering bills about same-sex marriage.

The chapter begins by evidencing the linkages for Americans among citizenship, public hearing participation, and religious talk. Then, after providing background on the legislative hearings, I describe six different ways citizens drew upon or oriented to religion in their testimony. In the chapter's conclusion I identify how deliberative democracy and rhetorical citizenship have been tied and suggest why the tie needs to be loosened.

Citizenship for Americans

How do citizens shape policy? In representative democracies, the main way ordinary folks influence what becomes policy is by voting for the representatives who will make the decisions. But there is another avenue for influence. Citizens can speak at public meetings in which a governance group is considering a particular policy issue (Laidman 2010). As a populist democracy the United State gives to its citizens a bigger role for speaking out in meetings than is the case in European countries that have an elite democracy philosophy. In elite democracies, deliberation is largely restricted to elected and appointed government officials. In the federalist system of governance, American citizens are extended an opportunity to testify at local and state levels that is rare in European countries. In a large survey that Conover, Searing, and Crewe (2002) carried out with American and British citizens they found that more than twice as many U.S. citizens reported speaking in public meetings than did British citizens (29 % vs. 13 %).

The American belief that there should be a place for ordinary citizens to speak in democratic institutions is accomplished through the design of local and state meetings in which speaking slots for members of the public are routinely included. Such is the typical structure in both regularly recurring governance bodies such as city council meetings (Leighter & Black 2010), school board meetings (Tracy 2007, 2010), and university trustee boards (West & Fenstermaker 2002), and in meetings that are specially set to decide about an action or policy that is controversial, such as building of a Wal-Mart (Buttny 2009, 2010) or introduction of a Disney Park (Olson & Goodnight 2004) in a community.

A second difference between American and (most) European notions of citizenship is the role religion plays in the American notion of democracy. The vast majority of Americans define themselves as religious. A recent survey by the Pew foundation ("Nones on the rise" 2012), in fact, treated it as news that the number of Americans defining themselves as not religious (agnostic, atheist, or nothing in particular) had increased from 15 % five years ago to slightly less than 20 % in 2012. In addition, 65 % of Americans report religion to be an important part of their daily life (Newport 2009). Wald and Glover (2007, 115) described the United States as a "nation with the soul of a church" that is also a secular society.

In the 1960s before the rise of the religious right, Robert Bellah (1967) popularized the idea that the United States had a "civil religion," a valuing of God in political life that permitted many different versions of belief. In his influential essay, "Civil Religion in America" he proclaimed that the relationship between politics and religion had been "singularly smooth." Writing a decade later Hart (1977, 1) described civil religion as the "ritualistic homage being paid by expedient politicians to a religious-conscious electorate." By the 1980s, though, the smooth relationship had disappeared (Hulsether 2007), and by the 21st century, legal scholar Noah Feldman (2005) described the relationship between government and religion as the issue that most divides Americans from each other.

Not only is the United States one of the most religious Western societies, but it has built into its constitution two principles of how government and religion are to be connected. The First Amendment to the U.S. Constitution asserts that the federal government will not establish any religion for the country and proclaims the rights of citizens to practice the religion of their choice. Exactly how these two clauses are to be weighed and put together tends to generate considerable controversy (Haiman 2003; Meacham 2005). In its initial form the First Amendment was designed to insure that decisions about religion stayed with the states. Well into the 1800s different states required their citizens to pay taxes or have affiliation with specific Christian religions. It was not until after the civil war and, practically speaking, following a series of court cases in the 1940s that contemporary notions about the separation of church and state began to be applied to individual states (Levy 1994).

Both Germany and the United States have clauses in their constitutions prohibiting the establishment of religion, but, as Haupt (2012) shows, the US allows religion to flourish in state matters much more than Germany. Although Thomas Jefferson wanted to build a wall between the church and the state, this never happened. Warren Burger, Chief Justice of the US Supreme Court during the 1970s, said of the constitutional battles over politics and religion: "the line of separation, far from being a 'wall,' is a blurred, indistinct, and variable barrier depending on the circumstances of a particular issue" (Meacham 2006, 240). This blurred boundary between religion and the state extends from interpreting law in the courts to the making of law in legislative hearings. When an American state considers changing its law with regard to a matter that ties to some people's religious beliefs and other people's rights, public discussions about what policy the state should adopt becomes a battlefield.

The public hearings

I obtained video/audio tapes of three judicial committee hearings by requesting them from the appropriate legislative office and then creating verbatim transcripts (Tracy 2005). Table 1 provides an overview of each hearing in terms of its date and length, the bill being debated, and the number of citizens speaking for and against the bill. In Colorado and Hawaii the proposed bill was about extending the rights of marriage but proposed labeling gays' committed relationships civil unions rather than marriage. In Rhode Island, there were two bills under consideration. The first bill proposed extending the rights of marriage and the name "marriage"; the second bill proposed that the issue be put to a popular vote rather than leaving it to the elected officials.

TABLE 1 OVERVIEW OF THE HEARINGS

State	Hawaii	Rhode Island	Colorado
Date	2/24/2009	2/8/2011	3/31/2011
Bill No.	HB444	HB5012 HB5260	SB 11-172
Hearing Length	18 hrs	8.5 hrs	7.5 hrs
Data	Video	Video	Audio
Total Speakers	176	108	79
Pro SS unions	76	67	61
Con SS unions	100	41	18

How "religion" entered citizen discourse

In this site of ordinary American democracy, religion entered citizen testimony in six distinct ways. The first way it entered citizen testimony was by a speaker referring to a religious text to argue for or against a proposal. When scholars (Audi & Wolterstoff, 1996) debate about the reasonableness of religious argument being part of public discourse, this is perhaps the key activity that is being contested.

1. Naming/quoting of religious text

In these hearings citizens referred to various books in the bible, with Leviticus being mentioned most often, in fact 47 times across the hearings. Citizens varied how specifically they referred to the bible, sometimes quoting chapter and verse and using the language of the King James bible (e.g., sodomites, fornicators) and at other times merely pointing toward "the scriptures." Excerpt 1 illustrates a detailed reference; excerpt 2 a general one.

Excerpt 1 (Colorado, Con)

Uh with all due respect, those people are not adhering to the teachings of the scripture. Leviticus 18:22 says if a man lies with another man, it is an abomination. Leviticus 22:18 says that if a man lies with a man as with a woman, they shall both be put to death for an abom- abominable deed, for they have forfeited their life ... In the words of St. Paul the apostle, you do not know- that the unjust will not inherit the kingdom of God. Do not be deceived, neither fornicators, nor adulterers, nor boy prostitutes, nor sodomites, nor thieves, nor the greedy, nor drunkards, nor slanderers, will inherit the kingdom of God. First Corinthians 9:10. Ladies and gentlemen of the committee, we're living in a world where the awareness of sins is ticking away. Let me show you that Jesus Christ is real, and he will judge us all at the moment of our death. If you're not a believer, at least consider the lessons of history.

Excerpt 2 (Hawaii, Con)

Um, let's start with God first ok? I'm a Christian, as most of us are, ok? And uh I'm not- I'm not gonna go through all the scriptures or whatever. But just to tell you that when God says something is not good, you better abide by what he says. Otherwise there's gonna be some serious consequences.

Religious texts were typically used by speakers as if they settled the dispute about what to do. In fact this was the only way that religious texts were used by speakers arguing against the same-sex marriage bills. Citizens passed on God's instructions to elected officials about how to vote.

Using texts as a vehicle to straightforwardly instruct officials, however, was not the only way these texts were used. Citizens favoring the bills highlighted the many different messages one could find in the bible, often quoting passages that emphasized God's loving character, or they cited a text to problematize its implications, as was seen when a citizen cited Leviticus to shows its datedness by noting how it condoned slavery and prohibited the eating of shrimp.

2. Praying for officials

A second way religious talk entered testimony was for a citizen to begin praying in the midst of testifying. Praying changed the footing (Goffman 1981) of the elected officials from the key addressed parties to that of overhearing third parties: officials were put in the position of listening in on a conversation between a testifier and God. Excerpt 3 illustrates an example, which occurred at the end of a lengthy speech.

> *Excerpt 3 (Hawaii Con)*
> Thank you Heavenly Father I apologize if I haven't always acted out of love. There are times when I would like to kick some peoples' butts. But I know it is out of love, Lord God that you called me and you loved me. And thank you for loving all of us and respecting the fact that you've given us the free choice to make our own choice. So it is with that love that I pray for our leaders and their families. Please guide them with your truth and your wisdom Heavenly Father. I pray also Lord God, for our nations and for the people of the nations, for every tender tongue and people. We are special, you made us, and you created us in your image and not to be degraded. I pray for our churches and our wonderful pastors and their wives and families and especially for those who have had the courage, thank you Jesus, to stand up for what God says is his word and to fear God rather than man. They took a risk and I thank you Jesus.

3. Labeling religious affiliation

A third way religion entered citizen talk was as a credentialing device, an implicit justification for why the judicial committee should listen closely. In citizen speeches in public meetings, a key move in openings is for the citizen to identify the features of self that warrant his or her views being taken seriously. What exactly a citizen will mention in this opening slot will vary with the issue and the context. In education governance meetings, for instance, speakers often mention their longevity residing in a geographic area, the number of children they had in the school district, their role as tax-payers, or an occupation that gave them expertise related to the focal topic (Tracy 2010). Because a speaker can describe self in a large variety of ways – by age, political party, ethnicity, occupation, place of residence – the category terms speakers select give us insight into what identities citizens regard as giving them credibility in that particular interactional site. Harvey Sacks (1992) would describe this practice as the use of membership terms. To describe persons using some membership terms rather than others is powerful because the selected term sets in motion inferences about activities, attitudes, and other people. In these hearings citizens used many different identity labels to self-describe, but what was striking was the frequency of religious identification. Both religious leaders and ordinary believers used category affiliation in their openings. In another study of three hearings, Tracy and Parks (2013) found 16 percent of the testifiers to be religious leaders. Excerpt 4 exemplifies two religious leader openings.

Excerpt 4

(a) Hello, my name is Dennis Dutton, I'm assistant pastor of the Family Chapel Estuwahu. … Today I'd like to provide three points of uh discussion concerning House Bill 444 (Hawaii, Con).

(b) After being identified as "Rabbi Mack" by the chair, she said, "Thank you so much. Um I'm here this evening, I think it's important um that you hear from me as- as the only formal representative of any Jewish community here in Rhode Island. Um just because I am the only representative, um does not mean that uh the Jewish community is not widely supportive of marriage equality. I'm the Associate Rabbi at Temple Bethel in Providence. Um we have 950 families" (Rhode Island, Pro)

In all the hearings, although particularly Hawaii's, ordinary believers also identified their religious categories with explicit identity terms. One example is seen in the opening of excerpt 2 where the speaker identified himself as a Christian; others included testifiers saying, "I'm a born-again Christian" or "We're Catholic," said by a husband/wife pair. These self-labeling moves underscore that the policy decision *is* a religion matter and function as an implicit reason that the legislative committee should give careful attention to the speaker. Many speakers who began by self-labeling brought religion into their message in others ways, but some did not. For those who did not, the self-labeling functioned to cue and reinforce the existence of important other unsaid argument grounds for being for or more often against the proposed bill.

4. Referring to the First Amendment of the U.S. Constitution

A fourth way religion entered testimony was by referring to one or the other of the religious clauses of the First Amendment. Which First Amendment clause a speaker gave attention to, however, depended on his/her position on the bill (Tracy & Hughes 2014). Speakers arguing in favor of their state's bill to extend marriage rights argued how it was a clear case requiring separation of church and state. An especially nuanced argument was made by one Christen minister. After describing differences in beliefs among various Christian groups with regard to several issues, he said:

> *Excerpt 5 (Rhode Island, Pro)*
> But here's the thing, there's a disagreement between religions, now it's a civil matter. And from a civil point of view, when two religions disagree, and you base your decision on Catholic teaching, or shall I say Orthodox Catholic teaching, there are many Catholic brothers and sisters who would agree with us, then aren't you recognizing an establishment of religion, one over the other?

In contrast, speakers arguing against proposed bills drew attention to the free exercise clause of the First Amendment. In the Colorado hearing the Senior Legal Counsel for the Alliance Defense Fund, an organization that describes its purpose as "build[ing] alliances between Christian attorneys and like-minded organizations to accomplish what none of us can do alone: protect and defend YOUR religious freedom" spoke extensively. After making a complex claim about a different issue, he launched an argument about how the proposed bill would violate religious freedom guarantees.

> *Excerpt 6 (Colorado, Con)*
> This bill is insufficient to protect the religious liberties in this state. People of- of faith an- and people of conscience. The only protection that this bill accords is by saying that clergy do not have to engage in the ceremonies of- of moralizing these civil unions. But it says nothing about uh Catholic Charities, who want to be involved in- in uh- in families. Or it doesn't say anything about businesses and what the impact would be on businesses and their policies internally. It doesn't say anything about the photographer who doesn't want to participate in filming civil ceremonies. Like we have a client in New Mexico that was sued because she chose not to do it. And now she has been faced with civil rights charges.

Religion entered testimony in two other ways, each of which requires inferential work to identify "religion" as being invoked.

5. Denying that a proposal is a matter of civil rights

In these hearings the central argument for extending the right of marriage or civil unions to same-sex couples was the need for equality: Marriage, proponents argued, is a basic civil right to which all citizens are entitled. This argument was repeatedly made with subtle kinds of variation by citizens favoring same-sex unions. As Michael Billig has shown (1987, Billig et al. 1988) everyday thought is fundamentally argumentative. Asserting one claim conveys an implicit assertion about the opposing claim. Often, too, the discourse reveals traces of the understood opposing claim. Many speakers denied that extending civil unions to gays and lesbians was an issue of civil rights. That an issue is *not* a civil rights issue does not necessarily make it a religious one, but in this context, it did. In Excerpt 7, an African American speaker uses his body and experience to assert the issue before them is not a civil matter, cuing that its alternative is religious with his preface about not getting into the religious aspect. In Excerpt 8 the fact that "religious issue" is the competing view to "civil rights matter" is formulated explicitly through the speaker's religious identity credentialing, claiming to represent Jesus Christ, and by describing the issue as a "moral" matter, a term that most would see as a cousin of religion.

> *Excerpt 7 (Colorado, Con)*
> I'm not gonna get into the religion expect- aspect of it. But I have a super problem with the civil rights thing about this. Now when the gay lesbian groups compare this issue to the issue of Americans who are black, and to civil rights, I find it very disingenuous. Let me just give you a story.

> *Excerpt 8 (Colorado, Con)*
> My name is uh Pastor Roger Angis, and I represent uh myself and I also r-represent Jesus Christ. I've been listening to the testimonies from both sides of the fence, I hear economic policies, I hear so-called civil rights. This is not a civil right. ... This bill has to be put up first. Is this a moral bill? And this is not a moral bill in any way shape or form.

We might say that the dominant counter-position in these hearings to same-sex marriage being a civil rights issue was to regard it is a religious, moral matter. Thus one way speakers brought religion into the debate was to deny that the issue before them concerned civil rights.

6. Claiming or disavowing (expected) neighbors of God and gays

Political attitudes and beliefs usually go together in clusters. When a speaker expresses a view on one issue, people will assume that the speaker has particular views on other issues and will make assumptions about what kind of person the speaker is (Conover, Searing, & Crewe 2002). To state it in a more discourse analytic way, stances toward an issue implicate identities and identities implicate stances (Tracy 2011). For instance, van De Mieroop (2011) shows how debt defaulters being interviewed by Belgian debt mediation services discursively work to disavow that they are irresponsible money managers and reframe themselves as caring parents caught in tough circumstances. Claims and disavowals, then, work in two ways. Such verbal acts seek to redefine what should be seen as going together – as part of a bundle – and they underscore what the taken-for-granted bundle is.

Citizen testifiers advanced claims about the goodness/badness of the proposed bills, but as they did they were also doing discursive work to show that they as persons possessed attributes not assumed to go with the stance they were advocating (pro or con same-sex marriage). That is, they did discursive work to draw attention to the fact that either (a) they did not possess undesirable attributes associated with the stance or (b) they did possess desirable socially valued attributes not typically associated with that stance. The American bundle of attitudes-identities, I would suggest, sees being religious as aligned with patriotism, which in turn goes with being hostile to gays. On the flip side, being gay is seen as not being religious and questionably patriotic. Evidence that this is the understood bundle is seen when gay speakers assert their patriotism and love of country/state or elaborate their positive connection to God as they argue for marriage rights. Excerpts 9 and 10 illustrate two gay speakers asserting their love of state and country. These comments could seem off-topic if the bundle of positions, which I articulated above, were not in operation.

Excerpt 9 (RI, Pro)

I really appreciate the opportunity to speak here uh this evening on behalf of marriage equality, uh and I will be brief ... I'm a proud Rhode Island native. I grew up here. I went to school here. I've enjoyed a terrific professional career here spanning 25 years.

Excerpt 10 (Colorado, Pro)

A lot has happened in the past 15 years. The good news is that our country has never been more just. Our country's founders would look at our country now and see the change that has taken place and look at us in admiration. I'm proud to be an American. In fact I work for our citizens everyday as a law enforcement officer.

Excerpt 11 from a pro-same sex marriage law professor illustrates a lesbian seeking to show herself, and the gay students for whom she speaks, to be "deeply religious." Although her utterance construction is not straightforward, the discursive proximity of her identification of the existence of inaccurate stereotypes and her claim that she and many of her gay students are religious function both to rebut and solidify the expected association.

Excerpt 11 (Hawaii, Pro)
Let me tell you a little about the students for whom I speak today. Most are local, born and raised in the islands, Hawaiian, Japanese, Chinese, Filipino, South Pacific Islander, European, Hapa. They give lie to the stereotype that gay rights are a mainland Haole issue. Many, myself included, are deeply religious people whose faith plays a central role in their and our lives.

A different strategy to seek to overturn the assumption that being gay is at odds with being religious is seen in excerpt 12 in which a lesbian comments about the character of the love she has for her partner.

Excerpt 12 (Colorado, Pro)
Living with Wendy in Loveland and being with Wendy for over 17 years has been the most stable, God-centered place I've ever been in my whole life.

Citizens testifying against the bill oriented to the opposite problem in the assumed bundle. As they argued against same-sex marriage, they proclaimed their love of gays or disclaimed that they were prejudiced. Excerpt 13 illustrates a typical proclamation of positive sentiment; excerpt 14 shows a speaker tackling the assumed bundle directly:

Excerpt 13 (Hawaii, Con)
I wanna state unequivocally that I love the gays, lesbians. Our church has some of them, the gáys. Our company has employed them, my kids have gay friends. I will also say that I love drug addicts, alcoholics. I've been ministering the homeless. I've been ministering to them for the last fourteen years.

Excerpt 14 (Rhode Island, Con)
To say that this traditional understanding of marriage as many people do believe, and they honestly believe it, is in fact based on uh, uh bigotry and discrimination,

> um I would say that we also have a new problem. And I do recognize that in society. Which is how do we demonstrate respect for our gay friends and family members and neighbors? And it is uh- It is a good question. It's a serious and important question. ... Um, I would say this in conclusion, that uh whatever else our marriage tradition is, it is not based on animus or hatred or bigotry or a desire to do harm.

In sum, because of the assumed bundling of religion, patriotism, and anti-gay sentiment (and the converse), speakers could indirectly bring religion into the exchange by referring to one or the other of the threads that comprised the attitudinal fabric.

Implications for rhetorical citizenship

In a response to Schudson's (1997) essay, "Why conversation is not the soul of democracy," Schroll (1999) remarks, "Some new way of talking about talking is needed that reflects the complexity of modern democratic life" (103). Two aspects of modern (American) democracies' complexities are the dominance of representative formats and the focal role that public meetings serve in giving elected officials knowledge of their citizen desires, principles, and preferences. Citizen testimony in public meetings is the bread and butter, or at least a main entrée, of American democracy. Any useful notion of rhetorical citizenship needs to take account of the frequency of citizens' speeches of advocacy in public meetings.

The dominant view of good citizenship draws a tight connection to deliberative democracy, highlighting communicative scenes in which there is back-and-forth talk, reason-giving, openness to others' views, and equality among participants (e.g., Gastil & Levine 2005; Habermas 1989; Hicks 2002). Such an ideal does not well match what citizens do in public hearings. As seen in the hearings on same-sex marriage, speakers evidenced little openness to the opposing position, and with only a few exceptions hearing talk involved no back-and-forth exchange. Delli-Carpini, Cook, and Jacobs (2004), in fact, rule out the public meeting as an activity that warrants the label "deliberative." Certainly if reason-giving and open-minded discussion among equals are needed for deliberation, then public hearings are not instances. But public meetings, I would argue, should not be conceived as flawed sites of democratic deliberation. Rather, they are a distinctive, valuable, and necessary site for citizenship that requires ways of speaking that differ from how discussion unfolds in small groups, the implied format for deliberation. Public meetings are places for advocacy and passionate expression, a type of expression that should be part of any notion of rhetorical citizenship.

Rhetorical citizenship and its companion concept, rhetorical democracy (Kock & Villadsen 2012), carry the promise of more useful norms of conduct for citizens' public participation than democratic deliberation. Public meetings, with their thin connection between citizens and elected officials, make possible expression of strong disagreement that enables clarity about issues and a deeper understanding of difference. In relationship-attentive, deliberative settings, the disagreements that do occur can be muted and not explored in depth (Karpowitz & Mansbridge 2005).

Given rhetoric's strong connection to strategic talk and persuasion, rhetorical citizenship would seem a useful counterweight to deliberative democracy. For rhetorical citizenship to be an effective ideal, however, it needs to keep a productive tension between deliberation and advocacy. Deliberation and advocacy are essential to a well-functioning democracy, but they are the antithesis of each other (Heindriks 2011; Mutz 2006). Rhetorical citizenship needs to keep its tie to democratic deliberation loose so that it can equally moor its meaning in the traditions of advocacy.

Given religion's importance in American life, including the understandings of what democracy entails, it seems essential to legitimate religious talk in the public sphere. For many Americans there would be no need to make this argument – religion is prominent in public debate as it well should be. But for others, especially academics and other intellectuals, the legitimation of religious talk in public debate may seem problematic. For those of us who are not religious there are two reasons why legitimating religious expression is important. First, in a pluralistic society with many different flavors of religion, legitimating religious expression in public meetings keeps visible that there is a diversity of opinions on just about any issue that connects to religion. There is rarely *a* religious point of view, although sometimes traditional factions of a religion, whether they be Protestant, Catholic, or Jewish, will claim to speak "the religious perspective." Lived religion – what ordinary religious people believe and do – often differs in a significant way from church religion, i.e., official doctrine (Wald and Glover 2007). Within most religious groups, progressive as well as traditional factions are to be found.

Second, legitimating religious expression in public meetings is likely to keep discussion of controversial issues as matters of public reason-giving and accountability. In the same sex marriage debates, one strategy used in a number of states by persons opposing particular bills was to argue that the issue should be settled by a popular vote. Direct democracy initiatives on socially sensitive issues, such as abortion or gay rights, move political discussion from accountable sites of public talk to private, informal discussions in which people speak mostly with like-minded others (Wojcieszak & Mutz 2009). Under such conditions law-making is likely to become more restrictive of people's civil rights (Carter 2011). Legitimating religious talk in the American public square is a reasonable way to encourage careful reflection among the many observing citizens and listening representatives as citizens strongly concerned about an issue advocate passionately for what they believe.

References

"Nones" on the rise. (2012). *Pew Forum of Religion and Public Life.*

Audi, R. and N. Wolterstorff. (1996). *Religion in the Public Square: The Place of Religious Convictions In Political Debate.* New York: Rowman & Littlefield.

Bellah, R. N. (1967). Civil Religion in America. *Daedalus* 96 (1), 1-21.

Billig, M. (1987). *Arguing and Thinking: A Rhetorical Approach to Social Psychology.* 1st Ed. Cambridge: Cambridge University Press.

Billig, M. and S. Condor, D. Edwards, M. Gane, D. Middleton and A.R. Radley. (1998). *Ideological Dilemmas.* London: Sage.

Buttny, R. (2009). Wal-Mart's Presentation to the Community: Discursive Practices in Mitigating Risk, Limiting Public Discussion, And Developing A Relationship. *Discourse & Communication* 3 (3), 235-254.

Buttny, R. (2010). Citizen Participation, Metadiscourse, and Accountability: A Public Hearing on a Zoning Change for Wal-Mart. *Journal of Communication* 60 (4), 636-659.

Carter, M. E. (2011). Regulating Abortion through Direct Democracy: The Liberty of All Versus the Moral Code of a Majority. *Boston University Law Review* 91, 305-346.

Conover, P.J., D.D. Searing and I.M. Crewe. (2002). The Deliberative Potential Of Political Discussion. *British Journal of Political Science* 32, 21-62.

Delli Carpini, M.X., F. Lomax Cook and L.R. Jacobs. (2004). Public Deliberation, Discursive Participation, and Citizen Engagement: A Review of the Empirical Literature. *American Review of Political Science* 7, 315-344.

Feldman, N. (2005). *Divided by God.* New York: Farrar, Strauss, and Giroux.

Gastil, J. and P. Levine. (Eds.) (2005). *The Deliberative Democracy Handbook: Strategies for Effective Civic Engagement in the 21st Century.* San Francisco: Jossey-Bass.

Goffman, E. (1981). *Forms of Talk.* Philadelphia: University Of Pennsylvania Press.

Habermas, J. (1989). *The Structural Transformation of the Public Sphere: An Inquiry into a Category of Bourgeois Society.* Cambridge, MA: MIT Press.

Haiman, F.S. (2003). *Religious Expression and the American Constitution.* East Lansing, MI: Michigan State University Press.

Hart, R. P. (1977). *The Political Pulpit.* West Lafayette, IN: Purdue University Press.

Haupt, C.E. (2012). *Religion-State Relations in the United States and Germany.* Cambridge, UK: Cambridge University Press.

Hendriks, C.M. (2011). *The Politics of Public Deliberation: Citizen Engagement and Interest Advocacy.* New York: Palgrave Macmillan.

Hicks, D. (2002). The Promise(s) of Deliberative Democracy. *Rhetoric and Public Affairs* 5, 223-260.

Hulsether, M. (2007). *Religion, Culture, and Politics in the Twentieth Century United States.* New York: Columbia University Press.

Ivie, R. L. (2002). Rhetorical Deliberation in the Here and Now. *Rhetoric and Public Affairs* 5, 277-285.

Karpowitz, C.F., and J. Mansbridge. (2005). Disagreement and Consensus: The Need for Dynamic Updating in Public Deliberation. *Journal of Public Deliberation* 1 (1), 1-17.

Kock, C. And L.S. Villadsen. (2012). Introduction: Citizenship as a Rhetorical Practice. In: C. Kock and L. S. Villadsen (Eds.) *Rhetorical Citizenship and Public Deliberation* (pp. 1-10). University Park: Pennsylvania State University Press.

Laidman, D. (2010). Constitutional Law – Free Speech – Ninth Circuit Uphold's City Council's Ejection of Audience Member Based on Nazi Salute. *UCLA Law Review Discourse* 57, 51-63.

Leighter, J.L. and L. Black. (2010). “I'm Just Raising the Question”: Terms for Talk and Practical Metadiscursive Arguments in Public Meetings. *Western Journal Of Communication* 74 (5), 547-569.

Levy, L.W. (1994). *The Establishment Clause.* 2nd Ed. Chapel Hill, NC: University Of North Carolina Press.

Meacham, J. (2006). *American Gospel: God, the Founding Fathers, and the Making of a Nation.* New York: Random House.

Mutz, D.C. (2006). *Hearing the Other Side: Deliberative Versus Participatory Democracy.* New York: Cambridge.

Newport, F.(2009). State of the States: Importance of Religion. *Gallup Poll.*

Olson, K. M. And G.T. Goodnight. (2004). Ingenium – Speaking in Community: The Case of the Prince William County Zone Hearings on Disney's America. In P.A. Sullivan and S. R. Goldzwig (Eds.), *New Approaches to Rhetoric* (Pp. 31-59). Thousand Oaks, CA: Sage.

Sacks, H. (1992). *Lectures on Conversation.* Vol. 1. Cambridge, MA: Blackwell.

Schroll, C. (1999). The Place of "Conversation" in the Omnilogue of Democracy: A Reply to Schudson. *Critical Studies in Mass Communication* 16, 99-106.

Schudson, M. (1997). Why Conversation Is Not The Soul of Democracy. *Critical Studies in Mass Communication* 14, 297-309.

Shiffman, G. (2004). Deliberation Versus Decision: Platonism in Contemporary Democratic Theory. In B. Fontana, C. J. Nederman and G. Remer (Eds.), *Talking Democracy: Historical Perspectives on Rhetoric and Democracy* (pp. 87-113). University Park: Pennsylvania State University Press.

Tracy, K. (2005). Reconstructing Communicative Practices: Action-Implicative Discourse Analysis. In K. Fitch and R. Sanders (Eds.), *Handbook of Language and Social Interaction* (pp. 301-319). Mahwah, N.J.: Lawrence Erlbaum.

Tracy, K. (2007). The Discourse of Crisis in Public Meetings: Case Study of a School Board's Multimillion Dollar Error. *Journal of Applied Communication Research* 35, 418-441.

Tracy, K. (2010). *Challenges of Ordinary Democracy: A Case Study in Deliberation and Dissent.* University Park, PA: Pennsylvania State University Press

Tracy, K. (2011). "Reasonable Hostility": Its Usefulness and Limitation as a Norm for Public Hearings. *Informal Logic* 31 (3), 171-190.

Tracy, K. and M. Durfy. (2007). Speaking Out in Public: Citizen Participation in Contentious School Board Meetings. *Discourse & Communication* 1 (2), 223-249.

Tracy, K. and J.F. Hughes. (2014). Democracy-Appealing Partisanship: A Situated Ideal of Citizen Participation. *Journal Of Applied Communication Research*, 43 (3) 307-324.

Tracy, K. and R. Parks. (2013). Managing the Problematic Relationship between God and Government: A Discourse Strategy Used in Legislative Hearings about Same-Sex Marriage. Presented at The International Communication Association. London.

Van De Mieroop, Dorien. (2011). Identity Negotiations in Narrative Accounts about Poverty. *Discourse & Society* 22 (5), 565-591.

Wald, K.D., and G.B. Glover. (2007). Theological Perspectives on Gay Unions: The Uneasy Marriage of Religion and Politics. In C. A. Rimmerman and C. Wilcox (Eds.), *The Politics of Same-Sex Marriage* (pp. 105-130). Chicago: University of Chicago Press.

West, C. and S. Fenstermaker. (2002). Accountability in Action: The Accomplishment of Gender, Race and Class in a Meeting of the University of California Board of Regents. *Discourse & Society* 13, 537-563.

Wojcieszak, M.E., and D.C. Mutz. (2009). Online Groups and Political Discourse: Do Online Discussion Spaces Facilitate Exposure to Political Disagreement? *Journal of Communication* 59 (1):40-56.

Voice, Listening, and Telling Stories: The Communicative Construction of Rhetorical Citizenship in Small Groups

CAROLYNE LEE & JUDY BURNSIDE-LAWRY

Introduction

We proceed from the assumption that rhetorical citizenship is constructed communicatively in its microcosmic form in small groups, in conversations about forms of social behavior, interpersonal and public, about prices or elections, or about general ethical issues, among other topics. Using a new theoretical lens comprised of the three linked aspects of voice, narrative, and listening, in synergy with theories of discursive democratic activity and rhetorical citizenship, and principles of Aristotelian rhetoric, we will examine opportunities for free and equal expression of voice in small group conversations, considering processes and characteristics of those initiating and exercising voice, and the quality of the listening. Much research into listening assumes something to be listened to – speaking, or "voice," a term that has recently been regenerated by Couldry to aid us in thinking about democracy and political/social change, and in recognizing that humans have a strong need for the process of voice, to narrate an account of oneself and to have that voice heard and taken into account. For this reason, narrative theory/ methodology (Boje 1991, 2001, 2008, 2011) can be a very useful theoretical strand, and will be drawn on to analyze and represent the content of discussion and performances of rhetorical citizenship in a small group.

In addition to voice, we include the linked concept of narrative in our examination of rhetorical citizenship, and we look to some important narrative theorists of the past three decades in order to show the centrality of narrative/storytelling to human communication in general, and rhetorical citizenship in particular.

For the third and final component of our new theoretical lens we draw on listening research, because even if both voice and narrative are produced, in any context, they are pointless unless someone is listening. We use this new lens to analyze rhetorical citizenship in a particular instance – that is, small group discussions about issues in society. We conducted an empirical study, and although our overall framework supporting this new lens has enabled us to analyze rhetorical citizenship in a tripartite way – looking at voice, narrative and listening – for the purposes of this chapter we look mainly at the narrative component. Because our theoretical framework is quite new, we will demonstrate why we think this particular framework is useful, and then will give an example of how we have used one strand of it to analyze the performance of rhetorical citizenship in a small group. We chose the small group as our context because, following Poole and Hollingshead (2004), we see the group as the basic unit of communication, believing the analysis of small groups facilitates "the detailed study of human communication exchange" (Poole and Hollingshead 2004, p. 359), allowing a focus on each individual in the group. It is also a practical choice when researching rhetorical citizenship, as it is within their small and informal friendship and family groups that citizens first construct their citizenship, perhaps to a certain extent testing out their rhetorical production before performing it anew in larger groups, for example, at a community meeting. So it is often in the small group context that citizens first deliberate about issues before doing so in a wider public sphere.

Theoretical framework

Whether the context is public or private, it could be said that citizenship is constructed communicatively every time we participate in conversations about forms of social behavior, about prices or elections, or about general ethical issues, among other topics. In such forms of discursive democratic activity – which is, by default, citizenship – the role of rhetoric has been explicitly acknowledged by many theorists for some time (e.g., Gutmann and Thompson 1996, Young 2000, Ivie 2002, Dryzek 2010). Most recently, these theories have been brought into synergy and considerably refined by Kock and Villadsen (2012), who focus on, among other things, the many informal ways in which citizens discuss issues of common concern in society, arguing that such civic engagement is rhetorical, that the whole process is always already rhetorical: we each use rhetoric to construct ourselves and represent the ideas and ideals we believe in, whether the process is conscious or not. While deliberative democracy has been theorized extensively and in many different ways, we align our conception with Cohen's view of it as public discussion or argument among equal citizens, about issues affecting them, as part of wider discussions taking place ideally across the whole of a society (Cohen, 1989). While it is widely acknowledged that the "most sophisticated account of deliberative procedures is from Habermas" (Passerin d'Entrèves 2002, p. 7), Habermas himself seems to want to distance his theories from rhetoric when he asserts that the "tradition of rhetoric ... is interested more in speech that convinces than in its truth content" (Habermas 1984, p. 27). And yet, Habermas is a rhetorician by default, given that he sees the study of society as the study of communication, which fits within the Aristotelian framework in which citizens need rhetoric to discuss and reflect on "those aspects of human affairs for which there are no experts and for which everyone is assumed to have an opinion" (Garver 1994, p. 21). Rhetoric is quite simply the means by which "a person advocates, or provides voice for, an idea" (Herrick 1997, p. 18), engages in public discourse and thus "communicative action" (Habermas in Foss et al. 1991, p. 252).

The process of communicating one's (or one's group's) views or position will, therefore, inevitably involve rhetoric. As Young states: "rhetoric constitutes the flesh and blood of any political communication, whether in a neighborhood meeting or on the floor of Parliament" (2000, p. 65). Such communication does not even have to be formally political, as it can take place in social or socio-political contexts, but it is inevitably enacted by citizens. Before discussing the theories and models we have drawn from, we need to make clear the specific way we use the concept of rhetorical citizenship in our project. Rhetorical citizenship describes the process of rhetorically constructing and articulating one's position regarding an issue or belief of concern in the particular social context. But we argue it is more than this: rhetorical citizenship occurs ideally in a continuous feedback loop of articulating one's position, listening to, taking into account, and responding appropriately to, the positions of others, resulting in a form of mutual sense-making.

When all components of the loop operate at optimum levels, we see mutual weighing up of citizens' differing views – that is, deliberation. As Kock and Villadsen point out, when applied to public issues, deliberation "implies holding together all reasons and considerations relevant to the issue – not only those of one's own that speak for a given policy but also others that may speak against it, and that one has not yet considered" (Kock and

Villadsen 2012, p. 4). We can see from this idealistic definition of deliberation just how mutual this sense-making process needs to be. Conversely, when one or more of the components is missing or inadequate, miscommunication occurs, the quality of rhetorical citizenship diminishes, and the level of debate and the quality of the communicative action of citizens in society can suffer.

Although it is tempting to dismiss the account of deliberation above as an almost impossible ideal, we argue that at least it gives us a sketch of what "best practice" rhetorical citizenship might look like, and how it relates to the automatic human activity of exercising voice. Indeed the concept of voice, recently taken up and theorized anew by Couldry, largely includes "exchange of narratives with others" (Couldry 2010, p. 8). A true exchange requires that one "takes into account" the views of others, which can surely only occur if one maintains a relatively open mind on an issue, thus constituting an equally idealistic description – albeit from another angle – of rhetorical citizenship. As with many significant concepts, however, the devil is in the detail, and details are often in short supply in ambitious theories. In an attempt to begin conceptualizing these details, we draw on literature from the fields of communication, listening, democracy theory, and narrative analysis to first develop a critical framework for identifying the conditions that enhance or, conversely, impede the thriving of rhetorical citizenship.

Listening

If, then, an important part of *ideal* rhetorical citizenship is taking into account the narratives that citizens tell each other, what does this mean exactly? "To take into account" is "to take into consideration" in other words "to consider" that is, to "give mental attention to; think over". We turn to the International Listening Association's definition of listening: "the process of receiving, constructing meaning from, and responding to spoken and/or nonverbal messages." Competent listening incorporates affective, cognitive and behavioral (verbal, nonverbal, interactive) dimensions. How can we determine whether a person is listening effectively or not? Or, to use Coakley, Halone and Wolvin's (1996) terms, how do we evaluate competent or incompetent listening?

In order to answer this question we turn to the organizational communication scholar, Thomas Jacobson, who studies participatory communication within the context of organizations that provide humanitarian aid to developing countries. Jacobson has found that organizations that do not listen to (in other words "take into account") local community needs risk developing projects that lack community engagement and ownership. Jacobson contends that participatory communication and listening are interchangeable terms, and has developed a participatory communication model, derived from Habermas's theory of communicative action, to assess whether an organization listens and gives voice to participants during specific communication events.

As with organizations, small group dynamics can include overbearing participants who dominate conversation and control inter-group communication, behaviors that reduce or completely obstruct listening. We therefore adapt Jacobson's (2007) participatory communication model to examine whether participants in small groups listen and give voice to each other as part of the process of rhetorical citizenship.

Narrative

But our examination of the quality of listening is not the focus of this presentation. It is, rather, narrative. We argue for the centrality of narrative in rhetoric/rhetorical citizenship, and base our argument on the work of many communication theorists over the past few decades who have researched narrative and argued for its centrality to human communication. Our species has even been renamed *homo narrans* by Walter Fisher (1987), one of the first theorists to see human communication as narration. Indeed Fisher believes that all forms of communication can be seen as stories; that is, they are "symbolic interpretations of aspects of the world, occurring in time, and shaped by history, culture and character" (Fisher 1987, p. xi). The relevance of this to rhetoric, we claim, is that these stories are – as theorised by Fisher – offered as "value-laden warrants for believing or acting in certain way" (1987, p. xi). In other words, the stories provide the means for persuasion, and readers probably do not need to be reminded that the universal description of Aristotelian Rhetoric is "the faculty of observing in any given case the available means of persuasion." The centrality of storytelling has also been argued for from an anthropological perspective: "Before human beings learned how to read and write, storytelling was the medium of collective memory" (Allan 2002, p. 2).

We can still see this today, for example, in the collective memory of Indigenous Australians. In Australia there have been a number of situations in which certain groups of Indigenous people, in arguing their case in legal processes for land rights claims, have acted and sung stories of their right to own areas of ancestral land. This is a very compelling example of storytelling as a main mode of rhetorical citizenship in a specific context. It is also an example of stories functioning as "windows into the emotional, political and symbolic lives" of people, as argued by Yiannis Gabriel (2000). As further support for this perspective, we can argue – following Bruner – that narrative is the form intrinsic to human thinking, that our brains are hardwired to organize experience as narratives, with the most important of these narratives being each person's autobiographical one.

The process of telling our stories, often using them as warrants for our beliefs or for our actions as citizens, aims to gain support, and thus to engage in a sort of collective sense-making. This was first demonstrated in an organizational context in Boje's seminal 1991 article in which he conducted an ethnographic study of a large firm, and showed "how people perform stories to make sense of events, introduce change, and gain political advantage during their conversations ... [He found] the stories were dynamic, varied by context, and were sometimes terse, requiring the hearer to fill in silently major chunks of story line, context, and implication" (Boje 1991, p. 106). This study brought into organisational theory the view of organisations as "collective storytelling systems ... in which the performance of stories is a key part of members' sense making." So in organisations and in citizen interaction more generally, sense making is a collective process enacted rhetorically, frequently via storytelling (Boje 1991).

Voice

So what happens if/when storytelling is insufficiently taken into account in society? It seems intuitive to suggest that there would be a deficit of shared sense-making among citizens. Some theorists go further than this, arguing that "society cannot work ... unless there is a good degree of shared meaning, and society's ills are due to a lack of shared meaning" (Bohm, 1996, cited in Allan 2002, p. 230). In other words, the state of our democracies is suffering. This view of the declining quality of democracy has been articulated by many theorists, in particular by media theorists, of which Couldry, Livingstone and Markham (2007) are notable examples According to them, citizens' shared orientation to the public sphere where matters of common concern are addressed has been waning since the middle of the twentieth century.

Significantly, in seeking a way forward from this, in a world divided by fundamental differences in values, Couldry subsequently argued for a turn towards Aristotle's ethics. This approach asks: "What do we need to do to live together well?" Couldry does not give us too many specifics, but he does say that we should aim for Aristotle's *phronēsis* – that is, practical wisdom. This would occur, Couldry believes, through the circulation of all necessary information and facts in society, and through opportunities for the expression of opinion and voice by as many citizens as possible. We don't all have to agree on everything, but we can agree on certain underlying conditions – respectful listening to each other's rhetorical constructions of their citizenship, shared sense-making, openness and reflexivity.

A development of this view is achieved in Couldry's 2010 book, *Why Voice Matters*, in which he terms the "recognition of people's capacities for social cooperation" as "voice" (Couldry 2010, p. 2) or, in other words, people's rhetorical citizenship, although he doesn't actually use this term. Couldry further defines "voice" as process, as "giving an account of oneself and what affects one's life ... an irreducible part of what it means to be human" (2010, p. vi). However, the opportunity to have one's voice heard is seriously diminished "across various domains: economic, political, cultural [because] we are now governed in ways that deny the value of voice and insist instead on the primacy of market functioning" (2010, p. xi). According to this view, voice ideally "involves us in an ongoing process of reflection, *exchanging narratives back and forth*" (2010, p. 8, emphasis added). And this sort of narrative exchange, this exercising of one's "voice" needs support – an atmosphere of cooperation, an optimum level of listening, and ongoing processes of reflection. Proceeding from Couldry's argument, our hypothesis is that a crucial part of how people construct themselves rhetorically and articulate their positions on issues (which is of course rhetorical citizenship), and this is done by way of narratives, an important element of voice. So the specific question that we want to address in this chapter is: What part do narrative and voice play in rhetorical citizenship and especially in small group deliberation? We will now proceed to the empirical case study we conducted in order to explore this question.

Methodology

We follow David Snowden's methodology (2000) which involves systematic collection of anecdotes using anthropological observation, capturing stories by recording them. The recorded stories are then transcribed, read, and systematically analyzed. We conducted a very brief analysis of this sort, and in our analysis we were guided by Boje's distinction between narrative and what he calls "ante-narrative." Boje argues for the use of "ante-narrative" analysis, because if we look only for neat, complete narratives, we will be disappointed. Boje argues that the stories we tell are more a sort of random flow of fragments, often not quite yet shaped into a coherent story. He says: "narrative is post, a retrospective explanation of storytelling" (Boje 2001, p. 3). We could equally call these fragmentary flows pre- or proto-narratives, but since Boje has theorized and trialed ante-narrative analysis, we are following that method, amalgamating it with Poole's analysis of small group talk, and with Snowden's ethnographic analysis – getting people to talk, recording it, and analyzing it.

Our small group was made up of three volunteers – two men and one woman, all in their twenties, who had just completed their masters' degrees at a large Australian university; two were born in Australia, the other was an exchange student from Italy (the pseudonyms of these three participants are Roy, Dino, and Gina). Each participant was asked to choose a current issue in society with which to start a brief conversation. We determined the order in which participants would choose topics by taking their names, unseen, out of a hat. The first conversation, chosen by Roy, was on the topic of university courses being put online by 39 of the largest universities in the world, including their own university. The other two topics were national identity, and refugees.

We started with the topic, university courses going online. This was Roy's first comment, in which he demonstrated that he wanted to make sure that the others understood the prevalent terminology:

> R: I would like to talk about university courses going online ... Does everyone know what MOOCs are? (R:1)

He went on to present his view, which we have decided in our analysis to categorize as *gently* pro online courses. The other two participants asked for some clarification. One participant, Dino, positioned himself, equally gently and respectfully, as not really in favor of the idea (D: 1).

The third participant, Gina, positioned herself as explicitly "neutral":

> I'm undecided on the fees versus free; like, I know it's open access and worldwide and global but, like, I'm pretty neutral, I don't really know where I stand because I see both sides. (G: 2)

Gina and Dino then asked short questions of Roy (the initiator of this topic), in order to get more information; once they felt confident about the topic, probably also about how their ideas, their "voices," would be received, each of the two who did not propose the topic gave a type of narrative. This is an example of what Couldry talks about when he says for voice to occur, there must be social support, for example, polite and empathic listeners and a feeling of comfort (Couldry, 2010, p. 9).

This is Dino's narrative:

> D: Before we were saying how people might be at work and need to have a degree... I could tell you a thing from personal experience: my mother at 50 years, decided to complete her degree in foreign languages while teaching, she's a primary school teacher, and while working she went to university and got her degree. It was ... as a person who works, I think it's even better to have someone, a teacher, who guides you because you don't have any experience, you're not used to studying, and you always need someone who guides you ... (D: 4)

We can see here how the way he expresses his voice in non-support of online courses is very much embedded in his personal narrative. He uses this story about his mother to make his argument, the crux of which is that all learning should occur with a guide. This argument is the last sentence of his story. We see here that by way of his story he is actually presenting "value-laden warrants for believing or acting in certain ways" (Fisher 1987, p. xi). Dino rhetorically constructs his position *but* he tailors it to the social context he is in by taking into account that his position is more "contra" the issue than those of the other two participants, and what we see here is an example of his responding in a manner that he considers appropriate – not too didactic, not saying, "online courses are bad; everyone needs an actual teacher" – but in giving the story of his mother, he's saying his position on the issue is contingent on this narrative.

What happens next is very interesting: Gina starts her narrative by creating a link from Dino's story to her own story, which gives validity to Dino's story, showing that she sees it as relevant, showing that she is "taking into account" his voice and his story, a crucial aspect of hearing the voice of others.

> G: ... well I'm not as old as your mum but ... but one of the reasons I chose [this University]... is because it's all on campus and you have to attend classes and everything; ... and I tried to juggle part time masters study with full time work and it didn't work, and for that reason I've decided ... to quit full time work so I have the ability to come to uni and interact ... because otherwise I could get my piece of paper on line but it would just be a piece of paper and nothing else. (G: 4)

What is notable here is that she has moved away from her original stated neutrality, to align more with the position Dino has articulated, and she voices her own personal story to reinforce her new position. Clearly Dino's story resonated with her – and as a result she instigated mutual sense-making (Weick 1995) as she responded by telling her own story, which followed the same line of argument as Dino's.

We argue that both these stories show themselves as part of a continuous feedback loop of articulating one's position, listening to, taking into account, and responding appropriately to the voices of others in which each articulates his or her own position; by way of these voiced narratives, participants enacted a mutual weighing up of differing views, a collective process of sense-making (Weick 1995), evincing a very egalitarian/democratic form of citizenship.

The next topic the three participants discussed was refugees. Dino proposed the topic and Gina was the first to respond:

> G: well **I got really irked...** [when someone used the term] "illegal asylum seekers", and I was ... "Well **that's just a really stupid take**"... but**... I don't actually know too much about the situation**, ... I've just started working at Amnesty International. ...we're a big country, we've got lots of land, why can't we share? **That's just my take**. None of **this political rubbish** ... no one comes here ... because they think, "Oh I'm going come to Australia and see how it is..."; they... can't leave [legally], **often it's a life and death situation**, ... it's their one chance of survival, and **that's my take on it**. (G: 6, emphases added)

There are narrative elements here (for example, she narrates where she works) but the narrative is very fragmentary, very much an example of what

Boje calls "ante-narrative," by which he means no "proper plot sequence and mediated coherence ... [but instead] unconstructed and fragmented" (Boje 2001, p. 3).

Gina's characters in her story are vague – for example, whoever used the term "illegal asylum seekers" is not given, is in fact absent, one of the gaps Boje mentions in ante-narrative, but Gina is still expressing her voice, embedding her perceptions in her own lived experiences – for example, her work for Amnesty International. We note also the rhetorical devices she uses to make her argument: she represents her own emotions quite strongly, using rhetorical pathos, linguistic features that we have represented by bolding the text above. At the same time she retreats a bit from this strong stance by saying "that's just my take on it," which we argue is to use rhetorical ethos to construct herself as someone who can at least see that others might think differently from her on this issue. In offering her own voice in this way she ensures she is not dismissing the voices of the others, is still "listening" to their voices; in other words, she wants to maintain an open mind, and see this discussion as very much an "exchange" of voices, not one person simply lecturing the others in a didactic manner without taking their views into account.

As the conversation proceeds, Gina becomes noticeably more comfortable in the position she's constructed for herself; from the implied acceptance of her position by the other two participants (they don't disagree with her, they take her voice into account); she clearly feels there's a certain mutuality to the sense-making, and she drops her "hedging" phrases ("that's just my take"), and expresses her voice much more strongly in favor of welcoming others into Australia and the need for assimilation:

> G: ... **my dad was one of the first Indians to come**, and at that time **all the Indians were the outcasts** and now they've assimilated, then maybe the Vietnamese ... If we actually look back, then it was like the Sudanese, Africans, and they are now assimilating and now it's all the people who are coming as asylum seekers coming from [Afghanistan]... and **we need to make more of an effort to assimilate them or to educate them** ... (G: 7, emphases added)

As we can see, here she is using the story of her father's migrant experience, which is also a way of constructing her own ethos – she's the daughter of someone who was initially an "outcast," but who over time became assimilated.

Conclusion

In this chapter we have presented our specific usage of the term rhetorical citizenship to include the concept that rhetorical citizenship occurs ideally in a continuous feedback loop of articulating one's position, listening to, and responding appropriately to the positions of others. We described the new theoretical lens that we have constructed for our analysis of rhetorical citizenship, comprised of voice, listening and narrative.

Our empirical study of a small group discussion shows that narrative (and/or ante-narrative) is employed by participants at various stages in the feedback loop – and, in fact, has led us to include another stage in the feedback loop. Our findings indicate that participants use narrative as a method to self-reflect verbally on a topic, in the early stages of a group discussion, to help one find one's position and to explore the "social environment" of public spheres; in our study narrative was also used by more than one participant to articulate feelings and to demonstrate taking account of others' views – illustrating one's understanding of, or extension of, another's viewpoint by using a story. Narrative was also used by participants as a means of responding to others, the final stage of our feedback loop. At times, we saw evidence of the use of very strong and explicit rhetoric in a narrative responding to another's position, using emotive or persuasive terms to advocate or to reassert one's own position in response to another's.

To conclude, we ask: what are the implications of our findings for the process of rhetorical citizenship? To answer this, we return to Habermas and his concept of the public sphere as a place for (the always rhetorical) exchange of views and argumentation by citizens. In this study, we have extended Habermas's conception of the public sphere from 19th century European salon society to the small group context (equally, it could be extended to contexts of public debate or community deliberation). For rhetorical citizenship to occur in its ideal form, the public sphere, in whatever context, will provide an environment where participants are able not only to use voice and narrative to formulate and then articulate their position, but also to facilitate listening to, taking into account the views of others, and to respond appropriately to, the positions of others. We believe our analysis of the micro public sphere has implications for the policy and practice of democratic participation in macro public spheres – for example, between organizations and local citizens during deliberation about the planning of projects that impact a community. Acknowledging that more sustainable societies cannot be achieved without the participation of local communities, stakeholders and interest groups in more open, deliberative processes, the UN Conference on Environment and Development formalized Principle 10 of the Rio Declaration on Environment and Development, stating the need for participation of all concerned citizens and the imperative of providing them with access to information, judicial and administrative proceedings (UNCED, 1992, Principle 10). In 1998, the adoption of the Aarhus Convention, Article 8, as part of the UN European Economic Commission, established citizens' rights to information and to fair participation in the development of environmental regulations (United Nations Treaty Collection, 1998).

Citizen participation has been embedded in France's national legal framework since the mid-1980s, following major conflicts concerning transport infrastructure projects. New legal procedures were enacted during the 1990s to enhance public and stakeholder participation, including the Law of Public Debate (CNDP, 1996), and creation of the National Commission of Public Debate (CNDP). The CNDP, as an independent administrative authority, was created to administer organization–citizen debates, to guarantee impartiality, to ensure the quality of debates, and to watch over the respective organization's methods of engagement.

The emerging theme from these and other international policies is the need for democratic empowerment of citizens in decision-making. Findings from this study can assist governments and organizations to ensure their policies for democratic public participation provide a public sphere for rhetorical citizenship that operates in a continuous feedback loop of articulating one's position, listening to the positions of others, and finally responding appropriately to them.

Given that stories are the main way humans share meanings, more research built upon our framework could assist in mitigating the noted present lack of voice in society, by suggesting conditions that would enhance the expression of voice and the construction of shared meanings among citizens.

References

Allan, J., G. Fairtlough and B. Heinzen (2002). *The Power of the Tale: Using Narratives for Organizational Success.* New York: John Wiley and Sons.

Boje, D.M. (1991). The Storytelling Organization: A Study of Story Performance in an Office- Supply Firm. *Administrative Science Quarterly* 36, 1, 106-126.

Boje, D.M. (2001a). *Narrative Methods for Organizational and Communication Research* (London: Sage, 2001).

Boje, D.M (2001b). *Storytelling and the Future of Organizations: An Antenarrative Handbook.* New York: Routledge.

Boje, D.M. (2008). *Storytelling Organizations.* Los Angeles, London: Sage.

Coakley, C. G., K. Halone and A.D. Wolvin. (1996). Perceptions of Listening Ability Across the Life-Span: Implications for Understanding Listening Competence. *International Journal of Listening* 10, 1, 21-48.

Cohen, J. (1989). Deliberation and Democratic Legitimacy. In A. Hamlin and P. Pettit (Eds.), *The Good Polity: Normative Analysis of the State.* Oxford: Blackwell.

CNDP (Commission Nationale du Debat Public), http://www.debatpublic.fr/ accessed 2 November 2014.

Couldry, N. (2009). Towards the Ethics of Global Media: Truthfulness, Hospitality, Care. (Closing plenary paper presented at *Journalism in the 21st century.* University of Melbourne, July 16-17, 2009.)

Couldry, N. (2010). *Why Voice Matters: Culture and Politics After Neoliberalism.* London: Sage.

Couldry, N., S. M. Livingstone and T. Markham. (2007). *Media Consumption and Public Engagement: Beyond the Presumption of Attention.* New York: Palgrave Macmillan.

Cragan, J.F., D.W. Wright and C.R. Kasch. (2004) *Communication in Small Groups: Theory, Process, Skills.* Belmont, CA: Wadsworth/Thomson Learning.

Dryzek, J. (2010). Rhetoric in Democracy: A Systemic Appreciation. *Political Theory* 38, 319-339.

Gabriel, Y. (2000). *Storytelling in Organizations: Facts, Fictions, and Fantasies.* Oxford: Oxford University Press.

Garver, E. (1994). *Aristotle's Rhetoric: An Art of Character.* Chicago: University of Chicago Press.

Fisher, W.R. (1987) *Human Communication as Narration: Toward a Philosophy of Reason, Value, and Action.* Columbia, SC: University of South Carolina Press.

Foss, S.K., K.A. Foss and R. Trapp. 1991. *Contemporary Perspectives on Rhetoric.* Prospect Heights, Ill.: Waveland Press.

Gutmann, A. and D.F. Thompson. (1996). *Democracy and Disagreement.* Cambridge, Mass.: Harvard University Press.

Habermas, J. (1984). *The Theory of Communicative Action, Vol.1: Reason and the Rationalization of Society*. Boston: Beacon Press.

Herrick, J.A. (1997). *The History and Theory of Rhetoric: An Introduction.* Scottsdale, Arizona: Gorsuch Scarisbrick Publishers.

Ivie, R.L. (2002). Rhetorical Deliberation and Democratic Politics in the Here and Now. *Rhetoric and Public Affairs* 5, 277-85.

Jacobson, T. L. (2007). Indicating Citizen Voice: Communicative Action Measures for Media Development. (Unpublished paper presented at *Workshop on Measuring Press Freedom and Democracy: Methodologies, Uses, and Impact*, University of Pennsylvania, Annenberg School of Communication, Centre for Global Communication Studies, 2007.)

Kock, C. and L. Villadsen (Eds.) (2012). *Rhetorical Citizenship and Public Deliberation.* University Park: Pennsylvania State University Press.

Passerin d'Entrèves, M. and S. Benhabib (Eds.) (1997). *Habermas and the Unfinished Project of Modernity: Critical Essays on The Philosophical Discourse of Modernity.* Cambridge, MA: The MIT Press.

Poole, M.S. and A.B. Hollingshead. (2004). *Theories of Small Groups: Interdisciplinary Perspectives.* Thousand Oaks, CA: Sage.

Snowden, D. (2000). Cynefin: A Sense of Time and Space: The Social Ecology of Knowledge Management. In: C. Despres and D. Chauvel (Eds.), *Knowledge Horizons: The Present and the Promise of Knowledge Management* (pp. 237-265). Boston: Butterworth-Heinemann.

Weick, K.E. (1995). *Sensemaking in Organizations.* Thousand Oaks, CA: Sage.

Young, Iris Marion. (2000). *Inclusion and Democracy.* Oxford: Oxford University Press.

Argumentative Literacy and Rhetorical Citizenship: The Case of Genetically Modified Food in the Institutional Setting of a Greek Primary School

FOTINI EGGLEZOU

Introduction

Ever since antiquity, rhetoric, as bipolar thinking and arguing upon every issue, has been interwoven with the instillation of virtues such as reflection, reasoning, awareness of the civil identity and of the sense of common good. In our era, characterized by rapid social and economic changes at both the *polis* and the *cosmopolis* levels, such an effort becomes essential for the formation of a more reasonable and humanistic social reality. Therefore, teaching rhetorical argumentation, even in the earliest stages of education, becomes one of the most powerful tools for the attainment of such a goal through the development of multi-level literacies and the concomitant construction of individual and social identities.

Theoretical framework

Rhetorical citizenship: from Isocrates to a critical and socio-cultural pedagogy of citizenship

Isocrates attributes to rhetoric as philosophy an essential role in the development of civic education. As a pioneer, he combined rhetoric – as good speaking (εὖ λέγειν/*eu legein*) – and literacy with the necessity of prudential action, of *praxis* (εὖ πράττειν/*eu prattein*). Within the Isocratean rhetorical *paideia*, literacy, the capacity of talking, reading and writing effectively, is accompanied by reflection (στοχάζεσθαι/*stokhazesthai*) and appropriate expression (πρέπον/*prepon*) of subjective opinions (δόξαι/*doxai*) upon current civic matters (καιρός/*kairos*). In particular, writing – an important feature of literacy – becomes a powerful "epistemic tool" that permits, first, the expression of *kairos* and *prepon* and, second, the formation of an ethos "within which both personal and public can work" (Walters 1993, p. 162). In this way, Isocrates shaped the individual and social values and identities of his students in the democratic context of his era. By cultivating their eloquence, literacy and the aptitude to take political decisions, Isocrates sought to instill in his students the quality of practical wisdom, of *phronēsis,* and to lead them to "a collective inquiry into the good" (Poulakos 1997, pp. 4-5). For Papillion, "precept, practice and example" (1995, p. 151) were the cornerstones of Isocrates' *technē* that combined rhetorical training and practice with civic education. In *Antidosis* (§ 184) Isocrates notes (1929, pp. 289, 291):

> … the teachers of philosophy impart all the forms of discourse in which the mind expresses itself. Then, when they have made them familiar and thoroughly conversant with their lessons then they set them at exercises, habituate them to work, and require them to combine in practice the particular things which they have learned, in order that they may grasp them more firmly and bring their theories into closer touch with the occasions for applying them …

Almost 2,500 years later, central notions of critical pedagogy are related to Isocratean principles of civic education for young citizens. For Freire (1985), Giroux (1988) and Welch (1999), the empowerment of citizenship is based on the interaction of a) the reflective challenge to political, socio-scientific and cultural data, b) consciousness raising, which instills social identity in individuals, and c) the improvement of current social data through the active learning and participation of citizen-agents. Active involvement in learning (Dewey 1933) is guaranteed by participatory, dialogic, situated activities that lead students to become informed participants and literate persons in a community (Shor 1999).

As regards the essential role of literacy in the acquisition of civic education (Knobel 1999), the modern socio-cultural approach (Christie 1990) confirms the primitive – although crucial – interrelation that Isocrates had pointed out during the middle of the 4th century B.C., when the passage from an oral to a literate culture characterized the socio-cultural reality of the era. According to UNESCO's definition (2004, p. 13), "literacy involves a continuum of learning in enabling individuals to achieve their goals, to develop their knowledge and potential and to participate fully in their community and wider society." The extension and plurality of the term literacy makes it a prerequisite to civic education. At the same time, active citizenship is identified as a form of literacy mutually interrelated with other forms or levels of it. Critical, genetic, argumentative and school literacy constitute some of these levels, as will be shown later in this paper.

Teaching citizenship and multi-level literacy in the modern Greek school context

Since the era of Isocrates' celebrated educational establishment of rhetoric in Athens, the school system, as a socio-cultural institution, offers a favorable "cultural environment" where students and teachers co-construct desirable civil virtues. In modern Greece, the *Single Interdisciplinary Curriculum* directs its gaze to a broader conception of citizenship following the demands created by the interdependence of events in different fields of the global social life (Keating et al. 2009). Therefore, besides the development of "Greek identity and consciousness," it aims at the intellectual, moral, social, economic, political and cultural development of young Greek citizens. The knowledge and understanding of universal and diachronic social values, critical evaluation of matters concerning liberty, equity, justice, human rights etc., the acquisition of necessary skills for free, responsible and active participation in the social, political and economic spheres are cited as necessary processes for attaining such goals. The whole effort takes a more systematic and organized form, once a week, in the 5th and 6th grade of primary school (11 and 12 year-olds) and the third class of High School (*Gymnasio*). Because of the limited time dedicated to formal civic education, its development is also attributed to an interdisciplinary approach ranging across the curriculum.

For example, in primary school the "semi-typical" lesson of *Flexible Zone* consists of an "umbrella" (Generalized Application ... 2005, p. 17715) under which various interdisciplinary programs are included. Emphasis is put on the development of critical thinking through collective forms of action and of dialectical communication (Ministry of National Education and Religion 2001, p. 10). The lesson aims at the students' cognitive development and the learning of values and pragmatic aspects of real life. Therefore, it offers an opportunity to develop "citizenship literacy" by examining socially contentious questions, such as the socio-scientific issue (SSI) of *Genetically Modified Food* (GMF). The interrelation of the genetic issue with argumentative and critical literacy facilitates the construction and expression of students' identities as members of a social group through purposeful literacy practices (Gee 1990).

In the case of genetics such an effort becomes necessary. The science of genes, as a field of scientific endeavor and of social interest, directs and imposes new modes of individual and collective thinking and decision making about the creation of life, health, the environment and, consequently, the global society. It demands the active engagement of individuals with various sources of information and knowledge as well as with the actions of debating and arguing about the application of bio-technology in modern human life.

On the other hand, argumentation, as the linguistic expression of a socio-cultural practice, contributes to civic education. First, it represents a form of social action based on rhetorical, situated practices and activities (Miller 1984, p. 163). Second, it favors the emergence of critical thinking and of participatory skills due to its interactive nature (Schwarz 2009). Also, argumentation becomes a necessary tool for exploring linguistic possibilities. The students engaged in argumentation discover the necessary linguistic and meta-linguistic expressions (e.g. argumentative markers) that facilitate the representation of their identities (Golder 1993) and the negotiation of their standpoints (Tseronis 2011). Finally, argumentation is the key factor in supporting Isocrates' rhetorical education: "to explore the senses in which *logos* can articulate communal purposes, address situational demands, induce cooperation and secure wise deliberations" (Poulakos 1986, p. 307).

In sum, rhetorical engagement in the global issue of GMF creates a parallel activation of multi-level literacies, capable of conducing students to "the expansion of [their] personal and social identity" (Intzidis and Karantzola 2008, p. 8). As will be obvious, the idea of the construction of a literate, social identity informs the present case study. At the same time, the paper examines whether the Isocratean ideal of *logōn paideia*, education in argumentative discourse (in oral and written form), may still lead modern students to "wisdom and involvement in their culture" in order to benefit the *polis* as well as themselves (Blair 1992, p. 4).

About the study

Purpose

The purpose of the study was the improvement of argumentative writing and the production of higher level argumentative texts through which students might express their opinions about the use of GMF.

Materials and methods

Theory and methodology

The study describes an experiment with 24 twelve-year-old students, in the sixth grade of a public elementary school in Alimos, an urban zone of Athens. The experimental group shared an homogeneous middle class social background. The intervention was carried out for a total of forty-four class hours.

Our program aimed at finding an appropriate method for the construction of a literate civic identity. To the social constructionist approach, the shape of an identity stems from the community in which we belong as individuals. Writing, as an "act of identity" (Ivanič 1998, p. 32) is influenced by the applied practices and interactions of the community in which it is generated. Therefore, the destabilization of pre-existent educational practices or *habitus* and of crystallized ways of thinking and acting, and the enhancement of a more reflexive monitoring of texts, of classroom practices, of the self and of the society, may lead to the genesis of conscious, literate and active citizens. As Vygotsky notes (1981, p. 157), both social life and argumentation determine the higher intellectual capacities and possibilities of each individual.

Theoretical and methodological models that informed our intervention were:

a) *The rhombus model of education* (Fig. 1). It represents the teaching of language as macro-genre. According to it, a bilateral relation may be shown to obtain between the promotion of literacy and the construction of identities of the participants-agents (Koutsogiannis and Alexiou 2012, p. 71). This relation is developed in a more complex web through the interdependence of all its factors such as: 1) *knowledge about the world* (values, attitudes etc.), 2) *knowledge about language* (meta-language), 3) *teaching practices*, 4) the intervention of *literacies* and 5) *identities*. The model seems to be influenced by *the sociological model*, which examines the development of *citizenship* as a complex process, directly interwoven with the acquisition of *identity* and of *civic virtues*, integration into a certain *community* (classroom) and access to various economic, cultural and political *resources* (school) (Turner 1997).

Other resources were: b) *The theory of social identity*: for Tajfel and Turner (2004) the formation of social identities depends on the meanings that individuals attribute to themselves as members of a particular social category and c) *the sociological analysis of emotions* (Stets and Turner 2008). According to it, there is a recursive and transformative interaction between,

FIGURE I THE RHOMBUS OF EDUCATION

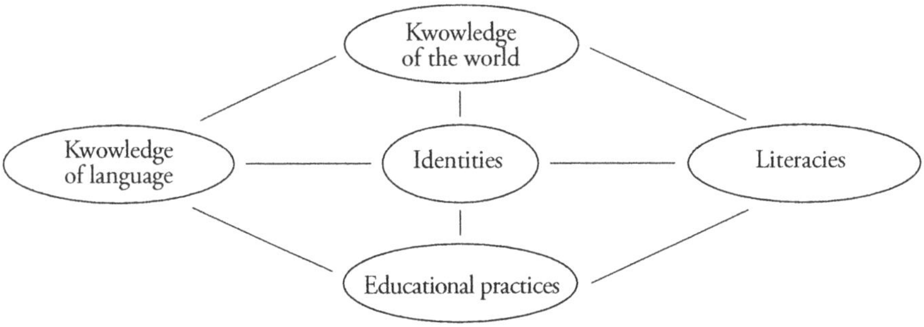

on the one hand, emotions and cognitive representations of the self and of features of the social reality and, on the other, with the social structure and culture which influence the expression of salient identities (Stets 2007).

The corpus of data consisted of: a) transcripts from audiotaped activities in the classroom and b) students' individual pre-test texts (Text A) and post-test texts (Text B) in the form of an argumentative opinion essay. The results of the students' oral activities and written texts were analyzed in qualitative and quantitative terms (triangulation of data). The qualitative analysis was based on the dialectical-relational approach of Critical Discourse Analysis. More specifically, Fairclough's three-dimensional model (1995) examines the linguistic choices that reveal the form and the texture of the produced texts, situated in a specific social context and interwoven with the practices that generate them (Wodak and Meyer 2009). The category system was identified as reliable based on the calculation of Cohen's Kappa coefficient for two raters (Cohen 1960). Alpha values of 0.60 (statistical significance: $p < 0.003$) and 0.833 ($p < 0.000$) were obtained for the observations regarding the level of the *decided* and *evaluativist* argumentative texts written after the intervention (Text B; see 4.2). Therefore, there was evidence that the observation system used by the researcher was valid.

Materials and treatment

The treatment was realized in two phases:

Phase I: The first phase included typical strategies such as: 1) the choice of the theme (1 hour): the issue of Genetics was included in the official manual of *Flexible Zone* and was freely chosen by the students among other issues for further research; 2) reading and analysis of textbook material (1 hour); 3) gathering and presentation of data (5 hours): students chose, and read in class, texts (journalistic, web-texts) and presented photos relative to the issue. A short discussion about GMF followed; 4) writing an argumentative text (1 hour): students developed their arguments for or against GMF (pre-test). The theme was: "What is your opinion of the use of GMF in your daily life?" During this phase, the oral interactions among teacher and students were limited to typical forms of questions and answers. The above habitual educational practices aimed at students' acquisition of a basic knowledge about GMF and their familiarization with the necessary vocabulary relating to the issue.

Phase II: The second phase included cognitive and social strategies of learning such as:

1) use of audiovisual media (1 hour): a short video from Greek educational television (http://www.edutv.gr) was presented in order to increase students' knowledge about GMF. Students were informed equally about the possible positive and negative consequences of genetically modified products;

2) expert opinions (2 hours): two experts, an industrial chemist and a member of the Greek World Wildlife Fund (WWF), visited the classroom in order to further cultivate the genetic literacy of the students. A short conversation about the role of bio-technology in foods followed;

3) drawing ideas (2 hours): after these visits, students were asked by the teacher to draw a picture illustrating the possible positive and negative effects of GMF. As evident in Figures 2 and 3, the visual antithesis among the drawings provoked a further classroom discussion of the controversial character of GMF in real life;

4) posing the problem (2 hours): students expressed and justified their initial attitude about GMF by playing the linguistic game *The chain of explanations*;

5) direct instruction (4 hours): students were taught basic elements of the argumentative genre such as: argumentative topics (cause and effect, antithesis etc.), types of evidence (statistics, testimonies etc.), expressions of modality (*should*, *must* etc.) and connectives (oppositional, concessive, etc.) in order to increase their knowledge about argumentation as a linguistic activity;

6) modeling (1 hour): a modeling of an argumentative text as a train (Egglezou 2010) was used, aimed at facilitating recall of its structure (thesis/reason(s)/counterargument(s)/rebuttal(s)/conclusion/evidence);

7) reading, listening and analysis of model texts (5 hours): five texts about GMF, brought to the classroom by the students, were re-read and broken down into their component parts by the teacher in cooperation with the students, in order to help them analyze the argumentation provided for or against GMF;

FIGURE 2 THE BUTTERFLY-APPLE

FIGURE 3 NO TO GMF

8) oral interactions between students (10 hours): students engaged in various oral interactions such as a) *linguistic games*: during the game "Tell the opposite" each student stated his/her opinion and asked the next classmate to state the opposite idea about GMF (1 hour); b) *role-playing debates*: these debates created the necessary context for the development of the students' arguments. For example, students acting as consumers asked the greengrocer of the 'laiki' market (a typical Greek farmers' market) why the tomatoes were so big, red and round or, as commercial agents of Monsanto, tried to persuade producers to buy GM tomato seeds (2 hours); c) the *Six Thinking Hats* of De Bono (1985; 3 hours). The students, as consumers, producers, citizens and scientists, worked collaboratively and developed their parallel argumentation considering the issue of GMF under multiple perspectives; d) *brainstorming*: students were divided into six groups of four and tried to find arguments for and against the use of GMF for (i) human health, (ii) the environment, and iii) society (1 hour); e) *Parliamentary debates* (3 hours): students exchanged arguments for and against GMF. All the above practices permitted the students' familiarization with various roles, allowed them to deliberate and/or arrive at justified opinions, while they shared common experiences and interacted pleasantly during the learning process;

9) *emotional arousal* (2 hours): students expressed their feelings and thoughts about a real case. Four of the biggest Greek dairy companies were accused by Greenpeace of using GM animal feed at a percentage of 90 %, with the result that the milk tested positive for GM substances;

10) *dyadic collaborative writing* (2 hours): students, in pairs, wrote a letter to the dairy companies, complaining, as responsible citizens, about the use of GM animal feed;

11) *observational learning* (4 hours): students, as observers, developed their metacognitive, metalinguistic and critical skills by evaluating and commenting the oral and written activities of their classmates;

12) *individual writing* (1 hour): students wrote a second text (post-test) stating their arguments on GMF.

Findings

Qualitative analysis of the oral activities

The aforementioned oral activities aimed at changing formal educational practices as well as students' knowledge about the world and the language. The game *The chain of explanations* provoked their skepticism about personal thoughts and attitudes and established the basis for their further deliberation on GMF. For example:

> (Antonis): "In the beginning I thought that it would be fun ... ehhh ... to ... create new products, but, then, Mrs. Helen made me understand that they are dangerous ...What about you?"
>
> (Konstantina): "I still don't know if they are good or bad. I am very confused ... What about you?"

The game *"Tell the opposite"* familiarized students with the expression of counterarguments related to the use of GMF and to the development of the art of controversy. The students exchanged different ideas on the issue of GMF:

> "The use of GMF will solve the problem of malnutrition worldwide, because the production will be increased".
>
> "Maybe you are right, but have you ever thought that the industries will control the production of goods? The farmers will be obliged to buy new genes every year!"

The role-playing debates, as an introduction to debate, made students assume various roles and produce arguments from those perspectives. At the same time this activity helped them develop the necessary civic qualities of *empathy* and *tolerance*, that is, the ability to recognize, understand and accept another person's perceptions:

> (Nikos as farmer/seller): "These tomatoes are improved. That's why they have this color and shape. Also, they are more tolerant to cold weather. So you can eat tomatoes all year long."

> (Apostolos as producer): "The crops that you are selling destroy bio-diversity. Nature knows how to improve its products by itself."

> (Despina as agent): "You are right to have doubts. But you must know that the crops produced by precise genetic engineering techniques are as safe as the crops which are generated by naturally selected intersections. You will have secure results and, trust me, your output will increase. So you will earn more money."

By wearing the *Six Thinking Hats* of De Bono (1985) students extended their thinking skills. Their argumentation varied according to the students' identification with different social groups (e.g. consumers, producers, citizens and scientists). For example:

> (Mary): "As a scientist, wearing the yellow hat of optimism, I assure you that you don't have to be afraid of GMF. Genetics is the science of the future, the science that will guarantee a better and healthier life to our children. The scientists will continue the research in order to prove that genetic modification does no harm to human beings. We want consumers to trust our products and choose them of their own free will because they prefer them."

Two debates were carried out in the classroom in order to offer students the opportunity to be engaged in public speaking, to "inter-think" (Mercer 2009, p. 182) and to understand the usefulness of audience-based discourse.

> (Evangelos): "I and my team, we are against the use of GMF. The opponent team said that GMF has beautiful shape and color. But I really don't understand how it is possible for you to like a purple tomato. Also, maybe some mice lived 20 more days in the labs in Great Britain ... but the researches refer only to animals not to humans ... and we all know that we are different organisms from mice. So, we don't really know if they are good or bad ..."

The information that the daily milk tested positive for GM substances acted in a catalytic way on the students' judgments. Intense feelings such as rage, anger, sorrow, insecurity, anxiety arose in students, proving that "increasing our capacity for emotion enhances our ability to reason" (Nelson 2005, p.8) and illustrating the role of passion in every rhetorical situation. At the same time, salient thoughts and judgments were activated. Students wondered about the role of legislation and the informative role of television, and as consumers they demanded official information about what they ate, asking for GMF labels in supermarkets, and criticizing, implicitly, current policies or failures to act on the part of the state or consumers:

> (Dimitris): "I don't feel safe because I don' know if what I eat is genetically engineered or not. Shouldn't the representatives of the milk industries be taken to court and put in jail? What they did was awful, since thousands of Greek children drink their milk. Fortunately Greenpeace revealed this big secret that concerns all Greeks ... If I could have the control of these industries I would try to change a lot of their practices ..."

> (Nikolas): "I feel angry because we pay a lot of money for our milk. I am wondering why TV didn't present this information."

Statistical analysis of the written texts

The evaluation criteria for students' pre-test texts (Text A) and post-test texts (Text B) were:

a) the argumentative level of the text. Following the taxonomy of levels of argumentative texts proposed by Mani-Ikan (2000) a rating scale from 1-5 was created. Each text was marked by a number representing a different argumentative level: a) *unwarranted* texts (1 point), b) *one-sided* texts (2 points), c) *multiplist* texts where despite the appearance of oppositional arguments no explicit conclusion was drawn (3 points), d) *decided* texts where the choice between the contrasting arguments was not grounded (4 points) and e) *evaluativist* texts where the adoption of the proposed argumentation was based on a refutation of the opposing argument(s) (5 points). Lower average means of the scale represented a lower argumentative level of the text while higher average means represented a higher argumentative level of the text;

b) argumentative markers (of claim and modality). A rating scale from 0-2 was created according to the following norm: a) no use of argumentative markers of claim or modality: 0 points, b) use of an argumentative marker of claim or modality at least once in the text: one point, c) use of both argumentative markers at least once in the text: two points. Lower average means of the scale represented limited use of argumentative markers in the text.

Two statistical tests were used: a) the McNemar non-parametric test, for measuring the significance of the percentage of the matched pre/post test results. In our case the test was applied in order to determine whether the intervention had an effect on argumentative writing according to the above criteria at a significant level; b) the Wilcoxon non-parametric test was used in order to detect the existence of differences at a significant level between the average means of texts A and B as regards the first and second criterion of analysis.

The activities during the second phase of the intervention were considered as the independent variable of the research (YES/NO) (Verma and Mallick 1999). The average mean of the argumentative level of the text and of the argumentative markers constituted the dependent variables.

As for the first criterion of analysis, the McNemar test showed significant changes in the percentage of the level of the texts written before and after the intervention (Text A vs. Text B). After the intervention a significant difference was observed in the percentage of the produced texts of the *unwarranted* level (Text A 33 % vs. Text B 0) (p = 0.008), of the *decided* level (Text A 0 vs. Text B 29.2 %) (p = 0.016), and of the *evaluativist* level (Text A 4.2 % vs. Text B 45.8 %) (p = 0.002), while no significance was noticed in the texts of *one-sided* level (Text A 54.2% vs. Text B 20.8 %), and of the *multiplist* level (Text A 8.2 % vs. Text B 4.1 %).

According to the Wilcoxon signed rank test the average mean M = 1.88 (SD = ± 0.9) of the argumentative level of the pre-test (Text A) increased in the post-test (Text B) (M = 4.00, SD = ± 1.18). The analysis showed a significant difference in the mean argumentative level between Texts A and B (p = 0.000). Positive differences in Figure 4 indicate that the students produced texts at a higher argumentative level after the activities of the second phase (Text B), while the negative difference expresses the final absence of "unwarranted" texts.

For the second criterion a significant increase in the percentage of argumentative markers was noticed. In particular, the proportion of the students (N=12) that used argumentative markers of claim varied from 50 % (Text A) to 91.7 % (N = 22) in Text B. The McNemar test confirmed

FIGURE 4 POSITIVE AND NEGATIVE DIFFERENCES IN THE ARGUMENTATIVE LEVEL OF THE PRODUCED TEXTS

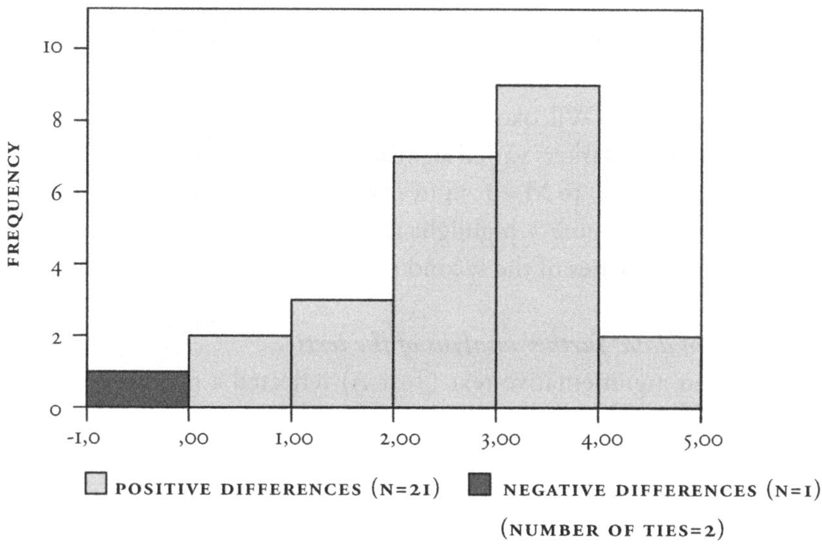

FIGURE 5 POSITIVE DIFFERENCES IN THE USE OF ARGUMENTATIVE MARKERS

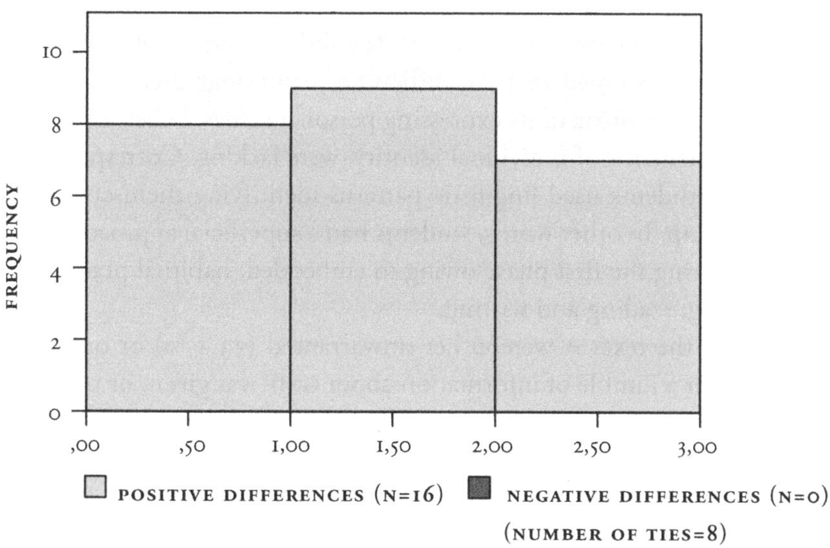

a significant difference in the use of argumentative markers of claim (p = 0.000). A significant difference relative to the use of argumentative markers of modality (p = 0.002) was also noticed. The percentage of the students that used argumentative modality markers increased between Texts A and B from 8.3% (N=2) to 62.5% (N=15) correspondingly.

According to the Wilcoxon signed rank test the average mean of the use of argumentative markers varied significantly (p = 0.000) from M = 0.58 in Text A (SD = ± 0.654) to M = 1.54 in Text B (SD = ± 0.658). The positive differences shown in Figure 5 highlight the increased use of argumentative markers after the activities of the second phase.

Triangulation of data: further analysis of the texts

The free written argumentative text (Text A) reflected a generalized negative reception and attitude (Gaskell 1999) towards GMF, which represents a broader public European and, especially, Greek perception of the issue (Marouda-Chatjoulis et al. 1998). Thirteen students (54 %) stated their opposition to GMF, four students (16.6 %) kept a positive attitude towards it, while seven students (29 %) were neutral on the use of GMF (Fig. 7).

Despite the results, the qualitative analysis of the produced texts showed that the generalized rejection of GMF wasn't supported by personal and conscious "discursive constructions" (Lankshear and Knobel 1997, p. 95). The students seemed to have difficulties expressing their "discursive self" as writers. Linguistic units expressing personal values, beliefs or experiences, that is, elements of individual identity, were lacking. Correspondingly, only three students used linguistic patterns identifying themselves with some social group. In other words, students had a superficial approach to the whole issue during the first phase owing to embedded, habitual practices of communicating, reading and writing.

Most of the texts A were either unwarranted (33.3 %) or one-sided (54.2 %). Either a jumble of information about GMF was given, or the arguments were clichés, mechanical reproductions of stereotypical ideas about human health. The negotiation and critical evaluation of opposite ideas were lacking (4.2 %) (Fig. 8).

> "The scientists modified fruits and vegetables in order to grow sooner than the natural ones and to be more nutritious and delicious. The label of GMF is a triangle with four circles inside, but, we rarely see it on the products."

The lack of personal interest and engagement in the issue was shown by the limited use of argumentative markers of claim (50 %) and of modality (8.3%) in text A (Fig. 6). Even the incidental use of modality markers weakened the argumentation presented, since their 'value' indicated either a possibility or an uncertainty of the writer about the position supported (*maybe*, *possibly*, etc.).

> "I believe that GMF is, possibly, harmful to our health, since they change the cells of the fruits or of the animals we eat. For example, they may put cells of lemon in a banana" (Mary).

FIGURE 6 ARGUMENTATIVE MARKERS (TEXT A VS. TEXT B)

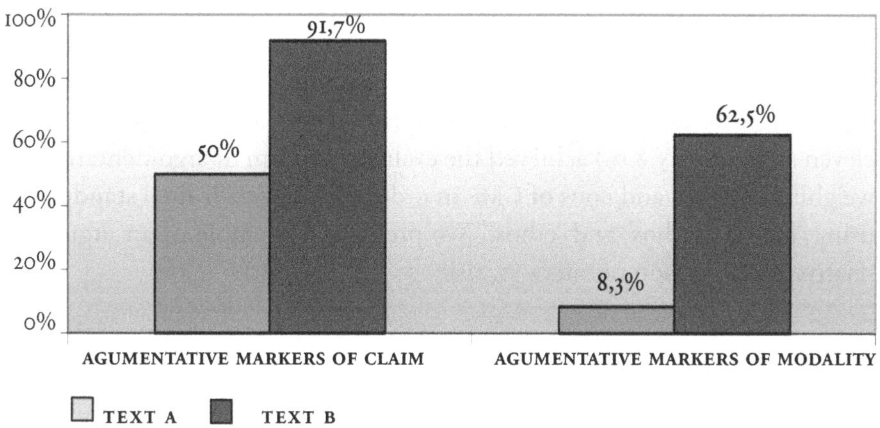

On the other hand, the activities during the second phase had a positive impact on the writing of Text B. The final attitude to GMF continued to be negative in most of the texts. Twenty-one students (87.5 %) were opposed to the use of GMF, two students (8.3 %) supported it, while one student (4.1 %) remained neutral (Fig.7). But what is most important is that the students discovered the linguistic "tools" which helped them a) support their position in a more authoritative way and b) construct their identities through writing. The form of the texts was improved, achieving higher levels of argumentation (Figure 8).

FIGURE 7 ATTITUDES OF STUDENTS (TEXT A VS. TEXT B)

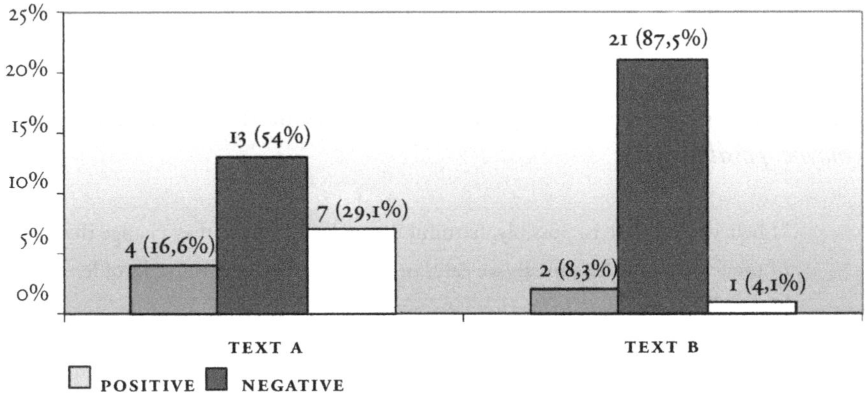

No unwarranted texts were produced, and the number of one-sided texts decreased to five (20.8 %). Seven students (29.2 %) managed to produce decided texts through the presentation of bilateral thinking and arguing, while eleven students (45.8 %) achieved the evaluativist form of argumentation by weighing the pros and cons of GMF in order to adopt their final standpoint, using 'logos', 'pathos' and 'ethos.' We present an example of an argument relative to the notion of safety vs. risk:

> "On the one hand, animal testing shows that the use of GMF made the animals live longer. On the other hand, their use provoked dangerous side-effects as toxins on the liver and the kidneys. I am afraid to risk my health since the researches are ambiguous. That's why I am against GMF and I advise all my fellow men to be so." (Zenia)

In the final texts (B), the use of argumentative markers increased significantly and highlighted an active commitment on the issue (Fig. 6). Twenty-two students (91.7 %) used markers of claim (*I believe that…, according to my opinion…etc.*) in order to express their personal opinions. Fifteen students (62.5 %) used modality markers. What is important to notice is not only the increase in the percentage but, mainly, their strong value (*should…, shouldn't…* etc.), which revealed a greater certainty about the students' standpoints.

Also, the use of argumentative markers in Text B was accompanied by an increased use of linguistic units that revealed the students' adherence to a certain social group (70.8 %). Mostly, the students were identified with the

FIGURE 8 LEVEL OF ARGUMENTATIVE TEXT (TEXT A VS. TEXT B)

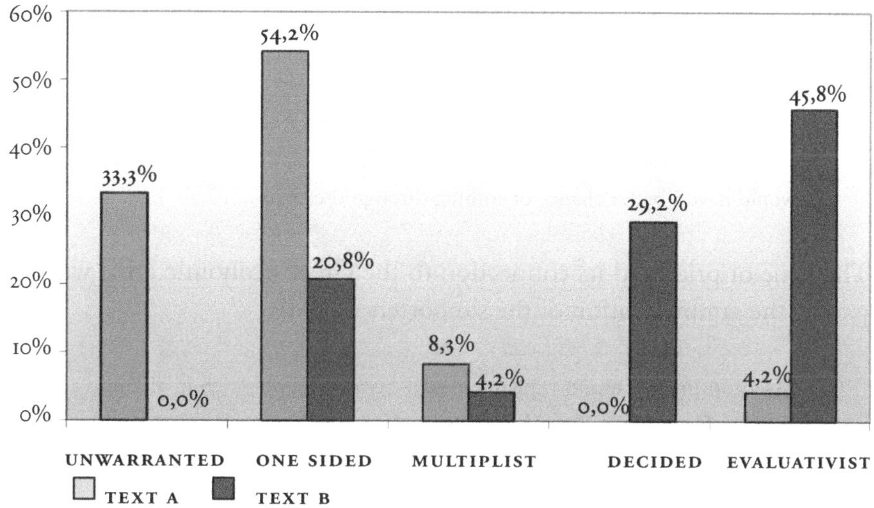

social groups of citizens and of consumers or both of them at the same time (*as consumer…*, *as citizen…*, *as a consumer and citizen…*). Besides that, the students either connected their interests to the practices of activist organizations or set themselves apart from the interests of other social groups – such as the industries. Also, the students proposed courses of action against GMF:

> "The big companies are afraid only of one thing: the informed citizens who protect their rights. If GMF was as safe as they want to present it, then why do they hide the identity of GM products and they don't write it on their packages?"

Sometimes the students' individual identity was absorbed by a collective one, as shown by the use of the plural personal pronoun *we*:

> "As citizens of a democracy we demand to know what we are eating…".

> "Because, when we play dangerous games with mother nature, we are lost from the very beginning. Her gifts are more than enough for all of us and we don't need anything more than the perfection of nature…",

Moreover, in some cases representing the social identity of the consumer/citizen the students produced arguments in favor of organic farming, converting the logic of GM crops and relating the problem of GM animal feed to the economic crisis of Greece, that is, to the social context in which they lived:

> "Since in Greece we have so many fields, why don't we cultivate crops such as chickpeas or peas that enrich the soil and may offer so many jobs?... In our economic situation such farming would bring development to the country and we would have a better chance of coming through the crisis ...".

The issue of price and its connection to the Greek economic crisis was also part of the argumentation of the supporters of GMF:

> "As a consumer, I support the use of GMF because they are rich in vitamins and may be cheaper than natural products and, as we all know, we are going through an economic crisis ... ".

Also it's worth mentioning that in Text B fourteen students (58.3 %) used, at least once, linguistic units which permitted the expression of their 'auto-biographical' discursive self through the writing of examples, personal experiences, testimonies, sentiments etc. Such discursive constructions were totally lacking in the first text. Their use in the post-test (B) helped the students to extend their argumentation, to formulate effective warrants and to give a more personal style to the texts produced.

> "My sister is allergic to various foods. How can I be sure that genetic modification has nothing to do with it, since several researches have shown that GMF provoke allergies?"

Some students declared that their participation in the activities of the program led them to form their final opinion, to reach a higher level of self-understanding and to gain a deeper knowledge of the socio-scientific issue of GMF.

> "After a long period of involvement in GM products I now have an opinion on them. My standpoint is negative and I drew my conclusion based on the information and the sources which I saw and heard...".

Conclusions

To conclude, the statistical results of the research showed that *logos* was a precious tool that allowed students to get in touch with reality, to promote their knowledge, to deliberate on a modern socio-scientific issue and to arrive at justified beliefs. The students succeeded in cultivating the Isocratean quality of *sophia* or *phronesis* (Depew 2004, p. 171), as future deliberating citizens and consumers. In other words, they developed their practical reasoning and made decisions about the use of GM products through rhetorical argumentation. So, the belief of Isocrates is still credible: that the unifying strength of the language embedded in rhetorical pedagogy helps the acquisition of literacy as well of civic engagement in young citizens. Today, more than ever, it is necessary to train the *politai* in a socially responsible rhetoric, affording opportunities for social change and for shaping the future *polis* through an emergent discourse of care (Ackerman and Coogan 2010).

In particular, our research revealed that the educational practices of the second phase of the intervention created a suitable context for a more active, dialogic, self-reflective and exploratory process of learning. The students' argumentative discourse on GMF permitted them to develop the skill of controversy and the capacity of evaluating and questioning the information provided. Rhetorical argumentation contributed to the expansion of their linguistic and metalinguistic, cognitive and metacognitive abilities. Students' knowledge about the language and the world, the self and society was broadened.

Apart from the students' oral argumentative activities, the writing facilitated articulation of their thoughts in written words in an orderly and disciplined way. The statistical analysis confirmed that written texts at a higher argumentative level were produced; that is, an improved form of argumentative literacy was achieved. Also, the departure from habitual teaching practices seemed to have positive implications for the construction of the students' individual and social identities. In the final texts, the increased use of argumentative markers and of various linguistic patterns relative to the auto-biographical and social selves of the students was a sign of active engagement with the issue. Their intellectual, emotional, practical and moral involvement in the issue of GMF moved them away from prior habitual attitudes such as indifference and apathy towards everyday social phenomena.

It might be objected that students reiterated commonsense notions about GMF, recycling bias and stereotypes. Indeed, this may be true up to a certain point. However, exploration of the self and of society, especially at this age, starts from commonsense argumentation in order to criticize, refute or transform it later. As Billig notes, "each repetition will be a creation, bringing the past towards its future" (1991, p. 22). What really matters is the internalization of rhetorical argumentation, implying criticism, evaluation and choice of the best alternative in every situation. Citizenship and civic virtues stem from such internalized processes and practices of individual thought and social existence.

References

Ackerman, J. and D. Coogan. (2010). *The Public Work of Rhetoric: Citizen-Scholars and Civic Engagement.* Columbia: University of South Carolina Press.

Billig, M. (1991). *Ideology and Opinions: Studies in Rhetorical Psychology.* London: Sage.

Blair, K.L. (1992). Isocratean Discourse Theory and Neo-Sophistic Pedagogy: Implications for the Composition Classroom. (Paper presented at the annual meeting of the Conference on College Composition and Communication, Cincinatti, OH, March 19-21, 1992.)

Christie, F. (1990). *Literacy for a Changing World.* Melbourne: Australian Council for Educational Research.

Cohen, J. (1960). "A Coefficient of Agreement for Nominal Scales." *Educational and Psychological Measurement* 20, 37-46.

De Bono, Edward. (1985). *Six Thinking Hats: An Essential Approach to Business Management.* Boston: Little, Brown and Company.

Depew, D. (2004). "The Inscription of Isocrates into Aristotle's Practical Philosophy." In T. Poulakos and D. Depew (Eds.), *Isocrates and Civic Education* (pp. 157-185). Austin: University of Texas Press.

Dewey, J. (1933). *How we Think.* Boston: Heath.

Egglezou, F. (2010). Argumentative Writing: Teaching of Language Arts in Primary School. PhD diss., University of Ioannina.

Fairclough, N. (1995). *Critical Discourse Analysis: The Critical Study of Language.* London: Longman.

Freire, P. (1985). *The Politics of Education: Culture, Power and Liberation.* Westport, CT: Bergin and Garvey Publishers.

Gaskell, G., M.W. Bauer, J. Durant and N.C. Allum. (1999). Worlds Apart? The Reception of Genetically Modified Foods in Europe and the U.S. *Science Magazine* 28, 384-387.

Gee, J.P. (1990). *Social Linguistics and Literacies: Ideology in Discourses.* London: The Falmer Press.

Generalised Application of the Program of Flexible Zone to the Primary Education.

(2005). In: *Journal of the Government of the Greek Republic, Vol.* 2, no. 1280 (13-9-2005): 17715-17726. Athens: The National Typography.

Giroux, H. (1988). *Teachers as Intellectuals: Towards a Critical Pedagogy of Learning.* Westport, CT: Bergin and Garvey Publishers.

Golder, C. (1993). Framed Writing of Argumentative Monologues by Sixteen-and Seventeen-year-old Students. *Argumentation* 7, 343-358.

Intzidis, E. and E. Karantzola. (2008). Literacies for Active Citizenship. In C. Medel-Anonuevo (Ed.), *Literacy and the Promotion of Citizenship: Discourses and Effective* (pp. 7-12). Hamburg: Unesco Institute for Lifelong Learning.

Isocrates. (1929). Antidosis. In *Isocrates* (Vol. II). Translated by George Norlin, pp. 181-367. London: William Heinemann Ltd.

Ivanič, R. (1998). *Writing and Identity: The Discoursal Construction of Identity in Academic Writing.* Amsterdam: John Benjamins Publishing Company.

Keating, A., D. Hinderliter Ortloff and S. Philippou. (2009). Citizenship Education Curricula: The Changes and Challenges Presented by Global and European Integration. *Journal of Curriculum Studies* 41, 145-158.

Knobel, M. (1999). *Everyday Literacies: Students, Discourse and Social Practice.* New York: Peter Lang Publishing.

Koutsogiannis, D. and M. Alexiou. (2012). *Study for the Design, Development and Application of Scenarios and Educational Activities for the Teaching of Greek Language to the Secondary Education.* Thessaloniki: Center of Greek Language, Ministry of Education, Lifelong Learning and Religion.

Lankshear, C. and M. Knobel. (1997). Critical Literacy and Active Citizenship. In S. Muspratt, A. Luke and P. Freebody (Eds.), *Constructioning Critical Literacies: Teaching and Learning Textual Practice* (pp. 95-124). New Jersey: Hampton Press.

Mani-Ikan, E. (2000). Writing as a Tool for Learning Biology: A Model for Learning Biology through Writing Skills. PhD diss., Hebrew University of Jerusalem.

Marouda-Chatjoulis, A., A. Stathopoulou and G. Sakellaris. (1998). Greece. In J. Durant, M. Bauer and G. Gaskell (Eds.), *Biotechnology in the Public Sphere: A European Source Book* (pp. 77-88). London: The Board of Trustees of the Science Museum.

Mercer, N. (2009). Developing Argumentation: Lessons Learned in the Primary School. In N. Muller Mirza and A.N. Perret-Clermont (Eds.), *Argumentation and Education: Theoretical Foundations and Practices* (pp. 177-194). Berlin: Springer,.

Miller, C. (1984). Genre as Social Action. *Quarterly Journal of Speech* 70, 151-167.

Ministry of National Education and Religion. (2001). *Guide for the Application of Flexible Zone: Teacher's Guide.* Athens: Pedagogical Institute.

Nelson, J. (2005). Emotions as Reasons in Public Arguments. *Poroi* 4, 1-26.

Papillion, T. (1995). Isocrates' Techne and Rhetorical Pedagogy. *Rhetoric Society Quarterly* 25, 149-163.

Poulakos, T. (1986). Gorgias' and Isocrates' Use of the Encomium. *Southern Speech Communication Journal* 51, 300-307.

Poulakos, T. (1997). *Speaking for the Polis: Isocrates' Rhetorical Education.* South Carolina: University of South Carolina Press.

Schwarz, B. (2009). Argumentation and Learning. In N. Muller Mirza and A.N. Perret-Clermont (Eds.), *Argumentation and Education: Theoretical Foundations and Practices* (pp. 91-126). Berlin: Springer.

Shor, I. (1999). *Empowering Education: Critical Teaching for Social Thought.* Chicago: University of Chicago Press.

Stets, J.E. (2007). Identity Theory and Emotion. In J. Stets and Jonathan Turner (Eds.), *Handbook of the Sociology of Emotions* (pp. 203-223). Berlin: Springer.

Stets, J.E. and J.E. Turner. (2008). The Sociology of Emotions. In M. Lewis, J. Haviland-Jones, L.F. Barrett (Eds.), *Handbook of Emotions* (pp. 32-46). New York: The Guilford Press.

Tajfel, H. and J. Turner. (2004). The Social Identity Theory of Intergroup Behavior. In J. Jost and J. Sidanius (Eds.), *Political Psychology* (pp. 276-293). New York: Psychology Press.

Tseronis, Assimakis (2011). From Connectives to Argumentative Markers: A Quest for Markers of Argumentative Moves and of Related Aspects of Argumentative Discourse. *Argumentation* 25, 427-447.

Turner, B. (1997). Citizenship Studies: A General Theory. *Citizenship Studies* 1, 5-18.

Unesco. (2004). *The Plurality of Literacy and its Implications for Policies and Programs.* Paris: United Nations Educational Scientific and Cultural Organization.

Verma, G.K. and K. Mallick. (1999). *Researching Education: Perspectives and Techniques.* Philadelphia: The Falmer Press.

Voelkl, K. and S. Gerber. (1999). *Using SPSS for Windows: Data Analysis and Graphics.* New York: Springer.

Vygotsky, L. (1981). The Genesis of Higher-Order Mental Functions. In J. Wertch (Ed.), *The Concept of Activity in Soviet Psychology* (pp. 144-188). New York: Sharpe.

Walters, F. (1993). Isocrates and the Epistemic Return: Individual and Community in Classical and Modern Rhetoric. *Journal of Advanced Composition* 13, 155-172.

Welch, K. (1999). *Electric Rhetoric: Classical Rhetoric, Oralism, and a New Literacy.* Cambridge, MA: MIT Press.

Wodak, R. and M. Meyer. (2009). Critical Discourse Analysis: History, Agenda, Theory and Methodology. In R. Wodak and M. Meyer (Eds.), *Methods of Critical Discourse Analysis* (pp. 1-33). California: Sage.

"People Power" in Philippine Presidential Rhetoric: (Re)Framing Democratic Participation in Post-authoritarian Regimes

GENE SEGARRA NAVERA

Introduction

Crucial to the development of democracy is the kind and level of civic engagement citizens perform in society (Diamond 2008, pp. 359-62; Dahl 2000, pp. 185-188). Needless to say, various societal contexts necessitate different forms and levels of citizen participation. In more mature democracies, citizen participation comes in the form of political debates and discussions that creatively draw upon various methods and technologies available in the 21st century (Dahl, p. 188; Diamond, pp. 361-62). For societies that have gone through years of authoritarianism and have, at some point in their history, chosen to reject autocratic leadership in favor of a democratic government, mass mobilizations and protests become the most manifest political expression. Such political expression was apparent in the democratization movements in Eastern Europe in the 1990s and in the Arab Spring at the turn of the second decade of the 21st century.

The Philippines, which transitioned from a long-standing dictatorial regime to democratization in the latter half of the 1980s, shares with other societies-in-democratic transition the penchant for mass mobilizations and protests in order to break free from the grip of dictatorship or quell autocratic tendencies. In fact, protests were waged even during the dictatorial regime of Ferdinand Marcos despite his leadership's notorious use of state terrorism. The protests culminated in what is now known as the "people power revolution" – a four-day mass protest of hundreds of thousands of Filipinos along a strip of highway called Epifanio delos Santos Avenue (EDSA). The peaceful convergence of Filipinos-in-protest overthrew Marcos from his 20-year rule and installed Corazon Aquino, wife of a slain opposition leader and the emergent leader of the anti-Marcos struggle, into power.

Corazon Aquino's assumption into the Philippine presidency somehow parallels the rise of the term "people power," an expression that, from then on, found its way into the political lexicon of the country. It may be argued that people power in the Philippines has served as a model for democratization movements in other parts of the world. More importantly, it has served as a resource for talking about and for performing democracy in the country. It may be worth asking then the question, how has people power been talked about and rhetorically constructed in the years following the fall of the Marcos dictatorship? People power is in itself a rhetorical phenomenon in that it requires the deployment of linguistic and semiotic resources in order to shape and create impact on politics and society; however, I wish to suggest that its definition and redefinition pose constraints to its realization in the Philippines' democratization project.

In this chapter, I examine how the notion of "people power" has been variably cast in the schemas of post-dictatorship Philippine presidencies. I specifically examine how the post-dictatorship presidencies – from Corazon Aquino to the incumbent president Benigno Aquino III – have conceptualized the notion of democracy in their presidential rhetoric. The State of the Nation Addresses (SONAs) delivered by these presidents are used as primary data for analysis.[1]

In the succeeding sections, I discuss the analytical framework used to analyze the national speeches of five Philippine presidents including Corazon Aquino (1986-1992), Fidel Ramos (1992-1998), Joseph Estrada (1998-2001), Gloria Macapagal Arroyo (2001-2010), and Benigno Aquino III (2010 to the present). I then provide a brief account of the socio-political and historical milieu of the five presidencies to contextualize their public addresses. This is followed by sections containing analyses of presidential texts and discussion of insights generated from the analyses. In the discussion, I argue that conceptualizations of people power across the post-dictatorship presidencies are motivated by presidential character, agenda, and the unique socio-political situation presidents find themselves in. I conclude by proposing that as conceptualizations of the presidencies are motivated by a host of

[1] The SONAs are annual reports to the nation delivered by the Philippine presidents before members of the legislative chambers. Mandated by the constitution, the SONA is the most publicized speech of the president and arguably the most talked about before, during and after its presentation.

factors, the notion of people power necessarily becomes malleable and this is realized in presidential text and talk. This malleability reveals the potential of presidential rhetoric to define the limits and possibilities of rhetorical citizenship.

Analytical framework

In my analytical framework, I assume that mental models (van Dijk 1998) mediate our sense making processes. When we make sense of texts, mental representations enable us to establish a link between linguistic or semiotic expressions and their socio-political contexts. In this paper, I examine these mental models by using concepts from cognitive linguistics. For the purpose of analysis, I use the terms "conceptual frames," "conceptualizations," "conceptual metaphors," and "metaphorizations" that have been largely informed by the works of Lakoff and Johnson (1980), Lakoff (1992, 2008), and Charteris-Black (2004, 2005). I generate what I call the conceptual frames of democracy through an analysis of conceptual statements including conceptual metaphors (Lakoff and Johnson 1980; Lakoff 1992, 2008; Charteris-Black 2005, 2007) that underlie metaphorical and lexico-grammatical expressions found in political texts and talk. Specifically, I focus on identifying, describing, and analyzing conceptualizations of Philippine democracy as realized in the presidential speeches and how they parallel or differ from each other. I suggest that the presidential conceptualizations of democracy reveal how the notion of people power is curiously rendered in the national leaders' visions of the state of the nation.

In the following sub-sections, I briefly discuss how the theme of democracy becomes a salient theme in post-authoritarian presidential rhetoric and illustrate (see Figure 1) how the analysis is done using extracts from the speeches of the first post-dictatorship president, Corazon Aquino.

The theme of democracy

This paper is derived from a larger study that looks into configurations of the various conceptualizations of the state of the nation across 23 national addresses delivered by four presidencies.[2] It solely focuses on the conceptualizations

[2] Navera, Gene Segarra, "Metaphorizing the Philippine Presidency: Schemas of Presidential Leadership in the Post-Marcos State of the Nation Addresses (1987-2009)", (PhD diss., National University of Singapore, 2012).

of democracy in the State of the Nation Address or SONA, a constitutionally mandated speech delivered by the Philippine president before the Congress every third Monday of July. The identification of democracy as a salient theme in the post-dictatorship presidential rhetoric is based on a careful examination of the 23 SONAs and published historical accounts and documents on the Marcos authoritarian regime (from 1972 to 1986) and the four post-Marcos presidencies to get a good grasp of the socio-political and historical milieu within which the public addresses were situated.[3] Crucial to the identification of the theme were accounts of the socio-political situation in the Philippines during the final year of the Marcos presidency[4] and the Aquino administration's assessment of its presidential term (see Abueva and Roman, 1993).

Based on my analysis of the primary texts and my critical appreciation of previous accounts of the major issues and concerns that confronted the four post-Marcos presidencies under question (Malaya and Malaya 2004, Cortes 1999, Martinez 1999), I identified democracy as an important theme in the post-authoritarian Philippine presidential rhetoric.[5] The theme of democracy subsumes the notion of "people power," a political expression that found its way into the national imagination during the fall of the Marcos dictatorship and at the beginning of "re-democratization" in the Philippines. Understandably, "people power" figures prominently when the theme of democracy is discussed in Philippine political discourse.

Method of analysis

In analyzing the SONAs of each president, I focused on portions of the speeches that explicate or discuss the focal theme. From these extracts, I

[3] The sources of these documents include the library and archival sections of the Philippine House of Representatives; the University of the Philippines Main Library's Filipiniana section; the library of the UP National College of Public Administration and Governance; the library of the Philippine Center for Investigative Journalism (PCIJ); and the library of IBON Foundation, an independent think tank that regularly publishes analyses on the socio-economic and political situation in the Philippines.

[4] They are significant in that they highlight the issues and concerns that the post-Marcos presidential leadership was positioned to respond.

[5] Other themes that surfaced in my analysis of the texts include national economy, peace and security, and the presidency. They are not covered in this paper, but are covered in the unpublished doctoral dissertation by the author.

identified the metaphorical expressions relevant to the said theme. Since metaphorical expressions having to do with the focal theme were varied (that is, various source domains were used to express a focal theme), several clusters of related metaphorical expressions were generated. From these clusters of metaphorical expressions, I derived the underlying conceptual metaphors, which are represented in the analysis as A is B (e.g., DEMOCRACY IS A CURE TO THE NATIONAL ILLS). To illustrate this point, I present the following extracts from the SONAs of Corazon C. Aquino:

> (1) I believe that *nowhere could you find more effective cures for the ills of our country* – such as the habit of oppression, the inclination to corruption, the betrayal of public interest – *than in the blessings of democracy*: freedom; rights; transparent dealings; and a government of the people by the people themselves. (1988)

> (2) The failed adventurism has underscored the fact that *our restored democracy has gone past its fledgling stage*. (1990)

> (3) Democracy, once a word, *is now alive*: this is our legacy. (1991)

The extracts above, taken from SONAs delivered in 1988, 1990 and 1991, all deal with the theme of democracy. Metaphorical expressions are indicated using italics. The first extract metaphorizes democracy as a "cure for the ills of the country" suggesting the conceptual metaphor DEMOCRACY IS A CURE TO THE NATIONAL ILLS; the last two express democracy as a living ("alive") and evolving ("has gone past its fledgling state") organism, thus, the conceptual metaphor DEMOCRACY IS A LIVING ENTITY. Further examination of the Aquino SONAs would show various metaphorical expressions that suggest other conceptual metaphors such as DEMOCRACY IS A BENEFACTOR OF THE PEOPLE, DEMOCRACY IS RESOURCE FOR PEOPLE POWER, and DEMOCRACY IS A FUNDAMENTAL REQUIREMENT TO A PEOPLE-POWERED ECONOMY. These conceptual metaphors relate to the conceptual metaphor DEMOCRACY IS A CURE TO THE NATIONAL ILLS suggested by extract 1. They are related in that the domains suggested by the terms 'CURE TO THE NATIONAL ILLS', 'BENEFACTOR', 'RESOURCE FOR PEOPLE POWER', 'FUNDAMENTAL REQUIREMENT TO A PEOPLE-POWERED ECONOMY' yield the broader conceptual metaphor DEMOCRACY IS A LIFE-SUSTAINING SYSTEM. In addition to the conceptual metaphors DEMOCRACY IS A LIFE-SUSTAIN-

ING SYSTEM and DEMOCRACY IS A LIVING ENTITY cued by extracts 2 and 3, several other conceptualizations relevant to the theme of democracy have been generated in the analysis of the Aquino SONAs. These conceptual metaphors include DEMOCRACY IS A NATIONAL ACHIEVEMENT and DEMOCRACY IS PEOPLE-EMPOWERMENT.

Now, the conceptual metaphors generated from the various clusters of related metaphorical expressions on democracy are considered in the analysis as constitutive of a macro-conceptualization on democracy, which is referred to in this article as the conceptual frame. The conceptual frame is an overarching or general statement that shows the relationship of these various conceptual metaphors on a focal theme and is represented in the analysis in bold caps, that is, **A is B.** In my illustration, the two conceptual metaphors DEMOCRACY IS A LIVING ENTITY and DEMOCRACY IS A LIFE-SUSTAINING SYSTEM combined with other conceptual metaphors posited from other extracts on democracy (i.e., DEMOCRACY IS A NATIONAL ACHIEVEMENT, DEMOCRACY IS PEOPLE-EMPOWERMENT) would yield the following frame: **DEMOCRACY IS AN EVOLVING ENTITY THAT SUSTAINS NATIONAL LIFE.** Figure1 below provides a visual representation of how the analysis works.

FIGURE 1 AN ILLUSTRATION OF THE LEVELS OF METAPHORICAL ANALYSIS

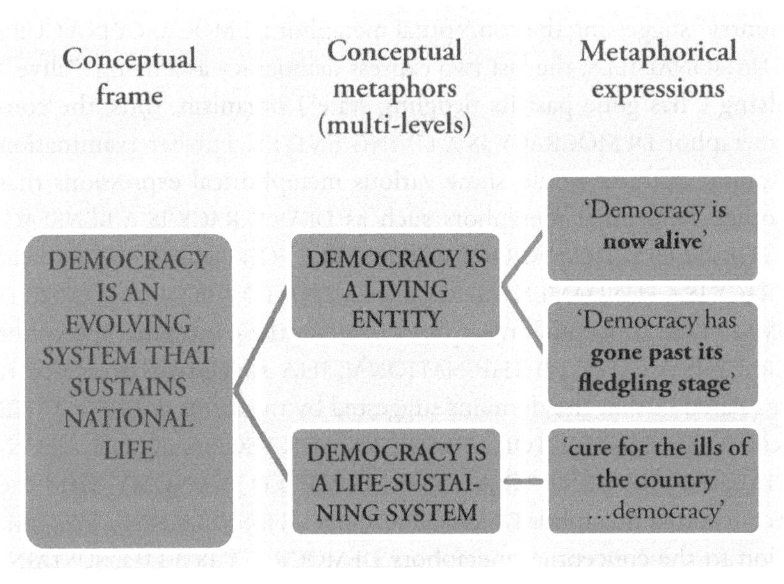

I now move on to a brief description of the socio-political historical milieu of the post-dictatorship presidencies to contextualize the analysis of the SONAs.

From mother to son: Presidencies after the dictatorship

When Corazon Aquino assumed the presidency after the people power revolution in 1986, she worked toward restoring democratic institutions and basic freedoms curtailed under the militaristic rule of Marcos. For instance, she issued presidential proclamations lifting the suspension of the writ of habeas corpus and granting amnesty to political prisoners. However, Aquino inherited from Marcos a fragmented Philippine society including a long-standing communist insurgency, a highly politicized military that challenged her government through several coup attempts, and a Moro rebellion fighting for an independent state in Southern Philippines. Notwithstanding these challenges, Aquino pursued economic reforms including economic liberalization and privatization of government-owned and -controlled corporations. Graft and corruption in the bureaucracy were addressed through the creation of the Office of Ombudsman to investigate complaints of illegal acts by government officials. In 1992, Aquino completed her term successfully with a peaceful transfer of power. She was succeeded by her defense minister Fidel V. Ramos, a cousin of the ousted dictator for whom he also served as the Chief of Staff of the Philippine Constabulary.

Considered an EDSA people power hero for breaking his allegiance to the Marcos regime on 22 February 1986, Ramos' rallying principles in his 6-year term were "people empowerment" and "global competitiveness." Ramos' presidency sustained the economic liberalization pursued by Aquino and her team and pushed for the implementation of the structural adjustment plans prescribed by the International Monetary Fund and the World Bank (IMF-WB) (Malaya and Malaya, 2004).

Economic growth and a relatively significant decline in poverty during the Ramos administration earned for the Philippines the label "emerging tiger" economy. His term is also noted for having signed peace agreements with military rebels and a major separatist Muslim group in Southern Philippines. Despite the modest economic gains and the historic peace accord with the two rebel groups, the Ramos presidency was marred by a number of challenges and controversies including the inconclusive peace talks with the communist movement and the 1997 Asian financial crisis (Malaya et al., p. 262).

Succeeding Ramos was his vice president Joseph Ejercito Estrada, who was a former senator and highly popular Filipino actor. Estrada was known for his tough persona – a stance that was particularly evident when he dealt with the problem of persistent communist and Muslim insurgencies (see for instance, Ecumenical Movement for Justice and Peace 2006). Criticized by the mainstream Philippine media for his laidback management style, Estrada faced a debilitating political crisis due to allegations of corruption. Barely two years after his election as president, an erstwhile friend of Estrada's made an exposé on his involvement in an illegal numbers game that led to his impeachment trial before the Philippine Senate. The trial was eventually aborted, but it resulted in a popular mass demonstration similar to the "people power" in 1986. Estrada was ousted from power and was replaced by his vice president, Gloria Macapagal Arroyo.

Arroyo's early months as president were hounded by questions on the legitimacy of her assumption to power. As there were still a considerable number of Estrada supporters, her successor presidency was confronted by a divided society. In her first SONA, she called for an end to political bickering and presented her agenda to win the war against poverty. She later established the link between her administration's war on poverty and the global war against terror by arguing that the commitment to the US-led war was necessary in building a "strong republic" (Navera 2011).

Arroyo ran for a full presidential term in 2004, won, but was later accused of rigging the elections. Public condemnation of her alleged involvement in electoral fraud resulted in congressional hearings, failed impeachment complaints, and mass protests to which the Arroyo government responded with a series of controversial executive orders and proclamations. These included, among others, an executive order that prohibited government officials under the executive branch attending congressional hearings unless permitted by the Office of the President, and the Calibrated Preemptive Response, which disallowed street protests without a permit.

In 2010, Arroyo was succeeded by Corazon Aquino's son Benigno Aquino III who vowed to make the corrupt during his predecessor's term accountable and who envisioned his presidency as a journey towards the straight and narrow path ("ang tuwid na daan").

"People power" in Philippine presidential talk

Table 1 below shows the conceptualizations of democracy that underlie the post-Marcos presidential rhetoric examined in this study.

TABLE 1 CONCEPTUALIZATIONS OF DEMOCRACY[6] IN THE SONAS FROM 1987 TO 2009

President	Conceptual frames

Aquino (1987-1991)	• **DEMOCRACY IS AN EVOLVING SYSTEM OF GOVERNMENT THAT SUSTAINS NATIONAL LIFE**
	• DEMOCRACY IS AN EVOLVING SYSTEM THAT HAD BEEN RENDERED WEAK UNDER MARCOS DICTATORSHIP
	• THE RESTORATION OF DEMOCRACY IS A NATIONAL ACHIEVEMENT
	• DEMOCRACY IS PEOPLE-EMPOWERMENT
	• DEMOCRACY IS LIFE-SUSTAINING SYSTEM
	  • DEMOCRACY IS A BENEFACTOR OF THE NATION
	  • DEMOCRACY IS A NURTURER
	  • DEMOCRACY IS A RESOURCE FOR PEOPLE POWER
	  • DEMOCRACY IS A CURE TO THE NATIONAL ILLS
	  • DEMOCRACY IS A KEY TO A PEOPLE-POWERED ECONOMY/ CAPITALISM CONDUCIVE TO GROWTH

Ramos (1992-1997)	• **DEMOCRACY IS AN EVOLVING SYSTEM OF GOVERNMENT THAT SUSTAINS NATIONAL LIFE**
	  • DEMOCRACY IS A SOURCE OF NATIONAL STRENGTH
	  • DEMOCRACY IS A RESOURCE FOR DEVELOPMENT
	  • DEMOCRACY IS A FOUNDATION FOR A GOOD SOCIETY
	  • DEMOCRACY IS A FUNCTIONAL SYSTEM THAT IS CAPABLE OF INITIATING CHANGE
	• **DEMOCRACY IS A PRECURSOR FOR COMPETITIVENESS**
	  • DEMOCRACY IS A COMPETITIVE EDGE
	  • DEMOCRACY IS A COMPARATIVE ADVANTAGE

Estrada (1998-2000)	• **DEMOCRACY IS AN OBJECT OF DEFENSE AND PROTECTION**
	  • DEMOCRACY IS A PRIZED IDEAL
	• **DEMOCRACY IS AN EVOLVING ENTITY**
	  • DEMOCRACY IS A STRUCTURE
	  • DEMOCRACY IS AN ORGANIC ENTITY

Arroyo (2001-2004)	• **DEMOCRACY IS A WEAPON** • **DEMOCRACY IS AN OBJECT OF THREAT** • **DEMOCRACY IS A NATIONAL FAITH THAT THE FILIPINOS HAVE FOUGHT FOR**
Arroyo (2005-2009)	• **DEMOCRACY IS A VALUE THAT FINDS EXPRESSION IN THE NATIONAL INSTITUTIONS AND PRACTICES** • DEMOCRACY IS A PRECURSOR FOR FIRST WORLD STATUS • **DEMOCRACY IS AN OBJECT OF THREAT**

[6] A detailed analysis of these conceptualizations can be found in the author's doctoral research. Excluded in the said study is the incumbent presidency of Benigno Aquino III who is president from 2010 to 2016.

The data show a multilayered conceptualization of democracy especially apparent in the first Aquino presidency. Corazon Aquino, having been the first post-authoritarian president, necessarily set off the scope and boundaries of post-dictatorship Philippine democracy. Her multilayered conceptualization was bound to be adopted and re-contextualized by her successors.

A conceptualization that had been sustained in the post-Marcos presidencies is the conceptualization of democracy as an evolving entity (see sections on Aquino, Ramos, and Estrada in Table 1). This conceptualization had been substantiated through the use of metaphors that suggest democracy either as a structure that goes through alterations or as an organic entity. This takes into consideration that several factors influence the way democracy moves from one phase to another. The influence of these factors – people power being a prominent one – suggests the specific and unique process of democratization in the Philippines, an understanding of which may possibly lead to the articulation of the Philippines' contribution to theorizations and practice of democracy at large.

Common to all of the four presidencies covered in this study is the framing of democracy as a national value. This is suggested in the following conceptualizations of democracy from each of the four presidents: RESTORATION OF DEMOCRACY IS A NATIONAL ACHIEVEMENT (Aquino); DEMOCRACY IS A FOUNDATION FOR A GOOD SOCIETY (Ramos); DEMOCRACY IS A PRIZED IDEAL (Estrada); and DEMOCRACY IS A VALUE THAT FINDS EXPRESSION IN NATIONAL INSTITUTIONS AND PRACTICES (Arroyo). The great importance given to democracy across the four presidencies suggests the presidents' commitment to the national ideals embedded in the 1987 Constitution, a major achievement in the re-democratization process. It also implies that public addresses of national importance like the SONA serve as an opportunity for national leaders to engage in what Campbell and Jamieson (2008) call "a public meditation on values."

In the latter presidencies – specifically those of Estrada and Arroyo – emphasis given to the conceptualization DEMOCRACY IS AN OBJECT OF THREAT is evident. Both presidencies had been criticized for being anti-democratic or harboring dictatorial tendencies and both responded by asserting that democracy was threatened under their watch. This common response channels that of Marcos. In his presidential statements, Marcos conceptualized democracy as an object of communist threat in order to justify his imposition of martial law (Marcos, 1971, 1972, 1977; Rebullida

2006). This rendering of democracy can be seen as a common feature of Philippine presidential rhetoric that had been fully utilized during the Marcos presidency and has been re-deployed even in post-dictatorship presidencies. That democracy is used to justify the use of state power to respond to the opposition and critical sectors of Philippine society makes democracy a problematic notion. It rekindles the discourse of constitutional authoritarianism that Marcos used to justify his imposition of martial law and consequently his abuse of presidential power.

While commonalities are evident among the conceptualizations across the four post-Marcos presidencies, the fluidity with which democracy had been conceptualized in the 23 SONAs cannot be denied. This fluidity may be explained by various factors. These include differences in key emphasis, shifts in domestic and global concerns, shifts or changes in presidential agenda, and the agency of the political actor. For instance, because Ramos emphasized the need to be "globally competitive" in order to attain the state of national industrialized country-hood (NIC-hood), there was a shift in the way he conceptualized democracy in his addresses. From rehearsing the conceptualizations rendered by his immediate predecessor, Ramos adopted and made more salient the conceptualizations of democracy as a "competitive edge" or a "unique comparative advantage." These conceptualizations were more attuned to his presidential agenda and the domestic and global concerns of his presidency that included the ratification of the General Agreement on Tariffs and Trade-World Trade Organization (GATT-WTO). The Philippine government's active involvement in the GATT-WTO marked the country's participation in the new global economic order primarily anchored on the discourse of neo-liberalization. In other words, each President conceptualized democracy in terms of how her/his administration could respond to existing domestic and global issues.

There also appears to be less articulation on democracy as a concept in the latter presidencies compared to those of Aquino and Ramos. If at all, the invocation of the democratic concept in the SONAs of Arroyo and Estrada was merely a reaffirmation of a national ideal – a "public meditation on values" as expressed earlier. This shows that other issues of national significance had through time taken the place of what was considered a primary concern in the early post-Marcos years. However, it takes a salient position in presidential discourse when a president is accused of resorting to authoritarian measures as in the case of Estrada in 1999 and Arroyo after the 2005 political crisis. That democracy is reaffirmed in the SONAs or any important presidential speech to dispel public perception of a return to martial law indicates the Filipino people's tendency to be skeptical towards a strong state and its propensity for abuse (see Abinales and Amoroso 2005, p. 242).

Evident in the rhetoric of the post-Marcos presidencies was a need to re-conceptualize people power to harness its potentials for the new order – the post-Marcos, post-authoritarian, and purportedly a re-democratized Philippines. There appeared a gradual shift from *people power as a form of resistance* to *people power as an essential element of nation building.* This is particularly evident in the presidencies of Aquino and Ramos. People power as protest remained visible during the first two post-Marcos presidencies. The new conceptualizations of people power as organized participation and as capital would have probably taken root in the succeeding presidencies, but there was a resurgence of massive street protests during the presidency of Estrada. He was accused of corruption and culpable violation of the constitution, which eventually led to his impeachment trial that culminated in his ouster from power two and a half years after he was elected to the highest office. Estrada, during his short-lived presidency would emphatically speak of democracy as a national value that his leadership reaffirmed. In his 1999 SONA, during which protests against his move to change the charter were rife, Estrada would assure his audience that people power was alive. He affirmed that it was a guarantee of the protection of freedom, but would make curious qualifications on the exercise of freedom: "[L]iberty without responsibility is license...freedom without responsibility is the formula for chaos, anarchy, and lawlessness."

Arroyo, who replaced Estrada, completed her successor term, and took on a full presidential term, downplayed the significance of people power as a symbol of protest (cf. Gonzaga 2011, p. 26). Arroyo's presidency – including both successor and full terms – was marred by questions of legitimacy. Throughout her presidency, she had to constantly reaffirm her position as "a constitutional successor" to the ousted president and as "a duly elected president" during her full term. After having faced a series of attempts to impeach her, Arroyo could no longer contain her disdain for people power as a form of resistance or protest. This is evident in the following passage from her speech delivered during a peace rally in commemoration of the people power uprising in 1986.

> 'Yung mundo pinagdiriwang ang EDSA 1[7]. Yung mundo pinayagan ang EDSA 2.[8] Yung mundo hindi patatawarin ang EDSA 3. Sasabihin ng mundo, ano ba yang Pilipinas? Pinakamagaling na manggagawa sa buong mundo kaya hinahanap sa buong mundo tapos parating binabaril ang sarili at hindi matatag? Kung ganon, sino ang darating na investor dito? [The world celebrated EDSA 1. The world tolerated EDSA 2. The world will not forgive us for EDSA 3. The world will say, what's wrong with the Philippines? Because its workers are the best in the world, they are sought after by the entire world. But then it always shoots itself and does not stand firm. If that's the case, which investor would want to come here?] ("PGMA's Speech during the Peace Rally at the Capitol grounds", 25 February 2008 in Gonzaga 2011, p. 26)

Though not explicitly expressed in Arroyo's SONAs, such sentiment appears to be salient in Philippine presidential discourse – Marcos or post-Marcos. When an economic environment conducive to business and foreign investment is emphasized in important political speeches, the call to reduce, if not dismiss, mass mobilizations almost always becomes imperative.

The incumbent president, Benigno Aquino III, son of Corazon Aquino, succeeded Arroyo in an election that other pundits would consider a form of people power – a repudiation of a reviled Philippine presidency. More than two years into his presidency as of this writing, he has also displayed disdain towards protest and mass mobilizations. In fact, he would make qualifications on the kind of citizenship that he considers beneficial to the nation – one that is "nakikilahok" (participative) not one that is "nakikialam" (meddlesome) (SONA 2011). He also indicts what he calls the "industry of criticism" especially instigated by the vibrant Philippine press.

The analysis reveals that over the last 25 years Philippine presidential rhetoric has worked in ways that constrain public participation. The gradual shift from people power as a form of resistance to people power as an element of nation building, which I mentioned earlier, reveals a drift from a radical notion of participation that propels change to one that is instrumentalized to serve the agenda of those in power.

I suggest that the shift is motivated by a host of factors: presidential

[7] EDSA 1 is considered another expression for People Power 1.

[8] EDSA 2 refers to People Power 2, the mass mobilization that ousted Joseph Estrada from the presidency.

personae, agenda, and the unique socio-political situation that presidents find themselves in. With these factors at play, the notion of people power has necessarily become malleable in so far as presidential rhetoric is concerned. The malleability makes it easy for the wielders of leadership to use the very notion of people power in order to affirm a privileged persona, assert legitimacy, justify political choices, constrain public participation, and even redefine socio-political reality. The table below (Table 2) summarizes the shifts in conceptualizations of people power across five presidencies vis-à-vis the presidents' varying personae, presidential agenda, and socio-political and historical milieu.

The shifts point to what Kock and Villadsen mention in the introduction to this book as the constructive potential of rhetoric. On the one hand, this potential, when tapped by powerful agents such as presidents, can encourage citizens to participate in platforms that are deemed appropriate and helpful to nation-building. On the other, it sets limits to what citizens can do; it constrains rhetorical citizenship. In such a scenario, the value of protest as a symbolic action is denied in order to privilege a less disruptive act but one that may be more in keeping with the interests of the state. This makes it imperative to examine presidential rhetoric not only for its potential "to induce deliberation" or to contribute to the "construction of an effective deliberative system", but also for its power to define rhetorical citizenship – how it limits and circumscribes possibilities for democratic participation in public policy formulation, in decision-making, and in charting the national course, at large.

Notwithstanding the influencing power of presidential talk, the Filipino people can reclaim and redefine people power in their favor. They can achieve this by being cognizant of how those in public office define "people power" and "democracy" and by taking possession of public platforms in order to assert their own definitions or counter-definitions of what it takes to participate in a democracy. For instance, a more active public involvement in memorializing and discussing the relevance of people power events that transpired in recent history would potentially provide a necessary counterbalance to how the current national leadership frames democratic participation. In this way, the malleability of democracy and people power works in favor of the general public and not just of those who hold power in public office. The Philippines is actually not bereft of examples of citizens and civil society groups who express and enact alternative visions and versions of people power. A vibrant Philippine press and a social media environment that is conducive to generating public opinion have in fact served as venues for citizens to offer alternative frames of people power. It is through these platforms, for instance, that Filipino citizens have pushed for more transparency and accountability in governance both in the local and national levels. However, these examples have yet to be examined more systematically from a discourse analytical and rhetorical perspective. Needless to say, rhetorical citizenship thrives in a society where the concerns of the majority go beyond putting food on the table. In the Philippines, where major structural inequalities exist, it may take more than rhetoric to make rhetorical citizenship work. Enabling conditions that are socio-economic in character can facilitate symbolic actions and discursive practices that are participatory and less elite-driven.

Conclusion

This paper, which examines how democracy has been conceptualized in post-authoritarian presidential addresses, reveals that the notion of people power has become malleable and this has implications on the kind and level of democratic participation the government expects from its constituents. "People power" as a political expression has evolved in that it is no longer just associated with mass mobilization employed to reclaim democratic space or to challenge (the threat of) autocratic power. This is because various leaders who have assumed presidential power since the first post-dictatorship president end up putting their stamp on "people power" by reframing or recontextualizing the political expression in ways that are consistent with their personae, their agenda, and their appreciation of the socio-political and historical moments they need to deal with during their terms of office. These varied and changing conceptualizations of "people power" potentially reveal how citizen participation has been valued and constrained by presidential leadership in a period of democratization following the end of a long-standing dictatorship. A rhetorically cognizant citizenry enabled by a more egalitarian socio-economic structure would provide a necessary counterbalance to what the current post-dictatorship leadership offers.

TABLE 2 CONCEPTUALIZATIONS OF PEOPLE POWER IN PHILIPPINE PRESIDENTIAL RHETORIC

Presidency	Conceptualizations of people power (associated with terms as democracy and freedom)	The presidential persona	Presidential agenda	Some highlights of the socio-political and historical milieu
Aquino, Corazon	Democracy is people power (people power as source domain)	The anti-thesis of Marcos; heroine of democracy	Transition from dictatorship to democracy; de-Marcosification	Installed to power through people power revolution; credited for reestablishing democratic institutions during her term
Ramos, Fidel	People empowerment is an instrument toward global competitiveness	The president is a manager	Global competitiveness	Anointed by his predecessor; presidential term saw decent economic growth which earned the Philippines the label 'emerging tiger' economy; faced Asian financial crisis toward the end of his term
Estrada, Joseph	People power as a defender of freedom; qualification of freedom – "liberty without responsibility is license…freedom without responsibility is the formula for chaos, anarchy, and lawlessness"	The president as macho; extended his cinematic persona as a tough guy with the heart of gold	Poverty-alleviation; war on poverty	Won the election by a huge margin; accused of involvement in the siphoning of excise taxes and receiving bribe money from an illegal numbers game; impeached and was ousted from the presidency through people power
Arroyo, Gloria	People power is the heart of democracy; people power is a sustaining element of democracy; voting is people power ('let us address the highest exercise of democracy, voting!')	Anti-thesis of Joseph Estrada; positioned herself to allay fears that she would perpetuate herself in power	A strong republic; war on terror	Constitutional successor of Estrada; completed her successor term and later elected for a full term; accused of corruption in government and of rigging the 2004 presidential and 2007 national elections
Aquino, Benigno	People power is citizen participation (pakikilahok) and not meddling through giving harsh criticism (pakikialam)	The president as incorruptible and the anti-thesis of Gloria Macapagal Arroyo	The straight and narrow path	Ran for president after generating popular support following the death of his mother, Corazon Aquino; elected in 2010 to replace Arroyo; enjoys huge political capital from high public satisfaction ratings

References

Abinales, P. N. and D.J. Amoroso. (2005). *State and Society in the Philippines.* Manila: Anvil Publishing.

Abueva, J.V. and E.R. Roman (Eds.). (1993). *Corazon C. Aquino: Early Assessment of Her Presidential Leadership and Administration and Her Place in History.* Quezon City: University of the Philippines Press.

Campbell, K. and K.H. Jamieson. (2008). *Presidents Creating the Presidency: Deeds Done in Words.* Chicago: University of Chicago Press.

Charteris-Black, J. (2004). *Corpus Approaches to Critical Metaphor Analysis.* New York: Palgrave Macmillan.

Charteris-Black, J. (2005). *Politicians and Rhetoric: The Persuasive Power of Metaphor.* New York: Palgrave Macmillan.

Charteris-Black, J. (2007). *The Communication of Leadership: The Design of Leadership Style.* New York: Palgrave Macmillan.

Chilton, P., H. Tian, and R. Wodak. (2010). Reflection on Discourse and Critique in China and the West. *Journal of Language and Politics* 9, 489-507.

Cortes, R.M. (2000). *Philippine Presidents: 100 years.* Quezon City, Philippines: Philippine Historical Association and New Day Publishers.

Dahl, R. A. (2000). *On Democracy.* New Haven: Yale University Press, 2000.

Diamond, L. (2008). *The Spirit of Democracy: The Struggle to Build Free Societies Throughout the World.* New York: Times Books.

Ecumenical Movement for Justice and Peace (EMJP). (2006). *Oplan Bantay Laya: A Primer.* Manila, Philippines.

Gonzaga, F.P. (2011). Rule of Law in the Philippines: The Reproductive Logic of Elite Democracy. *Asian Perspectives in the Arts and Humanities* 1, 17-37.

Kock, C. and L. Villadsen. (2014). "Rhetorical Citizenship as Conceptual Frame: What We Talk About When We Talk About Rhetorical Citizenship." In *Contemporary Rhetorical Citizenship* edited by C. Kock and L. Villadsen. Leiden: Leiden University Press, 9-26.

Lakoff, G. (1992). The Contemporary Theory of Metaphor. In A. Ortony (Ed.), *Metaphor and Thought* (pp. 202-57). New York: University of Cambridge Press, 1992.

Lakoff, G. (2008). *The Political Mind: Why You Can't Understand 21st –Century Politics with an 18th-Century Brain.* New York: Viking Penguin.

Lakoff, G. and M. Johnson. 1980. *Metaphors We Live By.* Chicago: University of Chicago Press, 1980.

Malaya, E. and J.E. Malaya. (2004). *So Help Us God: The Presidents of the Philippines and Their Inaugural Addresses.* Pasig City: Anvil Publishing.

Marcos, F.E. (1971). *Today's Revolution: Democracy*. Manila, Philippines.

Marcos, F.E. (1973). *Notes on the New Society of the Philippines*. Manila, Philippines.

Marcos, F.E. (1977). *Democratic Revolution of the Philippines* (3rd ed.). Manila, Philippines. (First published in 1974).

Martinez, M. F. (1999). *A Political History of Our Time: Presidential Policies from Aquino to Ramos to Estrada (A Study in Leadership)*. Paranaque City, Philippines: MFM Enterprises.

Navera, G.S. (2011). "WAR ON TERROR" IS A CURATIVE: Recontextualization and Political Mythmaking in Gloria Macapagal Arroyo's 2002-2004 State of the Nation Addresses. *Critical Inquiry in Language Studies*, 8, 313-343.

Navera, G.S. (2012). Metaphorizing the Philippine Presidency: Schemas of Presidential Leadership in the Post-Marcos State of the Nation Address (1987-2009). PhD diss.: National University of Singapore.

Rebullida, M.L.G. (2006). The Executive: Martial Law, Constitutional Authoritarianism, and the Marcos Administration. In T.S. Encarnacion-Tadem and N. Morada (Eds.), *Philippine Politics and Governance: An Introduction* (pp. 153-178). Quezon City: Department of Political Science, College of Social Sciences and Philosophy, University of the Philippines.

Strauss, C. and N.Quinn. (1997). *A Cognitive Theory of Cultural Meaning*. Cambridge: Cambridge University Press.

van Dijk, T. (1998). *Ideology: A Multidisciplinary Approach*. London: Sage.

On Being a Simple Judge: Exploring Rhetorical Citizenship in Aristotelian and Homeric Rhetorics

MARI LEE MIFSUD

The gifts of rhetorical history and theory

What does rhetorical history have to offer contemporary theorizing of rhetorical citizenship? Turning to Aristotle for answers to this question is commonplace.[1] Many resources reside within Aristotle, yet not without complications. Rhetorical citizenship in an Aristotelian mode could be defined as citizens enacting their duties to judge various contingent matters whether political, judicial, or cultural via civic discourse. The "citizen" as "judge" means at once someone requiring qualification, namely in ancient Greece birth into a qualifying family and gender, and someone requiring no qualification, as audiences are assumed to be unqualified, simple people. Aristotle tells us that the rhetorical audience serving as "judge" (*kritēs*) must be "simple" (*haplous*) (*Rhet.*1357a11-12). John Henry Freese translates *haplous* as "a simple person" (1982, 25), and Rhys Roberts translates "an audience of untrained thinkers" (1954, p. 27).[2]

[1] Recent work in rhetorical studies related to deliberative democracy, rhetorical citizenship, and publics demonstrates various returns to Aristotle. See for example van Haaften, Jansen, De Jong, and Koetsenruijter, eds. (2011); Kock and Villadsen, eds. (2012); and van Belle, Gillaerts, van Gorp, van De Mieroop, and Rutten, eds. (2013). The significance of the ancient Greek rhetorical tradition, in particular Aristotle's *Rhetoric*, is being noticed in political theory as well. Chantal Mouffe calls for politics to connect with the great tradition of rhetoric originating in ancient Greece (1993, pp. 4-6; see also qtd. in Ivie 2002, p. 278). Danielle Allen turns to Aristotle's *Rhetoric* for guidance on producing trust in democratic citizen discourse (2004). Iris Marion Young turns to Aristotle's *Rhetoric* to advance a communicative theory of political discourse that could, via empathy (ēthos and *pathos*), support the democratic inclusion of difference (2000).

[2] For working with Aristotle's *Rhetoric*, I use translations by J.K. Freese, Rhys Roberts, and

The contemporary view of the classical conception of audience is not a positive one, caricaturing the classical view as wrongly viewing the audience as passive, needing to be acted upon by the rhetor, like a billiard ball by a cue (Benson 1989, p. 293). This critique of classical notions of audience is not unwarranted – the Platonic Socrates actually does describe the rhetor's audience as so simple as to be persuadable to take an ass into battle rather than a horse based on resemblance (Plato, *Phaedrus*, 260c)! And immediately prior to the key passage in Aristotle's *Rhetoric* describing the audience as *kritēs ... haplous,* we can find another less than flattering description of audience members, namely that they cannot follow a long chain of syllogistic reasoning, hence need rhetoric to simplify complex matters (Aris. *Rhet.*, 1357a3-4). Plenty of evidence exists to warrant a contemporary critique of the classical conception of the citizen-judge as simple.

Yet, something about being simple seems lost in translation. Other places in Aristotle's *Rhetoric* suggest being simple is a *virtuous* quality of mind, one related to divining universals at play in any particular situation, universals that must be acknowledged to live happily together in a polity. But we do not hear much about these other places. If we want to make the argument that rhetoric matters to citizenship and that the two – rhetoric and citizenship – are mutually benefitted by their exchanges, then we need to deal with this charge of citizens as simpletons that rings through the rhetorical tradition. We need to go to these other places. In juxtaposition with an approach relegating classical conceptions of agency and audience as outdated and over, I wish in this essay to avoid such a negative approach, or perhaps I should say such a "negating" choice. I wish to take being simple as a citizen judge creatively. Rather than negating citizen judges as simpletons, might we create something new? In this essay, I wish to try.

What can be created anew from primary text when seen with different eyes, thought within other contexts, enacted with new tropes, lived in different bodies? Texts can be figured otherwise, or *alloiostrophically* (Sutton and Mifsud 2012, and Forthcoming). *Alloiostrophic rhetoric* make meaning otherwise: through turns toward difference, the other, the strange, *alloiosis.* And indeed something other, different, and strange lies lurking in the

George Kennedy, along with my own, to navigate the ancient Greek of the *Oxford Classical Text.* I consider as well William Grimaldi's commentary on Books 1 and 2, and Edward Meredith Cope's commentary in 3 volumes.

ancient Greek concept of being a simple judge, *kritēs ... haplous*. For the purposes of this preview, I call this *kritēs* (judge) who is supposed to be *haplous* (simple) "strange" for involvement in the divination of universals, the Homeric culture of the gift, and the *telos* of happiness. Rationality, contingency, the needs of the polis, and the *telos* of judgment continue to figure the conditions in which the *kritēs ... haplous* acts, but in this essay, I turn toward the weird parts of being simple, the parts that are not easy to represent. I do so lest these weird parts be forgotten, their resource lost for theorizing, envisioning, imagining contemporary rhetorical citizenship. Before starting though, we should call to attention how I have just set up my project for failure by way of claiming to represent the unrepresentable. We ought to be always aware that this and other such paradoxes of communication are ever-present, yet we must communicate anyway.

I begin with tracings in Aristotle's primary text on being a judge and being simple. These traces take us to the Homeric culture of the gift. Creating in the limen "betwixt and between" the archaic and the classical, I offer considerations of rhetorical citizenship through the figure of the rhetorical citizen as a judge, being *haplous*.

On being a judge: *kritēs*

Aristotle uses three different terms to identify the rhetor's audience: hearer, *akroatēs*, judge, *kritēs*, and observer, *theōros* (cf.1358b2-3). Scholarly controversy exists on whether Aristotle meant different things by the various terms he uses for the audience of rhetoric, in particular whether the subcategories of *akroatēs*, namely *kritēs* and *theōros*, mean different things. Some like Freese and Roberts hold the observer in a lesser position than the judge. Freese's translation takes a significant interpretive liberty by qualifying the "observer" as "mere:" "Now the hearer must necessarily be either a mere spectator or a judge" (Freese 1982, p. 33). Roberts' translation is not so loose, "The hearer must be either a judge ... or an observer" (Roberts 1954, p. 32), but his note affirms Freese's reading of the *theōros*: "a mere onlooker, present at a show, where he *decides* no grave political or legal issue (cp. 1391b16-20) and plays no higher role than that of speech taster, or oratorical connoisseur" (32 n. 1). Yet, when we follow Roberts' direction to compare with 1391b16-20, we find that even though Aristotle expresses some level of privilege about the audience as *kritēs* proper being those deciding questions at issue in civic controversies, he recognizes that judgment cannot be restricted just to deliberative and judicial rhetoric. He says that the *theōros* is also a *kritēs* for the epideictic speech is put together with reference to the spectator as a judge (Aris. *Rhet.* 1391b15).

I side with Grimaldi who affirms no evidential need to force a firm distinction between the *kritēs, theōros,* and *akroatēs,* though he says, "I believe it is clear that for A. as far as judgment is concerned the auditor in each class of rhetoric can rightly be called *kritēs*" (Grimaldi 1980, p. 81). I consider then *kritēs* as the operant term for the citizen who must judge the various contingent affairs of civic life, whether political, judicial, or cultural. Moreover, I see being *kritēs* as being in a position of power and an opportunity for agency, making for meaningful rhetorical citizenship, hardly the position of being simple, as in "simpleton."

On being simple: *haplous*

What quality of mind ought we to assume the *kritēs* has when the *kritēs* is described as *haplous*? While a translation of *haplous* is indeed "simple," the meaning in use is anything but. As Grimaldi notes (1980, p. 56), the term is related in use to "*haplōs*" which has several meanings:

> (a) "singly, by itself, without the admixture of anything else," and, so, "simply," in either a physical or moral sense. Connected with this use is one in which [*haplōs*] is employed in a derogatory sense, "negligently, without sufficient care"; e.g. *Met.* 987a21: "to treat a subject too simply." (b) A second meaning is a development out of the first; here [*haplōs*] is the same as [*kath' auton*], "in itself, absolutely, without reference to anything else," and thus is it opposed to [*pros ti*] "the relative"; e.g., *Top.* 115b33-35. (c) There is a third meaning, "generally, universally," which is used in opposition to *kath' ekaston* or *kata meros,* "individually, particularly, specifically." This third meaning is the meaning in our passage [1356a7] and is a common usage of the word (Grimaldi 1980, p. 41).

Only a small part of the semantic range of *haplous* suggests a "derogatory sense" of the word. The more prominent meanings are "singular," "universal," "without reference to anything else," "given," "simple."[3] Moreover, Lid-

[3] A review of Liddell, Scott, and Jones (LSJ) on *haplous* and related terms reveals evidence across Aristotle's corpus showing these terms signifying that which is singular, absolute, uncomplicated in its being, given for the whole to see or know or divine: See *Pol.*1268b.39, *EN.*1149a2, and *Metaph.*989b17, 1025b7, 1030a16.

dell, Scott, and Jones indicate that beyond the reference to Aristotle in his *Metaphysics* (which Grimaldi notes), only Isocrates, *To Nicocles* (2.46) uses *haplous* for its derogatory sense (LSJ 1977, p. 191). What if the interpretive industry has over-determined the translation of *haplous* to convey a derogatory sense of the audience as judge, with the simple judge then being akin to a simpleton, in need of rhetoric to make complex things simple? What if this regard for the judge eventuates in a democratic citizenry living in accordance with this diminished view of itself? Can we imagine democracy surviving if rhetorical citizenship were envisioned and embodied as such?

What if within the text lies something other lurking, something resourceful, forgotten, perhaps even never understood or turned into "knowledge" in the first place? Grimaldi's range of definitions of *haplous* gives us a sense that indeed something other is present, a sense Liddell, Scott, and Jones confirm. Following the traces in Aristotle's *Rhetoric*, which take us to the Homeric epics, will give us an even better sense.[4]

The use of the term *haplous* in the *Rhetoric* reveals a range of meaning suggesting not only much more than "simpleton," but perhaps just the opposite. In a key passage suggesting as much, 1367a 38, Aristotle describes being *haplous* as a virtuous quality of a person. When one needs to praise another who shows excessive qualities (*hyperbole*), one can turn to the best sense of these attendant qualities. For example, Aristotle tells us that if one who needs to be praised is *manikos*, or "manic," this person could be praised for the virtuous part of these qualities, namely in this case being *haplous*.

Common translation of this line takes *haplous* to mean "outspoken," "straightforward," and "frank and open" (Roberts 1954, p. 59; Kennedy 2007, p. 79; and Freese 1982, p. 97). But this seems to miss the significance of Aristotle's use of *manikos*. Mania in ancient Greece, albeit considered an excessive quality, was also recognized as a desire to speak the divined truth of a matter. Think of Kassandra in ancient Greek mythology, a priestess fated not to be believed; her divinations, never to be given credence, proved, nonetheless, true. Using Aristotle's suggestion, if we were to choose to praise

[4] For working with the Homeric epics, in addition to my own readings of the *Oxford Classical Texts*, I am guided by Richmond Lattimore's translations of both epics, as well as translations provided in the Loeb editions by A. T. Murray for both epics. Stanford's commentary on the *Odyssey* is a steady source of consideration, along with Kirk, et al., and Heubeck et al. commentaries on the *Iliad* and *Odyssey* respectively.

her rather than blame her, we could praise her for being *haplous*. The positive quality of *mania* is its connection to divination of the universal at play, and its capacity to discern the simple truth of any given matter. Think as well of Plato's *Phaedrus* in which the Platonic Socrates defines *mania* as connected with the noblest of arts, for it foretells the future, gives prophecy (Plato, *Phaedrus*, 244c). Later the Platonic Socrates calls true Love, as in the true Love of the ideal forms of Beauty, Truth, Justice, and the Good, a *mania* (249d). If being *haplous* is being *manikos* without the hyperbole then *haplous* is connected to all that *mania* is connected to, only in moderate form, hence all the more an Aristotelian virtue.[5]

This textual evidence suggests being *haplous* means something other than simple-minded in a derogatory or minimalizing sense. Another key passage demonstrating this point arrives when Aristotle is addressing a matter of style and organization. Here, Aristotle explains that a speech refraining from detail in the narrative (*diēgēsis*) about the facts is preferable in that it is a simpler (*haplousteros*) speech, and avoids being unnecessarily complicated. For example, you ought not to develop a complicated narrative "if you wish to praise Achilles; for all know of his actions" (Aris. *Rhet.*, 1416b 20-28).

One who is in a position to judge, namely any citizen, ought not need a long chain of reasoning or a complicated *diēgēsis* to discern what is good, just, and praiseworthy. That which is known by all is given, hence needs no complicated story. Givens are simple to discern. This discernment is something other than rational if "rational" is understood as syllogistic production. Aristotle tells us these givens, which he describes as general ideas of the just and unjust, can be divined (*manteuontai*) by all (Aris. *Rhet.* 1373b6-8). Note that Aristotle uses *manteuontai* and in doing so calls attention all the more to dimensions of *mania* that are involved in being *haplous*.

But what are these givens? One prime example of a given in Aristotle's *Rhetoric* is happiness. Exploring this given provides all the more insight into being *haplous*.

Happiness, being *haplous*, and the Homeric gift

Aristotle identifies happiness (*eudaimonia*) as the primary topos for rhetors needing to derive arguments for exhortation (*Rhet.*1360b4-7). With this topos, rhetors can argue that one should do the things that procure happiness

[5] For consideration of *mania* in ancient Greek culture see Dodds (1951).

or one of its parts, or increase instead of diminish it, and avoid doing those things that destroy or hinder happiness or bring about its opposite. Aristotle gives an extended account of the topoi of happiness, namely those things which are good such as a good birth, good children and numerous children, wealth, good reputation, honor, health, beauty, strength, stature, good old age, many friendships and good friendships, good luck, virtue (1360b19-21). He follows this list by going into some detail revealing the given beliefs and opinion in each topos, the *endoxa* at play.

Endoxa become topical resources for exhortation, and these *endoxa* are givens of Homeric gift culture. Moreover the *endoxa* can be seen circulating via Aristotle's citation of Homer and reference to his works. Grimaldi notes that the topoi of happiness that Aristotle uses are specifically noted as marks of honor in the *Iliad* (1980, p. 114), and again Grimaldi notes that when Aristotle cites "eloquence and capacity for action" as a given good at 1362b22-23 in the *Rhetoric*, that the same idea is "aptly expressed in Phoenix's words to Achilles" at *Iliad* 9.442 (Grimaldi 1980, p. 130). Moreover, Aristotle cites Homer three times in this section, to exemplify the significance of honor (*timē*) in these happiness topoi: 1) *Iliad*, 2.160 cited at Aris. *Rhet.*1363a6: Hera appeals to Athene to prevent the dishonor and unhappiness that would befall the Greek people if the Greeks were to retreat leaving Helen for the Trojans to boast of; 2) *Iliad*, 1.255 cited at Aris. *Rhet.*1362b36: Nestor uses an honor appeal to Achilles and Agamemnon to point out how their enemy would be happy if he heard all the truth about the Achaeans' quarrelling; 3) *Iliad*, 2.298 cited at Aris. *Rhet.*1363a6-7: Odysseus appeals to his men to hold out lest they be disgraced and bring upon themselves unhappiness returning unsuccessfully after having stayed so long.

Aristotle's happiness topoi draw their material substance from archaic *givens,* in particular the *endoxa* of honor, *timē*, exemplified in Homeric epic. *Timē* in the archaic archive is so immense that trying to track its presence is like trying to track the presence of *logos* itself. The paths go in every direction. But perhaps the most important point to make here is that in the Homeric lexicon, *timē* means first and foremost recompense, compensation, or indemnity (Cunliffe 1977, p. 383; see for example *Il.*1.159; 3.286; 16.92; *Od.*14.70, 117). Indeed *timē* also means honor in terms of the respect one is given, but so does *kleos* for that matter, a term that Aristotle does not use in these passages. The meaning of *timē* is more robust than "honor" as its primary register is that of exchange, in particular in an economy of reciprocity and mutual benefaction typifying ideals of Homeric gift culture. *Timē* is an act of giving honor as recompense for one who has done good deeds, who has benefitted many and in ways that are not easy to do.

In Aristotle's catalogue of happiness topoi, the specific topic of the gift is an organizing dynamic of the *endoxa*. The key passage on the gift occurs within this section on the topoi of happiness:

> Honor (*timē*) is a token of a reputation for doing good; and those who have already done good (*euergetēkotes*) are justly and above all honored, not but that he who is capable of doing good is also honored. Doing good relates either to personal security (*sōterian*) and all the causes of existence; or to wealth; or to any other good things which are not easy to acquire, either in any conditions, or at such a place, or at such a time; for many obtain honor for things that appear trifling, but this depends upon place and time. The components of honor are sacrifices, memorials in verse and prose, privileges, grants of land, front seats, public burial, State maintenance, and among the barbarians, prostration and giving place, and all gifts which are highly prized in each country. For a gift is at once a giving of a possession and a token of honor ... (Aris., *Rhet.*, 1361a 27-38).

Aristotle's description of the materials of happiness deriving from honor shows an intimate connection with the gift and giving. Honor is recompense for doing good, *euergetein (eu*=well*; ergon* = work*)* (1361a30). Doing good means giving well, hence Kennedy's translation of *euergetein* as "benefaction" (2007, p. 59). One who does good works is a benefactor, a giver of good things.

Continuing to follow the tracings in the text, we can see that to give well is to offer what Freese calls "personal security" (1982, p. 53), and Kennedy calls "safety" (2007, p. 59), along with all the causes of existence, and things that are hard to come by. To give security is to give not just the resources that support existence but also preservation. In divine form the *sōtēr* or *sōtērian* are providers of safety, givers of safe passage, preservers or maintainers of security. Zeus is known as a *sōtēr*. And Aristotle references the Savior Goddesses in Book 3 of the *Rhetoric* (1419a3), who were honored for protection and preservation. Human benefactors are *sōtēr*, doing good work to ensure civic safety and preservation.

Aristotle's description of the ways in which a benefactor should be justly honored brings to light the archaic ethic of reciprocity in gift-giving, mutual benefaction. As Marcel Mauss' classic work (1990) on archaic gift culture reveals, receiving a gift sparks a cycle of obligatory reciprocity, wherein the receiver honors the gift and the giver with some kind of return gift, typically either equal to what was received or surpassing it. Aristotle's passage on honor in happiness topoi shows how reciprocity forges civic relations as both givers and receivers are benefitted mutually, the receivers by way of safety and benefits for the happy life, and the giver by way of being honored for giving, ideally for giving in abundance and of those things which are hardest to come by. And nowhere in Aristotle's *Rhetoric* is it clear that the receivers and the givers are mutually exclusive persons.

These classical happiness topoi are figured through the Homeric gift in Aristotle's *Rhetoric* and serve as examples of *givens*. In short, giving well makes for a happy polis. The highest form of giving, like giving safety and honor, inspires the greatest happiness. This *endoxa* circulates from the archaic Homeric gift culture into the classical culture of the polis via Aristotle's *Rhetoric*, and envisions a rhetor's agency as a preparation for being *haplous*, and audience agency as discerning the simple givens that in their universal connection to all that is good ought to be judged simply. No need for lengthy and complex syllogisms exists when the principles at play are so easily divined, so universal, singular, so simple.

To complement this theoretical figure of being *haplous*, let's consider a poetic figure, one presented by Aristophanes' *Lysistrata*. Here is the scene: To forge a peace between the embattled states of Sparta and Athens, in the context of a Panhellenic sex strike by the women until peace is settled, Lysistrata, assuming the role of citizen out of care for the security of her home, appeals to the Magistrates via the gift. She reminds Spartan Magistrates about the time when Spartans came to Athens to sit at the altars as suppliants seeking defense against attack. Athenians responded with great generosity, rescuing them. She reminds the Athenian Magistrates how, when Athenians were enslaved by the Thessalians, the Spartans came to their aid, liberating them, and replacing slaves' rags with warm cloaks, as suits a free people (Aristophanes, *Lysistrata*, 1149-1156).

Lysistrata brings to light the circulation of the gift between the two warring states, mutual benefaction and solidarity. She then brings to light the violation of the gift ethic by displaying the disgrace of failed reciprocity. She asks the Magistrates why, after being treated with generosity by the other country, they are now out to ravage this one that treated them so well (1137-1146). More than once she asks, "So why, after so many mutual benefactions are you fighting instead of calling a halt to your misbehavior" (1161)? Aristophanes then portrays how Lysistrata's gift appeals, offered generously as questions rather than arguments, succeed. Reconciliation ensues, along with much feasting and dancing. Married couples are reunited. Peace and lovemaking resume. Solidarity in ever-lasting friendship becomes their lasting future.

What a poetic vision! In it we can see Lysistrata as the simple judge having no need for qualifications, no need for complicated reasoning, to make the simple offering of a universal happiness via solidarity and mutual benefaction. The magistrates, too, are simple judges, being asked by Lysistrata to discern the simple, universal goods at play. But of course these Magistrates, for more than once exclaiming their willingness to agree to anything for the return of sex, seem simple in the derogatory sense of being *haplous*, despite their qualification as Magistrates. Still my point holds. If they judge peace and friendship to be theirs, rather than war, based only on desire for the return of sex, then still they are being *haplous*. What is a more singular, universal principle of exchange than sex? As Georges Bataille writes, "It should come as no surprise to us that the principle of the gift, which propels the movement of general activity, is at the basis of sexual activity" (p. 41). Halting sex is not just a cunning comedic tactic in *Lysistrata*, it is the primary means of halting the gift.

We can see being *haplous* at work in *Lysistrata*, discerning that the simplest path to happiness is the idealized and friendly ritual of the gift. To be a rhetorical citizen in this Homeric mode of Aristotle's rhetoric is to be a simple judge of the gift, so that happiness via solidarity and mutual benefaction guides one's choices. Commonplace in gift studies is the expression that the theory of the gift is a theory of human solidarity. Likewise commonplace is the expression that there are no free gifts.[6] That which is given by way of the gift obligates simple acceptance. Something so simple about human solidarity ought not to need much by way of dialectical investigation, or proof by way of lengthy syllogistic reasoning. Such complications make the gift something quite other than a gift.[7] For the gift to be given, it must be

[6] See Douglass (1990), who frontloads these ideas in her foreword to Mauss' classic work on the gift.

[7] See Derrida (2000) and Calvin O. Schrag for their critiques of the conditions of the gift. Schrag's position is recorded well and in brief in Ramsey and Miller (2003, p. 41). See also Mifsud (Forthcoming) which offers a rhetorical history and theory of Homeric and Aristotelian rhetorics of the gift.

given *simply*. Yet lurking still is the possibility of the duplicitous gift, hostility in the guise of hospitality, the classic Homeric example being the gift of the Wooden Horse to the Trojans.[8] The gift, as many have pointed out, is both remedy and poison.[9] The gift offers no guarantees of happiness nor of the resolution of enmity between peoples, only a spark of possibility, and an agent of change in the rhetorical citizen as simple judge.

Contemporary resourcefulness of being *haplous*

How we do rhetoric's history and theory matters for what we can know about rhetorical citizenship. Perhaps for the very reason that being *haplous* is connected to divination means it must be negated as rhetoric's history gets written through the privilege of rationality. Ideas, terms, and practices that seem to undercut or at least fail to affirm the traditionally privileged ideas, terms, and practices get negated in any number of ways, all to ill effect. In a history privileging the rational means of knowledge production, divination falls into nothingness and the remnants of being *haplous* are reduced to a rather diminutive form of the simpleton. Negating these Homeric dimensions of being *haplous* leaves only a view and an attitude of the rhetorical citizen as simpleton. Or, said another way, negating these Homeric dimensions of being *haplous* is killing the spark of possibility that could have been the rhetorical citizen.

From recent work in rhetorical citizenship and in deliberative democracy, we can see a return to Aristotle as a source of affirming the significance of rhetoric to civic life and theorizing the art of citizens in a democracy.[10] Bolstering critical reception of what can be seen in this "eternal return" to Aristotle seems an imperative lest we create what Hélène Cixous calls "the empire of the self-same," a form of cultural colonization that has no place in

[8] See Derrida's deconstruction of hospitality in his response to Anne Dufourmantelle that shows hospitality's relation to hostility (2000). See also Serres' classic work on hostility and the parasite (2007). See also Davis (2010, p. 132).

[9] Benveniste (1997) points out that across Indo-European languages "to give" means simultaneously "to take." This paradox is addressed in a range of work from the original sociological work by Mauss (1990), to the philosophical deconstruction of the gift by Derrida (2000; 1997).

[10] In addition to work cited earlier, see Gross and Walzer (2000) as an excellent demonstration of the return to Aristotle and the significance such a return continues to offer.

democratic practice nor the happy life (2001, pp. 78-83). This exploration of being *haplous* offers what Cixous calls a "*sortie*" an escape from the traditional story of the death of the other (2001, p. 78). By way of going back to Aristotle to see that which is strange anew for its resourcefulness, acknowledgement is given to the resources within rhetorical history to create new structures for exchange, structures oriented towards what Cixous calls joy and Aristotle happiness. The strangeness that we see anew in this essay is the virtue of being simple in rhetorical judgment, exemplified theoretically and poetically through rhetoric and the gift. In Aristotle's *Rhetoric* and its related citation of Homeric epics we see the gift as directed towards happiness and the greatest universal good. In *Lysistrata*, we see the gift used rhetorically as a simple path to peace. To shape rhetorical citizenship in and through the gift is to allow the most singular and simple forms of human solidarity to be discerned, divined, judged, and lived.

But to conclude that a rhetoric of being *haplous* is a *technē* of rhetoric would be mistaken. Being a simple judge is a quality prior to *technē*, prior to the need to be persuasive about anything in particular. Being a simple judge is not an appropriative position where the given is only ever acknowledged for what it can give the rhetor by way of persuasiveness. Lysistrata is no technician. Nor Homer. Being a simple judge marks a kind of judgment other than one wrought by *technē*. To be simple is to be untrained, and to be appropriate as is, both qualities stand in juxtaposition to being *technē*. To be *technē* is to have an awareness of awareness towards the end of greater, even absolute, efficiency in achieving desired ends, namely rational judgment on the contingent matters of civic life. Technical efficiency works against the grain of democracy's messiness, and some describe *technē*'s *telos* as ensuring mutual destruction rather than mutual benefaction. Kenneth Burke describes the human condition as separated from its own nature by instruments of its own making, goaded by the spirit of hierarchy, and rotten with perfection (Burke 1966, p. 16). Henry Johnstone describes a brutalizing effect of technical communication (Johnstone 1982). David Lovekin argues that a technical orientation towards symbols and society has an alienating effect, turning us all into strangers in a political landscape (Lovekin 1991). Even Aristotle is careful to note that rhetoric deals with things about which we deliberate but for which we have no systematic rules, no *technai* (Aris. *Rhet.*, 1357a2), and this despite *technē* being much of the focus of and on Aristotle's *Rhetoric*. This paradox turns out to be a very good thing. Rhetoric has a *technē*, and rhetoric has this other dimension, this dimension that is other than *technē*, incapable of being translated into *technē*, this simple dimension, connected to that which is given, not technically produced, but free. To be free and enact freedom, rhetoric must be more than a *technē* of persuasion, or even a *technē* of rhetorical citizenship. Bringing this strange dimension of rhetoric to light, we see it can serve as an irritant to the whole of our thinking about rhetoric, like sand in an oyster making a pearl.[11]

[11] See Sutton and Mifsud (2012, p. 230) for discussion of *alloiostrophic* rhetoric as irritant. See as well, Sutton and Mifsud, Forthcoming. For a robust consideration of how theorizing rhetoric through the gift, beyond *technē*, offers resource to rhetorical citizenship in new media spaces via a concept of "netoric," see Petra Aczél (2013).

References

Aczél, Petra. 2013. Netoric: An Approach to New Media Rhetoric. In H. van Belle, P. Gillaerts, B. van Gorp, D. van de Mieroop and Kris Rutten (Eds.), *Verbal and Visual Rhetoric in a Media World* (pp. 311-328). Amsterdam: Leiden University Press.

Allen, Danielle. 2004. *Talking to Strangers: Anxieties of Citizenship since Brown v. Board of Education.* Chicago: University of Chicago Press.

Aristophanes. 2000. *Lysistrata.* Translated by Jeffrey Henderson. Cambridge: Harvard University Press.

Aristotle. (1947). *Metaphysics.* Vol 1-2. Trans. Hugh Tredennick. Cambridge: Harvard University Press.

Aristotle. (1954). *Rhetoric.* Translated by Rhys Roberts. New York: Modern Library.

Aristotle. (1959). *Ars Rhetorica.* Oxford: Oxford University Press.

Aristotle. (1975). *Nichomachean Ethics.* Trans. H. Rackham. Cambridge: Harvard University Press.

Aristotle. (1977). *Politics.* Trans. H.Rackham. Cambridge: Harvard University Press.

Aristotle. (1982). *The "Art" of Rhetoric.* Translated by John Henry Freese. Cambridge, MA: Harvard University Press.

Aristotle. (2007). *On Rhetoric: A Theory of Civic Discourse.* Translated by George A. Kennedy. Oxford: Oxford University Press.

Bataille, G. (1991). *The Accursed Share.* Vol. 1. Translated by Robert Hurley. New York: Zone Books.

Benson, T.W. (1989). Rhetoric as a Way of Being. In T.W. Benson (Ed.), *American Rhetoric: Context and Criticism* (pp. 293-322). Carbondale: Southern Illinois University Press.

Benveniste, E. (1997). Gift and Exchange in the Indo-European Vocabulary. In A. Schrift (Ed.), *The Logic of the Gift* (pp. 33-44). New York: Routledge.

Burke, K. (1966). *Language as Symbolic Action.* Berkeley: University of California Press.

Burke, K. (1959). *Attitudes toward History.* Los Altos, CA: Hermes.

Cixous, H. (1986). Sorties: Out and Out: Attacks/Ways Out/Forays. In H. Cixous and C. Clément (Eds.), *The Newly Born Woman* (pp. 63-131). Minneapolis: University of Minnesota.

Cope, E.M. (1966). *The Rhetoric of Aristotle.* Ed. John Edwin Sandys. 3 vols. Cambridge: Library Press.

Cunliffe, R.J. (1977). *A Lexicon of the Homeric Dialect.* Norman: University of Oklahoma Press.

Davis, D. (2010). *Inessential Solidarity.* Pittsburgh: University of Pittsburgh Press.

Derrida, J. 1997. The Time of the King. In A. Schrift (Ed.), *The Logic of the Gift* (pp. 121–47). New York: Routledge.

Derrida, J. and A. Dufourmantelle. (2000). *Of Hospitality: Anne Dufourmantelle Invites Jacque Derrida to Respond.* Translated by Rachel Bowlby. Stanford: Stanford University Press.

Dodds, E.R. (1951). *The Greeks and the Irrational.* Berkeley: University of California Press.

Douglas, M. (1990). No Free Gifts. Foreword to M. Mauss, *The Gift: The Form and Reason for Exchange in Archaic Societies* (pp. vii-xviii). New York: W. Norton.

Grimaldi, W. (1980). *Aristotle, Rhetoric I & II: A Commentary.* New York: Fordham University Press.

Gross, A.G. and A.E. Walzer (2000). *Rereading Aristotle's Rhetoric.* Carbondale and Edwardsville: Southern Illinois University Press.

Heubeck, A. S. et. al. (Eds.) (1992). *A Commentary on Homer's Odyssey.* Vols 1-3. Oxford: Oxford University Press.

Homer. (1920). *Homeri Opera: Iliadis.* Oxford Classical Texts. Vol I-II. London: Oxford University Press.

Homer. (1974). *Homeri Opera: Odysseae.* Oxford Classical Texts. Vol. III-IV. London: Oxford University Press.

Homer. (1984). *Odyssey.* 2 Vols. Translated by A. T. Murray. Cambridge, MA: Harvard University Press.

Homer. (1985). *Iliad.* 2 Vols. Translated by A. T. Murray. Cambridge, MA: Harvard University Press.

Homer. (2007). *Iliad.* Translated by Richmond Lattimore. New York: Harper Perennial.

Homer. (2011). *Odyssey.* Translated by Richmond Lattimore. Chicago: University of Chicago Press.

Isocrates. (1928). *Volume I: To Nicocles.* Translated by George Norlin. Cambridge, MA: Harvard University Press.

Ivie, R. (2002). Rhetorical Deliberation and Democratic Politics in the Here and Now. *Rhetoric and Public Affairs* 5, 277-85.

Johnstone, Jr., H.W. (1982). Communication: Technology and Ethics. In M.J. Hyde (Ed.), *Communication, Philosophy, and the Technological Ages* (pp. 38-53). Tuscaloosa: University of Alabama Press.

Kirk, G. S. et al. (Eds.) 1993. *The Iliad: A Commentary*, vols.1-6. Cambridge: Cambridge University Press.

Kock, C. and L.S. Villadsen (Eds.) (2012). *Rhetorical Citizenship and Public Deliberation.* University Park: Pennsylvania State University Press.

Liddell, H.G., R. Scott and H.S. Jones. (1968). *A Greek English Lexicon*. Oxford: The Clarendon Press.

Lovekin, D. (1991). *Technique, Discourse, and Consciousness: An Introduction to the Philosophy of Jacques Ellul*. Bethlehem: Lehigh University Press.

Mifsud, M.L. (2007). On Rhetoric as Gift/Giving. *Philosophy and Rhetoric* 40, 89-107.

Mifsud, M.L. (Forthcoming).) *Rhetoric and the Gift: Ancient Rhetorical Theory and Contemporary Communication*. Pittsburgh: Duquesne University Press.

Mauss, M. (1990). *The Gift: The Form and Reason for Exchange in Archaic Societies*. Translated by W. D. Halls. New York: W.W. Norton.

Mouffe, C. (1993). *The Return of the Political*. London and New York: Verso.

Plato. (1983). *Gorgias*. Translated by W. R. M. Lamb. Cambridge: Harvard University Press.

Plato. (1990). *Phaedrus*. Translated by Harold North Fowler. Cambridge: Harvard University Press.

Ramsey, E. and D.J. Miller (Eds.) (2003). *Experiences Between Philosophy and Communication: Engaging the Philosophical Contributions of Calvin O. Schrag*. Albany: State University of New York Press.

Schrift, A.D. (Ed.) (1997). *The Logic of the Gift: Towards an Ethic of Generosity*. New York: Routledge.

Serres, M. (2007). *The Parasite*. Translated by Lawrence R. Schehr. Minneapolis: University of Minnesota Press.

Sutton, J. and M. L. Mifsud. (2012). Towards an *Alloiostrophic* Rhetoric. *Advances in the History of Rhetoric* 15, 222-233.

Sutton, J. and M. L. Mifsud. (Forthcoming). *Alloiostrophic Rhetoric*. Baltimore: Lexington Books.

Thesaurus linguae Graecae. Irvine, [Calif.]: University of California, Irvine. Other title(s): TLG. Columbia URL: http://www.columbia.edu/cgi-bin/cul/resolve?AUV9026.

Young, I.M. (2000). *Inclusion and Democracy*. Oxford: Oxford University Press.

van Belle, H., P. Gillaerts, B. van Gorp, D. van de Mieroop and K. Rutten (Eds.) (2013). *Verbal and Visual Rhetoric in a Media World*. Amsterdam: Leiden University Press.

van Haaften, T., H.Jansen, J. de Jong and W. Koetsenruijter (Eds.) (2011). *Bending Opinion: Essays on Persuasion in the Public Domain*. Amsterdam: Leiden University Press.

The Rhetorical Citizen: Enacting Agency

RAYMIE E. MCKERROW

This essay will consider the nature of, and enactment of, agency in the guise of the rhetorical citizen. The essay considers the rhetorical citizen as a person whose actions within the public sphere encompass considerations of race, class, sex, gender lines. Two major criteria undergirding the enactment of citizenship will be explored: the constraints provided with respect to access – whether one can gain both presence in and express voice – and the role of motive in highlighting why one acts in giving voice to one's role as a citizen. The role of voice includes that of silence – the decision to remain silent in the context of an ability to access and present one's voice is itself a message to the community of which one is a part. The refusal to act is as much a rhetorical statement, provided the motive is clear, as is an overt action. The methodological grounding for this exploration will be premised on a Burkean sense of motive.

The rhetorical citizen

Karlyn Kohrs Campbell's treatment of rhetorical agency provides a useful starting point for an examination of the role that may be played by the rhetorical citizen: "Whatever else it may be, rhetorical agency refers to the capacity to act, that is, to have the competence to speak or write in a way that will be recognized or heeded by others in one's community. Such competency permits entry into ongoing cultural conversations and is the *sine qua non* of public participation, much less resistance as a counter-public" (2005, p. 3). The key term in this orientation to agency is "capacity"; while I will have reason to object to "competence" as the sole explanation of what it means to have capacity, an ability to state a position is one potential attribute of a person's agency. Stacey Sowards (2010) provides a useful listing of the "whatever else" in noting its varied nature includes terms such as enactment, performance, articulation, personal will, and resistance, among others. In noting the complex nature of this concept, Sowards offers a concise perspective that serves well for my use: "rhetorical agency is a function of individual dispositions, social contexts, and a rhetor's ability to respond to those situations as they change over time and negotiate social standings related to gender, race, ethnicity, class, and national origin status" (pp. 227-28). Agency, then, encompasses the complexity involved in any human interaction in which ideas are held in conflict. As such, it embodies issues of access to public space as well as motives for engagement (as will be addressed later). More precisely, this "agentic orientation" is at odds with what Joshua Gunn and Dana Cloud (2010) accurately label "magical voluntarism," as a reference to "any theory of agency that suggests one can fulfill one's needs and desires through the independent, willful manipulation of symbols irrelevant of structural limitation or constraint" (p. 62).[1] In Foucaultian terms, agency exists, not as a possession of a person, but as a capacity to act within relations between and among people and the lifeworld they inhabit at a moment in time (Martin 1988).[2]

Having considered the sense of "agency" in the title, I return to the first phrase. *Rhetorical citizen* has entered the lexicon in various manifestations over the past decade or so (see Greene, 2004, 2007; Martin, 2009; McKerrow, 2010, 2012). My purpose in this essay is to "trouble" the senses in which this term might be employed in relation to rhetorical agency. The central argument I want to advance is that current scholarly interest in articulating a conception of rhetorical democracy, within which the rhetorical citizen is presumed to act, excludes consideration of what it means, rhetori-

[1] Their essay is a trenchant critique of a 2007 essay by Sonja Foss, William Waters, and Bernard J. Armada. As Gunn and Cloud (2010) note, this is a more complex issue than an assumption that a person can choose agency and enact change as a result of that choice. Space does not allow a summary of their extensive review of recent rhetorical positions related to "What is agency?" Suffice it to note that the position they arrive at, which incorporates materialist and dialectic considerations, advances the discussion (See Geisler, 2005).

[2] Agency is a resource for change. In noting "My role – and that is too emphatic a word – is to show people that they are much freer than they feel" Foucault suggests that individuals can choose, but that freedom is not absolute; it is always constrained within a social matrix that pre-exists their presence (See Rux Martin, 1988, p. 10).

cally, to enact agency by not participating, via silence or the overt refusal to engage others within any of the public spaces reserved for interaction. The argument will proceed in two stages. First, it is important to frame the potential exercise of agency within a sense of rhetorical or "communicative democracy" as distinguished from highly anti-rhetorical conceptions of public deliberation (Young, 2000; McKerrow, 2012). With this as a conceptual backdrop, the essay then considers two principal issues – access, in reference to race, class, etc., and motive within which a sense of silence, or what is perceived as non-action is advanced as a potentially positive act on the part of the rhetorical citizen.

Framing rhetorical democracy

Chantal Mouffe, whose work has privileged the possibility of dissensus as the primary ingredient in a working democracy, provides a starting point. In a 2006 interview, she notes:

> I would argue that conflict is ineradicable, but there are different ways in which conflict can express itself. Democracy entails the legitimisation (sic) of conflict. Its aim is to enable forms of expressing conflict that are not going to destroy the political association. ... When a society does not allow for this agonistic form of conflict to express itself, you see the emergence of antagonistic forms of conflict. ... Public spaces should be places for the expression of dissensus, for bringing to the fore what forces attempt to keep concealed. (Carpentier and Cammaerts, p. 973)[3]

It is useful to contrast this assessment of the nature of a rhetorically oriented approach to democratic action with Robert Ivie's (2004) astute claim that "democratic dissent was rendered oxymoronic in America after 9/11 under the sign of a timeless war on global terror. ... [The] domestic dissenter symbolizes democracy's foreign threat, its enemy Other, a traitor to the people and their cause" (p. 20). America has forever been oriented toward exorcizing the perceived enemy within, when outside forces appear as a threat. Witness the creation of a House Un-American Activities Committee, the incarceration of Japanese-Americans in detention camps after Pearl Harbor, the attacks on German-American citizens in the same period, and post 9/11, the downfall of the Dixie Chicks after a brief utterance in relation to then

[3] For a brief review of Mouffe's sense of "agonism," see Mouffe (2007 and 2013).

President Bush's status as a Texan, and myriad other episodes in which the "foreign other" within American boundaries has been targeted as a symbol of the enemy without. We are forever marking the Other with difference as if it mattered in terms of our own safety and security.

The contrary force, consensus, is equally problematic as a response to the disciplining of dissent. As Jacques Rancière (2009) notes:

> Before becoming a preference for peace over war, consensus is a certain regime of the perceptible: the regime in which the parties are presupposed as already given, their community established and the count of their speech identical to their linguistic performance. What consensus thus presupposes is the disappearance of any gap between a party to a dispute and a part of society. ... It is the absolute removal of the sphere of appearance of a people. (pp. 102-03)

Instead of providing a measured, appropriate response to civil discord, consensus excludes those whose voice would otherwise impede progress. It is the privilege of those already in control of the processes of governance, acting on behalf of the people, to determine whose voice will be determined helpful, and which will be silenced via exclusion from the public spaces in which deliberative assembly might occur. From Rancière's (1999) perspective, the "appearance" relates to "a part of those who have no part" in the affairs of civil society (p. 99); their appearance serves to "trouble" the make-up of consensus society in articulating their right to be heard as equals. It should be noted, however, that Rancière's (2011) sense of dissensus differs markedly from that provided by Mouffe:

> Political dissensus is not a discussion between speaking people who would confront their interests and values. It is a conflict about who speaks and who does not speak, about what has to be heard as the voice of pain and what has to be heard as an argument on justice. (p. 2)[4]

[4] As a further example, consider Darrin Hicks' (1995) observation that "By limiting the range of what we persons can say and have count as a legitimate contribution to the discussion, deliberative models are not recognizable as what we know as actual human conversation oriented to practical questions" (p. 304). For a more comprehensive critique of procedural models of deliberation, see Hicks and Langsdorf (1999).

This broadens the compass of discourse from a specific argumentative encounter over differences to the more general sense of who is heard in speaking. From my vantage point, I want to see dissensus operating in this more general context, as well as in contradistinction to the kind of consensus Mouffe considers (e.g., in the narrower frame of dissensus over discussion of interests). That dissensus, at both levels, is an arguably better position from which to perceive the workings of democracy is, of course, not a new idea, nor is the sense that consensus may simply serve to protect hegemonic forces from those whose positions appear threatening. As Mouffe notes, "there is no consensus without exclusion" (Carpentier and Cammaerts, 2006, p. 967). This observation leads us to the first principle with respect to what constitutes the role of the rhetorical citizen – access. Agency, as well as the decision not to participate, requires the requisite resources to engage social others. As I've argued elsewhere, those deemed by hegemonic forces to be incivil are automatically excluded from the "civility table" (McKerrow, 2001). They are not invited to participate as their past reveals a disdain for regulative ideals of decorum and respect. It is much easier for those already accepted into the congregation of the civil to achieve consensus – but at what cost? What is the price paid in terms of exclusion? As Mouffe points out, however, there is no way around this particular "inclusion/exclusion" principle – exclusion is an inherent consequence of any attempt at reaching consensus. Rancière's question is worth noting in this context: "What indeed is consensus if not the presupposition of inclusion of all parties and their problems that prohibits the political subjectification of a part of those who have no part, of a count of the uncounted?" (Carpentier and Cammaerts, 2006; Ranciere, 1999, p. 116). If you are not among the counted, you have no role to play in presenting voice. As M. Lane Bruner (2010) notes, "all forms of consensus necessarily marginalize some set of discourses" (pp. 57-58). As I argue below, the uncounted may well exercise their voice as rhetorical citizens, if not in legally accepted terms, then in making clear their status as "part of those who have no part."

In working from Rancière's position, it needs to be noted that he upends the entire Western tradition of rhetoric that presumes communal connection is arrived at through the appropriation of discursive mechanisms already ensconced within the regulative ideal of a smooth-functioning democracy. As James Martin (2009) notes, Rancière's "analysis focuses on disagreement as a relationship that *exceeds* any effort to regularize persuasion through a typology of techniques and devices" (p. 23). Using "police" as a generic term encompassing all social efforts to control the activities of a people, the traditional conception of persuasion falls under this broad umbrella in dictating who speaks and how their discourse shall be shaped. If "the part that has no part" is to be heard as equals, the dimension of what constitutes "the people" has to expand in challenging the conventional dictates of who may speak.

Access

A key issue that needs to be addressed here is the nature of "citizen" in the context of recognizing rhetoric's province as a means of overcoming the kind of conflict that, in Mouffe's terms, is endemic in a vibrant democracy. I am in complete agreement with Robert Asen (2004), in arguing that we need to move from a concern over what a citizen "does" or "does not do" that marks their presence as a qualified citizen:

> Rather than asking what counts as citizenship, we should ask: how do people enact citizenship? Reorienting our framework from a question of *what* to a question of *how* usefully redirects our attention from acts to action. Inquiring into the *how* of citizenship recognizes citizenship as a process. ... A discourse theory conceives of citizenship as a *mode of public engagement.* (p. 191).

An example from the earlier experience of women in attempting to secure rights illustrates the paucity of a "citizen rights" perspective. Susan Zaeske's (2003) account of women's attempt to be recognized by the U.S. House of Representatives in submitting petitions arguing for the abolition of slavery serves as a reminder of how a "right" or "what is done" orientation serves the interests of those already possessing such rights:

> Women, they [Representatives] maintained lacked the requisite virtues of republican citizenship: they could not deliberate rationally, act independently, or fulfill a citizen's obligation to serve in the military. Not unlike the scenario in which the representatives formally abrogated the right of slaves to petition and questioned that of free blacks, members suggested that women possessed no citizenship rights. "Have women, too, the right of petition?" asked Wise at one point in the debates. "Are they citizens?" (p. 131)

What is suggested here, via Representative Wise, is a rejection of women's (and Blacks' as well) status as "citizen" because there is no action that "counts" in relation to the obligations set forth in a "rights" orientation. In seeking to petition, and later to vote, women played into this dominant sense of what citizenship meant. By changing from "what counts" to "how," the very act of petitioning becomes a "mode" of engagement; they were citizens by virtue of the varied processes they employed in seeking to be heard. Being heard is not, in itself, a condition of citizenship. This broader sense is explicit in Josue Cisneros' (2011) examination of the role of a "hybrid citizenship" enacted by Latina/o immigrants (some illegal) in the process of a major 2006 protest against legislation that would place new restrictions on immigration (p. 36). In this instance, the immigrants *enacted citizenship* through public forms of protest, and *problematized citizenship* through their recognition of border violations. The point I wish to draw from Cisneros' argument is that the protestors, especially those representing an "alien" or "illegal" status, enacted the role of the rhetorical citizen via their modes of engagement: they illustrated that "those who lack citizenship in the political, legal, or cultural sense can perform citizenship on a daily basis through rhetorical acts" (p. 40). From a legal or technical perspective, one might not *be* named a citizen, but one can enact that role in contributing to the discursive formation of their value as beings contributing positively to a community. As Cisneros notes, however, coming out publically in this way can produce a backlash, wherein real citizens–those already affirmed under the law – perceive protestors as unworthy of inclusion, and use their protest as affirmation of that judgment (p. 42). As the protestors' activity in 2006 suggests, they came together in accessing public space to air their views over their status as contributors to the national scene.

Another example, this time clearly one that illustrates that not all dissensus arrives at consensus, also serves to highlight the issue of access to public space. In this instance, a "five-acre empty lot simply known as Wilson Yard" in Uptown, a suburb of Chicago, remained undeveloped after a fire in 1996. As plans moved forward for a large apartment complex, "dozens of organizations and hundreds of Uptown stakeholders ... evoked democratic rhetoric ... to justify and support arguments both for and against affordable housing at Wilson Yard" (Rai, 2010, p. 41). As Candice Rai notes, over the next several years those involved pro and con in how best to develop the Yard were "completely unable to agree on a collective vision of their neighborhood's future" (p. 4). This did not occur due to a lack of rhetorical skill, an absence of access to public space in which to express opinions, or an inability to communicate with those in power. In the end, those opposed to the proposal lost their lawsuit against the city, and the units (and big-box store) were eventually occupied in 2010, some thirteen years after the initial conversations began. While dissent continued, planners planned, bureaucrats found financing, and a developer completed the project. A collective vision likely still is absent. As Douglas Ehninger (1970) observed long ago, arguments are never "over" even when events are concluded, such as the decision to build in the face of ardent opposition. Some residents of the Uptown neighborhood may yet refuse to shop in the new Target or grocery store now occupying the former vacant lot.

In the above examples, citizens (whether official or not) have exercised their rhetorical voice in public spaces. These function as illustrations of the possibility present for any person (in theory) to enter a public space and give voice to their interests. That this is not open to all is also evident, as is shown in Ivie's initial illustration of the difficulty for those calling attention to the possible complicity of the U.S. in creating conditions for Bin Laden's hatred – this in no way excuses or authorizes the actions on 9/11; it does, however, acknowledge the possibility that hatred toward another does not simply appear one morning; one does not initiate hate from a vacuum. Access may be limited by a commitment that suggests loyalty to country brooks no expression other than from those in support of a government's actions in opposing the enemy.

Access may also be a function of simple logistics. The meeting I wish to attend is in a small space, and I arrive too late to obtain a seat; my transportation to a meeting place is not available, either on my own or with assistance; my interest is not sufficient to overcome obstacles to attendance. I do not feel welcome in the public space; I do not see myself in that space – others of "my kind" are not present, or have not been valued when they attended. These are varied reasons that effectively silence the rhetorical citizen's enactment of citizenship.

Motivation

The last reason brings us to a consideration of a second principle underlying the enactment of citizenship – that of motive. My argument is simple: I wish to create a space for what may be perceived as "non-action" as a rhetorical expression – as an enactment by a citizen that is worthy of consideration in the same way as overt discursive acts might be seen. If citizenship, as Asen noted, is a process, that process includes motives that may culminate in silence or the overt refusal to participate in ways already "counted" as those fulfilling one's obligation as a citizen. Kenneth Burke's (1965) sense of motive as "shorthand terms for situations" grounds an extension of a citizen's enactment of rhetorical voice to encompass acts that are not explicitly included in prior discussions of what it means to be a rhetorical citizen (p. 29). Burke notes "motive is not a fixed thing" – you can't see one walking down the street, nor is it singular: "any set of motives is but part of a larger implicit or explicit rationalization regarding human purpose as a whole (p. 26)." A complex notion, motives function, in Burke's orientation, as "distinctly linguistic" properties which allow one to interpret reality (p. 35). As named, they do not reflect the one and only reality, but rather function as possible interpretations of why one has acted as they have. Burke goes to great lengths in *A Grammar of Motives* to illustrate the various ways in which motives are connected to the elements within the set of terms that function as a means of explaining situations: act, scene, agent, agency, purpose (1969, p. xv). One can locate a motive within each of these terms – they will be different, but hopefully will assist in explaining an event (see Benoit 1996; Blankenship, Murphy, and Rosenwasser 2012; Jasinski 2001). The indeterminacy present in this treatment of motive is purposeful; we do not know the mind of another (and perhaps the other doesn't either). The best we can do is to attribute, with an understanding of the cultural background or context within which an event occurs, possible motives that accord with our best judgment. In suggesting silence as a rhetorical act that engages an event, I cannot know that the motive for an action is as I've called it. I may be wrong. A person who does not vote in an election may have "failed" from the perspective of a normative sense of an almost mandatory act of citizen engagement. However, it remains possible that this alleged failure was itself an expression of disgust with the system, with the selection of candidates, etc. The reason for not voting may, as well, be that one was well-intentioned and simply forgot, that one was ill, or that one simply didn't like to get involved in any activity remotely connected to an expression of interest in their own lives (Romney's alleged 47 % perhaps?). In the absence of precise knowledge of one's motive, one may withhold judgment, or make whatever attribution seems most likely in the present context. The attribution of motive as contributing to one's actions as a citizen may be based on past information about the person's beliefs and/or actions, as well as nonverbal expressions, or other sources that would corroborate the accuracy of what one concludes about the actions of another.

To be more precise with respect to opening a space for silence as an act of citizenship: Is silence a means of engagement? First, consider Robert Scott's (1972) observation that "every decision to say something is a decision not to say something else, that is, if the utterance is a *choice*. In speaking we remain silent. And in remaining silent, we speak" (p. 146). Cheryl Glenn (2006) elaborates on this perspective in noting that "speech and silence depend on each other: behind all speech is silence, and silence surrounds all speech" (p. 7). This orientation to the rhetorical function of silence is evident in Zaeske's (2010) analysis of Lincoln's silence on issues that could have been noted in an 1842 speech to the Temperance Society:

> By talking about the temperance movement while staying silent on the issue of abstinence, Lincoln exploited the capacious indeterminacy of meaning afforded by the discourse of the flourishing temperance movement to articulate his notion of the ideal republican citizen and assert a new trajectory for the American republic. By silencing the public memory of Washington, he effected a parricide against the founding father and the slaveholding generation of the American Revolution so that the sensibilities of a new generation of men, the Whigs, could be heard. ... In what he said and, importantly, in what he did not say – in his silences – Lincoln articulated and demonstrated a rhetorical philosophy of public deliberation grounded in compassionate appeal to the self-interest of the opponent and the enveloping support of public opinion. (392, p. 412)

I think it is clear that silence may function to convey specific meaning. Lincoln's motive in speaking is implicit; he valued an appeal to his opponent's self-interest, and the desire to enhance potential for support served as the impetus to silence. Whether I am right is less critical (as Burke would suggest) than in noting that his silence had consequences. What would have occurred had he addressed abstinence, or more clearly addressed the memory of Washington in that setting is unclear. But in speaking and withholding, Lincoln served the role of rhetorical citizen.

As another illustration, consider the silence that is endemic within a Quaker meeting. Paula Lippard (1988) chronicles the various motives for silence as a procedural element in Quaker's consideration of proposals, as silence is a means toward consensus: "It is important to note here that, from the Quaker's perspective, the group's common centering in the silence constitutes the true 'gathering' of the meeting" (p. 149). Their motive for silence is to privilege a means of demonstrating respect and a willingness to listen to "inner voices" before speaking. Elizabeth Molina-Markham (2014) corroborates this orientation toward silence as a process in suggesting "A cultural premise could be formulated as: *Silence during meeting for business prepares participants to participate in spiritual decision making and allows space for participants to listen for a decision to emerge*" (p. 170). While this example does not suggest a role within public space, it gives support to the sense in which silence functions as a rhetorical device for, in this instance, a social good of value to the congregants. The same value-added nature of a motive for silence may underly a citizen's decision not to speak at a meeting.

Silence is not the only means of engagement in ways other than speaking within a public space. The refusal to allow a political sign in one's yard during election season may be motivated by a desire to avoid creating an unsightly or aesthetically unpleasing look on one's lawn. It may be that the candidate, even when of the same party as the resident, is one a person wishes not to support. In this latter instance, the motive suggests political engagement through its absence. That is, one acts in not acting. Agency remains present in the scene, as one has the ability to engage via sign placement or not, as one's own interests dictate. It may also be the case that placing a sign on one's lawn engages a conflict of interest, or a show of support for a candidate that violates an obligation to remain neutral. In a recent local campaign, for example, the police chief in an adjoining town allowed a campaign sign for one of the two candidates for sheriff to be placed on his lawn at home. The incumbent sheriff, not the one supported, took exception to a member of law enforcement being perceived to overtly campaign for his opponent. Given this circumstance, and the incumbent's later victory, the police chief's action could mean a rift in cooperation between the two offices. There can be ethically appropriate reasons for a refusal to engage politically. As Burke reminds us, judging the action based on one motive rather than another may change the perception of the act. In this latter instance, the police chief was within his legal rights to campaign, but the social consequences might argue against the overt nature of his action. In either case, his action is one of a rhetorical citizen.

Silence, as Shelby Bell (2014) notes, can be a risky enterprise, especially as one loses any control over the ultimate judgment others may make: "Rhetorical silence limits the silent rhetors' interpretive authority. Even when the rhetor later attempts to frame their silence, or is spoken for by another, the expectations still limit the silent rhetors' authority and give authority to other interpreters. This is one of the risks of silence as a rhetorical form" (p. 190). I would add "may" to the argument that authority is given over completely to others; in the legal case she examined, it is clear that justices reviewing an appeal possess the authority to ignore whatever the appellant thought was meant by silence as their judgment is placed within a consideration of prior and future legal actions. In other cases, relinquishing authority will depend on the circumstances, not the least of which would be the rhetor's own credibility as a past and future citizen.

When factors such as race and class are considered in the context of relations of power, the control over one's reason to remain silent may be limited. As Dana Cloud (1999) argues, "the rhetoric of silence points to *extra-discursive*, material relations of power which are perceived for various reasons to be unspeakable" (p. 179). When one is not part of what may speak, silence is perhaps the only protective mechanism one retains. As Cloud concludes:

> The process of being negated, or the formation of a silenced silhouette, can also apply to the speaker or rhetor. If the first persona is the rhetor, perhaps the phenomenon of self-silencing noted in these transcripts could be referred to the constitution of oneself in the role of "null persona." The null persona refers to the self-negation of the speaker and the creation in the text of an oblique silhouette indicating what is not utterable. (p. 200)

While we may never know in any certain sense what motivates a particular action, or its absence, we need to keep space available for motives that imply engagement with the political culture at a given moment in time. How a citizen engages encompasses more than the exercise of one's voice in public space. Potentially, it extends to one's silence, or one's refusal to participate as evidence of one's desire to send a specific message to others. Whether that message is heard is open to question, but it does not invalidate the person's attempt to engage, any more than when ideas expressed publically are ignored, misinterpreted, or simply not heard. The rhetorical citizen does not have to be successful in achieving goals in order to be "counted" among the parts of the social. In this sense, Campbell's sense of agency as tied to competence is too narrow a conception – as it assumes that one's inability to be seen as competent or be heard is one's fault; it may just as easily be the fault of those refusing to hear what is being said. That "the people" have ignored those who have counseled against particular actions does not, of necessity, mean that the counsel was wrong, nor does it mean that the person giving voice to ideas was incompetent.

Conclusion

As the above makes clear, while starting with Campbell's sense of rhetorical agency is a useful beginning, it is necessary to take a broader view of the consequences of one's attempt to act within a public space. That is the point with respect to the issue of access as well – while one may well be "a part that has no part" within the social matrix, this does not invalidate the attempt to give voice – to "trouble" democracy in a way that upsets what Rancière (2009) references as the "distribution of the sensible": "a relation between occupations and equipment, between being in a specific space and time, performing specific activities, and being endowed with capacities of seeing, saying, and doing that 'fit' those activities" (p. 275). This troubling brings those who are of "no account" into account through their active involvement – forcing those already "in place" to reconsider the role of those whose exclusion is being challenged. Although not a new conception, beginning from dissensus rather than consensus as the orientation toward how a rhetorical citizen enacts and problematizes engagement is a preferred point of departure. As theorized here, I am embracing a potentially contradictory sense of dissensus as the larger question of who may speak, as well as the more precise issue of how the argument is expressed within an agonistic (not antagonistic) environment. This consideration of both definitions allows for the sense of those who have no part to be considered in the context of a rhetorical citizen's enactment of agency. The role of motive introduces a second problematic beyond considerations of access, as it opens up the space for suggesting that inaction is itself an action, that silence may well function rhetorically as something other than simple disinterest and disengagement. That one disengages from what is perceived as an obligation to act in certain ways may be seen as motivated by something other than disinterest. Silence and the refusal to act are potential acts whereby a citizen expresses disgust with a particular party or process, and thereby indicates, through enactment, her or his motive.

References

Asen, R. (2004). A Discourse Theory of Citizenship. *Quarterly Journal of Speech* 90, 189-211.

Bell, S.P. (2014). What Does Silence Signify? Investigating the Rhetoric of Silence in Berghuisp v. Thompkins. *Western Journal of Communication* 78, 175-93.

Benoit, W. (1996). A Note on Burke on "Motive." *Rhetoric Society Quarterly* 26, 67-69.

Blankenship, J., E. Murphy and M. Rosenwasser. (2012). Pivotal Terms in the Early Works of Kenneth Burke. In J.K. Muir (ed.), *Coming to Terms: The Collected Works of Jane Blankenship* (pp. 165-85). New York: Lexington.

Bruner, M.L. (2010). The Public Work of Critical Political Communication. In J. Ackerman, and D. Coogan (Eds.), *The Public Work of Rhetoric: Citizen-Scholars and Civic Engagement* (pp. 56-75). Columbia, SC: Univ. of South Carolina Press, 2010.

Burke, K. (1965). *Permanence and Change.* Indianapolis: Bobbs-Merrill.

Burke, K. (1969). *A Grammar of Motives.* Berkeley, CA: Univ. of California Press.

Campbell, K.K. (2005). Agency: Promiscuous and Protean. *Communication and Critical/Cultural Studies* 2, 1-19.

Carpentier, N. and B. Cammaerts. (2006). Hegemony, Democracy, Agonism and Journalism: An Interview with Chantal Mouffe. *Journalism Studies* 7, 964-75.

Cisneros, J.D. (2011). (Re) Bordering the Civic Imaginary: Rhetoric, Hybridity, and Citizenship in *La Gran Marcha. Quarterly Journal of Speech* 97, 26-49.

Cloud, D.L. (1999). The Null Persona: Race and the Rhetoric of Silence in the Uprising of '34. *Rhetoric & Public Affairs* 29, 177–209.

Ehninger, D. (1970). Argument as Method: Its Nature, its Limitations and its Uses. *Speech Monographs* 37, 101-10.

Foss, S.K., W. Waters and B.J. Armada (2007). Toward a Theory of Agentic Orientation: Rhetoric and Agency in *Run Lola Run. Communication Theory* 17, 205-30.

Geisler, C. (2005). How Ought we to Understand the Concept of Rhetorical Agency? Report from the ARS. *Rhetoric Society Quarterly* 34, 9-17.

Glenn, C. (2004). *Unspoken: A Rhetoric of Silence.* Carbondale, IL: Southern Illinois University.

Greene, R.W. (2004). Rhetoric and Capitalism: Rhetorical Agency as Communicative Labor. *Philosophy and Rhetoric* 37, 188-206.

Greene, R.W. (2007). Rhetorical Capital: Communicative Labor, Money/Speech, and Neo-Liberal Governance. *Communication and Critical/Cultural Studies* 4, 327-31.

Gunn, J. and D. Cloud. (2010). Agentic Orientation as Magical Voluntarism. *Communication Theory* 20, 50-78.

Hicks, D. (1995). Disagreement and Democratic Pluralism. In S. Jackson (Ed.),

Argumentation and Values: Proceedings of the Ninth SCA/AFA Conference on Argumentation (pp. 302-07). Annandale VA: Speech Communication Association.

Hicks, D. and L. Langsdorf (1999). Regulating Disagreement, Constituting Participants: A Critique of Proceduralist Theories of Democracy. *Argumentation* 13, 139-60.

Ivie, R. (2004). Prologue to Democratic Dissent in America. *The Public* 11, 19-36.

Jasinski, J. (2001). *Sourcebook on Rhetoric: Key Concepts in Contemporary Rhetorical Studies.* Thousand Oaks, CA: Sage.

Lippard, P.V. (1988). The Rhetoric of Silence: The Society of Friends' Unprogrammed Meeting for Worship. *Communication Quarterly* 36, 145-56.

Martin, J. (2009). The Rhetorical Citizen. *CSD Bulletin* 16, no. 1 and 2, 21-23.

Martin, R. (1988). Truth, Power, Self: An Interview with Michel Foucault - October 25th, 1982. In L.H. Martin, H. Gutman and P.H. Hutton (Eds.), *Technologies of the Self: A Seminar with Michel Foucault* (pp. 9-15). London: Tavistock.

McKerrow, R.E. (2001). Coloring Outside the Lines: The Limits of Civility. *Vital Speeches of the Day* 67, 278-81.

McKerrow, R.E. (2010). Citizenship. In R. Jackson (Ed.), *Encyclopedia of Identity, Volume One* (pp. 78-80). Thousand Oaks, CA: Sage.

McKerrow, R.E. (2012). Principles of Rhetorical Democracy. *RÉTOR* 2, 94-113, http://www.revistaretor.org/.

Molina-Markham, E. (2014). Finding the "Sense of the Meeting": Decision Making Through Silence Among Quakers. *Western Journal of Communication* 78, 155-74.

Mouffe, C. (2007). Artistic Activism and Agonistic Spaces. *Art&Research: A Journal of Ideas, Contexts and Methods* 1, 2, 1-5.

Mouffe, C. (2013). *Agonistics: Thinking the World Politically.* London: Verso.

Rai, C. (2010). Power, Publics, and the Rhetorical Uses of Democracy. In J. Ackerman and D. Coogan (Eds.), *The Public Work of Rhetoric: Citizen-Scholars and Civic Engagement* (pp. 39-55). Columbia, SC: Univ. of South Carolina Press.

Rancière, J. (1999). *Disagreement.* Translated by Julie Rose. Minneapolis, MN: Univ. of Minnesota Press. Original work published 1995.

Rancière, J. (2009). Afterword. In G. Rockhill and P. Watts (Eds.), *History, Politics, Aesthetics: Jacques Rancière* (pp. 273-88). Durham, NC: Duke University Press.

Rancière, J. (2011). The Thinking of Dissensus: Politics and Aesthetics. In P. Bowman and Richard Stamp (Eds.), *Reading Rancière: Critical Dissensus* (pp. 1-17). London: Continuum International Publishing.

Scott, R.L. (1972). Rhetoric and Silence. *Western Speech* 36, 146-158.

Sowards, S. (2010). *Rhetorical Agency as Haciendo Caras* and Differential Consciousness

Through Lens of Gender, Race, Ethnicity, and Class: An Examination of Dolores Huerta's Rhetoric *Communication Theory* 20, 223-247.

Young, I.M. (2000). *Inclusion and Democracy.* New York: Oxford University Press.

Zaeske, S. (2003). *Signatures of Citizenship: Petitioning, Anti-slavery, & Women's Political Diversity.* Chapel Hill, NC: University of North Carolina Press.

Zaeske, S. (2010). Hearing the Silences in Lincoln's Temperance Address: Whig Masculinity as an Ethic of Rhetorical Civility. *Rhetoric & Public Affairs* 13, 389-420.

PART III

Crossing Borders: Disciplinary, Political and Otherwise

Online Civic Participation, Discourse Analysis and Rhetorical Citizenship

PETER DAHLGREN

Openings: a potential interface

It has been about two decades since the internet became a mass phenomenon, and even if this nexus of communication technologies – that I here simply and with some imprecision term the web – has in some ways become "normal" and no longer feels "revolutionary," from an historical perspective it does remain an unprecedented seismic societal transformation. The use of the web, not least social media, also called network sites (SNS), has altered just about all facets of social life, its organization, and its dynamics. SNS such as Facebook, Twitter and Instagram are truly vernacular contexts, where everyday rhetorical practices contribute to the construction of social worlds, communities, and identities.

Not least, these platforms facilitate new modes of political participation. Rhetorical analysis has often had political speech as its object of analysis; up until about two decades ago the site for such speech, aside from limited live venues, was largely the mass media. Today the mass media remain, while the web has incorporated much of the role of the mass media – major media outfits are now online. More significantly, the web also adds the dimension of interactivity, offering a whole new setting in which groups and individuals can express themselves politically. There are of course limitations and constraints: for example, politics remains a minor focus on the web compared to many other activities that transpire there, and it is much easier to launch a blog than to attract and hold an audience for it. Still, if deliberative rhetoric can be seen as constituting the core of democracy, its site has now shifted to the web, especially SNS. Indeed, the web has become the dominant public space for civic communication; this is where rhetorical citizenship today is largely enacted.

Within my own academic field of media and communication studies, the emergence of the web has been analytically followed with intensity, not least its use in the context of politics. Media and communication studies is rather eclectic, importing theories and methods from a range of other fields. This openness has in the past led to some interfaces with rhetoric – but unfortunately not enough, in my view. In this chapter I want to stage such an encounter between these fields by discussing web based online civic participation and addressing the notion of rhetorical citizenship in the process.

Along with the study of media institutions, publics, audiences, reception processes, and so on, media and communication studies also spends a lot of time and energy analysing media texts. We have at our disposal a rather wide array of intellectual traditions, research orientations and methodologies to draw upon, ranging from hard-nosed quantitative to qualitative currents. In terms of the latter, there are some approaches that seem to have some obvious connections with rhetoric; here I will take up two forms of related yet distinct discourse analysis. What is called Critical Discourse Analysis (CDA) has gained prominence over the past two decades – and seen considerable development by scholars within our field as well. A more recent import, still hovering on the periphery, is called Discourse Theory (DT). I will sketch the contours of these two traditions in order to highlight what I see as potentially mutual benefits from an exchange with rhetorical analysis. This of course is done without brushing under the rug the inevitable differences between them. Yet it is my sense that it can be edifying and fruitful to become familiar with what in essence I perceive to be potential allies: useful turns or developments may emerge unexpectedly on either side.

I begin with a brief scene setting of a few central themes concerning the changes in political participation in Western democracies, transformations that can provoke both despair and hope. I suggest that one important aspect here is the evolution of politics itself. This leads me into a discussion on the importance of the web and SNS for political participation; these media are both a reflection of and a factor in the transformation of political participation. From there I take up CDA as a mode of analysis of media texts; it can be seen in part as a more sophisticated successor to the older and problematic notion of the critique of ideology. Thereafter I turn my attention to DT, extracting from its rather dense philosophical program a basic methodological approach for dealing with media texts. In the final section I pull together the main threads from the two forms of discourse analysis, and juxtapose them with the field of rhetorical analysis, with the notion of rhetorical citizenship serving as the key conceptual link.

Democracy, participation and the web: transforming politics

While democracy has begun to take hold in many countries where it was notably absent only a few decades ago, in the established Western democracies we have seen how the functioning of democracy has become all the more problematic; a crescendo of international voices talk about "crises" and "dilemmas," or at the very least note profound and problematic "transformations." The causes are found in an array of factors (I offer a more detailed overview of this literature in Dahlgren 2013). Some analysts point to the late modern processes of individualization and socio-cultural fragmentation that can undermine collective purpose and action. Others argue that the onslaught of neoliberalism subverts democracy by depoliticizing public issues and allowing societal power to drift towards the democratically unaccountable private corporate sector. There are other explanations on offer as well, with considerable disagreement among various camps.

All observers, however, are in agreement that citizen participation in formal party politics is on the decline in most Western democracies, as citizens often feel marginalized, sensing that established politics offers few opportunities for meaningful engagement. Civic cynicism grows, especially in the face of financial and social crises; many citizens feel political elites subordinate the public interest for private gain, and that governments are inefficient in their use of the public's tax money. The consequences of this discontent have led to significant declines in participation in party politics on many fronts.

However, if such trends can lead to a generalized sense of political disenchantment for many citizens, for others it becomes a signal to engage politically, to participate – on local, national, regional and transnational levels. While we see some upsurge in engagement in party politics (including, unfortunately, a growth in extreme right wing parties in Europe), the biggest growth is in the alternative, extra-parliamentarian political domain, where on both the Left and the Right, innumerable advocacy groups, activist networks, citizen collectives, social movements, and transient moblizations enter the public sphere to pursue their own interests and/or their visions of a better world. There are movements on many fronts – human rights, economic justice, environment, gender issues, and so on – that cross national boundaries, generating the contours of global civil society; see, for example Manuel Castells (2012) and Paolo Gerbaudo (2012). The web can foster the sociality needed for political cooperation, as Nancy K. Baym demonstrates (2010), and connect citizens to discussions and causes in ways that are personally meaningful, as W. Lance Bennett and Alexandra Segerberg show from their research (2013). In particular SNS are effective in linking citizens to the political; see for instance *The Journal of Communication* (2012) and the collection by Brian Loader and Dan Mercea (2012). Such involvement, of course, manifests at least as much affective as cognitive engagement, which Zizi Papacharissi, among others, emphasizes (2014).

In these developments, many observers claim that the notion of politics itself is transmuting, as citizens broaden the notion of what constitutes political issues. Overarching traditional ideologies become less compelling for many citizens, especially younger ones, as they engage with issues that appear more personally meaningful to them, having to do with values, identities, life-style choices, and single issue movements. In the process, they are finding new ways of enacting citizenship, developing new practices for doing democracy. Chantal Mouffe (2013) and others use the notion of "the political" to point to collective contestations that can emerge anywhere in society; at times these issues may become incorporated into formal politics, but often they live a separate life, in a much expanded public sphere.

As stated at the outset, the location for much of this activity – and increasingly for politics in general – is of course the web. Since the advent of the internet as a ubiquitous phenomenon in the mid-1990s, there have been debates about how and to what extent these communication technologies enhance the public sphere or can "save" democracy. James Curran, Natalie Fenton and Des Freedman confront the wishful thinking often involved in such discussions (2012). We need to be cautious in making assumptions about the web and its affordances; Mathew Hindman (2009) and Evgeny Morozov (2011) from different angles argue strongly that there can be no techno-fix for democracy. The web cannot be seen as some simple solution to democracy's problems; going online per se does not make engaged citizens out of people who are otherwise uninvolved.

Civic online participation is shaped by the character of the web environment, which of course varies; YouTube has different technical affordances and discursive possibilities than, say, Twitter. More generally there are troubling factors built into the web's present architecture and political economy, as Robert McChesney points out (2013). José van Dijk addresses these issues in regard to social media, highlighting the now well-known issue of political surveillance and the gathering of personal data for commercial purposes. In addition many observers have noted the growth of "echo chambers," sites where like-minded people gather to confirm their views and avoid conflicting perspectives; this runs counter to the very ideal of the public sphere. Other problems have to do with "slackitivism" or "clicktivism," which points to the danger of having exclusively screen-based connection with the political world. As I discuss, with low levels of commitment, attention can easily be drawn from the political into online consumption, entertainment, gaming, and so on (Dahlgren 2013). Not least, the web can be and often is used for undemocratic purposes by all kinds of political actors, from individuals who harass public figures to political groups spreading lies and disinformation. However, despite these and other issues, the web remains a vital resource for civic participation; indeed, it is difficult to imagine political life today without it.

In today's world, on- and offline contexts have become ever more entwined. The web is interwoven with our social worlds, increasingly embedded in our daily activities of social interaction, gossip, entertainment, consumption, hobbies, and so forth. We usually demarcate politics from other domains of life, yet the boundary is also fluid: via the web, the political can arise unexpectedly in the mundane settings of the everyday. Web tools have become more effective, less expensive, and easier to use; access and collaboration are increasing, and we are evolving from being mostly media consumers to including many media producers – or "produsers," as they are sometimes called. The relatively easy mastery of web techniques is often an empowering experience in itself, leading to further innovative and creative uses.

Communication among citizens of course manifests many modes and can vary enormously according to local cultures, political traditions, historical experience, and organizational situations. On the web, the range of discursive registers is amplified, especially in SNS; political communication is often quite cacophonic and often most decidedly does not express formalized deliberation. Media genres hybridize; many citizens are doing versions of what might pass for journalism, further enhancing – or problematizing according to some commentators – how journalism is defined. Leah A. Lievrouw writes: "Media culture in the digital age has become more personal, skeptical, ironic, perishable, idiosyncratic, collaborative, and almost inconceivably diversified" (2011, p. 45). Politics and the political are an integral part of this messy online world, which offers innumerable concrete yet often shifting and contradictory discursive contexts for participation.

Specifying the factors that promote or hinder online participation among citizens is naturally a daunting undertaking, but I can briefly note that such discursive agency is facilitated by what I call civic cultures (Dahlgren 2009). These are taken-for-granted resources that need to be available to citizens in their everyday lives; they have to do with knowledge, democratic values, social trust, communicative practices and skills, and civic identities. That civic cultures could be translated into concepts from rhetorical analysis should be apparent. Civic cultures are strong in that they can enhance agency; citizens through their practices can in turn further develop civic cultures. Yet civic cultures are always vulnerable to the exercise of undemocratic power: civic trust can be undermined by sowing suspicion; knowledge and practices can be circumscribed. The point here is that – with sound social constructionist grounding – the sustained enactment of citizenship has the possibility of further strengthening democratic traditions as well as empowering citizens to participate.

Democracy is in turbulent transition, new practices and notions of the political are emerging, and the web has become a new location for discursive agency and political participation. Let us now turn to the two traditions of discourse analysis to see how they help us to analytically approach these circumstances of today's political communication among citizens.

Critical Discourse Analysis: updating ideology critique

By the 1980s, the Marxian paradigm was facing a number of serious conceptual (and political) problems; among them was the contested notion of ideology. Elements of Marxian analysis had been used in some corners of media and communication studies since the late 1960s; it examined how specific media form and content reproduce illegitimate and unacknowledged relations of power. Ideology in this critical sense implies some distortion of reality, which serves class interests (this stands in contrast the descriptive use of the term, which signifies, for instance, a party's political platform). John Corner describes how there were various attempts to "repair" the notion of ideology and to re-launch it in new, improved versions (2011). These efforts were not successful; the term had been overloaded and bent in too many different directions, and the time had come to put it to rest. Yet, it was still clear to many scholars that the interconnections between representation, meaning, value, social structure and power – whatever we choose to call these links – remained, and they demanded critical analysis.

At a general level, the notion of "critique," and its adjective form "critical," signify an analytic approach that problematizes power relations, confronting domination as the unnecessary and unjustifiable restrictions on human liberty and equality. Today this perspective extends far beyond class relations. Indeed, the single-minded focus on class was being challenged by voices pointing to other modes of subordination, arising from, for example, gender, ethnicity, and sexual orientation; not least the ascent of Cultural Studies played an important role here. Further, more sophisticated epistemological reflection was rendering the categories of "true" and "false" depictions of society as untenable. And in media studies, the view of audiences as victims of ideological media power began to give way to an understanding of them as active, sense-making agents, capable of independent (and critical) interpretation.

As the ideology concept drifted to the margins, another enterprise moved into some of the ground it had covered. CDA, in its various versions, began to emerge in the early 1990s, retaining some obvious connection with the critique of ideology tradition. Norman Fairclough (2010), Ruth Wodak and Michael Meyer, (2009) and Teun van Dijk,(1998) offer differing ports of entry into CDA, while an overview, by Marianne Jørgensen and Louise J. Phillips, provides an analytic and comparative overview of the field (2002). The "critical" in CDA signals precisely a central concern with power relations, and it is this that distinguishes it from other, more descriptive strands of discourse analysis.

In simple terms, discourse here is understood as patterned ways of using language in specific social contexts; when these patterns and contexts take on large societal proportions, some authors (for example Foucault) deploy the terms discursive formations. Significantly, theories of discourse underscore its constitutive character: discourses participate in the shaping of subjectivities, identities, social relations, objects, systems of knowledge, modes of cognitive and normative perception – while at the same time being shaped by such elements. (Again, we can see strong parallels with the rhetorical tradition.)

These theories of discourse are strongly influenced by social constructionism: discourses can serve to engender and sustain social order – as well as to challenge it – through patterns of meaning. Thus, discourses are more than just text; they are manifestations of (collective) social practice – while at the same time functioning as linguistic contexts, as symbolic environments for human action. Action, in turn, as the meaningful expression of agency, always has a discursive dimension to it. CDA, concerned with power arrangements, was rather quickly adapted by media and communication studies, which is not surprising: the media are ubiquitous carriers of discourses enmeshed in power relations.

For Norman Fairclough CDA examines the dynamics between three basic dimensions: text, discursive practice, and social practice/structures (1993). Moreover the opacity of the links between discourse and social power is in itself a significant aspect of power. Methodologically the approach is rather diverse and open, and specific methods tend to emerge in relation to the given discursive object, its social contexts, and the problems perceived in this triad of text-practice-context. The scope of its use in media and communication research is broad – in principle it can be applied to any media content and context.

The web offers of course almost endless contexts where discursive patterns are manifested, from the mainstream journalism of commercial media organizations to radical political organizations at both ends of the spectrum. Texts emanate from powerful organizations, but also from oppositional groups and individuals. CDA can help identify significant discursive and societal online contexts and elucidate discursive patterns within them – illuminating their implications for power relations between the concerned parties. On the web, "text" of course can mean all sorts of multimodal audio-visual productions, and a given discourse can be manifested across a variety of platforms such as Twitter and Facebook; Habermasian rationality is of course usually the exception in these settings. The discursive agents and their recipients are largely under-theorized, however; CDA does not delve extensively into conceptualizations about the subject. This concern, on the other hand, has a more pronounced position within DT.

Discourse Theory: hegemony, contingency and subjectivity

It must be said that Discourse Theory is a somewhat unfortunate label, since it easily leads to confusion with CDA and other variants of discourse analysis. An intellectual endeavor that derives from the work of Ernesto Laclau and Chantal Mouffe (1991), DT encompasses an extensive philosophical ontology and a politically radical understanding of democracy, but my focus will be on its discourse analytic toolkit. This has clear parallels with CDA, but goes further conceptually in linking discourse to other domains of social theory. DT has been used in a variety of contexts in social and cultural analysis with a political bent, but has only recently begun to be deployed within media and communication studies.

Laclau and Mouffe's by now classic text first appeared in the mid-1980s at a time when Marxism was confronted with growing dilemmas, and when post-structural thought, especially as expressed in the works of Foucault, Anne M. Smith (1999), Jørgensen and Phillips (2002), and Jason Glynos and David Howarth (2007) offer useful introductions to this tradition and the debates around it. In recent years media researchers have begun to make use of DT in a variety of ways, as exemplified by Nico Carpentier and Benjamin De Cleen (2007) and Lincoln Dalhberg and Sean Phelan (2011). Nico Carpentier and Erik Spinoy demonstrate its utility in other domains of cultural analysis (2008).

DT is post-Marxist in its efforts to better align critical social theory in keeping with historical realities, and it is clearly post-structural in its approach to society, knowledge, language, and the subject. This is quite evident in its emphasis on contingency: Laclau and Mouffe argue that all our knowledge, and the discursive modalities that it takes, are predicated on particular circumstances – a position not completely foreign to rhetorical analysis. No human practice or subjectivity exists outside the specific conditions that both make them possible and delimit them. DT's position is that there is no foundation or essence, no fixed meaning – for knowledge, language, subjects, or social phenomena. There are only possibilities, nothing is necessary. Not everybody would align themselves with such a stark version of contingency, but it does have the asset of clarity.

Turning to their methodological approach, in Laclau and Mouffe's lexicon, we find elements in DT that are clearly parallel to CDA. *Discourses* refers to relatively stable structures of meanings that arise as linguistic and material practices within a particular context relatively social and material practices. Having both linguistic and non-linguistic dimensions, this conception aligns itself with notions of language use as social action. DT posits that meaning arises via *articulation* – the positioning of signs, words, and actions in relation to others, which closely parallels the semiotic notion of "the play of signifiers." While meaning is never entirely fixed, it can attain a degree of social stability, and such meanings are called *nodal points* of discourses; we can think of them as the core concepts or established vocabularies. We see in DT's view of language the general poststructuralist perspective on meaning, as manifested, for example, in the later Barthes's semiology and in Derrida's deconstructionism (meaning is always to some extent "deferred," as Derrida says).

Given that the political is an inexorable dimension of all social relations, power is always already present in some way in any setting – yet is often not readily visible, remaining occluded, which becomes a key critical point for DT – to flush it out. And in many instances power is seen as lacking legitimacy, as unjust, and should be challenged, for the same reasons that CDA would assert. DT posits that some discourses, in relation to others, have *hegemonic* positions, that is, they offer preferred or dominant meanings. Here we have the pivotal point of politics, where such prevailing discourses are challenged by alternative, *counter-hegemonic* ones. While hegemonic discourses may operate as formalized political positions, mostly they seep into the micro-meshes of ongoing communication, for example in a Facebook group, surreptitiously framing assumptions and perception. Since meaning is always to some extent shifting and contested, even hegemonic discourses can never be fully secure – even if they are characterized by large degrees of inertia.

Where DT most clearly goes beyond CDA is in its notion of the subject and the processes of identity. If politics has to do with antagonisms between groups, between an "us" and one or more "them," discourses can serve as mechanisms of inclusion and exclusion. Discourses *interpellate* subjects, addressing them and providing them with *subject positions,* i.e. identities, in relation to contested issues and those who take opposing views. In the context of public spheres and politics, subject positions can be understood as political identities made available by pertinent discourses. However, given the often contested and disorderly state of discourses circulating in society, it is often the case that subjects are to varying degrees *over-determined,* which means that they are not fully at home in any one discourse, but are pulled in different directions and positioned by competing discourses. Their political identities thus are decentered, fragmented, and the us-them divisions become less self-evident (for example, one may strongly identify with an ecological position that argues for less industrial development in one's region, yet also be a union member who wants to generate more jobs in industry). DT's post-structural character is underscored by its insistence on ambivalence – certainly a disposition well suited to the character of the online world with its chaotic array of nodal points offering over-determined subject positions.

Though shaped by discourses and seen more as a process than a solidified entity, the subject is also a political actor, a contingent discursive agent. Conceptually there is a force-field of power between discourses and agency, between hegemony and counter-hegemony. DT is engaged in exploring the conditions that make specific identities, meanings, and practices possible, and how the dynamics of power support or alter them. Public spheres, not least online, become not just sites of political communication, but also the spaces where political subjectivities, with all their complexities and contradictions, are constructed, negotiated, and contested. There is a vast range of discourses that offer (and seductively compel) subject positions on a constant flow of issues on the web – via blogs, tweets, Facebook groups and other digital platforms. There is no finality here, assuming that democracy is functioning reasonably well: politics is never finished, new contestations and antagonisms always arise.

Discursive subjects, rhetorical citizens

Pulling together the discussion thus far, we have seen that both CDA and DT are oriented towards critical analysis of discourses (as opposed to merely descriptive rendering), trying to illuminate how meaning is structured via discursive practices and elucidating their significance in societal contexts. There is an emphasis on power relations, which are often not overtly visible. Discourses have a constitutive character: they participate in the shaping of subjectivities, identities, social relations, systems of knowledge, modes of cognitive and normative perception – while at the same time being shaped by such elements. Discourses are more than just text; they are manifestations of (collective) social practices; they *do* things. Action, in turn, always has a discursive dimension to it, to the extent that it is meaningful. In terms of the differences between them, DT can be seen as adding theoretic weight beyond the program of CDA, particularly in regard to contestation between discourses (hegemonic and counter-hegemonic) and in particular notions about the subject as an often tension-ridden entity.

Much of this should be rather familiar territory for rhetorical analysis, even if the terminology varies. Most rhetorical scholars today share some version of a social constructionist view of language and see language as a form of social action whereby humans constitute meaning as well as their identities and relationships. At bottom, rhetorical analysis addresses discourse, and all discourses have rhetorical dimensions. More broadly, today rhetorical analysis addresses all manner of human communication in just about all types of situations, from institutional settings such as law, science, and journalism to expressions from popular culture as well as everyday life. Fiction, visuals, works of art, even objects and their manner of display – indeed, all symbols – can be understood as having a persuasory dimension and can thus be of potential relevance for rhetorical analysis. And in most such settings the potential for the political, and thus for rhetorical citizenship, is ever present.

At the epistemological level, most rhetorical analysts today assume that we are always already immersed in language; there is no extra-linguistic escape, as Burke (1969) argues (cf. White 1984). Language operates in social contexts to shape what we know and how we see the world; we use language, but language also uses us, as it were. This stance is found throughout 20th century philosophy, from the later Wittgenstein to post-structuralism via social constructionism (and can be traced back not least to Kant's *Critique of Pure Reason*, with its emphasis on the contingencies of our knowing). As with discourse analysis, rhetorical analysis addresses discrepancies in knowledge or assumption about social reality between communicators and their audiences. This suggests links with the ideas of what Paul Ricoeur calls the three "masters of suspicion": Nietzsche's idea of power-knowledge (adopted by Foucault), Marx's concept of class-based ideology, and even Freud's notion of the repressive unconscious: all critically exemplify social consequences of language-based knowledge discrepancies (1970).

The door to an interface between rhetorical analysis and CDA/DT appears open. With its keen eye for contingency and indeterminacy, rhetoric is equipped to deal with the protean realities of communication on the web and its SNS. If rhetorical analysis has traditionally tilted towards the audience side of civic communication, the realities of the web signal an unprecedented historical shift that actualizes the imperative to energetically address the participatory side of civic interaction. Via the web, democracy has gained innumerable rhetors who are altering the fundamental character of the public sphere, not least through their at times dizzying displays of post-rational, affective communication.

Here the concept of rhetorical citizenship becomes cogent. As underscored in the Introduction to this volume by the editors Christian Kock and

Lisa Villadsen, rhetorical citizenship signifies participation via language in the processes of democracy. Publics are understood as processes – constantly emerging and dissipating. Thus, publics are embodied in practices, and these are largely of a communicative-rhetorical character. Individuals who comprise publics can thereby be seen as rhetorical political agents, enacting rhetorical citizenship. Moreover, such agency varies according to prevailing contingencies, empowering – or disempowering – citizens according to specific circumstances.

We can see here some parallels with discursive subjects, especially as conceptualized by DT. The differences reside chiefly in how and the extent to which the subjectivity of discursive-rhetorical agent is theorized. Rhetorical analysis can extrapolate readers' and listeners' responses to communication, yet the subject as such remains for the most part less theorized within rhetorical analysis, somewhat on a par with the situation in CDA. Psychoanalytic perspectives are mobilized on rare occasions; most specifications of the subject traditionally do not go beyond basic distinctions such as cognitive vs. affective or classic models of the psyche such logos, ethos and pathos. More recently, however, theories of rhetorical agency have been underscoring the situational factors that impact on the rhetor – a development that could facilitate links to DT.

It could readily be argued that rhetorical analysis can manage just fine without further ado about the dynamics of subjectivity; there is much it can do to illuminate civic agency on the web as it is. My assumption, however, is that to the extent that it wants to pursue the notion of rhetorical citizenship in a deeper manner, it would benefit from enhanced reflection on the dimensions and contingencies of subjectivity. DT's view of the subject as radically contingent and often fragmented need not be swallowed whole, but could be considered in small doses. Also, if rhetorical citizenship is about political participation, more attention to the power relations that enable and constrain civic participation in concrete situations would be an asset.

Additionally, rhetorical analysis tends not to deploy a highly developed social theoretic perspective in contextualizing its studies; the so-called "rhetorical situation" tends to be rather micro-contextual. Pursuing the notion of context further may involve taking some steps into political sociology or other social science endeavors, but in my "undisciplined" view – that research in the humanities and social sciences often benefit from crossing disciplinary boundaries – the gains usually outweigh the efforts required.

Indeed, with DT, the notion of discourse itself refers to both linguistic and material practices: there is no border to defend between them.

And certainly CDA and DT in turn could derive methodological inspiration by engaging with and adapting elements of rhetorical analysis, since so much of the analysis of discourse in fact has to do with how discourses impact their addressees. Thus, questions having to do with how discourse interpellates receivers, the compelling power of nodal points within discourses, the interplay of text, discursive and social practices, and so forth, are aspects that can be productively subjected to rhetorical analysis within the overarching logics of CDA and DT. Rhetorical analysis on the one hand, and Critical Discourse Analysis and Discourse Theory on the other, should not be seen as orthodoxies, but sets of tools of potential utility – that may be complemented and combined with each other. Such ventures of course require a degree of conceptual rigor to maintain coherence, but they may all have something to gain by getting to know each other better. And in the process we may deepen our understanding of the dynamics of citizens' political participation online.

References

Baym, N. K. (2010). *Personal Connections in the Digital Age.* Cambridge: Polity Press.

Bennett, W.L. and A. Segerberg (2013). *The Logic of Connective Action: Digital Media and the Personalization of Contentious Politics.* Cambridge: Cambridge University Press.

Burke, K. (1966). *Language as Symbolic Action: Essays on Life, Literature, and Method.* Berkeley: University of California Press.

Carpentier, N. and B. de Cleen (2007). Bringing Discourse Theory into Media Studies. *Journal of Language and Politics* 6, 265-293.

Carpentier, N. and E. Spinoy (Eds.) (2008). *Discourse Theory and Cultural Analysis.* Cresskill, NJ: Hampton Press.

Castells, M. (2012). *Networks of Outrage and Hope: Social Movements in the Internet Age.* Cambridge: Polity Press.

Corner, J. (2011). *Theorising Media: Power, Form and Subjectivity.* Manchester: Manchester University Press.

Curran, J., N. Fenton and D. Freedman (2012). *Misunderstanding the Internet.* Abington: Routledge.

Dahlberg, L. and S. Phelan (Eds.) (2011). *Discourse Theory and Critical Media Politics.* Basingstoke: Palgrave.

Dahlgren, P. (2009). *Media and Political Engagement.* New York: Cambridge University Press.

Dahlgren, P. (2013). *The Political Web: Media, Participation and Alternative Democracy.* London: Palgrave.

Fairclough, N. (1993). *Discourse and Social Change.* Cambridge: Blackwell.

Fairclough, N. (2010). *Critical Discourse Analysis,* 2nd ed. Harlow: Longman.

Gerbaudo, P. (2012) *Tweets and the Streets: Social Media and Contemporary Activism.* London: Verso.

Glynos, J. and D. Howarth. 2007. *Logics of Critical Explanation in Social and Political Theory.* Oxon: Routledge.

Hindman, M. (2009). *The Myth of Digital Democracy.* Princeton, NJ, and Oxford: Oxford University Press.

Jørgensen, M. and L.J. (2002). Phillips *Discourse Analysis as Theory and Method.* London: Sage.

Journal of Communication (2012). Special Issue: Social Media and Political Change, 62(2).

Laclau, E. and C. Mouffe (2001). *Hegemony and Socialist Strategy: Towards a Radical Democratic Politics,* 2nd ed. London: Verso.

Lievrouw, L.A. (2011). *Alternative and Activist New Media.* Cambridge: Polity Press.

Loader, B. and D. Mercea (Eds.) (2012). *Social Media and Democracy.* Abingdon: Routledge.

McChesney, R.W. (2013). *Digital Disconnect.* New York: New Press.

Morozov, E. (2011). *The Net Delusion: How Not to Liberate the World.* London: Allen Lane.

Mouffe, C. (2013). *Agonistics: Thinking the World Politically.* London: Verso.

Papacharissi, Z. (2014). *Affective Publics: Sentiment and the New Political.* Oxford: Oxford University Press.

Ricoeur, P. (1970). *Freud and Philosophy: An Essay on Interpretation.* New Haven: Yale University Press.

Smith, A.M. (1999). *Laclau and Mouffe. The Radical Democratic Imaginary.* London: Routledge.

van Dijk, J. (2013). *The Culture of Connectivity: A Critical History of Social Media.* Oxford: Oxford University Press.

van Dijk, T. (1998). *Ideology.* London: Sage.

White, J.Boyd. (1984). *When Words Lose Their Meaning.* Chicago: The University of Chicago Press.

Wodak, R. and M. Meyer (2009). *Methods of Critical Discourse Analysis,* 2nd ed. London: Sage.

"A Stowaway of Emigration": Polarization in Hafid Bouazza's Work

HILDE VAN BELLE

Introduction

An important subject of rhetorical criticism is the study of polarization, the process by which public opinion divides and goes to the extremes. Rhetoricians can examine how, in public discourse, opposition is constructed throughout texts, how competing choices of oppositions are put to work, or how fixed oppositions are changed into new ones. They can explore how groups are formed around certain oppositions and how different parties react to one another's challenges and arguments. The rhetorician's focus is often double, as both style and argument are involved in the analysis. Inspired by Perelman & Olbrechts-Tyteca, scholars of rhetoric use the intersection of style and argument as a way to typify rhetorical discourse and characterize types of practices (Perelman & Olbrechts-Tyteca 1969, p. 168).

A case in point for this study is the Dutch author Hafid Bouazza (born 1970), whose initial refusal to take part in public debate on matters such as intercultural relations gradually evolved into strong participation and outspoken positions. I will study a collection of his non-literary work in general, and particularly his stance toward the politically correct polarization warnings he emphatically rejects. In an evaluation of Bouazza's own "inverted" strategy I will examine both the arguments Bouazza comes up with in his defense of polarization and the polemical style in which he often tries to make his point. In order to obtain a better view of Bouazza's polarization strategies, I will study his ethos and involve his personal history and the reception of his literary work in the discussion. It will appear that despite the apparent differences both in style and argument, his literary and essayistic works have more in common than first assumed, and his polarization strategies have a clear and well-defined focus.

Hafid Bouazza and polarization

> That's how I know my Muslims: after the murder of Pim Fortuyn many talked about demonization of Islam; now they learned a new word: polarization. It is a riddle to me why the many Islamite organizations are not polarizing, but an association of ex-Muslims is (Bouazza 2011, p. 292).[1]

These explicit words are found in a text in defense of a Dutch committee of ex-muslims. The author is the Dutch writer and columnist Hafid Bouazza, and the tone of his argument is clear: he reproves a Dutch muslima for adopting the politically correct term *polarization* in her critique on the new organization. This text "Noble Savages" is part of a collection of columns and essays, in its turn a chapter of a larger collection of essays and reviews that Bouazza published in 2011, *Heidense vreugde: gepeins en gezang* (*Heathenish Joy: Pondering and Chant).* The chapter "A Stowaway of Emigration" ("Verstekeling van de Emigratie") is a compilation of work on intercultural relations published recently in Dutch quality newspapers.

Morocco-born author Hafid Bouazza, who left his homeland for Arkel (the Netherlands) at the age of seven, presents himself as a clandestine passenger (stowaway) of emigration. As a Moroccan-Dutch writer of short stories, novels, plays, reviews, columns, essays and polemical pieces, and a translator of Arabian and English poetry, Bouazza generally is considered an important representative of so-called migrant literature in the Netherlands.

In "A Stowaway of Emigration" the author tackles present-day questions such as the way western cultures and politics ought to look at Arab or Muslim culture, religion and politics, and vice versa. The occasion for these articles can be a current event, such as the murder of film director Theo Van Gogh (2004) or the expulsion of the Dutch-Somali politician Ayaan Hirsi Ali (2006), but also a less dramatic occasion such as the publication of a book or a debate on television, as is the case of "Noble savages." Gender issues come into the picture, evidently, as well as more autobiographical stories and childhood memories about Ramadan in the last pages of the collection (pp. 314, 317). Generally, the reviews are written in an unmarked, matter-of-fact tone and style; they are well documented and well argued. Some texts, however, are animated by a satirical, ironical, and polarizing touch.

[1] Unless otherwise indicated, all translations are mine (HvB).

The question is now how to assess the polarization issue. As rhetoricians, we tend to believe in the power of persuasion by means of rhetorical strategies such as audience adaptation and a drive for consensus, but what about the places where those modes are bluntly denied and the discussion is set in an openly polemical style? Bouazza satirizes the kind of public debate that shuns intense discussion and condemns conflict of ideas. This so-called politically correct thinking is naïve and self-destructive, he claims, as it does not properly counter the violence of fascist, fundamentalist or right wing populist discourse (pp. 284-289).

Bouazza's polarizing style is not new, nor is it unique. It refers to a rich tradition of polemic work all through Western history, from Martin Luther to Karl Marx, from Robespierre to Noam Chomsky, from Desiderius Erasmus to Michael Moore. Polemics is a widely accepted and appreciated genre,[2] not least by the media, which hunt for the wittiest polemicist and the spiciest controversy.

Moreover, antithetical thinking refers to fundamental human cognitive structures. We try to interpret and organize our world essentially through frames such as analogy and opposition. In other words, the construction of an argument in terms of opposition is nothing more than a basic mode of thinking. Trudy Govier defines the apparent inevitability of this phenomenon as such:

> Dare I say it? It even seems (somehow) *natural* for human creatures to think in binaries. And this despite the fact that two is a small number, a fact that we all know perfectly well (Govier 2007, p. 3).

Scholars such as George Kennedy suggest that thinking in oppositions might be a typically Western habit that originated in antiquity and still dominates our argument structures. His interpretation is based on cultural rather than natural tendencies:

> It would doubtless be an exaggeration to say that speakers in other cultures do not understand logical contradiction, but it is perhaps true that Western contentiousness tends to identify and sharpen contradictions. In other cultures, and now in poststructural thought in the West, there is a greater inclination to entertain

[2] For an excellent introduction, see Angenot (1982).

> the possibility that two seemingly contradictory statements may both be true in some sense; for example, if a term is used metaphorically in one of the statements. Yang and yin in Chinese thought are complementaries, not opposites; ... Western thinking, beginning with the Greeks, has tended to polarize truth and fiction, good and bad, body and soul, conservative and liberal, and other such concepts, for the sake of clarity but often unnecessarily (Kennedy 1998, p. 206).

In an attempt to delineate the phenomenon, Govier observes that polarizing discourse comes with our tendency to inflate a distinction into a dichotomy, to confuse contradictories (e.g., *a* / not *a*) and contraries, and to commit the *error of contrariety* by excluding a middle (e.g., safe / unsafe, wise / unwise, healthy / unhealthy). In what she calls a "slippery journey," Govier proposes to differentiate between forms of distinction reaching all the way from *difference* to *de-humanization*.

Difference
Distinction 1(early exclusion)
Distinction 2 (exclusive disjunction)
Dichotomous framework
Opposition (logical > social opposition)
Polarization (us/them)
Demonization
De-humanization

This scalar method shows similarities with Ruth Amossy's proposal for a modal conception of the argumentation that recognizes polemics. According to her, different positions can be defined along a continuum that goes from the co-construction of answers in the middle to the shock of antagonistic ideas at the far ends of the continuum. The arguments are the same, but they can appear in different modalities (Amossy 2014, pp. 54-55).

This perspective, focusing on the way arguments are delivered, shows that polarization is not only a way of thinking, but a rhetorical strategy as well. We present ideas and arguments within a particular interpretation, perspective or action. We choose which opposition we will highlight and what solution we will present. For example, nationalist political discourse presents the national or regional identity as basic, creates an opposition between "us" and "them," and suggests solutions that promote "us" and punish "them."

Thinking in binaries is one of our most fundamental cognitive structures, just as arguing along those lines determines the basic dynamics of argumentation in general. Scholars such as Christian Kock, Chantal Mouffe and Ruth Amossy endorse these structures when they stress the importance of conflict and opposition in the social and political field and argue that, despite the risk of excess, conflict represents a constructive and vital dynamism in our democracy. The model of dialogue as a verbal exchange along the lines of rationality that aims at one party convincing the other and reaching a consensual solution is too limited (Kock 2009, p. 105, Amossy 2014, p. 208). In a pluralistic democracy, differences and tensions should be voiced and heard, despite the utopian or theoretical ideal of consensus. Polemics are situated in the rhetoric of *dissensus*, where the existence of differences is considered not as a sign of failure, but rather as a fundamental characteristic of democratic functioning (Kock 2009, pp. 105-6, Amossy 2014, pp. 214-5).

The Belgian political theorist Chantal Mouffe stresses the potentially positive aspects of certain forms of political conflict as an essential and constructive aspect of pluralist democracy. It is the aim of democratic politics to transform *antagonism* into *agonism*, so that the other is not an enemy but an adversary. Chantal Mouffe rejects the model of deliberative democracy as it aims at a rational consensus in the public sphere. This consensus is impossible, because the idea is based on the negation of conflict as the essence of modern pluralism. Denying elements of conflict and passion denies the very nature of politics, thus creating not only political apathy but also the possibility of dangerous antagonisms that try to undermine democracy itself (Mouffe 2009, p. 8).[3]

So, when Bouazza writes in defense of polarization, he positions himself within a long and powerful (Western) tradition. Now the question is

[3] The dismissive attitude towards conflict is common in our own field as well. To quote just one arbitrary scholarly work – on the topic of dispute mediation: "Conflict is a problematic event, and as such, it needs to be managed. Also, it is natural to look for ways to resolve the conflict, because it undermines and endangers existing relationships. It triggers alliances and oppositions which polarize [!] the parties' positions; it creates a situation of precarious rapport that may block any constructive initiative; and it focuses attention and energy on the parties' reciprocal endeavour to hinder the realization of each other's desires. ... Yet human beings strongly desire not only to close conflict but also to have the possibility of saving valuable relationships and to live in a stable and friendly environment" (Greco Morasso 2011, pp. 14-15).

why he feels the need to do so, why he passionately claims the right to camp near one end of the pole. I argue that Bouazza manages to defend the right to polarize and the need for dissensus and conflict, without however dropping the concept of rationality. By building a strong ethos, he is able to defend passionately a whole series of democratic values, and to reject other perspectives just as vehemently. In order to prove this point, I will analyze both Bouazza's arguments and his ethos.

No doubt Bouazza's polarizing strategies can be connected to his ethos, i.e., his personal development and his public position on the one hand, and the way he presents himself in his literary and his polemical work on the other hand. This concept of ethos as presented by Ruth Amossy reconciles the pragmatic viewpoint where all ethos is discursive and the sociological perspective where discursive elements are nothing but the alibi of the "real" power battle that is going on elsewhere. Amossy proposes a rhetorical point of view, not least because the appeal to the audience and the process of persuasion play a significant role in the creation of ethos. The effectiveness of discourse is neither exclusively external (institution), nor purely internal (language), she claims, and it plays simultaneously at different levels. The discursive ethos cannot be cut off from the institutional position of the *locutor*, nor can discourse be cut off from social interaction in its symbolic exchange à la Bourdieu (Amossy 1999, p. 147).

Bouazza's essays cannot be separated from his literary work, or from his personal history. The key to his polarizing strategies is to be found in the way he manages his triple ethos as a writer, a polemicist and a public figure.

A first and superficial rhetorical analysis of the *Stowaway* set of essays does not reveal any specific features or anomalies. Bouazza clearly plays his role as an intellectual and a writer who takes part in public discourse. His arguments concern the domain of politics, religion and culture, and his rhetorical strategies often consist in a questioning of prevailing lines of thought, proposing new perspectives and oppositions.

The bulk of the seventy pages take on a wide public scope as it consists of book reviews, essays and columns. In one way or another, they all display a well-documented, engaged, often satirical and ironical plea against religious fundamentalism, misogyny, and all sorts of orthodoxy and repression. Bouazza favors reason, language, freedom of speech, imagination, individual responsibility and diversity. Without any doubt, most of this intellectual work comes down to the impassioned and sustained defense of free speech.

The case for free speech: Politics

Time and again, Bouazza warns his fellow Dutchmen that their comfortable belief in the power of rationality and human goodwill denies the agonism and the conflicts that mark the political sphere. For example, he blames the leftist political parties for treating muslims as noble savages that form a "perfect screen on which to project their own meekness and understanding" (Bouazza 2011, p. 292). He rejects the politically correct interpretation of terms such as diversity because politics should not be confused with morals. He claims the right to ridicule a project called *In Praise of Diversity* by bluntly stating that the distribution of poems in 48 languages will not have any effect on the promotion of mutual understanding between different cultures (p. 320).

Bouazza's main argument against politically correct discourse is the elementary right to free speech as a basic achievement of enlightenment and an indispensable condition for democracy. Politics is to be interpreted in its agonistic sense, and freedom of expression guarantees debate and the constant reinterpretation of any issue. It is remarkable how Bouazza stresses the Western principles of free speech and democracy again and again, wondering why Westerners seem to have forgotten the very values that this newcomer so dearly appreciates.

Bouazza claims the right to speak up and call the oppositions and conflicts by their names, in the name of political freedom. According to him, conflicts should be recognized before they can be tackled, and argument is no pathology but rather a means of communication. Bouazza refers to political, cultural and economic history in order to reveal the complex relation between disappearing and emerging conflicts. The wish for peace does not absolve one from recognizing the multiple appearances of political conflict, Bouazza claims. And when minorities *create* conflict in their desire to change inequality and injustice, this conflict may very well carry the positive-sounding name of revolution and make its way into the official history books.

Bouazza understands the righteous concerns about right-wing populist discourse, but he refuses to let anybody set the terms of the debate.[4]

[4] Indeed, one might wonder whether it is actually possible to agree upon them. To give one example: in his study of manipulative racist propaganda techniques Manfred Kienpointner judges right-wing populists by the content of their standpoints, for example the call for capital punishment or for repatriation of legal immigrants, or by the fact that their arguments

Figures such as hyperbole or metaphor are very familiar and popular tropes in many kinds of discourse (Ritter 2012, p. 407, Angenot 1982, p. 254), and in his arguments rejecting polarization warnings and paralyzing paternalism Bouazza does claim the unconditional right to use them. Likewise, he could not be more explicit in his argument on the Theo Van Gogh murder than when he bluntly declares that the profile of a victim never ever excuses criminal acts (Bouazza 2011, p. 286).

When confronted with the increase of "hate speech" in the public sphere,[5] Bouazza argues in his defense that he stands by his basic right to free speech as long as he takes responsibility for his words and does not incite people to harm or kill others:

> Of course it's not a bad idea to reflect before you say something. But I think: even the sharpest comment should be possible, as long as there's no call for violence – that is most important. What is the alternative? Should we cosily hold each other's hands and treat one another with plain silky respect and subservience? That is outrageous! (Geels 2011).

He is more concerned with dissecting current topics than with attacking particular people, and as such he sees a difference between vital political polemics and hate speech that runs wild in excessive enemy construction.

Interestingly, at some point Bouazza himself recognizes the roles of both style and argument when he explains how Hirsi Ali is caught in a double bind between Muslims who attack her arguments and Western politicians who blame her for her polemical style.

only mention the negative effects of immigration. Stylistic techniques that distinguish racist populist discourse are the use of "emotionally exciting language, for example, hyperbolic exaggerations" (Kienpointner 2005, p. 226), or metaphors like "invasion" and "flood" that "arouse dangerous emotions such as fear and hate" (p. 229). This example reveals how problematic it is to pin down and condemn right-wing populist discourse: Kienpointner's arguments and his references to alleged manipulative techniques do not really observe his own caveats, which warn against the begging-the-question fallacy in assuming that right-wing populism is a dubious, dangerous and irrational tradition, or against the straw man fallacy, while blotting out the evident fact that "populist techniques of persuasion have even been used within the whole political spectrum, from the far right to the far left" (pp. 214-215).

[5] This term is coined by Judith Butler (2007).

> Ayaan Hirsi Ali is caught between two fires. Muslims want to impose on her what to say, the ladies and gentlemen of politics want to command her how to express herself (Bouazza 2011, p. 290).

He keeps insisting on the opposition between the "meek Dutch" who underestimate the problem and downsize the problems of intercultural society to matters of style, and fanatical Muslims who entirely reject the democratic principle of free speech. His opinion is as clear as it is ambitious: the "meek Dutch" should be more fanatical about their democratic principles, the fanatical Muslims should embrace free speech and democracy, and he himself should definitely have the right to say so. Bouazza shows that the opposition is not only a matter of style, but also the reflection of a fundamental conflict between religious thinking and democratic politics.

The case for free speech: Religion

Next to politics, one of Bouazza's key topics is, understandably, religion. Many articles in the collection reject all forms of religious fundamentalism (not only the Muslim type) as "monolithic," i.e., having no place for different perspectives or debate. The opening quote of the "Noble Savages" article is followed by the remark that "If anything should be called polarizing, then it is the sectarian character of Islam, with its virulent, excluding monoperception of Allah" (p. 292). This exemplifies Bouazza's recurring reflection that some Muslims tend to adopt the terms of the "meek Dutch" in order to explain away their own stubbornness. The idea that Westerners fail to see how Islamic fundamentalism attacks the foundational principles of democracy – similar to a predator that pretends to be a prey – dominates the collection: "Why should the obstinacy of Muslims be seen as loyalty to a religion, while the defense of Western values should be considered racist?" (p. 298).

Bouazza reviews much work that brings him to this topic. For example, his review of *God Against the Gods* (Jonathan Kirsch), a historical work about the evolution from polytheism to monotheism, gives him the chance to promote diversity as the basis of paganism or polytheism, and to contrast the gentle pagans to the rigorous and misogynic Christian monotheists in the ages before the fifth century A.D. "The core of paganism or polytheism is diversity," Bouazza concludes (p. 257).

A biography of Mohammed serves as an occasion to condemn religion as a desire for myths and to celebrate science and the quest for facts.

The review then evolves further into a plea for question marks, but also for literature – apparently Mohammed is a frustrated poet – for irony, for criticism and jest (p. 284): "Believers will take care of themselves. Only skepticism, curiosity and doubt lead us, other mortals, further. And let's not forget humor" (p. 270). The author clearly defends the enlightenment ideas that consider religion to be a personal and private matter.

Gender issues are treated in a most expressive way, as in Bouazza's defense of Ayaan Hirsi Ali and her right to attack Islam, or in his fulminations against macho-imams:

> It is a travesty to think that the Netherlands, or Ayaan Hirsi Ali, or Theo van Gogh are responsible for the radicalization of the Islam (p. 286).

> Ambassadors of Islamic countries complain to Gerrit Zalm that Ayaan Hirsi Ali 'doesn't handle carefully the right to free speech.' Of course not, for Islamists this right is only to be handled 'carefully' in order to rage against gentiles, Jews, Christians, women, homosexuals and dissidents (to macho-imams these are all synonyms) (pp. 290-291).

Bouazza plainly calls Islamic extremism a worldwide phenomenon that combines totalitarian ideology with masculine aggression, and concludes with a merry recital of wishes in a salutation to Ayaan: "long live you, long live womanhood, long live free speech, long live jest, long live verbal anarchy" (pp. 286-289).

The main argument in this refutation is again freedom of speech, thinking and religion, as this symbolizes civil society in the light of the American and French Revolutions. In his attacks on Islamic fundamentalism, Bouazza time and again invokes the roots of Western democracy that encompasses the possibility of change through debate, calling for a separation of the religious and political domains. The archaic wording of the very book title is not without meaning in this context, as *Heathenish Joy: Pondering and Chant* explicitly evokes the old times of religious suppression in the West. As such, Western history is strategically linked to contemporary Muslim regimes in order to remind Westerners of their own (former) struggle with religious institutions and repression.

Bouazza tries to persuade his fellow Dutchmen that the most important aspect of the diversity question is public and political. He dismisses the dominant view that reduces the discussion to "essential" differences between cultural or religious groups, redirecting it towards the political domain, where dominant patterns of argument can be questioned again and again, and where the struggle for different social groups to make themselves heard should be considered part of the political enterprise.

The case for free speech: culture, language and literature

Intercultural references. The third argument in Bouazza's refutation of "politically correct thinking" concerns the domain of culture, language and literature, i.e., the domain where most of his work is situated. Again, free expression serves as a basic argument, this time presented as a plea for a colorful individual patchwork of styles, genres and cultural references. The book shows a substantial cultural and literary breadth. Bouazza presents elaborate reviews and essays on, e.g., Nabokov, Shakespeare, Wagner, on musicals such as *Moulin Rouge*, and in those various topics more often than not we see intercultural associations emerge.

In the "Stowaway of Emigration" pieces suggestive and striking passages evoke the literary power of the author: "I quickly zapped away: the fragment gave me the spiritual equivalent of a swig of beer from a can that has been used as an ashtray" (p. 292). The reference to the *sins* of smoking and drinking in this metaphor that expresses his disgust with politically correct polarization warnings is clever and effective. Note that "Noble savages," the title of this piece, is a playful reference to the rich cultural tradition of fascination for the primitive and exotic, as displayed by authors such as Jean-Jacques Rousseau, Daniel Defoe, John Dryden, James F. Cooper and Henry W. Longfellow, to name but a few. Not surprisingly, similar intercultural references and associations appear in Bouazza's literary works. To give but one example:

> Like a Bridal Veil we Children followed the Crowd of Women that my Mother with Abdullah in her Hands led towards the Mosque: I can't express the narcotic magnificence of the moment any better than with the use of Teutonic capitals (1996, p. 34).

This "Teutonic" way of evoking the otherwise very Moroccan setting of this story is but one of Bouazza's many ways to play with cultural references and mix perspectives.

Overall, the reception of Bouazza's literary work has been positive; he has received several prizes[6] and has appeared on prestigious cultural TV shows such as *Zomergasten* (Summer Guests). Critics praise his sensual, flowery and baroque style that reveals his love for exuberant language and multiple perspectives (Louwerse 2007, pp. 37-39). Bouazza's essays definitely have a more polemical and polarizing style. It would be misleading to say that the openness and diversity of Bouazza's literary work simply counterbalance his sharp statements elsewhere, but it does make sense to identify the stance of an author who proclaims the power of language to be the centre of his intellectual life and who concentrates his political arguments around the principles of free speech.[7]

This double focus can enrich our conception of Bouazza's ethos and our understanding of his polarizing strategies.

Bouazza's arguments

Hafid Bouazza's debut collection of short stories was published in 1996, and from that very moment he shows irritation for the way he is being typecast by critics and academics. He refuses to play an exemplary role in accordance with the new ideal of the so-called multicultural society.

> I write because I want to write, not because I aim to further intercultural relations. Get over it. And I certainly don't write because I feel a spokesperson for second-generation migrants. I am not a social worker. Does a Dutch author write in the name of others? (Louwerse 2007, p. 15).

[6] In 1996 he was awarded the *E. du Perron* prize for *De voeten van Abdullah*. In 2003 he was awarded the *Amsterdamprijs voor de Kunsten*. In 2004 he received *De Gouden Uil* for his novel *Paravion*.

[7] The suggested interaction between literary and non-literary work aligns with Alain Lempereur's notion of the two separate domains within the study of rhetoric: one that focuses on literature and cherishes constant rupture and innovation, while another emphasizes persuasion and efficiency and cherishes constant identity (Lempereur, 1990). The former fosters the original and the marginal, the latter goes for the stereotypical. As both domains suffer from this restriction, Lempereur proposes that theories of literature should not deny the reference to the topical, while theories of persuasive rhetoric should not aim exclusively at closure but rather leave enough room for innovation and questioning.

Personal history has nothing to do with art, he claims, and it is neither a driving force nor an excuse for success, even if the stories of his debut collection are set in Bertollo, the actual Moroccan village he left with his family in 1977. He refuses the label "migrant writer" and ridicules the literary establishment for its biographical obsession and its fixation on the exotic: "A French writer is somebody that writes in French, an immigrant writer is somebody that writes in Immigrantese, and a Dutch writer is somebody that writes in Dutch" (Bouazza, *NRC-Handelsblad* 21-6-96). And indeed, while at first some critics interpret his unique baroque and archaic style as a reminiscence of Arab poetry, others soon take to criticizing this view (Anbeek 2002). Hans Goedkoop ridicules its paternalism: "We take the Dutch for something exotic, tremendously fascinating and we pay the author a compliment because as a non-native he is so charmingly different" (p. 39).

Even more significantly, in her outstanding study on the reception of Bouazza's literary work Henriëtte Louwerse stresses the fact that Bouazza's style and perspective are actually based on the Dutch art movement *De Tachtigers*, known to many Dutchmen for the statement by Willem Kloos that "art is the most individual expression of the most individual emotion." According to her, this absolute fascination with language, individual expression and imagination, far from everyday worries, is what constitutes Bouazza's real homeland (pp. 48-49).

In 2001, Bouazza was selected to write the national Dutch *boekenweekgeschenk* (the CPNB Book Week Present): a commissioned essay with the theme "Country of Origin: Writing between Two Cultures." The most famous quote from *Een beer in bontjas* ("A Bear in Fur") goes:

> If I were to believe most critics, I am a Moroccan writer. But I don't believe most critics. According to other, benevolent people I am a Moroccan-Dutch writer. However, this signification sounds uncomfortable. It walks at the same time in a slipper and a clog – quite a tricky way of walking! Then there are the careful people who aim at integration (they are a minority), for whom I fabricated the title D.A.M.D.D.N. (Dutch Author of Moroccan Descent with Dutch Nationality). This is socially speaking the only correct signification, but it prevents you from making friends. It sounds like a rare disease. The D.A.M.D.D.N. syndrome. You don't walk into the pub with it (2001, p. 49).

An author finds inspiration for his subjects and style in art and literature, not in his personal background or social, religious, sexual or racial circumstances – that was Bouazza's claim at that time. Individual maturation, creative imagination and artistic freedom are to guarantee an escape from compulsory classification. However, as Louwerse observes:

> Hafid Bouazza's strategy in *Een beer in bontjas* is characteristically paradoxical: he writes an autobiography in order to emphasize that the author's life-story is irrelevant when it comes to producing or reading literature (Louwerse 2007, p. 227).

Indeed, the interplay between the role(s) he is expected to assume and the strategies he develops to resist is more complex than one would assume at first sight. The strict line between the literary and the extra-literary cannot be drawn all that clearly, and Bouazza cannot really escape his role of "migrant writer." In 2002, shortly after the publication of *Een beer in bontjas*, he enters the public scene and engages in a "full-fledged genre of public discourse" that goes under the name of "debating diversity" (Blommaert and Verschueren 1998, p. 11). He gives up the embargo on his private identity and tries to find a new way to challenge his readers in their perception of him as both an insider and an outsider to "their" culture. This did not go unnoticed; in November 2011, for example, Bouazza won the Scalpel 2011 prize for his polemics about the Arab Spring.

According to Louwerse, Bouazza's essays differ considerably from his literary work, both in topic and in tone. She claims: "Despite of his sharp statements in his political publications, in his literary texts he resists the need to reduce multicultural tensions to unambiguous oppositions" (Louwerse 2008, p. 10). It is remarkable that there seems to be an inconsistency between Bouazza's literary and non-literary work. A closer look at Louwerse's appreciation of his literary work, however, rather reveals a striking similarity between the literary and political issues: "Much of Bouazza's writing foregrounds communication gaps – between orient and occident, between man and woman, between animal and man, between reality and the imagination, between oppositional places, between character and narrator." (Louwerse 2007, p. 96) If anything, Bouazza in his polemical work tries to define these communication gaps as clearly and explicitly as possible. Also the notion of the preconceived ideas and stereotypical expectations is mentioned:

> Bouazza playfully exploits cultural expectations by painting an Arab setting which echoes the one-dimensional Western views of the Arab world ... What had initially seemed a 'safe' opposition between us and them, is now revisited upon the readers as a confrontation with their own preconceived ideas (p. 231).

In "A Stowaway of Emigration," time and again, Bouazza warns his readers about their preconceived ideas and their "Noble-Wild" projections. Louwerse perfectly captures Bouazza's rhetorical strategies when she describes his literary work in polemical terms: "What appears to start off as an exposure of cultural opposites ... evolves into a literary attack on the notion of unified, homogenous societies or cultures" (p. 233).

From the start, Bouazza refuses to follow the standard course of the political debate and develops a personal way of thinking and writing. In his public life, time and again he takes up the defense of free speech, argumentation, imagination, style play, humor, education, and individual maturation. He rejects religious and political fundamentalism in general (not just Islamic fundamentalism) and the excesses of fear and naiveté that go with it. Misogyny and all kinds of orthodoxy are disapproved of, as well as literary norms and stylistic restrictions. To Bouazza, imagination and argumentation do not exclude one another. His literary and polemical writings are closely connected and intertwined: they frame and reinforce one another. The right to develop both imagination and argumentation could be considered to be the basic tenor of his ethos.

Throughout all of his work, Bouazza shows his audience that openness towards the diversity of cultures and literatures does not stand on its own, but has a political dimension as well. It is no coincidence that he connects his very personal intellectual and cultural life with the fundamental concept of democracy. His own history reveals that "the basic biological fact of diversity" is part of the *condition humaine* (Blommaert and Verschueren 1998, p. 14). He is fully aware of the decision to enter the political debate and try to find ways out of the prevailing polarizations that classify people into certain groups with certain fixed features that promote homogeneity as the norm and makes diversity a problem (p. 117).

Conclusion

Louwerse's earlier remark that Bouazza's political work is characterized by "sharp statements" and "unambiguous oppositions" needs reservations, I suggest. The rhetorical construct Bouazza presents in his non-literary work shows clear oppositions indeed, but they are oppositions of a specific kind: they draw the sharp line between fixity and repression on the one hand and political freedom and imagination on the other hand. This corresponds to Louwerse's appreciation of Bouazza's literary work as a constant challenge of comfortable identities and a powerful confirmation of hybrid positions, movement and interaction.

> Opposing versions of the truth do not cancel each other out. In Bouazza's works, the representation of the 'real' has also come unhinged, and this reality is engaged in a ceaseless struggle against the desire for a fixed, fossilized reality that believes in the essential, in the absolute, in purity and authenticity. Undermining that belief is the essence of Bouazza's writing (Louwerse 2007, p. 233).

Bouazza's literary work is marked by the shifting and energizing of existing polarizations; in his non-literary work, he reveals the political conditions that make the shiftings possible. In this light, it is perfectly possible to read Louwerse's comment on his literary work as an evocation of his political program: "His work is a study of sustained opposition, but at the same time, an engagement with the underlying assumptions of these same oppositions. Interpretative closure or unity is not an option. Fixity is there to be squashed." (p. 76)

While Bouazza "squashes fixity" in his literary work by presenting a multitude of interpretations and shifts, in his polemical work he aims at the same target by revealing and safeguarding the very borders of this freedom of expression. His well-argued pleas for reason, freedom of speech, imagination, individual responsibility and diversity show that he wants the public domain to be rich and diverse. That is why he draws a sharp line between all kinds of fundamentalism and the politics of free speech.

Bouazza clearly endorses a concept of democracy that accepts dissensus and a concept of language that embraces polemics. This does not mean that his occasional harsh rhetoric should be interpreted as blind aggression or incitement to violence. Far from it. By pursuing related themes across different contexts, he manages to build a powerful ethos. In light of this ethos, my analysis of his polarization strategies has brought to the fore that Bouazza's polarization practices and his passionate plea for free speech reflect a deep involvement with the Dutch language, a commitment to very diverse audiences, and a sustained creativity in the fostering of mutual understanding.

References

Amossy, R. (1999). L'ethos au carrefour des disciplines: rhétorique, pragmatique, sociologie des champs. In *Images de soi dans le discours. La construction de l'ethos. Edited by* Ruth Amossy. Lausanne: Delachaux et Niestlé, pp. 127-154

Amossy, R. (2014). *Apologie de la polémique.* Paris: PUF.

Anbeek, T. (2002). Over Marokkaans-Nederlandse auteurs en hun critici. In *Europa buitengaats. Koloniale en postkoloniale literaturen in Europese talen,* Edited by Theo D'haen. Amsterdam: Bert Bakker. Accessed July 15, 2013: www.dbnl.org/tekst/dhae007eur001_01/dhae007eur001_01_0008.php

Angenot, M. (1982). *La parole pamphlétaire. Contribution à la typologie des discours modernes.* Paris: Payot.

Blommaert, J. and J. Verschueren (Eds.) (1998). *Debating Diversity. Analysing the Discourse of Tolerance.* London: Routledge.

Bouazza, H. (1996). *De voeten van Abdullah.* Amsterdam: Arena.

Bouazza, H. (2004). *Een beer in bontjas. Autobiografische beschouwingen.* Amsterdam: Prometheus.

Bouazza, H. (2011). *Heidense vreugde. Gepeins en gezang.* Amsterdam: Prometheus.

Butler, J. (2007). *Opgefokte taal. Een politiek van de performatief.* Translated by Niels Helsloot. Amsterdam: Parrèsia.

Geels, B. (2011). Hafid Bouazza: "Waarom zou ik mijn toon matigen?" HP-De Site 3 augustus 2011. Accessed July 15, 2013, http://www.hpdetijd.nl/2011-08-03/hafid-bouazza-waarom-zou-ik-mijn-toon-matigen

Govier, T. (2007). Two is a small number: False dichotomies revisited. In H.V. Hansen, C.W. Tindale, J.A. Blair, R.H. Johnson and D.M. Godden (Eds.), *Dissensus and the Search for Common Ground.* CD-ROM.Windsor, ON: OSSA.

Greco Morasso, S. (2011). *Argumentation in Dispute Mediation. A Reasonable Way to Handle Conflict.* Amsterdam: John Benjamins.

Kennedy, G. (1998). *Comparative Rhetoric. An Historical and Cross-Cultural Introduction.* New York and Oxford: Oxford University Press.

Kienpointner, M. (2005). Racist Manipulation within Austrian, German, Dutch, French and Italian Right-Wing Populism. In L. de Saussure and P. Schulz (Eds.), *Manipulations and Ideologies in the Twentieth Century* (pp. 213-235). Amsterdam: John Benjamins.

Kock, C. (2009). Constructive Controversy: Rhetoric as Dissensus-Oriented Discourse. *Cogency* 1, 89-111.

Lempereur, A. (1990). Les restrictions des deux néo-rhétoriques. In M. Meyer and A. Lempereur (Eds.), *Figures et conflits rhétoriques* (pp. 139-156). Bruxelles: Editions de l'Université de Bruxelles.

Louwerse, H. (2007). *Homeless Entertainment. On Hafid Bouazza's Literary Writing.* Oxford: Peter Lang.

Louwerse, H. (2008). Hafid Bouazza. In S. Bax, H. Brems and A. Zuiderent (Eds.), *Kritisch Lexicon van de moderne Nederlandstalige Literatuur*, nr. 108. Edited by Groningen: Noordhoff Uitgevers.

Mouffe, C. (2009). *The Democratic Paradox.* London: Verso.

Perelman, C. and L. Olbrechts-Tyteca. (1969). *The New Rhetoric. A Treatise on Argumentation.* Notre Dame: University of Notre Dame Press.

Ritter, J.R. (2012). Recovering Hyperbole: Rethinking the Limits of Rhetoric for an Age of Excess. *Philosophy and Rhetoric* 45, 406-428.

Extending Civic Rhetoric: Valuing Rhetorical Dimensions of Global Citizenship in Civic Education

REBECCA A. KUEHL

In a March 8, 2011 article in the *New York Times*, columnist David Brooks writes about "the new humanism." He explains that a new body of research provides additional insight into humanity: that "emotions assign value to things and are the basis of reason," and that "we are social animals, deeply interpenetrated with one another, who emerge out of relationships" (2011, p. A27). This essay builds on the idea of "new humanism," positing that civic rhetoric[1] could benefit from a rhetorical view of global citizenship[2] in

[1] Civic rhetoric is sometimes used to refer to classical accounts of rhetorical or speech education, but I see the terms as mostly interchangeable, depending on the context. Civic rhetoric describes a specific area of scholarship, whereas rhetorical or speech education tends to focus on the practices of how rhetorical scholars specifically teach students the necessary skills to enact citizenship. I use rhetorical or speech education interchangeably in this essay, since the terms are used differently based on historical context. See: Gehrke 2009.

[2] I purposefully use global citizenship, and not concepts such as cosmopolitanism, world citizenship, or transnational citizenship. Historically, global citizenship is a concept that evolved from philosophies of cosmopolitanism and world citizenship; see: Carter 2001. Because I am concerned with civic rhetoric and teaching rhetorical strategies for practice in citizenship, I use global citizenship as a concept and a practice. Additionally, I do not use transnational citizenship, a common turn in cultural and feminist studies, because I am concerned with conceptualizing citizenship not primarily through the state or territory, but instead through social belonging. For an analysis of the characteristics of transnational activism, see: Keck and Sikkink 1998, pp. 8-16. Transnational citizenship theorists are often concerned with keeping the nation-state intact when analyzing international activism, especially with international funding mechanisms and organizations such as the United Nations or World Bank. In contrast, I am more concerned with thinking

extending the practices of rhetorical education. This perspective describes how human beings identify with one another through different emotional attachments, developing a sense of social belonging to be able to work together to address shared global problems.

Civic rhetoric falls under the larger umbrella of civic education; education has a goal to prepare students to become citizens. Gerard A. Hauser explains the concept of civic rhetoric and its role in civic education: "[Rhetorical scholars] also have a birthright: rhetoric's role in civic education. That role is not just in the public performance of political discourse but in the education of young minds that prepares them to perform their citizenship" (2004, p. 52). Civic rhetoric is a specific component of civic education, focusing on teaching skills such as critical thinking, speaking, and writing.

Within the area of civic rhetoric, rhetorical scholars often concern themselves with more specific questions of rhetorical citizenship. William Keith and Paula Cossart define rhetorical citizenship as a "set of communicative and deliberative practices that in a particular culture and political system allow citizens to enact and embody their citizenship, in contrast to practices that are merely 'talking about' politics" (2012, p. 46). Such a view necessarily includes embodiment and enactment, which are often connected to emotions.[3] Rhetorical citizenship is contingent on arousing people's emotion

beyond the nation-state, specifically through relationships grounded in social belonging. For an analysis of this shift away from cosmopolitan or world citizenship and toward global citizenship as conceptualized through global connections and a commitment to the collective good, see: Rhoads and Szelényi 2011, pp. 22-27.

[3] In this essay, emotions and passions are synonymous, because they are often used in contrast to reason and rationality. The difference in usage is often because of historical context. Philip Fisher suggests that it is only through the modern turn (and the split of what is now called psychology from philosophy) that passions have been replaced by the term emotion: "We can see in mid-eighteenth-century English philosophy and rhetoric the banishing of the term 'passion' and its replacement by the new term 'emotion'" (2002, p. 6). For a book length study of this transition from passions in philosophy to emotion in psychology, see: Dixon 2003. Rhetorical scholar Daniel M. Gross does not differentiate between affect, emotion, or passions: "Theory can meaningfully differentiate between different affects (or passions, or emotions) and even between different instances of the same affect, by way of *history*..." (2006, p. 9). Gross seems to see these concepts as generally meaning the same idea; they are used as different terms based on the historical context.

about political issues: "People become engaged [in politics] because issues touch their lives" (Hauser 1998, p. 51). A fully developed understanding of civic rhetoric should involve analyzing the interaction of emotion *with* reason, whether the idea of civic rhetoric is based on civic republicanism or civic liberalism as the political philosophy underpinning civic education. Daniel M. Gross writes that scholars in the humanities rarely turn to the rhetorical tradition when analyzing emotions (2006, p. 9). In conceptualizing global citizenship, a rhetorical perspective analyzes the role of emotional attachments, such as feelings of concern or trust, in how activist groups reach people around the globe, often across identity differences such as culture, religion, ethnicity, and nationality.

To support the claim that rhetorical scholars should extend civic rhetoric to include global citizenship, this essay proceeds in four parts. In analyzing civic education, I first evaluate the lack of analysis of emotion in two political philosophies, civic republicanism and civic liberalism, that often undergird civic education itself. I then show how the civic rhetoric tradition has often relied on national understandings of citizenship. Third, to remedy this emphasis on the nation, I recommend adding global citizenship to the civic rhetoric tradition, as both a concept and a practice. Finally, I suggest two rhetorical dimensions to global citizenship: emotional attachments and social belonging.

Analyzing reason in civic education

Civic education can be connected to two different political philosophies that explain citizenship and its practice: civic republicanism and civic liberalism.[4] I briefly analyze examples in each tradition that emphasize reason to the det-

For example, Aristotle wrote about "passions," David Hume wrote about "emotion" and "sentiment," and 20th and 21st century theorists write about "affect," but they are all working with a similar meaning, that these concepts indicate intuitive modes of feeling with others. For a summary of some of the current approaches in rhetorical studies regarding the study of affect and emotion, see: Condit, 2013, pp. 3-5.

[4] I do not address democratic theory writ large or democratic deliberation here, for the purposes of focusing on the different strains of citizenship crucial to understanding civic rhetoric and how citizenship is taught to students in rhetoric classrooms. Democratic deliberation is often included in these discussions as an important part of the process of rhetorical education, and democratic deliberation itself is often grounded in a political philosophy of civic liberalism or civic republicanism.

riment of a full analysis of emotion in articulating citizenship. Because civic rhetoric is a component of civic education, civic rhetoric scholars should consider emotional attachments in addition to reason or rationality, especially since emotions are an important characteristic of how and why people become motivated to take action on a given issue.

Generally, civic republicanism conceptualizes citizenship as a practice (see: Longaker 2007, p. 6; Peterson 2009, p. 57; Peterson 2011, p. 3). Civic republicanism focuses on the characteristics and interests shared by individuals in a community. Some scholars assert that civic republicanism is communitarian (see: Longaker 2007, p. 212; Oldfield 1990, p. 145; Olsen 2006, p. 1), while others keep these two ideas distinct, preferring to compare communitarianism to liberalism more generally as two sides of a continuum (see: Boyte 2003, p. 86; Peterson 2011, p. 9; Vandenberg 2000, p. 9; Voet 1998, p. 133). Erik J. Olsen explains that "republicanism," "neorepublicanism," "communitarian republicanism," and "civic republicanism" all refer to the various theories of virtue and community that emerged in the 1980s as a critique of civic liberalism as a political philosophy that emphasized the "rights, interests, and choices of the individual" (2006, p. 1). Both civic republicanism and communitarianism emphasize the social aspect of citizenship yet do not elaborate on the emotional connections we share with others as part of what motivates us to care and to eventually take action.[5] For example, Adrian Oldfield asserts that "civic faiths, when they are devised with intent and consciously propagated, are not effective in encouraging a rational commitment to a practice of citizenship" (1990, p. 154). Rationality becomes a defining characteristic of civic republicanism.

In contrast, civic liberalism values the different characteristics of individuals and individual motivation in political and social issues. Reason and rationality become important to the exclusion of emotion in any discussion on civic liberalism, likely because of this tradition's connection to Immanuel Kant's universal reason (Peterson, 2009, p. 60). Andrew Peterson explains civic liberalism in terms of rationality: "Based on the understanding of individuals as able to rationally choose and revise their own ends, liberals have advanced a negative understanding of freedom in terms of non-interference" (2011, p. 11). In the classical civic rhetoric tradition, civic rhetoric entails building the individual's capacity for political involvement, especially the

[5] See especially Gerard A. Hauser's scholarship for an important exception to this claim.

capacities of reason and speech (Jackson 2007, p. 185; Walzer 2007, pp. 271-72). Indeed, most traditions of civic rhetoric tend to operate with the assumption that reason is one of the most important capacities to cultivate in individual citizens.[6] Reason is an important capacity for public discourse; however, the civic rhetoric tradition's understanding of reason needs to be supplemented with a rich analysis of the role of emotion.

Both the civic republican and civic liberal perspectives tend to use the language of rationality and reason to define citizenship. Civic empathy, the ability to feel what others feel in becoming engaged citizens, has "received little critical attention to date" in the scholarship of civic education (Peterson 2009, p. 62). Some rhetorical scholars view emotion as a problem for public discourse and communicating about the world's problems (Jackson 2007, p. 190). In studying the history of speech education, discussion movements relied on certain principles of reasoning that held reason above emotion (Gehrke 2009, p. 42; Keith 2007, p. 158). Civic education – and in turn civic rhetoric – has not yet given sufficient attention to how emotional attachments play a key role in persuading citizens to interact with strangers to resolve global problems.

Reason and emotion are not separate, but shape one another. This is not a novel argument for rhetorical studies; theories of persuasion have long acknowledged that commitment cannot come from reason alone. For example, many teachers of public speaking reference the Aristotelian appeal of *pathos* in evaluating persuasive appeals. However, the political philosophies that undergird civic education, and in turn civic rhetoric, have investments in rational approaches to citizenship rather than accounting for emotion. Since emotional attachments are important to cultivating social belonging, rhetorical citizenship scholars should more fully analyze how emotion works to motivate people to practice citizenship, and civic rhetoric seems especially well-suited to this task.

Extending the civic rhetoric tradition to global issues

Most scholarship on civic education, of which civic rhetoric is an important component, relies on national understandings of citizenship that exclude

[6] One exception is Hauser's scholarship, which tends to give equal attention to emotion in addition to reason in any rhetorical analysis of public discourse. See especially: Hauser 1999, 51; 2004, 41.

global issues. Scholarship about civic education is mostly centered on nation-states or nationalism (Longaker 2007, p. xii; Vandenberg 2000, p. 15), rather than a more comprehensive view of citizenship in a global setting. For example, Peterson outlines civic education programs in England, Australia, Canada, and the United States (2011, pp. 25-29). However, he approaches each program on a national level, instead of highlighting global concerns. Most civic rhetoric scholars also emphasize civic education on a local, state, or national level, but fail to take citizenship to its next logical step – the global. Mark Garrett Longaker writes: "Academics are encouraged to research public issues, to design classes that engage national, state, and local communities, to teach students responsible democratic citizenship" (2007, p. xi). Such a focus on the national, state, and local is important, but so is teaching students that many issues extend beyond these scales. Conceptualizing global citizenship as an outgrowth of these other types of citizenship, and inclusive of these other types of citizenship (Nussbaum and Cohen 1996, p. 135), can be a productive move in helping students understand how to take action on issues that have global causes and consequences.

Young people's ability to articulate their ideas to others is one of the most important skills in producing citizens who engage the world. Civic rhetoric is a vital component of civic education, since discourse, discussion, and debate are fundamental to active citizenship (Peterson 2009, pp. 56, 67). Cheryl Glenn writes that "rhetorical education enables people to engage in and change American society" (2004, p. viii). Indeed, civic rhetoric generally involves the tradition of teaching students the skills and basic concepts of persuasion and the art of argumentation, so that students are enabled to participate, criticize, and engage in public life. Longaker suggests that the "civic turn" in rhetoric signifies a move in research, theory, and teaching to promote public discourse, where citizens come together to communicate over shared concerns (2007, p. xii).

Historically, civic rhetoric scholars often derive their approach from two traditions – a classical and a more recent historical tradition in the United States, which originates from the colonial era. Rhetoric has long been connected to the civic republican tradition, especially because of its classical roots in Greek and Roman history (Arthos 2007, p. 198), including the work of Isocrates, and Cicero and Quintilian, respectively (Walzer 2007, p. 271). Specifically, the Greek tradition, *paideia*, includes the instruction of the Sophists, as well as Aristotle (Jackson 2007, p. 183). Greek *paideia* means that instructors have the goal of helping students lead the lives of active, engaged, and responsible citizens (Hauser 2004, p. 40).

In contrast, some scholars have outlined a more recent history of speech education in the United States and its role in cultivating citizens during the 18th, 19th, and 20th centuries.[7] Speech education in the United States, especially during the 20th century, served nationalistic purposes in furthering American democracy and government (Gehrke 2009, p. 43). Rhetorical scholars should be aware of civic rhetoric's ideological past (Longaker 2007, pp. xx, 216), and especially its history in contributing to wartime propaganda during the 20th century (Gehrke 2009, p. 34). Aware of that past, scholars should extend the tradition of speech education outward, beyond the nation-state. Global citizenship is not a necessary extension of ideologically-focused or nationalist perspectives on civic education. However, global perspectives help complicate the history of speech education for students, through bringing in examples from other cultures, places, and contexts and relating those examples to their own lives.

Global citizenship as a concept and a practice

I suggest that global citizenship, as a concept and a practice, is useful in extending the civic rhetoric tradition. Robert A. Rhoads and Katalin Szelényi note that global citizenship has not been clearly defined (2011, p. 22), but explain that their view of the concept "incorporates both local/national awareness with a growing sense of the interconnectedness of all nation-states and the importance of forging common ties and connections in terms of global rights and responsibilities" (p. 26). Although Rhoads and Szelényi's definition of global citizenship is still connected to the nation-state, the emphasis on interconnectedness and the importance of rights and responsibilities concerning all human beings is helpful in defining global citizenship. They go on to create a chart that details different types of citizenship, using locally and globally informed on the *x* axis and individualist and collectivist on the *y* axis. Global citizenship, for them, is the globally informed collectivist (p. 27).

While I applaud Rhoads and Szelényi's efforts to create different typologies for citizenship in higher education (2011, p. 27), a rhetorical view

[7] For recent histories of the relationship between the discipline of speech communication, now known as communication studies, and citizenship, see: Denman 2004; Gehrke 2009; Keith 2007.

of global citizenship is more complex. For example, let us analyze a woman who participates with others in a local food share program, through purchasing food from a farm located just outside her city. By participating with others in the food share, this is clearly a collectivist action. We might be quick to say that this woman is practicing global citizenship, because she is acting in a socially responsible way that shows she is globally aware – that her consumption affects others around the world. However, maybe she is also acting as a locally informed citizen. Perhaps another motivation for participating in the food share is because she likes the taste of locally grown food, because it is fresher than food at the grocery store that travels hundreds of miles. In talking to other citizens about her reasons for participating in the food share, her advocacy is more complex than simply local or global. In analyzing her rhetorical citizenship, or how she communicates with others to persuade them to participate in this food share, we must be careful not to oversimplify her motivations. In this case, the woman would be a locally and globally informed citizen in choosing to participate in and advocate for a food share. This case would not fit neatly into Rhoads and Szelényi's chart (p. 27). Because of the complexity of people's actions, and multiple reasons for those actions, global citizenship is probably too difficult to categorize in such a narrow typology.

Global citizenship can be conceptualized as a specific type of rhetorical citizenship, and can include numerous local and/or global issues that span nation-states. For example, some human rights groups use the concept to argue a connection to strangers, across national, ethnic, or gendered lines. Environmental groups also use global citizenship to describe citizenship in practice, through activism surrounding issues such as reducing pollution. Many issues extend beyond national borders, including hunger, water access, women's rights, online privacy, and the use of natural resources. These commonly debated topics illustrate that the world is interconnected beyond the nation-state.

Global citizenship is not without its limitations, however. Common counterarguments include postcolonial critiques of Western privilege and power, problems connected to globalization and the movement of global capital, including migrants, and the rise of nationalism. When scholars and citizens see global citizenship as merely a way of denoting Western privilege or access to global travel and resources, the concept remains hollow. Homi K. Bhaba suggests scholars start first with analyzing and evaluating local contexts, before carefully considering global issues in a way that complicates systems of privilege, economic progress, and globalization (1994; pp. xiv-xv). April Carter explains that with the rise of nationalism, global citizenship for some scholars is simply impossible. She analyzes the contributions of Hannah Arendt, David Miller, and Michael Walzer, arguing that each has problems with the idea of cosmopolitanism, or global citizenship. Limitations include the difficulty of citizens' participation at a national scale, let alone a global scale, problems with moral universalism, and a lack of institutional enforcement on a global level (2001, pp. 167-170). Although each counterargument has merit, some scholars suggest that global citizenship has still gained traction in public discourse as a useful concept, especially in practice. Additionally, if the concept is deployed responsibly alongside these counterarguments, students will have a better understanding of a critical reading of power and privilege associated with other concepts such as nationalism, globalization, and the problems accompanying global capitalism and the movements of migrants and refugees.

Despite these limitations, I believe global citizenship is useful for rhetorical studies, especially since numerous scholars have used the concept in diverse fields such as higher education, philosophy and political science (see: Carter 2001; Rhoads and Szelényi 2011; Schattle 2008). As human problems become larger in scope and implicate people across boundaries (Lister 2003, pp. 55-56), scholars need to expand their view of civic rhetoric. Universities are one place in which to introduce the concept and practice of global citizenship (Boyte 2003, p. 96), especially through courses in rhetoric, such as composition, argumentation, public speaking, rhetorical criticism, and persuasive writing. Many colleges and universities are incorporating a global orientation into their mission and value statements (Rhoads and Szelényi 2011, p. 21; Stearns 2009, p. 191). To meet these missions, rhetorical educators should better incorporate global issues into their teaching.

Extending speech education to focus on global issues helps students gain an understanding of other cultures and traditions as well as an ability to then criticize such practices, without being ethnocentric. In teaching students about global citizenship, instructors should include the "study of different cultural traditions and institutional frameworks…but also an appreciation of the kinds of forces that bear on societies around the world… and how these forces have emerged" (Stearns 2009, p. 15). In a summary of the History of Rhetoric Discussion Groups at the 2004 ARS Conference,

Patricia Bizzell and Susan Jarratt noted that the future of rhetorical studies should address multiculturalism and transnationalism (2004, pp. 21-22). Some rhetorical scholars have begun to answer this call, but more work needs to be done, especially in rhetoric classrooms. As a concept, global citizenship illustrates the importance of being able to communicate and interact with strangers who might be geographically removed from students' own local context. If coupled with counterarguments of global citizenship, students will have a more nuanced understanding of the tensions that occur when practicing citizenship among various peoples, places, and cultures, and how to incorporate critiques of power and privilege in their communicative interactions. This critical view of practicing global citizenship means beginning with local actions but recognizing the implications of those actions on others around the world.

Rhetorical dimensions of global citizenship

In this last section, I advance two rhetorical dimensions important to global citizenship: emotional attachments and social belonging. Emotions help us identify with others, which grounds global citizenship in social belonging. Rhetorical educators can teach students how to practice global citizenship, enabling an awareness of how to work across differences while being mindful of critiques of global citizenship.

Valuing emotional attachments in global citizenship

A rhetorical approach to global citizenship does not dismiss emotional means of persuasion, but instead analyzes emotion as a necessary aspect of the decision-making process, especially in choosing to take action on an issue. Rhetorical scholars are shifting their views about the role of emotion in politics and decision-making. For instance, Gross writes that emotions are rhetorical through a power differential, or "uneven distribution" of emotion, between two individuals or groups (2006, p. 5). However, such an "uneven distribution" may be bridged by emotion itself in order to incite action on a particular social or political issue. After all, without a power differential, it would be difficult to convince individuals to support resolving a particular global problem. Emotion is an important component in motivating individuals or groups with less power to change their situation. In contrast, Celeste M. Condit focuses on the possibilities of emotions for social action. Condit views *pathos* as "the deliberate art for the construction of shared public emotion" (2013, p. 5). People have mistrusted rhetoric's role in cultivating emotional responses for a long time, especially in rhetorical studies of mobs and propaganda (Gehrke 2009, p. 53). However, humans need emotion to be able to make rational decisions.

Emotion works *with* reason to help us make decisions to become involved in global issues. Kenneth Burke explains that identification is really about people understanding their "joint interests:" "A is not identical with his colleague, B. But insofar as their interests are joined, A is *identified* with B" (1969, p. 20). This definition of identification as "joint interests" seems important for crafting a rhetorical view of global citizenship. For example, consider human rights. People can have a joint interest in recognizing certain basic human rights for all through an overlapping consensus. That consensus is not achieved through a legal or territorial definition of global citizenship, but instead through discussion and deliberation among people, which are in turn influenced by both rational and emotional appeals.

Burke further explains that identification is linked to consubstantiality in that we become one with another person through identification yet still retain our individual differences. Burke writes: "In being identified with B, A is 'substantially one' with a person other than himself [sic]. Yet at the same time he [sic] remains unique, an individual locus of motives. Thus he [sic] is both joined and separate, at once a distinct substance and consubstantial with another" (p. 21). When considering how emotional attachments reinforce identification, identification can be understood as a process that connects us to other people through joint interests while simultaneously recognizing individual differences. For example, take the issue of reducing pollution in a city. People working together on that global issue would have a common goal of reducing pollution for the sake of the planet, although their work is locally focused. In working together to build advocacy campaigns and change polluting behaviors, these people will experience emotional attachments, such as compassion or trust, which will shape their interactions with each other. In coming together around the joint interest of pollution reduction, they are able to work together in advocacy across identity markers, such as race, ethnicity, and gender.

Just as identification can connect human beings across locations and cultures, rhetorical strategies can also be negatively used to diminish a sense of community and create division among people (Tonn, Endress, and Diamond 1993, pp. 167-168). Burke is well-known for theorizing identification with division (1969, p. 45). Creating emotional connections across individuals, borders, and cultures can be challenging. Cultivating compassion for other human beings is difficult because people often distance themselves as too different from the people who are suffering, especially with geographical distance. Martha C. Nussbaum notes that this distancing is always a possibility in societies that are "divided by class, race, gender, and other identities, particularly when disgust and stigma are involved" (2013, p. 262). Hans Schattle similarly notes that developing a cross-cultural empathy can be almost impossible when faced with racism, sexism, and discrimination (2008, p. 50); however, he cites multiple examples of citizens who overcome their fears in working across difference to practice global citizenship. Citing the ancient Athenian tragic and comic dramas, Nussbaum explains that these plays "were occasions for deep emotion," and were an important part of civic education. She writes, "These emotions, however, were not considered antithetical to the idea of a democracy based upon deliberation and argument: indeed, just the opposite. They were considered important inputs for political discussion" (2013, p. 260). Both emotion and reason are interconnected ideas that can be used in productive or destructive ways in the context of rhetorical citizenship. Rhetorical scholars need to understand how emotion operates in citizenship so that we can critique destructive strategies and promote productive strategies, especially in analyzing and evaluating public discourse with our students.

Rhetorical educators should teach students the importance of debate and critical thinking as students begin to make their own value judgments about cultures, traditions, and various political issues, always considering the shared interests between students and strangers as well as the power and privilege that might be at work in a larger process of globalization. Peter N. Stearns writes that students need to master global-analytical skills, but that such skills must be practiced through debate and discussion when students are asked to begin making value judgments about global issues (2009, 16). In the classroom, I introduce the concept of global citizenship through using various contemporary news magazines, books, and documentary films that focus on controversial global issues, such as human trafficking. In class, I ask students to read a segment of a book or a brief article, or watch part of a film. Together, we discuss and debate how and why the author or director uses different rhetorical strategies to reach across identity markers, including nationality. Usually, students quickly realize that the rhetor's goal is civic empathy, or the capacity to feel what others feel within a civic context. As a class, we interrogate structures of power that shape communicative interactions and public discourse about the issue, including political and economic contexts. For the issue of human trafficking, we discuss economic incentives for traffickers, as well as the political barriers to prosecuting those responsible. To enable students to relate the issue to their own lives, we also try to connect the global issue to a local context. We also take time to discuss various emotional attachments, such as feelings of concern, and how engaging these texts might cultivate empathy inside and outside of the classroom, once students leave the university.

Grounding global citizenship in social belonging

People identify with one another through emotion, which helps us to develop a sense of social belonging to be able to come together with others who are different from ourselves. The view that global citizenship should be grounded in social belonging differs from the more common view that citizenship should be connected to a state or territory, often through law, in scholarship about global citizenship (see especially: Armstrong 2006, p. 356; Butler and Spivak 2007, pp 3-4; Ford 2001, p. 210; Kivisto and Faist 2007, pp. 128-29; Miller 2007, pp. 39, 45; Ng'weno 2007, p. 196; Weil 2001, p. 19). Haldun Gülalp explains this traditional view: "The modern nation-state is (ideally) a territorially circumscribed entity, exercising legitimate power within its boundaries. Citizenship in the modern state is (ideally) linked to territorial sovereignty, so that individual members of that community are accepted as equals" (2006, 1). Grounding global citizenship in social belonging makes the mission of civic rhetoric one of teaching students the importance of advancing global social relations and communicating with strangers. Using Rhoads and Szelényi's concept of the social dimension of citizenship, social belonging involves "shared experiences one has within various social collectivities" (2011, p. 17). I would add to this view in suggesting that the "social collectivity" expands outward to the rest of the world in conceptualizing global citizenship. This approach shapes how student-citizens engage issues in the world, especially as these issues become more complex and intertwined in the activities of many different nations.

Social belonging has been conceptualized through ideas such as the union, state, nation, and religion; however, these are not examples that advance social belonging as essential to global citizenship. Instead, I suggest stranger sociability (Hariman and Lucaites 2003, pp. 36, 58; Warner 2002, p. 75) and vulnerability (Butler 2004, pp. 22-24) are two specific modes of social belonging that ground global citizenship. Stranger sociability involves the necessity of being open to interacting with strangers. Vulnerability entails the understanding that, as human beings, we are never alone. Our identity and actions are shaped through others' perspectives of us. Identification seems to precede emotional attachments, because a person needs to first see similarity to then develop an emotional connection to someone. People can acknowledge division yet still identify with others, however, and this recognition of cultural difference while still being able to work together for a shared political goal seems to echo this understanding of how division and identification work together in human interaction. Current conceptions of state-based or territory-based global citizenship that rely on reason as the primary mode of being able to identify with others fail to recognize how people connect to one another emotionally to be able to relate to a larger social world.

Global citizenship should be based on social belonging, rather than on the state or territory, partly because the technological changes in the world have changed social relations and therefore call for a new view of citizenship (Agosin 2001, p. 10; Rhoads and Szelényi 2011, p. 7). Indeed, the idea of communal obligation is not new to an understanding of civic education (Arthos 2007, p. 190), and is an important characteristic of global citizenship as understood through a rhetorical lens. Rhoads and Szelényi outline one major organizing principle in the variety of terms and definitions associated with global citizenship as "the notion of greater or lesser degrees of ethical responsibility toward human rights and other individual and community rights, as well as moving beyond the nation-state ... in acting upon one's sense of responsibility" (2011, p. 23). Considering our own rights and responsibilities, and how these affect others, is important in explaining global citizenship as a practice to students. The civic rhetoric tradition should strive to include a global ethic as part of the curriculum to instruct students to become engaged citizens.

For students, global citizenship as a practice should become an orientation to engage global issues and to consider the consequences of their actions for their own and others' lives. Civic rhetoric can help students in "developing an awareness and mastery of globally relevant issues, skills, and phenomena and using such understandings in approaching and enacting citizen rights and responsibilities in a local, national, regional, or global context" (Rhoads and Szelényi 2011, p. 264). Global citizenship does not exclude local, regional, or national contexts, but instead builds upon these contexts in how people conceptualize social relations. This is similar to Nussbaum's theory of cosmopolitanism as a series of concentric circles of concern, spreading outward from the self toward all humanity (Nussbaum and Cohen 1996, p. 135).

As rhetorical educators, we have a responsibility to cultivate citizens who can engage the world as a result of their university education. Rhoads and Szelényi write: "Just as we have used our sharpest university minds to advance science and technology, we must do the same in terms of advancing global social relations" (2011, p. 8). In conceptualizing global citizenship through creating relationships with others around the world, social belonging becomes more important than the state or territory.

Extending civic rhetoric through global citizenship

If one of civic rhetoric's goals is to prepare students to engage others in the world through discussion and debate, then global citizenship is a useful addition to the civic rhetoric tradition in expanding students' awareness of public problems and their role in those issues. The goal of using global citizenship in rhetorical education is to help students see global citizenship as a useful concept and practice, while complicating their understandings of globalization and nationalism. By doing so, students should feel better prepared to contribute to public arguments surrounding global issues and hopefully consider their own actions accordingly.

Accounting for global citizenship in the civic rhetoric tradition is important as students increasingly face political issues and discussions that extend beyond national boundaries. Whether theorizing civic education through a civic republican or civic liberal tradition, this essay suggests that both political philosophies underemphasize the role of emotion in citizenship. Grounding global citizenship in social belonging values different emotional attachments that inform citizens' decision-making and engagement with often distant strangers. Global citizenship highlights the importance of social relations, which becomes an important model for rhetorical education.

References

Agosin, M. (2001). Introduction. In M. Agosin (Ed.), *Women, Gender, and Human Rights* (pp. 1-11). Piscataway, NJ: Rutgers University Press.

Armstrong, C. (2006). Global Civil Society and the Question of Global Citizenship. *Voluntas: International Journal of Voluntary & Nonprofit Organizations* 17, 348-356.

Arthos, J. (2007). A Hermeneutic Interpretation of Civic Humanism and Liberal Education. *Philosophy & Rhetoric* 40, 189-200.

Bhaba, H.K. (1994). *The Location of Culture.* London and New York: Routledge.

Bizzell, P. and S. Jarratt. (2004). Rhetorical Traditions, Pluralized Canons, Relevant History, and Other Disputed Terms: A Report from the History of Rhetoric Discussion Groups at the ARS Conference. *Rhetoric Society Quarterly* 34 (3), 19-25.

Boyte, H.C. (2003). Civic Education and the New American Patriotism Post-9/11. *Cambridge Journal of Education* 33 (1), 85-100.

Brooks, D. (2011). The New Humanism. *The New York Times*, March 8, A27.

Burke, K. (1969). *A Rhetoric of Motives.* Berkeley: University of California Press.

Butler, J. (2004). *Undoing Gender.* New York and London: Routledge.

Butler, J. and G. Chakravorty Spivak. (2007). *Who Sings the Nation-State? Language, Politics, Belonging.* London; New York: Seagull Books.

Carter, A. (2001). *The Political Theory of Global Citizenship, Routledge Innovations in Political Theory.* London; New York: Routledge.

Condit, C.M. (2013). Pathos in Criticism: Edwin Black's Communism-As-Cancer Metaphor. *Quarterly Journal of Speech* 99, 1-26.

Denman, W.N. (2004). Rhetoric, the 'Citizen-Orator,' and the Revitalization of Civic Discourse in American Life. In C. Glenn, M.M. Lyday and W.B. Sharer (Eds.), *Rhetorical Education in America* (pp. 3-17). Tuscaloosa: University of Alabama Press.

Dixon, T.. (2003). *From Passions to Emotions: The Creation of a Secular Psychological Category.* Cambridge: Cambridge University Press.

Fisher, P. (2002). *The Vehement Passions.* Princeton and Oxford: Princeton University Press.

Ford, R. (2001). City-States and Citizenship. In A. Aleinikoff and D. Klusmeyer (Eds.), *Citizenship Today: Global Perspectives and Practices* (pp. 209-236). Washington, D.C.: Carnegie Endowment for International Peace: Distributed by Brookings Institution Press.

Gehrke, P.J. (2009). *The Ethics and Politics of Speech: Communication and Rhetoric in the Twentieth Century.* 1st ed. Carbondale, IL: Southern Illinois University Press.

Glenn, C. (2004). Rhetorical Education in America (A Broad Stroke Introduction). In C. Glenn, M.M. Lyday and W.B. Sharer (Eds.), *Rhetorical Education in America* (pp. vii-xvi). Tuscaloosa: University of Alabama Press.

Gross, D.M. (2006). *The Secret History of Emotion: From Aristotle's Rhetoric to Modern Brain Science*. Chicago: University of Chicago Press.

Gülalp, H. (2006). *Citizenship and Ethnic Conflict: Challenging the Nation-State, Routledge Research in Comparative Politics*. London; New York: Routledge.

Hariman, R. and J.L. Lucaites. (2003). Public Identity and Collective Memory in U.S. Iconic Photography: The Image of "Accidental Napalm." *Critical Studies in Media Communication* 20, 35-66.

Hauser, G.A. (1999). *Vernacular Voices: The Rhetoric of Publics and Public Spheres, Studies in Rhetoric/Communication*. Columbia, S.C.: University of South Carolina Press.

Hauser, G.A. (2004). Teaching Rhetoric: Or Why Rhetoric Isn't Just Another Kind of Philosophy or Literary Criticism. *Rhetoric Society Quarterly* 34 (3), 39-53.

Jackson, B. (2007). Cultivating Paideweyan Pedagogy: Rhetoric Education in English and Communication Studies. *Rhetoric Society Quarterly* 37, 181-201.

Keck, M.E. and K. Sikkink. (1998). *Activists beyond Borders: Advocacy Networks in International Politics*. Ithaca, N.Y.: Cornell University Press.

Keith, W.M. (2007). *Democracy as Discussion: Civic Education and the American Forum Movement*. Lanham, MD: Lexington Books.

Keith, W. and P. Cossart. (2012). The Search for "Real" Democracy: Rhetorical Citizenship and Public Deliberation in France and the United States, 1870-1940. In C. Kock and LS. Villadsen (Eds.), *Rhetorical Citizenship and Public Deliberation* (pp. 46-60). University Park: Pennsylvania State University Press.

Kivisto, P. and T. Faist. (2007). *Citizenship: Discourse, Theory, and Transnational Prospects, Key Themes in Sociology*. Malden, MA: Blackwell Pub.

Lister, R. (2003). *Citizenship: Feminist Perspectives*. 2nd ed. New York: New York University Press.

Longaker, M.G. (2007). *Rhetoric and the Republic: Politics, Civic Discourse, and Education in Early America*. Edited by John Louis Lucaites, *Rhetoric, Culture, and Social Critique*. Tuscaloosa: University of Alabama Press.

Miller, T. (2007). *Cultural Citizenship: Cosmopolitanism, Consumerism, and Television in a Neoliberal Age*. Philadelphia: Temple University Press.

Ng'weno, B. (2007). *Turf Wars: Territory and Citizenship in the Contemporary State*. Stanford, Calif.: Stanford University Press.

Nussbaum, M.C. (2013). *Political Emotions: Why Love Matters for Justice*. Cambridge, MA and London: The Belknap Press of Harvard University Press.

Nussbaum, M.C. and J. Cohen. (1996). *For Love of Country: Debating the Limits of Patriotism*. Boston: Beacon Press.

Oldfield, A. (1990). *Citizenship and Community: Civic Republicanism and the Modern World*. London; New York: Routledge.

Olsen, E.J. (2006). *Civic Republicanism and the Properties of Democracy: A Case Study of Post-Socialist Political Theory*. Lanham: Lexington Books.

Peterson, A. (2009). Civic Republicanism and Contestatory Deliberation: Framing Pupil Discourse within Citizenship Education. *British Journal of Educational Studies* 57, 55-69.

Peterson, A. (2011). *Civic Republicanism and Civic Education: The Education of Citizens*. New York: Palgrave Macmillan.

Rhoads, R.A. and K. Szelényi. (2011). *Global Citizenship and the University*. Stanford, CA: Stanford University Press.

Schattle, H. (2008). *The Practices of Global Citizenship*. Lanham, MD: Rowman & Littlefield Publishers, Inc.

Stearns, P.N. (2009). *Educating Global Citizens in Colleges and Universities*. New York; London: Routledge.

Tonn, M.B., V.A. Endress and J.N. Diamond. (1993). Hunting and Heritage on Trial in Maine: A Dramatistic Debate over Tragedy, Tradition, and Territory. *Quarterly Journal of Speech* 79, 165-181.

Vandenberg, A. (Ed.) (2000). *Citizenship and Democracy in a Global Era*, edited by. New York: St. Martin's Press.

Voet, R. (1998). *Feminism and Citizenship*. London, Thousand Oaks, New Delhi: Sage Publications.

Walzer, A.E. (2007). Blair's Ideal Orator: Civic Rhetoric and Christian Politeness in Lectures 25-34. *Rhetorica* 25, 269-295.

Warner, M. (2002). *Publics and Counterpublics*. New York: Zone Books.

Weil, P. (2001). Access to Citizenship: A Comparison of Twenty-Five Nationality Laws. In T.A. Aleinikoff and D. Klusmeyer (Eds.), *Citizenship Today: Global Perspectives and Practices* (pp. 17-35). Washington, D.C.: Carnegie Endowment for International Peace: Distributed by Brookings Institution Press.

Rhetorical Citizenship beyond the Frontiers of Capitalism: *Marx Reloaded* and the Dueling Myths of the Commodity and the Common

CATHERINE CHAPUT

> The problem of the left hasn't been our adherence to a Marxist critique of capitalism. It's that we have lost sight of the communist horizon.
> *Jodi Dean, 2012*

Rhetoric and capitalism share strikingly similar myths of origin. Rhetoric, we are told, emerged in Greek city-states where citizens who deliberated in the *polis* needed to be skilled orators.[1] The fate of rhetoric subsequently waxed and waned with the fate of democracy – thriving in the classical Greek age, suffocating during the Roman Empire, and reappearing, along with so many other things, during the Renaissance. Theorists from Karl Marx (1990) to Giovanni Arrighi (1994) note that capitalism's nascent form begins in the same Italian city-states that ushered in rhetoric's rebirth. Capitalism does not, of course, reach its full development until it becomes culturally and discursively tethered, like rhetoric, to the democratic myth. Important to this process, according to historian Peter Burke (1990), is the movement of Renaissance humanism from Italy, through northern Europe, into the Netherlands, and culminating in the British Isles, where capitalism, rhetoric, and democracy acquire their particularly modern appearance. Thus, by the early modern period, the democratic political system so connected to rhetoric also

[1] Historians of classical rhetoric, including such renowned scholars as George Kennedy (1994), James Murphy (2013), as well as David Timmerman and Edward Schiappa (2010), work from the commonplace that rhetorical training emerges with and is unique to democratic states. This myth is challenged by Jacques Rancière (2004), who argues that people without property who are treated as part of the *polis* have what amounts to a fictitious freedom.

attached itself to capitalism. English and Scottish enlightenment thinkers such as John Locke, David Hume, and Adam Smith propagated a theory of liberty simultaneously embedded in the democratic state and the market economy. Noting this crucial linkage, Deirdre McCloskey (2006; 2010) recently embarked on what is surely her magnum opus – a four-volume rhetorical history of capitalism that assesses its triumph through a revaluation of bourgeois identity. Yet this chapter suggests that those domains that McCloskey skillfully ties together, rhetoric and economics, were joined already by the history of myth-making. Indeed, the story of freedom, liberty and citizenship that connects deliberative political participation to market economies is the origin myth shared by both rhetoric and capitalism.

Myth, as Roland Barthes (1972) long ago contended, operates through a semantic doubling in order to further ruling class ideology. As theorized by Barthes, a myth functions through a signification that works twice. For example, capitalism and rhetoric do not simply refer to a specific economic configuration and a form of persuasion, but also reference democracy and its attendant virtues. This additional signification functions on behalf of class interests, transforming capitalism and its representatives from economic actors into defenders of freedom. Kenneth Burke (1961) identified the same kind of function in words he called "god-terms" (p. 2). He suggests that these highly charged words contain multiple referents within the single term; they house, that is, a diversity of meanings. No doubt some concepts fall beyond the reach of god-terms, but the vast majority can be subsumed within them. Burke (1966) later elaborates on the relationship between language and myth by discussing what he calls a "terministic screen" or a framework for reflecting one selection of reality and deflecting other possible selections. According to this theory, the terms we use to describe reality "necessarily constitute a corresponding kind of screen; and any such screen necessarily directs the attention to one field rather than another" (p. 50). Myths are, for Burke, different frames for understanding the same reality. Each frame highlights some things and downplays others. Rather than understanding this semantic work as a particular subset of language practices, Burke comes to appreciate myth as the means by which one meaning, as opposed to another, bubbles to the surface and animates our way of life. So conceived, myth necessitates the notion that language constitutes the world in which we live by virtue of its framing metaphor.

The persuasive function of metaphors, especially within an historical narrative, is not missed by early economists, most of whom received rhetorical training as part of their formal education. Adam Smith, for instance, explains metaphors as rhetorically crafted language. Before the publication of his famous *Wealth of Nations* he gave public lectures on rhetoric in which he discussed such things as the use of metaphor. His *Lectures on Rhetoric and Belles Lettres* (2001) define a metaphor as an allusion between one thing and another. But such an allusion works on its audience, he says, only if "it gives the due strength of expression to the object described and at the same time does this in a more striking and interesting manner" (p. 29). Metaphors bring an object or idea to life by giving it a particularly remarkable and, consequently, enduring character. The extraordinary quality shared by capitalism and rhetoric is the supposedly unfailing democratic nature of each. As a founding metaphor or terministic screen, democracy makes capitalism and rhetoric untouchable for all those committed to such things as freedom and equality. In other words, to espouse communism or to suggest the limits of rhetoric is, because of their mutual democratic frame, to welcome tyranny and propaganda. This conclusion is mythical in the sense that it functions through rhetorically delimited metaphors and not in the sense of being false or unreal. Thus, like all great metaphors, the myth connecting rhetoric, capitalism, and democracy requires constant propagation.

To take a relatively recent example, the fall of state communism at the end of the twentieth century offered a rhetorical opportunity to reinforce this mythical triple helix of freedom. Among the most memorable claims during this period of post-cold war elation was Francis Fukuyama's "end of history" thesis. In contrast to a Marxist teleology forecasting communism as the final stage of human social organization wherein class struggle is erased, Fukuyama (1989) cites capitalism, or liberal democracy, as the culmination of ideological struggle. During the 1990s this triumphalist rhetoric burgeoned into a "Washington Consensus" purportedly capable of managing all economic and political challenges across the globe. The mismatch between what this discourse on liberal democracy claimed and the environmental, social, and individual destruction for many of the world's citizens, however, did not escape notice among rhetoricians of globalization. Wendy Hesford's (2011) recent *Spectacular Rhetorics* addresses the human rights violations attendant in this stage of history, and Kendall Phillips and G. Mitchell Reyes's (2011) edited volume *Global Memoryscapes* challenges a unified global narrative with a collection of complex, networked, and diversified memories from around the globe. Even more recently, Rebecca Dingo and J. Scott Blake's

(2012) collection *The Megarhetorics of Global Development* examines and critiques the specific rhetorical strategies used by governments and corporations to facilitate capitalist agendas. Further adding to this body of work, Jennifer Wingard's (2012) *Branded Bodies, Rhetoric, and the Neoliberal Nation-State* explores how economic neoliberalism has constricted the rhetoric of political media, limiting the available range of information within the narrow framework of economic triumphalism. These important rhetorical critiques participate in the ongoing struggle to define our dominant social myth – do we articulate the world through the framework of capitalist individualism or do we frame it through the lens of a more social-oriented collectivism? Just as the myth of a triumphant knot among rhetoric, capitalism, and democracy seems to be permanently secured, it begins to loosen, unravel, and require diligent tightening.

A claim to the natural intersections among these spheres of social practice remains especially tenuous in our post-2008 world of global economic disarray. The counterclaim that communism may be more aligned with democratic citizenship than capitalism is by no means new, and yet it has garnered renewed strength of late. In just the last few years Verso has published nearly a dozen titles in its new Pocket Communism series that invites authors to pose contemporary versions of what Alain Badiou (2010) calls the "communist hypothesis" or the exploration of ethical social organizations (98).[2] Even though this series engages the possibility of communism, other efforts reject the feasibility of a working communist state. For instance, the University of Chicago, the intellectual home of neoliberal economic thought, runs a series, through its Seagull Books, titled *What Was Communism?* Framed in the past tense, the series basically chronicles the failures of communism with titles that focus on particular states and work from the assumption that communism, a well-intended idea, cannot hold up its promise of equality and freedom. Still, the series editor, Tariq Ali (2009), comes to much the same conclusion as does Slavoj Žižek (2009) in his *First as Tragedy, Then as Farce*: the future of democracy exists as some blend of free marketism and socialism. This argument, although logically defensible, fails

[2] Further illustrative of this communist revival is a recent conference "On the Idea of Communism" held by The University of London's Birkbeck Institute for the Humanities. The conference organizers anticipated fewer than 200 participants but had to accommodate an audience of 1200 people.

to garner much political strength because it asks us to envision the future through two different frameworks, a task that runs contrary to the polarized world we occupy.

The production of knowledge about political economic possibilities tends to represent and therefore reproduce a bifurcated world view. The Chicago book series leans toward capitalism and balances the Verso series which leans toward communism. Recent film documentaries exhibit a similarly political dichotomization on the question of capitalism's virtues. Offering something like an updated version of Milton Friedman's hugely successful *Free to Choose,* PBS's 2002 production of *Commanding Heights: The Battle for the World Economy* claims to provide the public with a better understanding of globalization, world trade, and economic development. The three part series, based on a book of the same name by Daniel Yergin and Joseph Stanislaw, declares global capitalism the winner in the battle between free and controlled markets. In contrast, Michael Moore's *Capitalism: A Love Story* (2009), while it tends to eulogize the good old days of monopoly capitalism when U.S. factories mass produced domestic goods and workers were paid an increasingly livable wage, critiques the more ruthless stage of global capitalism. Despite their apparent opposition, these films squabble over what amounts to different versions of market economies. Adhering to the rhetorical mythology that connects democracy with capitalism, they both assume that democracy cannot be enacted within communism.

Taking an entirely different perspective, Jason Barker's *Marx Reloaded* poses this opposition between capitalism and communism in terms made famous by the blockbuster film *The Matrix.* The film suggests that a choice exists between a blue pill that will induce blissful ignorance and a red pill that will reveal the painful truth of reality. These pills function as metaphors for the elaborate configuration of things, ideas, and processes that fall under the umbrella of democracy. What becomes clear from the documentary, especially the segments on production and consumption, is that ideological adherence to private property in the form of commodities delivers the blissful inoculation of the blue pill while an ideological investment in something called the common yields the reality of the red pill, though suspiciously without its delivery pains. I explore this film more closely to suggest that the commodity and the common are decisive metaphors – ones upon which entire fantasy structures emerge – for the production of two different versions of democratic citizenship. Before doing so, however, I provide a brief overview of the commodity and the common as competing metaphors through which to understand not only economics, but also social, political, and cultural relations.

Marx used the commodity to introduce his critique of capital because he believed that a single item produced through the division of wage labor represents, or bears the traces of, the entire economic system of capitalism. As he famously asserted in the much debated first chapter of *Capital*, the key to our understanding "begins with the analysis of the commodity" (p. 126). In his conception, a commodity produced by wage labor contains the value of the products transformed into the new product, the value of the labor paid to the worker in wages, and the value of the labor not paid to the worker or what he calls surplus value. This surplus value is simultaneously the mark of exploited labor and the source of profit. In Burkean terms, the metaphorical value of the commodity stems from framing it as the source of individual wealth and deflecting the collective labor also contained in it. Thus, if we take account of the rhetorical nature of the community, we can see additionally that the entire belief system of capitalism begins with an identification of property with owners and not with producers. To identify an item with the producers requires a notion of the common.

I believe such reidentification is the key to realigning democracy within the communist horizon. This horizon – distanced in space and time and yet setting the agenda for a path toward it – represents, as Jodi Dean (2012) explains it, faith "that collective determination of collective conditions is possible" (16). That is to say, a mythology or terministic screen of the common will reorganize language around an understanding that life is collectively produced and can be collectively regulated.

The commons, in a traditional sense, denotes the commonly held means of production in the precapitalist era. The destruction of the commons (through such state mechanisms as the British Enclosure Acts) separated individuals from the means of providing for themselves and subsequently forced them into wage labor. This version of the commons as the precondition for capitalism is undermined by Michael Perelman, who argues that primitive accumulation – the process of privatizing such commons – plays an ongoing role in capitalism.[3] Capitalism must intervene into self-

[3] The notion that "primitive accumulation" functions on an ongoing basis is evidenced by the global land grab in which rich countries buy up and privatize resources – both property and indigenous knowledge – in the global south. See, for instance, "Outsourcing's Third Wave."

sufficiency of all sorts (homespun health remedies, sustainable farming, or shared cultural texts, for instance) so that it can turn communal knowledge and products into commodities. To expand the capitalist marketplace requires the continuous process of commodifying previously non-commodified items, which requires government intervention to mandate and regulate this endless social restructuring. Just as surely as this is an economic and political process it is also a rhetorical process: people must believe in the commodity and its world in order to assent to its ruling order.

Because this continuous appropriation of common resources is not limited to land, air, and water but includes socially produced products, knowledges, and practices, theorists have turned to the common, in the singular, to signify both our natural resources as well as our invented resources. Michael Hardt and Antonio Negri, for instance, contend that the "common is not only the earth we share but also the languages we create, the social practices we establish, the modes of sociality that define our relationships, and so forth" (2009, p. 350). The common produces things, but it also produces social relations, lifestyles, and agentive subjects, all of which, according to Hardt and Negri, create value. Commodities put this collectively produced value in the hands of individuals and thus delimit its use value. To combat this problem, David Harvey argues that the "collective laboring that is now productive of value must ground collective, not individual, property rights" (p. 105). Recall that in Marx's configuration, collective labor, in its exploited form, produces the value, invisible and yet present, within the commodity that creates profit for the capitalist.[4] Harvey extends this theory by suggesting that we leverage the common value within the commodity to fuel a democratic transformation beyond the frontiers of capitalism – one in which wealth is socially accessible rather than privatized. A mythology of the common, contrary to a mythology of the commodity, emphasizes the collective labor constituting products. These two metaphors for understanding the division of contemporary labor practices, both outlined in *Marx Reloaded,* provide different discursive platforms on which to build a democratic myth pegged either to a capitalist or to a communist horizon.

Written and directed by Jason Barker, *Marx Reloaded* explores the relevance of Marxist theory to the contemporary political economy. It includes

[4] Marx claims that commodities are merely "the visible incarnation, the social chrysalis state, of all human labour" (p. 159).

interviews by scholars at the forefront of reviving and revising Marxism as well as leading economists and financial advisors who dismiss such ideas. All of this is structured through a four-part animation sequence which follows Marx through the matrix of his own thinking, beginning with the commodity and ending with the common. Using the global financial crisis of 2008 as the historical event from which to launch its revaluation, the film asks, "Have we been living in a dream? Is the capitalist world about to be unmasked as an ideological illusion and replaced by the communist system we thought was gone for good?" Although this framing represents capitalism as an imagined world opposed to the possibility of a communist reality, the prevailing metaphors – the commodity and the common – indicate that both pills offer a mythology and are thus two rhetorical sides of the same proverbial coin. Consequently, the film determines the political task as less oriented toward the overthrow of capitalism and more directed toward what Jason Read (2010) calls "the actualisation or manifestation of the common" (p. 121). Before we can create this new democratic imagination, we first must understand the common in relationship to the commodity.

According to the documentary, the commodity is the single most important metaphor for the entire mythology of capitalism. The narrator explains, in a voice parodying Marx, that "in order to grasp capitalism's true power and hold over us, we must delve into the strange and mystical world of the commodity." This section of the film is signaled by an animated shot of an industrial street with smoke floating up from a manhole cover. The figure of Karl Marx falls through the manhole and, just like Alice tumbling down the rabbit hole, he descends into a fantasy world; but, unlike Alice, the creatures populating this world are commodities. The documentary continues with the narrator quoting Marx who says that a commodity changes an everyday thing "into something transcendent."[5] This transcendent quality is value – the social labor that goes into the commodity, allowing it to be exchanged at a particular price and to be converted into profit. For Marx, value is an abstraction that standardizes the cycle of exchange and not a quality inherent in the material body of the commodity. Rather than being intrinsic to the commodity, value is intrinsic to the human labor that goes into a commodity.

[5] Marx uses the example of wood crafted into a table and sold as a commodity to explain this transcendence. As a commodity, the once simply wooden table comes to life and takes on a new existence. (See *Capital*, p. 163.)

It is precisely this transcendent power of working human beings that accounts for Marx's conception of commodity fetishism. As he (1964) explains in the *Economic and Philosophical Manuscripts of 1844*, commodities contain the innate quality of our very species. The value-adding power of life emerges in labor wherein "all the natural, spiritual, and social variety of individual activity is manifest" (p. 66). Workers transfer life value into commodities, and this accounts for why we invest special powers in these things. In the documentary, media theorist Norbert Bolz summarizes this process by stating that, in addition to fulfilling our needs, commodities "convey a spiritual surplus value and this value is the real reason for the purchase." Peter Sloterdijk puts it even more boldly, arguing that "the immortal part of Marx's doctrine" is that he "discovered the fact that things live." Commodities acquire this remarkable attribute from socialized human labor. The exploitation of wage labor means that social agency becomes externalized within commodities and thus alienated from large segments of the population. Commodity fetishism, although it emphasizes a negative critique of capitalism, contains the seeds of a more positive theory of collective agency promoted as the common.

To explore the common the documentary interjects yet another animated scene. Here the camera pans down a hallway, zeroes in on a door, and then moves through the keyhole of that door. Inside is a room with a bewildered Karl Marx musing over a doll of Slavoj Žižek clashing cymbals together as if he was a wind-up toy. In this segment Žižek explains in an interview how commodity fetishism is an illusion, but it is, he claims, an "illusion that is part of reality itself." From this perspective, we can unmask the illusion of capitalism and its commodity fetish, but we nevertheless live according to its myths. At heart, this argument, one central to all Žižek's work, maintains that a framing myth or organizing fantasy cannot be separated from pragmatic action. Consequently, if we debunk the myth of capitalism, we must either live as though we have not done so or we must replace the commodity with another equally strong fantasy. For this documentary and many contemporary theorists, the common provides the structure for such an alternative.

The common, which designates the collective and cooperative labor of production rather than its exploitation, offers a rhetorical spin on global economic interconnectivity. Besides stressing the shared nature of our natural resources, it highlights the socialization of labor. According to critical theorist Jodi Dean, the common "designates and takes the place of human labor power (Marx's source of value), now rereconceived in the broadest possible terms of the potential of creativity, thought, knowledge and communication" (pp. 134-135). The power of the common stems from the same power of capital – value production. The difference is that the common highlights the collective labor that goes into products while the commodity emphasizes individual profit. Through this shift in perspective, a rhetorically constructed mythology of the common enables and authorizes us to argue with impunity that the capitalist class, the now infamous one percent, "are not free to do as they will but are governed, controlled, and limited by the rest of us" (Dean 71). Because the common provides a conception of citizenship that nudges us toward a different democratic terrain without embracing the legacy of state communism, the film challenges us to create social structures based on the common rather than the commodity. Fittingly, its final image is of a crane removing the bust of Karl Marx from its unspecified location, suggesting that the answer to the conundrums of democracy can be found in what Antonio Negri (1989) calls "Marx beyond Marx" – the creative use of Marxist theory to bypass the stale political manifestations of Marxism.

As I have discussed through this reading of *Marx Reloaded,* the myth that rhetorically links democracy and capitalism begins with the commodity as a metaphor for the self-contained individual whose talents are crafted in relationship to private property. Such a metaphorical frame ignores not only the necessity (and often exploitation) of other individuals; it also turns a blind eye to the destruction of our natural environment. To engage the possibility of citizenship beyond the horizons of capitalism requires replacing this metaphor with the metaphor of the common, which calls attention to collaborations among people as well as to the need to care for our shared worlds, both those that are natural and those that are built. No doubt, McCloskey is correct to attribute part of capitalism's success to a rhetorical revaluation of self-interest, individual dignity, and other bourgeois values, and yet it is wrong to think that this decision was made for us several hundred years ago and that we have no traction on how that choice plays out for us today.[6] Our collective agency is obviously circumscribed by a nexus of ideas, institutions, habits, and traditions, but it is nonetheless open to change. The

[6] See also Albert Hirschmann's classic *The Passions and the Interests* (1997) for an earlier explanation of how self-interest shifted from a short-coming to a virtue.

goal for citizenship, from this view, begins by redefining itself through the common in order to engender a different democratic politics. I end with a brief summary of how a shift in our framing metaphors from the commodity to the common might adjust our other social relations.

TABLE 1 OPPOSING MYTHS OF CAPITALISM

Commodity	Common
Value in individual consumption	Value in collective production
Individual identification	Community identification
Economic and juridical relations	Cultural and deliberative relations
Citizenship as universal suffrage	Citizenship as an engaged publics

The above table charts the two foundational myths at hand within a Marxist critique of capital. The first myth is one that Marx opposes. Referring to the commodity as a mere representation or form of appearance, Marx understands its myth as one that obscures the source of profit in capitalism, which he (and liberal political economic theorists before him) identifies as labor. According to this myth, individuals are forced to seek value in consumption. As he says with characteristic sarcasm, "what I *am* and *am capable* of is by no means determined by my individuality. I *am* ugly, but can buy for myself the most *beautiful* of women" (1964, p. 167). The commodity myth and its object fetishism stress individualism and individual identification. Citizens, in this conception, find their relationship through the economy and the political regulation of private property. This myth aligns liberal economics with liberal democracy as each takes the individual to be a rational member of society whose freedom is exercised by voting at the ballot box or in the marketplace. In his critique of capitalism, Marx implicitly presents another myth – one that I am calling the common. His assessment of classical political economy depends on a notion of the common that values collective labor rather than individual consumption; community rather than individual identification; cultural and deliberative relations rather than economic and juridical ones; and a sense of citizenship based on shared resources (from history and knowledge to the environment to the surplus wealth) rather than citizenship based on individual rights. The common, that is, offers a different framing myth, one with the capacity to reorient democracy toward deeper and more engaged practices.

Rhetorical citizenship, under the myth of the common, might emerge as more pervasive and more active publics. A broad range of social movement and counterpublic theorists have been exploring this form of rhetorical citizenship since at least the 1960s.[7] Among their founding positions, however, is that this form of rhetorical citizenship is oppositional to the dominant structures. Indeed this is explicit in the notion of counterpublics. What I am suggesting is that the myth of the commodity helps maintain a structural relationship to both the civic and civil sphere such that the kind of active citizenship advocated by rhetorical theory becomes relegated to the margins of society and takes on the status of opposition. A shift in this framing myth, it seems to me, might reorient citizenship from a passive, rights-based activity to an active, public-formation activity, taking what is on the periphery and making it central to our very notions of citizenship. Indeed, the work of framing society through the common is itself an act of such citizenship: reimagining public space that is more environmentally sustainable and has people as opposed to profits at its core; working toward accessible public health care for all citizens; revising citizenship education by teaching deliberation rather than a prescribed list of historical facts; and advocating for an understanding of labor as an unavoidably collective activity in which all its participants receive its benefits – these are simultaneously rhetorical projects and ones in which a future common form of citizenship emerges.

[7] For an example of counterpublic investigations, see Robert Asen and Daniel Brouwer's collection *Counterpublics and the State* (2001); an equally strong articulation of contemporary social movement theory can be found in Christina Foust's *Transgression as a Mode of Resistance* (2010).

References

Ali, T. (2009). *The Idea of Communism.* New York: Seagull Books.

Arrighi, G. (1994). The Rise of Capital. In *The Long Twentieth Century: Money, Power and the Origins of Our Times* (pp. 85-158). London: Verso.

Asen, R. and D. Brouwer. (2001). *Counterpublics and the State.* Albany: SUNY Press.

Badiou, A. (2010). *The Meaning of Sarkozy.* Trans. David Fernbach. London: verso.

Barker, J. (2010) (Dir.) *Marx Reloaded.* Medea Film.

Barthes, R. (1972). *Mythologies.* New York: Farrar, Straus and Giroux.

Burke, K. (1961). *The Rhetoric of Religion.* Berkeley: U of California Press.

Burke, K. (1966). *Language as Symbolic Action.* Berkeley: U of California Press.

Burke, P. (1990). *The Impact of Humanism on Western Thought.* New York: Longman.

Dean, J. (2012). *The Communist Horizon.* London: Verso.

Dingo, R. and J.S. Blake. (212). *The Megarhetorics of Global Development.* Pittsburgh: University of Pittsburgh Press.

Foust, C. (2010). *Transgression as a Mode of Resistance: Rethinking Social Movement in an Era of Corporate Globalization.* Lanham, MD: Lexington Books.

Fukuyma, F. The End of History? (1989) *The National Interest* 16, 3-18.

Hardt, M. and A. Negri. (2009). *Commonwealth.* Cambridge, MA: Harvard University Press.

Harvey, D. (2011). "The Future of the Commons." *Radical History Review* 109 (Winter 2011): 101-107.

Hesford, W. (2011). *Spectacular Rhetorics: Human Rights Visions, Recognitions, Feminisms.* Durham: Duke University Press.

Hirschmann, A.O. (1997). *The Passions and the Interests.* Princeton: Princeton University Press.

Kennedy, G. (1994). *A New History of Classical Rhetoric.* Princeton: Princeton University Press.

Marx, K. (1964). *Economic and Philosophical Manuscripts of 1844.* Trans. Martin Milligan. New York: International Publishers.

Marx, K. (1990). *Capital: Volume One.* Trans. Ben Fowkes. New York: Penguin.

McCloskey, D. (2006). *The Bourgeois Virtues: Ethics for an Age of Commerce.* Chicago: University of Chicago Press.

McCloskey, D. (2010). *Bourgeois Dignity: Why Economics Can't Explain the Modern World.* Chicago: University of Chicago Press.

Moore, M. (2009) (Dir.) *Capitalism: A Love Story.*

Murphy, J. et al. (2013). *A Synoptic History of Classical Rhetoric.* London: Routledge.

Negri, A. (1989). *Marx beyond Marx: Lessons on the Grundrisse.* Trans. Michael Ryan. New York: Autonomedia Press.

Outsourcing's Third Wave. (2009). *The Economist* 21 May.

Perelman, M. (2000). *The Invention of Capitalism: Classical Political Economy and the Secret of Primitive Accumulation.* Durham, NC: Duke University Press.

Phillips, K. and G.M. Reyes. (2011). *Global Memoryscapes: Contesting Remembrance in a Transnational Age.* Tuscaloosa: University of Alabama Press.

Rancière, J. (2004). *Disagreement.* Trans. Julie Rose. Minneapolis: University of Minnesota Press.

Read, J. (2010). The Prodution of Subjectivity: From Transindividuality to the Commons. *New Formations: A Journal of Culture/Theory/Politics* 70, 113-131.

Smith, A. (2001). *Lectures on Rhetoric and Belles Lettres.* Oxford: Oxford University Press.

Timmerman, D.T. and E. Schiappa. (2010). *Classical Greek Rhetorical Theory and the Disciplining of Discourse.* Cambridge: Cambridge University Press.

Wingard, J. (2012). *Branded Bodies, Rhetoric, and the Neoliberal Nation-State.* Lanham, MD: Lexington Books.

Yergin, D. and J. Stanislaw. (2002) (Dir.). *Commanding Heights: The Battle for the World Economy.* PBS.

Žižek, S. (2009). *First as Tragedy, Then as Farce.* London: Verso.

A Game with Words: Rhetorical Citizenship and Game Theory

TOM DENEIRE, DAVID EELBODE & JEROEN LAUWERS

PART I: Rhetoric and Game Theory

Introduction

The idea of rhetoric as a contest or a game goes back to the very cradle of rhetorical theory in ancient Greece. Famous rhetoricians like Gorgias performed in a context that can aptly be characterized as a game, participating in debates or displaying their proficiency and giving impromptu replies (cf. Slethaug 1995, pp. 64-65). Moreover, the parallel between persuasive speaking and a game seems to operate as a conceptual metaphor in our intuitive understanding of rhetorical behavior, like in political discourse. Think for instance of Julius Caesar's (in)famous *Alea iacta est* ("The die has been cast"). The first part of this paper takes its point of departure in this omnipresence of game metaphors in rhetorical contexts and will explore the theoretical question whether we can use the model of mathematically formalized game theory for rhetorical criticism.

This conception of rhetoric will in turn allow us to demonstrate game theory's remarkable critical potential to address the systemic structures in which rhetorical citizenship is carried out. In an era that is driven by individualistic concerns with rhetorical effectiveness, our game-theoretical reflections offer a vantage point to question the so-called "natural" character of the rhetorical situations in present-day politics as stemming from a rational response to the arbitrary rules of the political game. Specifically, we will analyze current electoral dynamics as a rational result of the particular way in which we cast our political votes, and we will show how an alternative voting system can more effectively reward constructive political discourses.

State of the art

Game theory has often been integrated in non-exact fields like psychology or social studies. In sociolinguistics, for instance, it is used to explore interpersonal dynamics like politeness, vagueness and deniability (Pinker 2008, pp. 373-425). In political studies, a whole subfield of political game theory has been developed, which researches specific political games such as jury voting, veto threats, etc., alongside more general social dynamics like collective choice or negotiating (McCarty and Meirowitz 2007). Game theory has also found its way into literary studies, where it is used to illuminate the rational choices made by characters in literary narrative.[1] Yet for all this reflection on game theory's broad potential, the secondary literature does not appear to have considered the specific question of game theory and rhetorical criticism. Three contributions seem to broach the topic, without however really going into it.

Before discussing a particular example of conflict rhetoric from the Korean War, Bennett explains "basic game theory concepts and its potential relationship with rhetorical criticism" (Bennett 1971, p. 34). However, his parallel remains rather limited, as Bennett focuses on the link between speaker/player and speech/move. In this way, his paper uses game theory to interpret the *results* of rhetorical behavior rather than the dynamics of rhetorical behavior itself.

Herman (1998) describes how the interactive strategies of communal behavior observable in classical Athens are the same as those simulated by a computerized model of the Iterated Prisoner's Dilemma. Still, Herman's contribution amounts to an analysis of socio-political interaction, not public speaking.

Finally, Zamora Bonilla (2006) interestingly develops a game-theoretical model to analyze how scientists choose different claims as interpretations of the results of their research in a rhetorical context. However, Zamora Bonilla focuses exclusively on the rhetoric of science without really considering rhetorical behavior in general and does not describe the basic parallels between the mathematical game model and rhetorical theory.

It thus becomes clear that the fundamental question of the possibilities of game theory as a hermeneutic model to interpret rhetorical discourse is as yet unresolved.

[1] See Brams (2011). Cf. de Ley (1988), who engages with Brams' earlier ideas of game theory and literature, and Slethaug (1995), which deals with the general critical notion of "game" and "play," and therefore far exceeds game theory *stricto sensu*.

A basic exploration

In mathematical game theory, a "game" is usually defined as "a description of strategic interaction that includes the constraints on the actions that the players *can* take and the players' interests, but does not specify the actions that the players *do* take. A *solution* is a systematic description of the outcomes that may emerge in a family of games. Game theory suggests reasonable solutions for classes of games and examines their properties" (Osborne and Rubinstein 1994, p. 2). In other words, games consist of players who make choices that lead to actions with consequences or outcomes, bound by rules or constraints, and motivated by interests or preferences. Comparing that to a basic definition of rhetoric, viz. Bitzer's analysis of the rhetorical situation (Bitzer 1968) – in short "the necessary condition of rhetorical discourse," which "needs and invites discourse capable of participating with situation [sic] and thereby altering its reality" – we can already see clear parallels between rhetoric and game theory.

Rhetorical discourse can be interpreted as a game in which speakers are players and the rhetorical situation provides the constraints on the actions the players can take. These actions lead to consequences with certain pay-offs, or, rhetorically speaking, to discourse capable of participating with the situation or altering reality.

Utilitas *and rational decision-making*

It is worth exploring just how deep the conceptual similarity goes between rhetorical discourse and games. When rhetoric is viewed from the perspective of the speaker, rhetorical theory recognizes the crucial importance of *utilitas*, i.e., the fact that all rhetorical actors are partisan, serving their own particular interests, based on their estimation of the rhetorical situation at hand (see Lausberg 1990, §1060).[2] Similarly, game theory operates from the basic premise that it studies the behavior of a *rational* decision-maker – "'rational' in the sense that he is aware of his alternatives, forms expectations about any unknowns, has clear preferences, and chooses his action deliber-

[2] We are aware that our conception of rhetoric here only takes the speaker's rational perspective into account, and thus focuses on the speaker's estimation of his audience rather than on the actual interaction between the speaker and the audience. In the conclusion to this paper, we will further reflect on the limits and consequences of this approach.

ately after some process of optimization" (Osborne and Rubinstein 1994, p. 4). Accordingly, defining a player's rational choice is the first step of any game-theoretical analysis.

In short, we can say that rational choice and optimization can be applied to rhetorical *utilitas* in three different ways:

(1) The speaker is certain of the consequences of his actions and accordingly takes the action that offers the maximal consequence.

(2) The speaker is uncertain of the consequences of his actions, but does know the range of possible consequences and their probability vis-à-vis his actions, and accordingly takes the action that maximizes an expected result.

(3) The speaker is uncertain of the consequences of his actions and does not know the range of possible consequences nor their probability vis-à-vis his actions. Still, he takes the action that he assumes will maximize an expected result, based on a subjective idea of the possible consequences of his actions and their probability.

In other words, rhetorical optimization happens in one of the following three ways:

(1) The experienced rhetor knows that only in very simple cases can he be certain of the consequences of his rhetorical choice. An example of this is the choice to argue against nuclear energy before an audience of *Greenpeace* members.

(2) More often, however, the models of uncertainty apply to the rhetorical situation (even in situations that might at first seem quite straightforward). Indeed, in many cases the rhetor will be conscious of his uncertainty of the outcome of his rhetorical choices. However, he will often have information about a number of possible outcomes and their respective probability. An example of this is the rhetorical choice to hold a fairly left-wing speech before an audience of non-specified students, among whom the rhetor expects there to be more left-wing than right-wing supporters.

(3) Finally, there is the case in which the rhetor's information on the possible outcomes of his actions and their probability is imperfect. A concrete manifestation of this is the situation where a rhetor is unaware of the fact he is speaking to a different audience than the one expected.

Rhetoric as a strategic game

In previous literature, rhetoric tends to be compared to games of the so-called 'strategic'" type (players choose their strategies simultaneously and independently). The classical example of a strategic game is the *Prisoner's dilemma*, where the police offer two arrested criminals the same deal: if one man betrays his partner, and the other remains silent, the betrayer goes free and the one that remains silent receives the full one-year sentence. If both remain silent, both are sentenced to only one month in jail for a minor charge. If they betray each other, they both receive a three-month sentence.

In this game, both players have the same options, i.e., either *betray* or *remain silent* (B; RS). This game is then often visualized in terms of a matrix (Table 1):

TABLE 1 THE PRISONERS' DILEMMA

	B	RS
B	3/3	0/12
RS	12/0	1/1

As appears from the Table 1, a player's best decision is to betray when the other does not betray, since he will be free instead of spending a month in jail. Moreover, when the other betrays the player's best decision is *also* to betray, since he will be sentenced to three instead of twelve months. Each player thus gets a higher pay-off when betraying the other, regardless of the latter's decision. As this game is symmetrical, we may conclude that the best action for both players is to betray (the so-called *Nash equilibrium*). This is not a matter of the safest bet, but of the mathematical reasoning of each individual player: the optimal decision is to *betray*, although the lowest combined sentence (two months, one for each) would be reached if they cooperated.

When rhetoric is interpreted as a strategic game, it is tempting to replace the actions to *betray* or *remain silent* by to *persuade* (P) or *not persuade* (NP). However, unlike betraying or remaining silent, which are real-life actions, persuading or not persuading are not *actions* one can strategically choose to perform *in reality*. Rhetorically speaking, it would make more sense if we could define a game where to persuade or not are the *consequences* of the game. This would take the following basic form: players can choose from a set of rhetorical actions (e.g., to use a certain argument, style, ...), which have the consequence, respectively, of persuading or not persuading. Importantly, we could then also introduce the aforementioned *certainty/uncertainty* governing P and NP as consequences of certain actions. This model would then describe the actual rhetorical game more aptly, as it can conceptualize a speaker who strategically chooses that rhetorical action which maximizes the expected result. However, two problems remain. First, this model no longer allows for an analysis of the players' interaction, as we do not know the effect of pairing the players' actions, unlike what was the case in the *Prisoner's dilemma* or our first model. And second, the main result of the present model is that it poses the crucial question of the relation between actions and consequences. In other words, to understand the strategy of the rhetorical game we need to know which actions are more likely to persuade. Starting from a Bitzerian view of rhetorical discourse as a response to a rhetorical situation, this paper is especially interested in the analysis of how rhetorical persuasion is generated, not of the analysis of interaction and strategies where the outcome, persuasion or non-persuasion, is a given fact.

PART II: Location games

Rhetoric as a location game

A more fruitful model for our specific purpose is the *location game* (see Hotelling 1929 and Downs 1957): imagine a stretch of beach (say 100 m long), limited by rock at both ends. On this beach there are two people (P1 and P2) with hot dog stands, offering the same products at the same prices. The beach is evenly filled with bathers (i.e., they are uniformly distributed), and they always buy hot dogs from the nearest stand. What is the optimal position for a stand? This is a symmetrical game, and the Nash equilibrium results when both players position themselves in the middle. Moreover, as long as, e.g., P1 is *not* exactly in the middle (say, somewhere to the left), it is better for P2 to position himself between the middle and P1, as this implies that he gets all the customers to his right (who are closer to him than to P1) plus half of the customers between both players. As a matter of fact, the *worst* that can happen to a player who chooses the middle of the beach is a tie, making this strategy dominant.

Note that the model above starts from a *uniformly distributed* crowd. This condition is obviously not always fulfilled, and to model an *arbitrary* distribution of people mathematicians use density functions $f(x)$. The value

FIGURE 1 THE LOCATION GAME

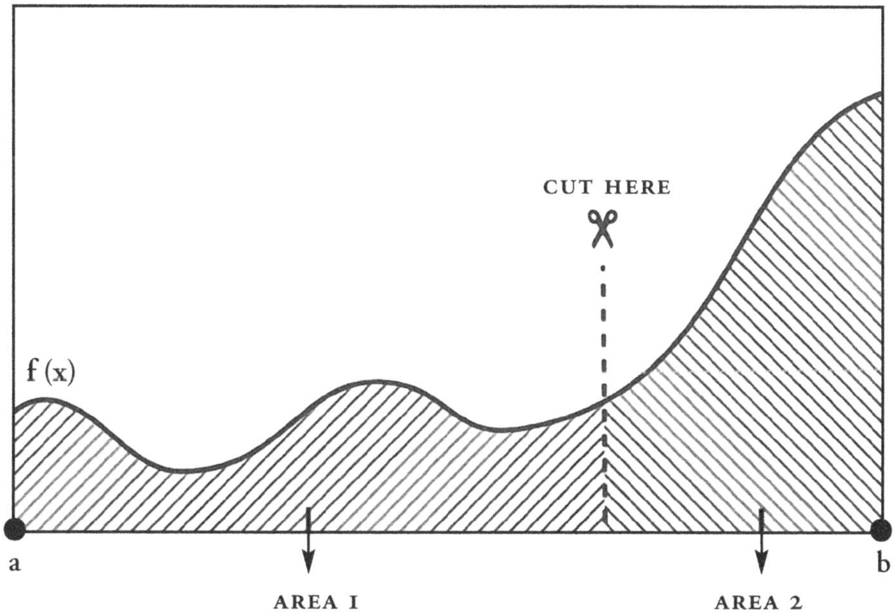

f(x) in a point *x* (say, between 0 and 100) is then interpreted as a measure of the number of people at that point in the domain. However, this does not change the core of the mathematical analysis: in case the crowd is distributed in terms of a *known* density function *f(x)* there still exists a Nash equilibrium, which can be found by solving an *integral equation* (one needs to locate the point *x* with the property that the number of people up to that point is half of the total crowd). Thinking of this density as a curve (see Figure 1), the solution for the non-uniform location game is then to be understood as the point where one can cut the picture in two pieces (along a vertical line) in such a way that the *area under the curve* is the same on both pieces (area 1 and area 2 are equal in the picture).

In order to see how the location game helps to model the rhetorical game, it suffices to adapt Downs' argument (Downs 1957, p. 142, using Hotelling's "spatial market" to analyze political ideologies as market shares and political parties as positions within that market), defining rhetorical behavior as manifesting itself in a spatial market of beliefs and convictions and choosing a certain position to claim a share of the market. Indeed, rhetorical theory teaches that persuasion always occurs against the background of shared common knowledge, on the basis of which new truths or values may be generated through rhetorical discourse. In this way, we can map the audience as a market of truths and values (represented by a density function) and the speakers, defending a specific set of truths and values, as positions within that market.

Besides offering an interesting way to analyze rhetorical situations and responses, the location game model of rhetorical behavior reveals the rhetorical importance of *the middle position*. For instance, when speaking to an audience with a symmetrical distribution of people in favor of and against certain environmental policies (i.e., a symmetrical density function), a "green" speaker wanting to abolish nuclear energy will best use a set of truths and values that is neither too green nor the opposite, in order not to alienate too many in his audience. At the same time, game theory shows what this middle position really means, as it is not necessarily the same as the "middle of the beach" position. Indeed, when facing a distribution of people that is *not* symmetrical, the mathematical analysis teaches us that we may actually find another value representing the rhetorical position that will best serve as a pivot of common knowledge. For example, when speaking before an audience of university students on the matter of freedom of speech, there will be almost no people holding the opinion that freedom of speech is a bad thing and a steadily increasing number of people believing in the absolute value of freedom of speech. The ideal position for a speaker is therefore not neutral, but a markedly positive one. We will refer to this position as "the middle," to be understood as the point "where to cut the paper." Figure 2 shows the formal density function for this example, and the analytical solution to the location game (the cut is to be made at a point on the horizontal axis defined as the square root of two minus one).

So, the location game model teaches that when the speaker is aware of his opponent's position (and the density function), the optimal strategy is to stay as close as possible to his opponent's position, yet slightly more towards the "middle." When the speaker is not aware of his opponent's position, the optimal strategy is to take the "middle" position. However, speakers do not always take the optimal position and therefore necessarily alienate a part of their audience, e.g., when they are forced to take a position that is not ideal in the spectrum of common knowledge. For instance, when a conservative Christian politician has to address a group of Gay Rights activists, it is im-

FIGURE 2 WHAT THE "MIDDLE" POSITION REALLY MEANS

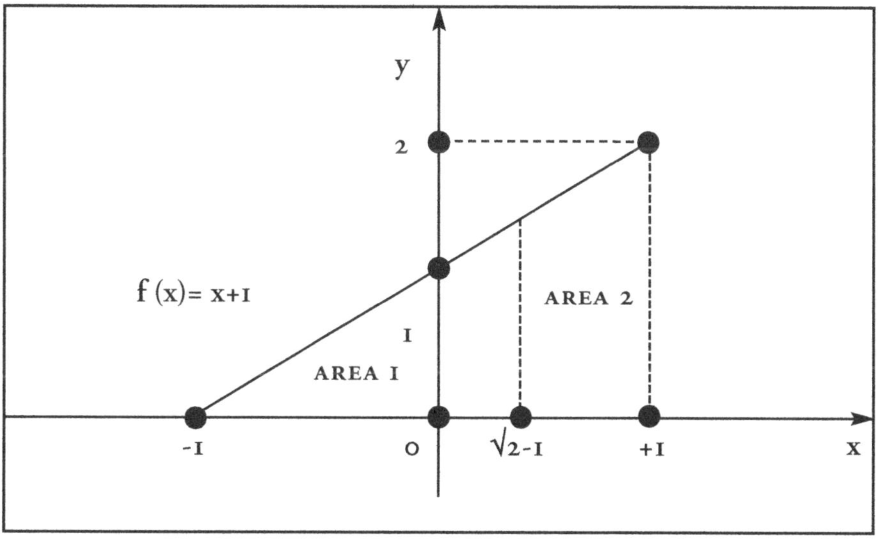

possible for the speaker, considering his convictions, to take the optimal position (markedly on the right, see the example above). Even if this speaker were to choose a neutral position, an almost impossible concession on the part of the Christian conservative, it is clear that the Christian speaker's results would be considerably worse than if he had taken the optimal position.

Location games in hyperspace

So far, our model has focused solely on the dimension of *logos*. Applying Aristotle's terminology, persuasion obviously also comprises the components *ethos*, *pathos* and *lexis*. Indeed, while a rhetor might lose the location game in terms of argumentation (*logos*), he might win it, and therefore compensate for his loss, on the level of authority (*ethos*), emotional appeal (*pathos*) or speaking competence (*lexis*). All of these can individually be conceived as location games, which have to be mathematically combined to make up the whole rhetorical game. While the game-theoretical approach thus tries to analyze rhetorical behavior as rational choice, it does not reduce rhetoric to mere rationality. By analyzing highly emotional aspects such as *ethos*, *pathos* and *lexis* as individual, but mutually interacting parts of the rhetorical "equation," so to speak, this model aims to account as fully as possible for the realities that govern the rhetorical and indeed rational choices made by speakers.

Formally, this leads to a location game in several dimensions (i.e., in *hyperspace*), in which we switch from a density function $f(x)$ in *one* variable x to a density function $f(x_1,\ldots,x_n)$ depending on *several* variables. As for the rhetorical application mentioned above, it seems worth considering density functions depending on *four* variables. Although this is much harder to represent graphically, it can be handled conceptually using multivariate analysis. In a sense, the location game is then to be understood in terms of vendors looking for the best position in a park (2 dimensions) or a building (3 dimensions). Let us, for simplicity's sake, stick to the former example. Although we can now only take two relevant parameters into account (e.g., *logos* and *pathos*), this does have the advantage that we can graphically represent the mathematical details. Density functions $f(x_1,x_2)$ can now be likened to a (not necessarily aesthetically pleasing) cake: the "number of people" is then proportional to the volume of the piece of cake, whereas finding a Nash equilibrium amounts to cutting the cake in equal halves. Despite the simplicity of this metaphor, it already illustrates the main difference from the previous situation: even perfectly symmetrical cakes can be cut in two equal halves in several ways (along the length of the cake, or orthogonally to this direction).

More formally, this is due to the observation that the relative position between 2 players is now fixed in terms of two parameters: there still is the *relative distance* between the players, measured along the line connecting them. But the big difference is that also the *orientation* of the players can change. This is important, because as the orientation changes (think of a player as "walking on a circle centered around the other player") the line along which the cake will have to be cut also changes. This is illustrated in Figure 3, in which two different positions for player 2 (P2) result in two different cutting lines (the full lines).

Note that this is not just an image: one can mathematically prove (but this would lead us too far astray) that by optimizing his orientation, a player can turn a loss into a win. The strategy is thus governed by the following principles:

- Optimize your market share by *minimizing the relative distance* in the domain.
- Optimize your market share by *choosing the angle* that maximizes the difference.

Instead of giving a formal proof of this, we will refer to a recent example from

FIGURE 3 A TWO-DIMENSIONAL LOCATION GAME

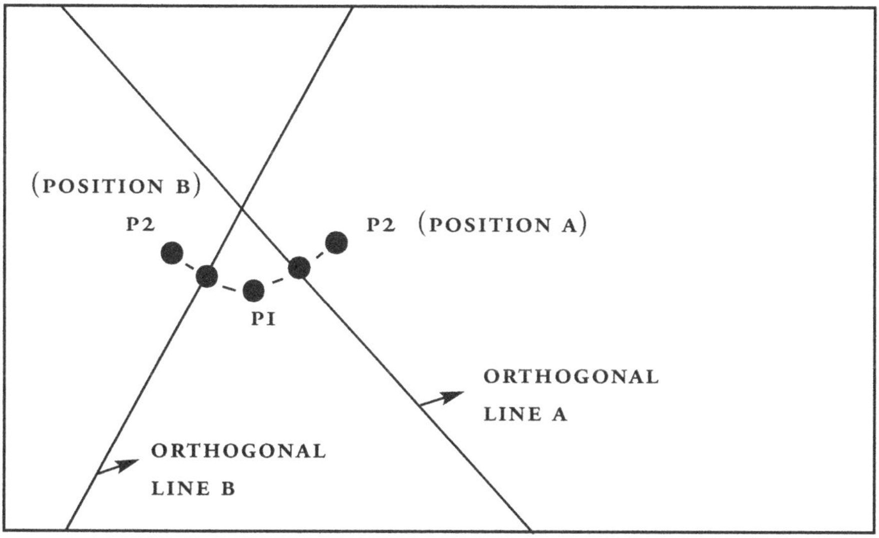

the 2012 US Presidential election campaign, featuring Barack Obama and Mitt Romney. Struggling to get his message across in the poorer communities, Romney on September 19, 2012, appeared on Univision, the most important Spanish-language television network, to make his case. As media sources pointed out by contrasting photographs taken on the same day,[3] Romney's complexion looked artificial, with the shape of protective goggles seemingly printed on his face, causing rumors that Romney had got a spray tan. This was interpreted as an effort on his part to look more Hispanic. This seemingly outlandish rhetorical ploy, obviously intended to strengthen Romney's *ethos*, can be perfectly understood in our hyperspace model. Confronted with an unfavorable position for the *logos*-game on the X-axis (there were obvious limits to the positions Romney could take), Romney's strategy to win the rhetorical game was maneuvering his position in the *ethos*-game on the Y-axis. By trying to look more Hispanic Romney intended to persuade more people than he would have been able to with strictly political arguments. For now the model cannot say *how much* spray tan Romney actually needed to win the debate (this would require knowledge of the density function), but the location

[3] See, e.g., http://www.huffingtonpost.com/2012/09/20/mitt-romney-dyed-face-brown-fake-tan-univision_n_1900707.html.

game in hyperspace certainly explains the idea how two rhetorical games can be 'combined' for "strategic maneuvering" (cf. van Eemeren 2009 and 2010).

PART III: Politics

As a final part of this paper, we would like to discuss how rhetorical discourses as heard in present-day politics are not automatic results of human nature, but rather of the legislative conditions under which people vote for their democratic representatives. These conditions are largely coincidental, in that a group of people who are convinced that a different system would be better for them has the power to change them.

The ideals of (deliberative) democracy and political deviations

According to certain deliberative democrats such as Rawls and Habermas, democratic ideals are often defined as a reconciliation of ideas on a higher societal level as a result of rhetorical processes of persuasion. We can ask ourselves why, when so many are convinced of the desirability of such a model, there are only few communities who manage to achieve this blissful democratic condition.

One of the problems is that for a society that believes in the values of free speech and open deliberation, it is impossible to exclude any kind of discourse from the deliberation floor, which means that people who resist being persuaded by others cannot be banned from the deliberation floor on system-internal grounds. The need for some kind of adjudication committee undercuts the idea of full freedom, and the ideal of deliberative democracy – that everyone's opinion should be respected – is no longer possible to maintain. This fact prevents deliberative democratic models from shrugging off their utopian appearance and manifesting themselves in real democratic debates.

We will here suggest a different approach to this problem by looking at politics as a game in which the existing rules define the best strategies for politicians. By suggesting an alternative voting system, we want to open a debate concerning the most appropriate conditions under which the ideals of rhetorical citizenship can be attained in the political sphere.

Politics as a game

It is a sad yet telling cliché that politicians and political parties are mostly perceived to chase their own individual success instead of the common good.

Other popular complaints about politicians are related to their alleged refusal to display ideological consistency; instead they make every impression of simply adjusting their rhetorical strategies to the audience in front of them.

Do these complaints imply, then, that politicians are *essentially* a class of less moral citizens than ordinary people? We do not think this cynical attitude offers the most appropriate approach. Rather, we would like to focus on the 'rule book' of the political game and show how antagonisms and free-rider behavior are inscribed in the electoral system that governs the field of politics.

In order to define politics as a game (in a simplified manner), we can see politicians as the players who undertake (rhetorical) actions in order to maximize their impact on society. The main moment when political power is negotiated in a democracy is during elections. Politicians, both idealists and pragmatists, all have good reasons for not wanting to lose an election.

To complete our formal description of the field of politics: during elections, each voter gives one vote to one particular party. As a result, in our present system it is entirely pointless to be a voter's second choice, because the voter can only give his vote to the party of his first choice. This aspect has some crucial consequences.

Zero-sum game and its impact on discourses

The voting game as described above has the structure of what we call a "zero-sum game." We know beforehand how many votes/points will be given, and a political party can only make progress if one or more of the other parties lose votes.

This zero-sum aspect has two important discursive implications for the way in which political parties rationally assess their best strategy. First, parties tend to present their own merits in antagonistic terms, in a fierce competition with other parties. Instead of emphasizing ideological resemblances and looking for ways to collaborate, it is often more beneficial to radically oppose oneself to parties that are nevertheless ideologically quite close to one's own position (think of the location game: the toughest opponent is the one closest to your own position, not the one who is extremely far away!). These antagonistic tendencies, which seem to annoy many people nowadays, are thus rational responses to the constraints of a system in which votes can only be won if one can convince the voter that one is the single best representative. We can thus label this as a "non-cooperative game."

A second implication is that, even though political parties would ideally like to gain 100% of the votes, the most rational response to the present political situation in many countries is to focus on a certain segment of the population and win over their sympathy at the expense of other sectors of society. There is as yet no mechanism that prevents politicians from bluntly ignoring the rights and wishes of a substantial part of the population, which contributes to a sense of discontent in many voters, because they do not feel that their political government reflects their societal choices.

Imagining an alternative

In order to see that a voting system does not inevitably need to be a zero-sum game, suppose that everyone were not given just one vote, but could rate each political party on a scale from 0 to 5. The result is that a party can only focus on its proper score and is no longer dependent on how other parties fare to achieve its own maximum score. As a result, parties who collaborate well in a government can all be rewarded by the voting public. Conversely, parties who present themselves in strongly antagonistic terms are not very likely to reach a high score, since the absolute support of a group of hardline believers is quickly leveled out by the punishment of non-believers (unless, of course, the group of believers is so large that the party is still successful; in that case, a democracy has to respect these voters' decision).

It thus appears that a simple change in the voting game could bring about a radical change in the most rational strategy one has to adopt in order to win the political game. By rewarding cooperative strategies, the rules of the game themselves become responsible for installing a certain type of political etiquette that brings us closer to the ideals of deliberative democracy.

This explorative suggestion strongly opposes those political analysts who state that current political behaviors reflect the nature of human beings.[4] In a sense, these analysts are quite right, but only in so far as it is part of human nature to develop a rational response to a certain situation. The

[4] One influential example of this trend in thought is generally labeled neoliberalism. In neoliberal discourse, it is maintained that human nature is thoroughly competitive and that liberalist economic logic could be freely applied to the level of politics as well. What neoliberalist thinking ignores is that this way of viewing politics is not natural, but the result of coincidental rules in our legislative system. For a critique on (neo-)liberalism, see, e.g., Bourdieu (1998), or the influential study by Negri and Hardt (2000).

way in which we vote, however, is largely coincidental, in that there is no cogent reason why we must vote in the way we do nowadays, apart from the fact that it is probably the easiest system we can think of. If we believe, however, that there are important reasons to get rid of this voting system in order to reward conciliatory discourses, it is entirely within our power to change the present structures and develop an alternative sense of democracy. We believe that such a decision could strongly improve the citizens' trust in their representatives, and could bring the field of politics more in line with the complexities of our postmodern society, in which paternalistic representation may no longer be an appropriate method to satisfy an individual's viewpoints and desires.

Questions for the political game

The model we propose here probably entails its own structural or practical pitfalls. However, we believe that the heuristic value of imagining an alternative to present structures allows us to ask some precise questions about what we expect from our present-day democracies. Some questions that can effectively guide such a discussion about the goals of democracy could be:

(1) On what level do we believe that the reconciliation of ideological positions in a society should occur? On the level of individual choice (in a nuanced voting system) or on a higher level (as a sum of individual votes)?

(2) Do we believe that a constructive attitude in politicians leads to better societal results?

(3) Do we need extreme positions on the deliberation floor (cf. Lund Klujeff 2012), or do they distract from actual results?

(4) Does our system, which originated from a paternalistic understanding of political representation, still work in our postmodern society?

(5) Can a redefinition of the political game alter the way in which we think of politics, so that it is less seen as a spectacular clash between opposed ideologies, and more as a creative undertaking in which attempts at reconciliation of positions are generally rewarded during elections and thus encouraged in future enterprises?

PART IV: Conclusion

Given the novel character of this paper, we have had to cover quite a lot of ground before we could demonstrate the effective value of our model for the study of rhetorical citizenship. Our collaborative work on rhetoric and game theory has indicated to what extent mathematics can help assess the most ideal rhetorical position of a speaker in a given situation. In closing, two final remarks are in order: one methodological, and one ethical.

First, a methodological *caveat*. In trying to analyze rhetorical behavior using game theory, we are not claiming to describe an exhaustive model for all aspects of such rhetorical behavior. What we hypothesize is a model of how speakers gauge their audience and accordingly adapt their rhetorical strategies. Our game theoretical analysis only offers an abstract model of the speaker's rational choices when making a speech, not a concrete interpretation of the audience's particular and often irrational response to that speech. This irrational side has been recognized already in antiquity, for instance in Pseudo-Longinus' account on the sublime, which allegedly has the power to strike a listener like a thunderbolt.[5]

As such, this tool is better suited to map the interaction between different competing speakers than that between one speaker and his audience. The whole of rhetorical deliberation cannot possibly be reduced to the notion of pure *utilitas* upon which the methodological foundation of our theory is based. Yet, quite interestingly, in representing the mental estimation of the audience distribution by the rational speaker, this model implicitly recognizes the interaction of audience and speaker that is fundamental in rhetorical theory; this interaction, however, ought not to be understood in the sense of active participation of the public in the actual speech delivery but in its mere presence as a factor in the orator's assessment of the appropriate rhetorical action.[6] While this model thus solely seems to focus on the speaker, there is also a distinctive place for the audience in the composition of the orator's discourse, at least for as far as it is conceptualized in the speaker's mind. A similar conception informs the final part of our paper, in which we suggested an alternative way to empower the voting citizens in a democracy to punish selfish political behavior and thus contribute to a more collaborative process of political decision-making.

Finally, this *caveat* will also make clear that while our approach of-

[5] See Ps.-Long. *Subl.* 1.4.

[6] This position is not all too different from canonical rhetorical works by Aristotle or Quintilian. It also comes quite close to the function of "public knowledge" in Bitzer (1978).

fers a model of how speakers try to predict their audience's response (since antiquity, oratorical theory has recognized the rhetor's need to do so), the model itself in no way claims such predictive powers. The game-theoretical approach to rhetoric does not interpret the audience as a passive body whose responses can easily be calculated, but only offers a model to understand the speaker's strategic deliberation of his or her audience's opinions, values and emotions.

Second, an ethical remark. As we have tried to show in part III of this study, it is important to realize that even purely "liberalist" rhetoric (understood as a form of rhetoric that searches for the most successful strategy regardless of ethics or moral beliefs) operates on a playing field that is shaped and constrained by laws, tenets, and societal values, and the assessment of the most ideal rhetorical position always needs to happen in consideration of these "rules." It is worthwhile to use this game-theoretical framework to question the conditions under which rhetoric and discourse function in a given society, and to imagine alternative "rules" according to which the ideals of rhetorical citizenship can be more fully realized. We hope this undertaking may inspire others to engage in a similar mode of reasoning, so that we can come closer to a societal model that will reward constructive democratic discourses and acts of responsible rhetorical citizenship.

References

Bennett, W. (1971). Conflict Rhetoric and Game Theory: An Extrapolation and Example. *Southern Speech Communication Journal* 37/1, 34-46.

Bitzer, L. (1968). The Rhetorical Situation. *Philosophy & Rhetoric* 1, 1-14.

Bitzer, L. (1978). Rhetoric and Public Knowledge. In D.M. Burns (Ed.), *Rhetoric, Philosophy, and Literature: An Exploration* (pp. 67-93). West Lafayette: Purdue University Press.

Bourdieu, P. (1998). *Acts of Resistance: Against the New Myths of Our Time.* Translated by Richard Nice. Cambridge: Polity Press.

Brams, S.J. (2011). *Game Theory and the Humanities.': Bridging Two Worlds.* Cambridge, MA: MIT Press.

de Ley, H. (1988). The Name of the Game: Applying Game Theory in Literature. *SubStance* 17/1, Issue 55, 33-46.

Downs, A. (1957). An Economic Theory of Political Action in a Democracy. *The Journal of Political Economy* 65/2, 135-150.

Herman, G. (1998). Reciprocity, Altruism, and the Prisoner's Dilemma: The Special Case of Classical Athens. In C.Gill et al. (Eds.), *Reciprocity in Ancient Greece* (pp. 199-225). Oxford: Oxford University Press.

Hotelling, H. (1929). Stability in Competition. *The Economic Journal* 3, 41-57.

Lausberg, H. (1990). *Handbuch der literarischen Rhetorik. Eine Grundlegung der Literaturwissenschaft.* Stuttgart: Steiner.

Lund Klujeff, M. (2012). Provocative Style: The Gaarder Debate Example. In C. Kock and L.S. Villadsen (Eds.), *Rhetorical Citizenship and Public Deliberation* (pp. 101-114). University Park: Pennsylvania State University Press.

McCarty, N. and A. Meirowitz. (2007). *Political Game Theory: An Introduction.* Cambridge: Cambridge University Press.

Negri, A. and M. Hardt. (2000). *Empire.* Cambridge, MA, and London: Harvard University Press.

Osborne, M.J. and A. Rubinstein. (1994). *A Course in Game Theory.* Cambridge, MA: MIT Press.

Pinker, S. (2008). *The Stuff of Thought. Language as a Window into Human Nature.* London: Penguin Books.

Slethaug, G.E. (1995). Game Theory. In I.R. Makaryk (Ed.), *Encyclopedia of Contemporary Literary Theory* (pp. 64-69). Toronto, Buffalo, and London: University of Toronto Press.

van Eemeren, F. (2009). *Examining Argumentation in Context: Fifteen Studies on Strategic Maneuvering.* Amsterdam: John Benjamins Publishing.

van Eemeren, F. (2010). *Strategic Maneuvering in Argumentative Discourse: Extending the Pragma-Dialectical Theory of Argumentation.* Amsterdam: John Benjamins Publishing.

Zamora Bonilla, J.P. (2006). Rhetoric, Induction, and the Free Speech Dilemma. *Philosophy of Science* 73/2, 175-93.

Contributors

Hilde van Belle, KU Leuven Campus Antwerpen, Antwerp, Belgium
hilde.vanbelle@arts.kuleuven.be
Judy Burnside-Lawry, RMIT University, Melbourne, Victoria, Australia
judy.lawry@rmit.edu.au
Catherine Chaput, University of Nevada, Reno, Nevada, USA
cchaput@unr.edu
Peter Dahlgren, Lund University, Sweden
Peter.Dahlgren@kom.lu.se
Tom Deneire, University Library of Antwerp, Belgium,
Tom.Deneire@uantwerpen.be
David Eelbode, University of Antwerp, Belgium,
David.Eelbode@uantwerpen.be
Fotini Egglezou, Athens, Greece
fegglezou@yahoo.gr
Maureen Daly Goggin, Arizona State University, Tempe, Arizona, USA
maureen.goggin@asu.edu
Kati Hannken-Illjes, Universität Marburg, Germany
kati.hannkenilljes@uni-marburg.de
Charlotte Jørgensen, University of Copenhagen, Denmark
chlt@hum.ku.dk
Christian Kock, University of Copenhagen, Denmark
kock@hum.ku.dk
Nathalie Kuroiwa-Lewis, Saint Martin's University, Washington, USA
nkuroiwalewis@stmartin.edu
Rebecca A. Kuehl , South Dakota State University, Brookings, South Dakota, USA
rebecca.kuehl@sdstate.edu
Jeroen Lauwers, Catholic University of Leuven, Belgium
Jeroen.Lauwers@arts.kuleuven.be
Carolyne Lee, University of Melbourne, Parkville, Victoria, Australia
carolyne@unimelb.edu.au
Raymie McKerrow, Ohio University, Athens, Ohio, USA
mckerrow@ohio.edu

Mari Lee Mifsud, University of Richmond, Virginia, USA
mmifsud@richmond.edu
Gene Segarra Navera, National University of Singapore, Singapore
gene.navera@nus.edu.sg
Paula Olmos, Universidad Nacional de Educación a Distancia, Madrid, Spain
polmos@fsof.uned.es
Karen Tracy, University of Colorado-Boulder, Colorado, USA
Karen.Tracy@colorado.edu
Anne Ulrich, Eberhard Karls Universität Tübingen, Germany
anne.ulrich@uni-tuebingen.de
Lisa S. Villadsen, University of Copenhagen, Denmark
lisas@hum.ku.dk
David Zarefsky, Northwestern University, Illinois, USA
d-zarefsky@northwestern.edu

Index of Scholarly Sources

16W01269/ T1/ 9789087282165